A BROKEN WORLD

1919–1939

*the text of this book is printed
on 100% recycled paper*

THE RISE OF MODERN EUROPE

*A SURVEY OF EUROPEAN HISTORY
IN ITS POLITICAL, ECONOMIC, AND CULTURAL ASPECTS
FROM THE END OF THE MIDDLE AGES
TO THE PRESENT*

EDITED BY

WILLIAM L. LANGER

Harvard University

A
BROKEN
WORLD

1919–1939

BY

RAYMOND J. SONTAG

*University of California
at Berkeley*

ILLUSTRATED

HARPER TORCHBOOKS

Harper & Row, Publishers

New York, Hagerstown, San Francisco, London

First HARPER TORCHBOOK edition published 1972

ISBN: 0-06-131651-2

79 80 12 11 10 9

To My Students

CONTENTS

CONTENTS

ILLUSTRATIONS

These photographs, grouped in a separate section, will be found following page 138.

MAPS

INTRODUCTION

Our age of specialization produces an almost incredible amount of monographic research in all fields of human knowledge. So great is the mass of this material that even the professional scholar cannot keep abreast of the contributions in anything but a restricted part of his general subject. In all branches of learning the need for intelligent synthesis is now more urgent than ever before, and this need is felt by the layman even more acutely than by the scholar. He cannot hope to read the products of microscopic research or to keep up with the changing interpretations of experts, unless new knowledge and new viewpoints are made accessible to him by those who make it their business to be informed and who are competent to speak with authority.

These volumes, published under the general title of *The Rise of Modern Europe,* are designed primarily to give the general reader and student a reliable survey of European history written by experts in various branches of that vast subject. In consonance with the current broad conception of the scope of history, they attempt to go beyond the merely political-military narrative, and to lay stress upon social, economic, religious, scientific, and artistic developments. The minutely detailed, chronological approach is to some extent sacrificed in the effort to emphasize the dominant factors and to set forth their interrelationships. At the same time, the division of European history into national histories has been abandoned, and wherever possible attention has been focused upon larger forces common to the whole of European civilization. These are the broad lines on which this history as a whole has been laid out. The individual volumes are integral parts of the larger scheme, but they are intended also to stand as independent units, each the work of a scholar well qualified to treat the period covered by his book. Each volume contains about fifty illustrations selected from the mass of contemporary pictorial material. All noncontemporary illustrations have been excluded on principle. The bibliographical note appended to each volume is designed to facilitate further study of special aspects touched upon in the text. In general every effort has been made to give the reader a clear idea of the main movements in European history, to embody the monographic contributions of research workers, and to present the material in a forceful and vivid manner.

In this, the chronologically penultimate volume of the series, Professor Sontag has undertaken to review the confused and ominous events of the twenty years that lay between the conclusion of the peace treaties in 1919 and the renewal of general conflict in 1939. It was indeed a "broken world" that emerged from the ordeal of a four-year war marked by human suffering and material losses unprecedented in the annals of mankind. What followed was a vengeful peace imposed by the victors on the vanquished, a peace which involved a drastic revamping of the European map and all but ruined the European economy. Worse yet, the legacy of resentment and hate was such as to divide the continent into hostile camps and facilitate the rise of dictatorships whose prime objective was to destroy democracy and unmake the European settlement, by force if necessary. Professor Sontag traces these developments judiciously and with the skill and understanding derived from long experience not only in the teaching and writing of history, but also in the practice of international affairs. His synthesis of so thorny and problematic a period is an achievement of high merit.

WILLIAM L. LANGER

PREFACE

The interwar years defy more explicit characterization than *A Broken World,* a title borrowed from Gabriel Marcel's play of 1933, *Le monde cassé.* Marcel used the word broken in the sense that we say a watch is broken when the mainspring does not function: we live, his heroine seemed to say, in an age when the values which once gave meaning to life no longer animate us. Many Europeans shared his despair, or rather the despair of his heroine; he himself looked ahead with hope.

The belief that the world of European thought, feeling, and action was broken, but not broken beyond repair, was more usual than despair. Some thought the "progress" interrupted in 1914—"normalcy," President Harding called it—could be resumed by minor adjustments like currency stabilization. Some placed their faith in social reform, or in a return to the eternally binding laws of economics which social reformers were violating. Some looked to the triumph of Marxism-Leninism, others to the triumph of the "myths" of Fascism; sometimes individuals and even masses of voters swung from one to the other. Loyalties shifted with bewildering rapidity. In the twenties the businessman was for many a hero possessed of wisdom in all fields of knowledge; in the thirties for many he became a fool or a villain; science and technology were now the hope of the future, now the destroyers of everything humane. Possibly the harshest contrasts were in the feelings aroused by the word nationalism. In 1919 nationalism was for many a term of opprobrium. By the thirties, and not just in professedly nationalist countries like Italy and Germany, nationalism was becoming a good to be cherished and intensified; in scarcely disguised form nationalism was exalted even in the Soviet Union.

Behind these and other bewildering shifts and contradictions lay what was usually called the Great War. Every aspect of European life was permanently and profoundly affected by the effects and by the memory of the terrible years from 1914 to 1918. Almost as pervasive and lasting were the effects of the Communist revolution in Russia, and both the revolution and the impact of the revolution on the world outside Russia were intimately connected with the war. Finally, it is above all the war which explains the tragic outcome of the Paris peace conference of 1919. At the time and since, down to our own day, the peacemakers of 1919 have been castigated because from their labors emerged, not simply a punitive peace but a peace without effective power behind it. Here I have been content to set down what seem to me the forces which resulted in a defective settlement and in divisions between the victors, and the consequences of the defects and divisions.

Throughout, I have had to wrestle with two problems of focus. The first was the problem of seeing this segment of the past as a historian without losing the fresh, if defective, vision of the contemporary observer. It seemed to me worthwhile to preserve the sense both of loss and of liberation which grew as wartime idealism gave way to scepticism, if not to cynicism; to many young Europeans, as to young Americans, the mocking wail of the saxophone perfectly expressed that mood. Again, to have been a student in Europe during the occupation of the Ruhr in 1923 was to learn that international conflict was very likely to be a conflict, not between right and wrong, but between deeply felt rights. Similarly the outside observer in Europe during the Locarno era could see that all the old breaks were there, unhealed, and yet could understand that after so many years of privation and fear it was bliss to have the ordinary good things of life again, and natural to hope that time and prosperity would suffice for healing. Finally, from the dark days of the thirties there is the memory particularly of young people in Paris, or Rome, or Vienna, or Munich, or London; these are only fragmentary and narrow views, but they help, possibly, to a better understanding of an official document, a painting, a poem, even of the total deepening catastrophe of those years.

The other problem of focus results from the fact that European history had become, in quite a new way, part of world history. Earlier, at least until the last years of the nineteenth century, it could be plausibly argued that world history was becoming an extension of European history. Certainly the history of Europe was substantially complete in itself, with only occasional and usually incidental reference to what was going on in the rest of the world.

This was not possible after 1918. What happened in Europe was affected, vitally affected, by what went on outside Europe. This was clearly true of the effects of American action, and substantially true of Japanese action also. Less directly, but strongly, Europe was affected by what went on in Turkey and Egypt, in China and India. In a sense, therefore, to write a history of the years 1919–1939 centered in Europe is both parochial and badly out of focus. My defense—apart from the name of the series of which this volume is a part—must be that it was hard enough to see with any clarity the historical significance of what was going on in Europe without attempting to place that story within the still largely uncharted history of the world.

The bibliographical footnotes and the bibliographical essay do not, of course, list all the publications upon which the text is based. In theory, the footnotes are to aid the reader who wishes to pursue a particular subject further, while the essay is intended for the reader who wishes to go further into the period as a whole, or large segments of the period. In practice, it was impossible to distinguish clearly between these two; I can only hope that the result is not seriously defective. In selecting studies for inclusion, as indeed in the work as a whole, I have tried to keep in mind the needs of those who wish to use the volume as an aid to further serious study of the period.

When Dr. Langer projected The Rise of Modern Europe series, this volume was to have been written by my teacher and friend, William E. Lingelbach. He became absorbed in his work with the American Philosophical Society and eventually decided not to proceed with the volume. From many conversations with him, I am convinced this was a great loss.

For long after I had agreed to stand in his place, I also despaired of writing a coherent account of so fragmented a period. If, at the end, there is coherence, my students are to be thanked. It is impossible to list all those from whose suggestions I profited; it is to these students that the volume is gratefully dedicated. Two were of especial help, not least on those questions where we found ourselves in complete disagreement: with James Sheehan, now of Northwestern University, I argued endlessly about what may loosely be called cultural history; with Marc Trachtenberg of Berkeley, there were similar arguments over economic history. One or another draft profited from the criticism of Gordon Wright of Stanford, of Richard Kuisel of Stony Brook, of David Kieft of Minnesota, and of Edward Segel and Thomas Beck of Berkeley. Like all contributors to this series, I am indebted for advice, but above all for patience and persistence, to the editor, William L. Langer, and to Beulah Hagen, the representative of Harper & Row. The typist, Grace O'Connell, was not only accurate; she was a good critic.

In my search for pictures, I drew heavily on the experience of my colleague Herschel B. Chipp, and of Franz Lassner and Agnes F. Peterson of the Hoover Institution. I received much help also from representatives of the collections and agencies who were good enough to furnish the pictures which will, I trust, throw light on the period.

Two debts are too great for more than mention: to the University of California, Berkeley, which has been my home for thirty years, and to my family.

RAYMOND J. SONTAG

A BROKEN WORLD

1919–1939

Chapter One

THE PEACE OF PARIS

1. BETWEEN ARMISTICE AND PEACE

FROM 1914 to 1918, through more than fifty months of war, the peoples of Europe were sustained by hope that peace, when it came, would be worthy of the death and the suffering with which it was being purchased. When, on November 11, 1918, the armistice signed at Compiègne did bring the fighting on the western front to an end, what had been done, and what remained to be done, seemed compressed into the message of President Wilson to the American people:

The armistice was signed this morning. Everything for which America fought has been accomplished. It will now be our fortunate duty to assist by example, by sober, friendly counsel and by material aid in the establishment of just democracy throughout the world.[1]

The war, it seemed, had vindicated democracy. The czarist autocracy had collapsed; Russia had fallen under Bolshevik rule, but this was thought a tyranny nourished by misery. On the ruins of the Hapsburg monarchy new democratic nations were being formed. The empire of Turkey, so long in decay, was now in complete disintegration. Above all, Hohenzollern Germany, the center of resistance to the Western democracies, now had a democratic government, at least precariously; in any event, the terms of the armistice and the continuance of the economic blockade made certain the military impotence of Germany while peace was being made. On the other hand, the power of the three great democracies—the United States, Britain, and France—towered over the world. Momentarily, the numerous other "Allied and Associated Powers" scarcely seemed to count. Even Japan, the one great power in Asia, certainly no democracy, and with its imperial aspirations heightened by the collapse of Russia, showed little interest in the

---

1. For the armistice as the background of the peace conference, see Harry Rudin, *Armistice, 1918* (New Haven, 1944), and Pierre Renouvin, *L'Armistice de Rethondes* (Paris, 1968).

European settlement. Italy was called a great power, but its claims to the territorial gains promised in the Treaty of London of 1915 were clouded by the unimpressive achievements of Italian arms during the war. Very quickly, it became usual to speak of the Big Three—Woodrow Wilson, David Lloyd George, and Georges Clemenceau—as the peacemakers who would shape a new and better world on the ruins of the old.

Even during the wild rejoicing of November 11, Wilson spoke with apprehension of the task ahead—"to see that the world did not fall into chaos"—and before the peace conference opened in Paris on January 18, 1919, the magnitude of the task confronting the victors was becoming apparent. The great influenza epidemic spread over the world, taking more lives than had all the battles of the war and leaving weakened populations susceptible to new epidemics.[2] Within Russia civil war and economic breakdown were creating famine. Along the frontiers of Russia subject nationalities were fighting for independence from Russian rule. The new nations rising from the ruins of Germany, Austria-Hungary, and Turkey were fighting not only against their old masters but with each other, and within the new states there was civil strife. In the West, Bolshevism was thought a deadly political disease to which despairing peoples fell prey; during the first winter of peace it seemed that all Europe east of the Rhine was ripe for Bolshevism.

Most ominously, divisions were opening within and between the Western democracies. In the United States the elections of November, 1918, gave the Republican rivals of the Democratic President a majority in the Senate, which had to ratify the peace treaty. Already, some Republican leaders were affirming their opposition to the President's declared objectives of a peace of reconciliation and continued American involvement in European affairs through membership in a league of nations.

In Britain, Lloyd George won a large parliamentary majority in the election of December, 1918, but in order to ensure the majority he had been forced to promise that the peace with Germany would be harsh, and specifically that Germany would be forced to pay a huge indemnity. Lloyd George himself had no settled objectives beyond the attainment of gains, territorial and financial, for the security of the

2. Great Britain, Ministry of Health, *Report on the Pandemic of Influenza, 1918–19* (London, 1920), p. xiv. The total number of deaths from influenza is commonly given as 20 millions, with 5 millions in India alone.

British Empire and for the economic position of Britain. After the election, however, it was more difficult for him to cooperate with Wilson, although both men were convinced that continued Anglo-American cooperation was essential. After the election, too, it was harder for him to resist the demands of British dominions for territorial compensation in German colonies, and to block French demands which, he believed, would both establish French hegemony in Europe and prevent the attainment of stable peace.[3]

There was no election in France, and Clemenceau was in sympathy with the demand for a peace which would wreck German power and ensure French hegemony. Unlike newspaper writers, however, and unlike leaders like President Poincaré and Marshal Foch, he did not believe either of these objectives obtainable. He was painfully aware that France had won only because of British and American support. Some day, he was convinced, Germany would revive and seek to reverse the verdict of 1918. When that day came, France must again have British and American aid. More immediately, France needed economic assistance, particularly from the United States, to restore the disordered finances of the country and to rebuild the northern provinces devastated by war. Therefore, while Clemenceau would go as far to break German power and to enhance French power as the Americans and British would permit, he was determined not to lose American and British support.

It is against the background of this strife and misery, this fear of the spread of Bolshevism, and this struggle to maintain Allied unity in face of Allied discord that the labors of the Big Three must be seen.[4] In

3. The best biography of the British prime minister is Thomas Jones, *Lloyd George* (Cambridge, 1951).

4. There is an excellent bibliography of the Paris conference in Arno J. Mayer, *Politics and Diplomacy of Peacemaking: Containment and Counterrevolution at Versailles, 1918–1919* (N.Y., 1967). Valuable older guides are Nina Almond and R. H. Lutz, *An Introduction to the Bibliography of the Paris Peace Conference* (Stanford, 1935); Robert Binkley, "Ten Years of Peace Conference History," *Journal of Modern History*, I (Dec., 1929), 607–29; Paul Birdsall, "The Second Decade of Peace Conference History," *Journal of Modern History*, XI (Sept., 1939), 362–78. A useful volume, giving the text of the Treaty of Versailles and factual notes on the history of most of the provisions is: United States Department of State, *The Treaty of Versailles and After, Annotations of the Text of the Treaty* (Washington, 1947). For the work of the conference, Arno Mayer's volume cited above should be compared with Paul Birdsall, *Versailles Twenty Years After* (N.Y., 1941). For a suggestive discussion of the conference, see Hellmuth Rössler, ed., *Ideologie und Machtpolitik 1919: Plan und Werk der Pariser Friedenskonferenzen 1919* (Göttingen, 1966).

particular, the appalling defects in the organization of the peace conference were a result of the need to make peace quickly, and of the lack of agreement among the victors. Ironically, in their preparations for the conference, the Allied leaders had resolved to avoid the errors of earlier peacemakers, particularly the errors made at the Congress of Vienna in 1815. The peacemakers of 1815 were thought to have failed in large part because the Congress of Vienna was so badly organized and particularly because the statesmen did not have the advice of experts who knew the problems Europe must face in the nineteenth century. Therefore the Allied statesmen came to Paris in 1919 surrounded by social scientists and other experts; on the ship taking the American delegation to Europe, President Wilson promised his experts that if they would tell him what was right, he would fight to achieve what was right. At Paris the experts found their views had little weight, not because the President had lost his eagerness to do what he believed was right, but because he found that what was politically possible could not be determined by experts. Because there was no agreement on what kind of a peace should be made, it was impossible to negotiate with the defeated powers; negotiation with the defeated would have brought into the open the division among the victors. Therefore, the defeated states were simply presented with the completed treaties and ordered to sign. Because there was no agreed basis for peace, the committees of Allied experts could not work out compromises; even trivial disputes were referred to the harassed, overworked heads of the delegations. As a result, the Big Three soon were deciding one question of detail and then another, without any clear view of the total settlement which these separate decisions were shaping. Lloyd George, when he finally read the draft treaty submitted to the Germans, was appalled by the cumulative weight of the exactions, each one of which had seemed reasonable when accepted by the Big Three.

2. THE TREATIES

The Paris peace conference would never have completed its work if, overshadowing all differences, there had not been the conviction, shared by Clemenceau, Lloyd George, and Wilson, that there could be no peace worthy of the name unless France, Britain, and the United States continued to work together. During the conference, however, what stood out was the conflicting objectives of the Big Three.

Inevitably, the French saw the problem of peacemaking in terms of their national security. Ceaselessly, the French press went over the arguments for a harsh peace. It had taken more than four years for a coalition of most of the world, including six great powers, to break the German will to dominate Europe. In the struggle northern France had been devastated and France had been drained of her young men and her wealth. There must not be another such ordeal. Now, while German power was temporarily broken, the map of Europe must be redrawn, and German power must be reduced, so that a new German bid for supremacy would be impossible. Moreover, now that Russia was an enemy and bidding for alliance with Germany, the states between Germany and Russia must be made as large and strong as possible. Therefore, French leaders demanded that German territory on the left bank of the Rhine be made an independent buffer state between France and Germany, and that the industrial region of Upper Silesia be included in Poland. They also demanded that German military power be permanently limited and that Germany be obligated to make reparation payments which would strengthen France and weaken Germany.

Finally, the French leaders believed it was the duty of the allies of France to help keep Germany in permanent subjection. To the French, it seemed that the war had left France as the one bulwark of civilization in Europe, facing still dangerous Germany and Russia. In time the new states, the *cordon sanitaire* between Germany and Russia, would become strong enough to redress the balance of power. Until then, France was entitled to assistance in the task of protecting and organizing Europe.[5]

The British representatives were pledged to partial support of the French position. During the election campaign of December, 1918, Lloyd George had promised to punish the Germans for starting the war, and in particular to exact vast sums as reparation for the cost of the war to Britain. But the British view of continental Europe was inevitably different from that of the French. In the British view, both Germany and Russia were bound to revive, and the states of the *cordon sanitaire* could not develop sufficient strength to provide an effective balance for these giants. Moreover, a Europe dominated by France had

5. J. C. King, *Foch vs. Clemenceau: France and German Dismemberment* (Cambridge, 1960).

no appeal for Britain. During the nineteenth century, British imperial interests had clashed violently with those of Germany, Russia, and France. For the moment, two of these powers were weak, and Lloyd George intended to exploit this situation to strengthen the position of the British Empire. Few Englishmen, however, were willing that their country should permanently maintain by force of arms an artificial distribution of power on the continent, and in particular maintain the hegemony of France. Therefore, Lloyd George refused to support the separation of the Rhineland from Germany—refused to create, as he said, another Alsace-Lorraine to poison the peace of Europe. And in the closing days of the debate on the Treaty of Versailles he forced the submission of the fate of Upper Silesia to a vote of the inhabitants. On reparation, he went along with the French in demanding unspecified but obviously vast sums from Germany.[6]

Wilson, like his French and British colleagues, had no doubt that Germany was responsible for the war, and he thought the Germans should be made to pay for the misery they had inflicted on the world. However, he was primarily concerned with the future, not the past. In his pronouncements during the war, and in particular in his Fourteen Points speech, he had outlined his program for the peace settlement. When the Germans had sought an armistice, he had wrested both from Germany and from the European Allies an agreement that peace would be made on the basis of the Fourteen Points and of his other speeches, with reservations only on freedom of the seas and reparation.

Wilson's program rested on the belief that if the peoples of the world were free to choose their own governments, a union of these governments could preserve peace: a combination of self-determination, democracy, and a league of nations would make possible reduction of armaments, removal of economic barriers, open diplomacy, and, as the highest good, peace. Wilson believed that outside of Europe many peoples were not yet ready for self-government, but he insisted that the interests of the natives, as well as the interests of the colonizing powers, be considered in regard to colonial claims. In his program as originally formulated, there had been no place for indemnities, but to secure Allied acceptance of the program he had agreed that the Germans must make reparation for the damage done to the civilian population of the Allied countries.

6. Seth Tillman, *Anglo-American Relations at the Paris Peace Conference of 1919* (Princeton, 1961); excellent, with valuable bibliography.

By the time the peace conference began its deliberations, Wilson and most of the American delegation had become aware of the strength of popular feeling in Britain and France, as well as in other Allied countries, and of the consequent need for compromise if Allied unity was to survive after the conference. This awareness increased as Wilson worked, week after week, with his colleagues on the supreme council. He continued to talk in terms of impartial justice, but his strategy was to maintain Allied unity by compromise and to keep the way open for reconsideration of the settlement after war passions had subsided.[7]

Through much of the Treaty of Versailles, Wilson's program was implemented only at the expense of Germany, with the hope that the precedents thus established would prove of value later in dealing with other countries. For instance, Germany lost all of its colonies, which were distributed among the victorious powers. However, the colonies were given to the Allies as mandates of the League of Nations, and the mandatory powers were required to report on the development of the territories to the League. The hope was that as the League supervision of these territories demonstrated its efficiency, other colonial territories would be placed under the jurisdiction of the League. Again, disarmament was imposed on Germany but not on the Allies. However, the disarmament section of the treaty was preceded by a statement which was later much quoted: "In order to render possible the initiation of a general limitation of the armaments of all nations, Germany undertakes strictly to observe the military, naval and air clauses which follow."

The most fateful series of compromises related to reparation. By the prearmistice agreement, Germany was required to make compensation "for all damages done to the civilian population of the Allies and their property." The American experts estimated the damage at between $15 billion and $25 billion; they also estimated that Germany had the capacity to pay this amount. In Britain and France, however, there was strong pressure for the recovery of the entire cost of the war from Germany; no responsible person believed Germany could pay such an astronomical sum. In an effort to move the discussion back to the prearmistice agreement, the experts formulated an introductory clause which affirmed German theoretical responsibility for total war costs; this clause was followed by another which stated that Germany did not

7. Arthur Link, *Wilson the Diplomatist* (Baltimore, 1957); N. G. Levin, *Woodrow Wilson and World Politics* (N.Y., 1968).

have the capacity to make complete reparation. This was the genesis of Article 231, which read as follows:

The Allied and Associated governments affirm and Germany accepts the responsibility of Germany and her Allies for causing all the loss and damage to which the Allied and Associated Governments and their nationals have been subjected as a consequence of the war imposed upon them by the aggression of Germany and her Allies.

The acceptance of this clause disposed of total war costs, but did not produce agreement on a sum which the American and some other experts believed was within Germany's estimated capacity to pay. The German obligation was soon stretched, with Wilson's consent, to include pensions and separation allowances for the Allied armies: this raised the obligation far above the American estimate of capacity to pay. In the end, the conference decided not to fix the amount of the German obligation in the treaty, but to require the reparation commission to fix the total by May 1, 1921; before then, Germany was to make payments totaling $5 billion.

As it became evident that the pressure of British and French public opinion was raising the reparation bill beyond what Germany could pay, the American experts sought to increase the powers of the reparation commission, which would have the task of implementing the reparation clauses. As the Americans saw the situation, the chairman of the commission would be an American, and he could use his influence to moderate the financial demands on Germany when war feeling subsided in Europe.[8]

In the reparation question, Wilson was forced to be satisfied with the hope of securing a reasonable settlement at a later date. So far as the territorial settlement in Europe was concerned, even before the discussions in Paris had begun, it was evident that the principle of self-determination, which had seemed both a noble and a practical aim to the Allied peoples during the war, would in practice yield very imperfect results and would in many places run counter to what the Allies considered essential for the security of Europe. Moreover, in large areas of eastern and southeastern Europe, application of the principle would have entailed new hostilities, upon which the peoples of the victorious

8. Philip Burnett, *Reparation at the Paris Peace Conference: From the Standpoint of the American Delegation* (2 vols., N.Y., 1940); documents, with a valuable introduction (I, 3–157) and bibliography (I, 158–66).

powers were unwilling to embark. Along the Baltic, along the undefined eastern frontiers of Poland, and in territory north of the Danube claimed by Rumania, actual warfare was in progress between the Bolsheviks and the people of the territories in dispute. Here the power of the supreme council in Paris vanished, once the decision was made to avoid direct hostilities with the Bolsheviks.

Turkey was for the moment powerless, but Allied claims to Turkish territory were in such conflict that the Treaty of Sèvres was not signed until August 20, 1920, the last of the five treaties which together formed the Peace of Paris. By then, however, the power of the sultan, whose representatives signed the treaty, was challenged by the rise of Mustafa Kemal, the leader of aroused Turkish nationalism in Anatolia. The Treaty of Sèvres never went into effect, and the final settlement with nationalist Turkey was not made until 1923.

Bulgaria presented no real problem to the peacemakers and was unlikely in itself to cause trouble in the future. The neighbors of Bulgaria had already satisfied most of their claims to Bulgarian territory after the Second Balkan War in 1913. By the Treaty of Neuilly, signed on November 27, 1919, Yugoslavia was given a few fragments of strategically desirable territory, and Greece took Eastern Thrace, thereby barring Bulgaria from the Aegean. Bulgaria was left with a population of some 5 million which included large numbers of troublesome exiles from Macedonia.

The division of the Dual Monarchy was more difficult, not because what was left of Austria and Hungary could offer effective resistance, but because the claims of the succession states went far beyond what could legitimately be asked on the basis of self-determination, and in many cases the claims conflicted. Through large parts of the old Monarchy, fighting went on while the peace conference was deliberating. The conference in the end compelled a settlement of all territorial questions except the quarrel of Italy and Yugoslavia over Fiume, but the Treaty of St. Germain, signed by Austria on September 10, 1919, and the Treaty of Trianon, signed by Hungary on June 4, 1920, did not bring peace to the Danube basin. Austria was reduced to an impoverished landlocked state of 6½ million, of whom nearly 2 million lived in the derelict imperial capital of Vienna. Hungary, with a population of 8 million, was equally powerless to offer effective protest against the settlement. However, to provide strategically or economically desirable frontiers for the successor states, the principle of self-determination had been flagrantly violated; these German and Magyar minorities within the successor states would be slow to accept subjection to peoples they had so recently dominated. Moreover, tension continued between those who had profited from the inheritance of the Dual Monarchy: the division of Teschen satisfied neither the Poles nor the Czechs; Rumania and Yugoslavia were at odds over the division of the Banat of Temesvár; relations between Italy and Yugoslavia were embittered, not only by the still unsettled problem of Fiume but by the whole eastern Adriatic settlement. Finally, the new frontiers tore apart what had once been a closely integrated economic unit, separating factories from raw materials and markets, creating here a dearth, there a surplus, of administrative talent, depriving old lines of communication of traffic, and forcing the building of new roads and railways. At best, economic dislocation of the Danube basin would take years of patient, cooperative effort to remedy, and it was clear to all at Paris that neither patience nor cooperation could be expected from the impoverished and distracted peoples of the basin.[9]

So far as the rebuilding of economic life and the security of the new frontiers in the Danube basin were concerned, the strength of the Allied powers and the pressure of world opinion through the League of Nations were counted on to protect the settlement made at Paris. A more direct effort was made to protect the minorities within states. Not only the defeated states (except Germany) but the successor states of central and southeastern Europe were required to sign treaties promising equitable treatment for minorities. The provisions varied, but in general the treaties sought to protect minority peoples against discrimination and to guarantee them the right to the use of their own language and the exercise of their own religion. Minorities were entitled to appeal for redress of grievances either to domestic courts or to the League of Nations. These treaties were accepted only under protest and after Wilson had bluntly declared that the victorious Great Powers could not be expected to guarantee the peace of the world unless the smaller powers were prepared to give guarantees against disturbance of the peace by persecution of minorities.

9. David Mitrany, *The Effect of the War in Southeastern Europe* (New Haven, 1936), and C. A. Macartney, *Problems of the Danube Basin* (Cambridge, Eng., 1942), are good introductions.

In distributing the territory of the Dual Monarchy among the successor states, the peacemakers were bound only by the promises of self-determination they had made during the war. By the prearmistice agreement, however, a formal pledge had been made that the settlement with Germany would conform to President Wilson's Fourteen Points and his other wartime pronouncements. Where the promise of self-determination entailed the loss of territory which had been part of prewar Germany, the only clear violation of the promise was the few hundred square miles given to Belgium in Eupen and Malmédy. The Saar basin was temporarily put under League administration, and ownership of the coal mines of the basin was given to France as compensation for German destruction of French mines, but after fifteen years the inhabitants of the Saar were to decide their own fate. German territory on the left bank of the Rhine, together with a strip fifty kilometers wide on the right bank, was to be permanently demilitarized; but the Rhineland remained under German rule. The efforts of Clemenceau to increase French security by separating the Rhineland from Germany were firmly and successfully resisted by Lloyd George and Wilson. Clemenceau gave way only after he had received assurance that in case of another German invasion France would not be forced to fight alone. By treaties signed on June 28, 1919 (the day the Treaty of Versailles was signed), the United States and Great Britain guaranteed assistance to France in case of unprovoked aggression by Germany; the treaties were to come into force only when ratified by both guarantors.

Alsace-Lorraine was returned to France; that cession had been somewhat ambiguously demanded in the Fourteen Points. The part of Schleswig which went to Denmark was ceded only after the wishes of the population had been ascertained. The cessions to Poland, including the placing of the German city of Danzig under League rule as a free city, could be justified by a rather strained interpretation of the Fourteen Points, although the resultant separation of East Prussia from the remainder of Germany and the large German minorities within Poland were certain to arouse lasting resentment. The separation of Memel from Germany and Allied acquiescence in the seizure of the city by Lithuania were harder to justify.

In the first draft of the treaty with Germany, Upper Silesia was given to Poland. Lloyd George contended, however, that this would be a flagrant violation of the principle of self-determination. In the end, the Treaty of Versailles called for a plebiscite to determine the fate of this valuable industrial area.

If the victors could claim that in taking territory from Germany they had not done great violence to the principle of self-determination, it was impossible to deny that in the partition of Austria-Hungary the principle was ignored when its application would add territory to Germany. Derelict Austria sought to join Germany. With Austria, however, Germany would be more populous than before 1914, and would also be in a position to dominate the Danube basin. Therefore, the peacemakers prohibited the union of Austria with Germany. Again, Germans lived in the mountainous border regions of Bohemia and Moravia. A strong argument was made, however, that the mountain barrier was essential for the defense of the new state of Czechoslovakia against German aggression. Therefore, the Sudeten Germans were put in Czechoslovakia. In the South Tyrol, also, there were Germans; but Italy had been promised the strategic frontier of the Brenner Pass. So the South Tyrol went to Italy. With reason, therefore, Germans could say that the principle of self-determination was applied only when it worked to the disadvantage of Germans.

To supervise the execution of the treaties and to cope with future international problems, the Peace of Paris set up two continuing bodies. Questions which related directly to the peace treaties and their enforcement were reserved for the supreme council of the victorious powers or for agencies of the victors such as the reparation commission. Wilson, Lloyd George, and the other heads of government returned home immediately after signing the Treaty of Versailles with Germany on June 28, 1919, but the supreme council continued to meet in Paris; the governments of the victorious powers were represented by their foreign ministers or deputies designated by the foreign ministers.

The other body was the League of Nations. The covenant, or constitution, of the League formed Part I of each of the treaties made at Paris. Wilson insisted from the outset that the League be an inseparable part of the treaties. To him, and to many at Paris, what was of lasting importance was that questions of war and peace, together with all of the questions which, if unsettled, might menace the peace, should be under the continuing scrutiny of world opinion and subject to review by representatives of governments of the world.

The covenant did not set out to create a world government: decisions, except on procedural matters and on the admission of members, required unanimous approval. This did not usually mean the unanimous vote of all members. The assembly of the League, in which every member was represented, had the right to consider "any matter within the sphere of action of the League." Decision, however, was reserved on most questions for the council of the League. Permanent membership in the council was given to "the Principal Allied and Associated Powers" (Britain, France, Italy, the United States, Japan); there were to be four nonpermanent members, selected by the assembly. At the outset, membership in the League was given to all the signatories of the Treaty of Versailles—except Germany. Most neutral states were invited to join—but not Russia. These exceptions made it easy for Germans to describe the League as an organization of the victors to protect their victory, and for Russians to say the League was a union of capitalist states against Communism.

While all important decisions of the League required the unanimous approval of the council, the covenant did seek to define the obligations of members so precisely that refusal to make a decision or failure to live up to the obligations of membership would be clear for all the world to see. The central obligation was spelled out in Article X: "The Members of the League undertake to respect and preserve as against external aggression the territorial integrity and existing political independence of all Members of the League." Every war or threat of war was declared a matter of concern to the League; every member agreed to submit all disputes to arbitration, judicial settlement, or inquiry by the council of the League; by Article XVI, if any member resorted to war in disregard of its obligations, "it shall *ipso facto* be deemed to have committed an act of war against all other Members of the League," and the other members agreed to impose penalties (sanctions, as they came to be called) against the offending member.

Articles XI to XVI of the covenant spelled out in great detail the measures to be taken to prevent any forcible disturbance of the existing situation in the world. Provision for peaceful change of the existing situation was made, much less explicitly, in Article XIX, which stated that the assembly "may from time to time advise" changes in treaties or "the consideration of international conditions whose continuance might endanger the peace of the world." On reduction of armaments also, Articles VIII and IX went no further than the creation of a permanent commission to advise the council, and the injunction that the council "shall formulate plans for such reduction for the consideration and action of the several Governments."

What was not included in the covenant is instructive. The French representative sought repeatedly to insert provision for armed forces under the control of the League, either an international force or national contingents at the disposal of a permanent international staff; these proposals were blocked by the United States and Great Britain. To many, not only in France, the refusal to put armed force behind the provisions of the covenant meant that League decisions would inevitably be ineffective. In a very different way, confidence in the ideal purposes of the League was impaired by the dispute over racial equality. The Japanese wished to include a sentence endorsing the equality of all nations and their people; the American and British representatives refused, because they feared League action against racial discrimination in immigration laws. When Wilson proposed a clause guaranteeing religious freedom, the Japanese representative promptly countered with the proposal that since religious and racial discrimination were equally bad, both should be condemned in a single article. As a historian of the League tersely commented: "The Japanese argument combined disconcertingly, from the British and American point of view, the qualities of being unanswerable and unacceptable. The only course, therefore, was to abandon both suggestions."[10]

As the peace treaties began to take form in the spring of 1919, relations between and within the delegations of victorious powers became increasingly strained. Within the American and British delegations, some who had wholeheartedly supported Wilson's promise of a peace based on impartial justice became convinced that the punitive clauses of the treaties and the violations of the principle of self-determination were merely made more reprehensible by the moral language in which these clauses were clothed. Some experts resigned; others, and even some of the delegates, made no secret of their disgust with the vindictive character of the treaties and with the failure of the Big Three to make any settlement with Russia. On the other hand, all of Clemenceau's prestige was required to silence the dissatisfaction of

10. F. P. Walters, *A History of the League of Nations* (2 vols., London, 1952), I, 64. This is in many ways the best study of the formation and history of the League.

those who, like Marshal Foch and President Poincaré, believed he was sacrificing the security of France in order to maintain unity with America and Britain. The conflicting claims of China and Japan proved impossible to reconcile, and China refused to sign the Treaty of Versailles. When Wilson made a public appeal for the Italian people to abandon their claim to Fiume, there was an explosion of wrath in the Italian press and the Italian delegation left the conference for a time. The Big Three could take comfort from the fact that some thought their compromises too lenient to the enemy states, while others thought they were too harsh; similarly, if some wished friendly negotiations with the Bolsheviks, others wished a war of extermination against the Bolsheviks.

3. THE VICTORS DIVIDED

Working together, Clemenceau, Lloyd George, and Wilson had come to understand, if not to share, one another's points of view. They were united in the conviction that the peace settlement could endure only if their countries continued the wartime alliance and if each of the Big Three made compromises in order to maintain unity. They were conscious that their work was imperfect and that no real settlement had been made of some problems, particularly reparation. However, agencies like the reparation commission had been created to review the work of the peace conference; the representatives of the victors, working together on the supreme council, could make adjustments on other problems; and the League of Nations could cope with threats to peace as they arose. The important thing, it seemed, was to end the uncertainty which kept all Europe in turmoil; therefore, many clauses of the peace treaties were accepted in admittedly imperfect form. When Lloyd George and Wilson left Paris, they and Clemenceau felt that they had put Europe and the world on the way to recovery by their labors and had preserved the unity of Britain, France, and the United States.

The fact that, very early, it became customary to regard the settlement as the work of the Big Three suggested some loss since the conference opened. In the first weeks of the conference the representatives of Japan and Italy formed part of the inner circle. However, the Japanese delegates took little part in discussion of the European settlement, and by the end showed no concern over anything except problems which directly affected Japanese interests, such as racial equality and German rights in the Shantung peninsula. Whether it would have been possible to draw Japan into full participation in the problems of peacemaking, no one can say. But Japan was the one Asian power on the supreme council, and the withdrawal of Japan from full participation in the peacemaking meant that the most populous continent was unrepresented.

The Italian delegates left the conference in anger over the Fiume question on April 24, 1919, and although they returned for the signing of the Treaty of Versailles, the Italian people were angered by the inferior status of Italy at the conference. Little effort was made by the Big Three to conceal their conviction that Italy was not entitled to full equality with the Three. Italy signed the peace treaties, but Italy was, and remained, a "revisionist" power, determined to change the settlement made at Paris. To make clear Italian determination to win a share of the Turkish spoils, Italian troops were landed at Adalia in southern Asia Minor on March 29, 1919. On September 12, 1919, the nationalist poet Gabriele D'Annunzio, with a group of volunteers, seized the disputed city of Fiume. While the Italian government disavowed his coup, his seizure of the city could easily have been blocked—and indeed he could easily have been ejected by the Italian armed forces—but nothing was done. The passiveness of the Italian government in the face of D'Annunzio's defiance encouraged the small but noisy groups of nationalists who were beginning to look for leadership to the ex-socialist editor of the Milan newspaper *Popolo d'Italia*, Benito Mussolini. The first Fascio di Combattimento (literally, bundle or group of combat) was organized in Milan on March 23, 1919, with a program which was vague on everything except insistence on action to further Italian nationalism. At the time, the birthday of Fascism passed almost unnoticed, even in Italy.[11]

The withdrawal of Japan into exclusive preoccupation with Japanese interests in East Asia and the restless dissatisfaction of Italy made more obvious the need for united defense of the still incomplete Peace of

11. A useful guide to recent studies on the history of Italy in the years immediately following the war is Roberto Vivarelli's "Italy 1919–1921: The Current State of Research," *Journal of Contemporary History*, III (1968), 103–12. See also Vivarelli's *Il dopoguerra in Italia e l'avvento del Fascismo (1918–1922)*, Vol. I, *Dalla fine della guerra all'impresa di Fiume* (Naples, 1967).

Paris by the Big Three. Already, however, that unity was disintegrating.

In the United States, approval by two-thirds of the Senate was necessary for ratification of the Treaty of Versailles. The Republican party had a slim majority in the Senate, and Republicans were naturally not eager to add luster to a Democratic President's name by simply approving the treaty he brought home from Paris. Possibly if Wilson had shown the skill in political negotiation which had marked his early years in the White House he could have secured ratification without vital change in the treaty. However, in this crisis he showed instead the unbending stubbornness which also had been evident in parts of his earlier career. His chief opponent, Senator Henry Cabot Lodge, adopted delaying tactics, hoping that time would weaken popular support for the treaty. These tactics were successful. Soon those who did not like this or that part of the treaty were insisting on deletions or additions, and Lodge was quick to formulate reservations to satisfy all the objectors. More important, Lodge concentrated his attack on Article X of the League covenant. To Wilson, Article X was the "heart" of the covenant; to an increasing number of Americans it meant that the United States must take part in every quarrel anywhere in the world. During the war Americans had convinced themselves that all peoples on the Allied side possessed all virtues and that the enemy powers were evil incarnate. Now that the war was over, there was an increasing disposition to see the Allied peoples as selfish and ungrateful, the liberated peoples of central and southeastern Europe as insatiable in their demands for American aid, and the defeated Germans, in their misery, as worthy of sympathy. Wartime idealism was giving way to disillusionment, even to a cynical disposition to dismiss all idealism contemptuously as "propaganda."

In a similar situation William Ewart Gladstone, the British statesman from whom Wilson had drawn inspiration in his youth, had successfully carried his case to the British people in the Midlothian campaign. Now the American disciple of the great British liberal set out in his turn to speak directly to the American people, despite warnings that after the strain of the war and the peace conference he should not further tax his strength. His strength did give way, and he was forced to break off his campaign. On October 2, 1919, he suffered a severe stroke. Thereafter, he was unable actively to support the treaty, but he remained President and leader of the Democratic party, and he remained determined to block what he considered crippling amendments to the treaty.

The decisive votes were taken in the Senate on November 19, 1919. Under orders from Wilson, most of the Democratic senators voted against ratifying the Treaty of Versailles with the reservations which Lodge had attached to it; the resolution failed to win even a majority.

During the winter repeated efforts were made to rephrase the Lodge reservations so that ratification could be effected. All failed. When the final vote was taken on March 19, 1920, a majority voted for the treaty with the reservations, but the vote was seven short of the necessary two-thirds majority. Wilson continued confident that the treaty would be ratified after the national elections in November, 1920; but even Democrats who, on his instructions, voted against ratification with reservations realized that the popular mood had shifted and was now indifferent if not hostile to treaty and League. On August 25, 1921, after the new Republican administration took office, a separate treaty of peace was made with Germany. The United States, which had played a decisive part in determining the issue of the war and in shaping the Peace of Paris, had refused to accept responsibility for upholding the peace settlement.

The confused debate in the United States was followed with mingled feelings in Britain and France. Woodrow Wilson's unconcealed conviction that while he stood for the general interests of mankind, the rulers of Britain and France could see no further than the selfish interests of their own nation, indeed no further than the selfish interests of the dominant minority within their country, had inevitably created resentment. To many it seemed that the United States had been very late in recognizing the justice of the Allied cause, had made few sacrifices for victory, and had grown rich from the war while the European democracies were draining themselves of manpower and wealth; then, victory achieved, Wilson had come to Paris claiming a monopoly of virtue and presuming to sit in judgment on European problems of which he was ignorant. At the other extreme, those who had put their confidence in Wilson rather than in their own national leaders were disillusioned by the compromises he had accepted to maintain Allied unity. As Wilson came under attack in his own country, therefore, there was a disposition to take comfort from the prospect that European problems would not, in the future, be complicated by Wilsonian meddling. Moreover, some of the reservations attached to the treaty by the Senate did not appear as important to Europeans as they did to Wilson. In particular, to most who accepted the League, the promise contained in Article X of the covenant that all members would come to the defense of a member state in case of aggression, and the sanctions of Article XVI, had not really meant that if there was war anywhere all members of the League must fight. Just as Europeans had been unwilling to accept the Fourteen Points as a yardstick for every European problem, so they did not regard the text of the League covenant as a criminal code which must be enforced by the total military and economic force of every member state.

As, however, the prospect of withdrawal of the United States from the League and from the defense of the world settlement became first a possibility and then a certainty, there was mounting alarm particularly in France, but also among those in Britain who could look beyond the momentarily strong position of the Empire.

Lloyd George returned from Paris confident of the future. Behind his coalition government there was a secure majority in the House of Commons. The opposition was small and divided. The Labour party had increased its popular vote from 400,000 to well over 2 million in the election of 1918, but it had elected only fifty-nine members and many of its leaders had been defeated. The Liberals outside the coalition had elected only twenty-six members, and the party was never to recover its old position in Parliament. The country was enjoying a boom which permitted the rapid absorption of demobilized troops into civilian occupations: within a year nearly 4 million men were demobilized, and unemployment remained small. In the flood of prosperity, wartime controls and rationing were ended. During the last months of the war there had been widespread fear of social revolution, and there had been much talk of the danger of Bolshevism during the election campaign. There were severe strikes in 1919, but they were touched off by the rapid rise in the cost of living, and in 1920 fear of social revolution subsided temporarily.

The position of the Empire seemed as strong as in the years immediately following Waterloo. The German navy and merchant marine were gone, and German overseas colonies were divided among the victors, with those of strategic importance in the hands of Great Britain or the British Dominions. Russia, the rival of the British Empire until common rivalry with Germany brought a truce in 1907, was now weakened by revolution and civil war. Turkey was powerless, awaiting partition. The great "Red Triangle," with its base in South Africa and Australia and its apex in India, seemed completely secure. Along the short route to India the British position had been strengthened by the ending of Turkish suzerainty over Egypt during the war; Egypt was now a British protectorate. Gone was the Russian menace in Iran and at the Turkish Straits; to screen the approach to the Mediterranean from the Aegean, Greece was encouraged by Lloyd George to land troops at Smyrna on May 14, 1919. Lord Curzon boasted, "The British flag never flew over a more powerful or a more united Empire than now; Britons never had better cause to look the world in the face; never did our voice count for more in the councils of the nations, or in determining the future destinies of mankind."[12]

Curzon's boast was made in November, 1918; to most Englishmen it still was valid a year or even two years later; but to the more discerning his words had an increasingly hollow ring. Even while in Paris, Lloyd George had occasional misgivings about the world he was helping to shape. Like most British statesmen, he had been trained in the tradition that the best guarantee of British security was the balance of power, preferably with Britain in the position of balance wheel between rival powers or groups of powers. In 1919 there was no balance, in Europe or in other parts of the world. In Europe, France was for the moment the only great power, and the French were seeking to solidify their position by building up the new or enlarged states of central Europe as counterweights against temporarily weakened Germany and Russia. British leaders were convinced that the French policy was bound to fail. Germany and Russia would inevitably regain their strength. The temptation of the two to unite would be great; and if they did unite, the states which separated them would be no match for them.

In the Far East also there was no balance. To create such a balance, Britain had allied with Japan in 1902, and after the Russo-Japanese War and the formation of the Anglo-Russian entente, there had been relative stability. Now that Russian strength was broken, Japan was the only great power with formidable strength in East Asia, and Japan was

---

12. Earl of Ronaldshay, *The Life of Lord Curzon* (3 vols., N.Y., 1928), III, 199.

using that strength to advance at the expense of both Russia and China. The Japanese advance aroused resentment in the United States: the concessions made to Japan in the Shantung peninsula were effectively exploited by senatorial opponents of the Treaty of Versailles. Moreover, the American opponents of Versailles were suggesting that it was the Anglo-Japanese alliance which gave Japan the courage to push ahead in Asia, and that the Alliance was now directed against the United States. Here a new and dangerous unsolved problem obtruded. The United States had embarked on a program of naval construction in 1916 which, if completed, would challenge the naval supremacy of Britain, and the Anglo-Japanese alliance was becoming an effective argument for American advocates of "a navy second to none."

One other potential source of Anglo-American discord weighed heavy on the British government: the loans made to Britain during the war and in the months following the close of hostilities by the United States government. These war debts were, in British thinking, inseparably connected with the still unsettled problem of German reparation; but the Americans denied that the two problems were connected in any way.

While, therefore, the campaign against ratification of the Treaty of Versailles offered to Britain the pleasing prospect of relief from American tutelage, it also raised the possibility not only of complicating the shift from war to peace but of stimulating Anglo-American rivalry. Very tactfully, the British government intimated through Viscount Grey, the elder statesman who enjoyed most respect in the United States, that American ratification of the treaty with reservations was preferable to rejection, but Grey's efforts antagonized Wilson without winning concessions from opponents of the treaty.

When the treaty was rejected by the Senate, the British could at least take comfort from the fact that their own obligations had been lightened by the American action. The joint Anglo-American treaty of guarantee to France was to go into effect only if ratified by both guarantors. The refusal of the United States to ratify relieved Britain of all obligation to protect France from invasion, apart from Article X of the covenant, and comment both in Britain and in the Dominions showed with increasing clarity that with America out of the League, Article X would not be regarded as an automatic obligation to use force to resist aggression. The triumph of isolation in America released a wave of isolationist sentiment in Britain which had, almost un-noticed, been gathering force since the conclusion of the armistice. A British scholar, writing in the years between the wars, concluded that "the desire for isolation, the knowledge that it is impossible—these are the two poles between which the needle of the British compass con-tinues to waver."[13] By the early months of 1920 the needle had moved toward isolation. On the one hand, there was unwillingness to main-tain a peace settlement which increasingly seemed both inequitable and unworkable; on the other hand, confidence in the ability of Britain to go it alone, already great at the end of the war, was heightened by the economic boom, now at its climax. The new mood was reflected in a disposition to criticize the peace settlement, and at the same time to avoid responsibility.

When, immediately after the Senate vote of November 19, 1919, the American government decided to bring home the American delegation at Paris, the French protested vigorously. The effect would be deplor-able if the Americans "were to shake the dust of France off their feet." The response of the American Secretary of State, Robert Lansing, was chilling: "Public opinion in the United States is against further American participation in and responsibility for the settlement of political questions which are largely subjects of European concern."[14] The only concession he would make was that the American ambassa-dor to France might attend meetings of the supreme council as an observer but not as a participant. On December 9, 1919, the American delegation left France.

The French felt they had been duped. To secure the Anglo-American treaty of guarantee, Clemenceau had surrendered the mate-rial guarantee of French security demanded by Foch and Poincaré, the permanent separation of the Rhineland from Germany. Now the strongest of the victorious powers had repudiated any responsibility for the defense of the European settlement. Many Americans, even Presi-dent Wilson, were beginning to criticize French "militarism" and to complain that France was determined to dominate Europe by force of arms. The British, to be sure, joined with France in compelling Ger-

13. R. W. Seton-Watson, *Britain in Europe, 1789–1914* (N.Y., 1937), p. 37.
14. United States Department of State, *Papers Relating to the Foreign Relations of the United States: 1919. The Paris Peace Conference*, Vol. XI (Washington, 1945), pp. 674, 691, 696, 697.

many to bring the Treaty of Versailles into effect on January 10, 1920, but influential voices in Britain were already calling for a revision of the treaty, and it was clear that the treaty of guarantee was dead.

Clemenceau was quick to feel the anger of his countrymen. He had allowed his name to be put forward as a candidate for president of France. At the election on January 17, 1920, he was defeated. The next day he resigned as premier and the long career of the indomitable old patriot came to an abrupt end.

Soon both the British and Germans experienced the new temper of France. In order to suppress a left-wing rising in the Ruhr, German troops were sent into the demilitarized zone. Immediately, and without consulting the British, French troops occupied Darmstadt and Frankfurt on April 6, 1920, and remained there despite British protests until the German troops left the demilitarized zone.

Seen from the outside, the new temper of France was bellicose and vengeful, determined to enforce every clause of the Treaty of Versailles no matter what the cost to Germany, to Europe, or even to France. Seen from at home, or at least by the members of the *bloc national* which had emerged victorious from the election of November 16, 1919, France was fighting single-handed to defend European civilization and receiving only abuse from false allies who had tricked Clemenceau and who would now, if they could, complete the ruin of Europe.

So many members of the center and right-wing *bloc national* were war veterans that the new Chamber of Deputies was called, from the color of the French uniform, the horizon blue chamber; but fear rather than militarism dominated the bloc. Even with the addition of Alsace-Lorraine, postwar France had fewer citizens than before the war. Despite territorial losses, Germany remained more populous than France; and the French birth rate remained lower. For the moment Germany was weak and disarmed, but the French government was convinced that if the Treaty of Versailles was undermined by concessions, or by inaction in face of German violations of the treaty, German power and the German lust for domination would lead to a repetition of 1914. By enforcing obedience to Versailles, therefore, France was protecting Europe. Moreover, France could protect Europe only so long as French military strength remained unimpaired and German strength remained fettered. American and British criticisms of French "militarism" aroused resentment, but did not weaken conviction of the rightness of French policy. Similarly, the French were impatient with British suggestions that to hold Russia away from Germany and to bring about an economic revival in eastern Europe a more conciliatory policy should be adopted toward the Bolsheviks. To France, Bolshevik Russia was an ally which had deserted at the crisis of the war, a debtor which had defaulted on its obligations, and an antagonist which struck at the social unity of France. To maintain unity with Britain at the end of 1919, France agreed to urge the Poles to accept the "Curzon line" as their eastern frontier, but when the Poles refused to surrender their claim to the Ukrainians and White Russians east of the line, France reverted to the idea of a large and strong Poland as a buffer between Russia and Germany.

When the Treaty of Versailles was ratified on January 10, 1920, it was already doubtful whether there was effective force behind the treaty, much less behind the other treaties which, together with Versailles, formed the Peace of Paris. Japan was preoccupied with defending its gains in the Far East and with extending its influence in that area. Italy was dissatisfied with the gains made at Paris and resentful of the secondary role allocated to Italy by the Western democracies. The British, confident of the strength and security of the Empire, had demobilized, not only militarily but in spirit, and were turning away from problems connected with the war to the more congenial task of world-wide economic reconstruction. The Americans were rapidly convincing themselves that Europeans were incorrigibly belligerent and that isolation from the quarrels of Europe was both desirable and possible. Of the great powers, only France was wholeheartedly committed to the defense of the peace settlement.

4. DISENCHANTMENT

In the closing days of 1919, during holiday celebrations of unparalleled extravagance, there appeared in London a small book which cast a somber shadow over the gaiety of the season, John Maynard Keynes's *The Economic Consequences of the Peace*.[15] Keynes was then only thirty-six, but he had already won recognition as a brilliant Cambridge economist and as a member of Bloomsbury, the group of artists and

---

15. (N.Y., 1920.) Unless otherwise indicated, subsequent page citations in this section are from *The Economic Consequences of the Peace*.

writers which included Lytton Strachey, Virginia Woolf, E. M. Forster, and Roger Fry. During the war Keynes served the British treasury, and he was treasury representative at the peace conference in 1919; early in June he resigned, sick and disgusted. After some hesitation, and encouraged by the South African statesman General Jan Smuts, he decided to attack the treaty. His book was written hurriedly, but the economic condition of Europe and the probable effects of the economic clauses of the Treaty of Versailles had been his constant preoccupation.

He began by sketching the magnitude of the economic achievement of Europe in the years before 1914. During those years, Europe had not only accumulated capital sufficient to support an ever larger population on an ever higher standard of living; Europe had also exported vast amounts of capital which developed the economy of the non-European world and increasingly made the world an extension of Europe. This amazingly productive system was dislocated by the war. "A great part of the Continent was sick and dying; its population was greatly in excess of the numbers for which a livelihood was available; its organization was destroyed, its transport system disrupted, and its food supplies terribly impaired."[16]

All this was painfully familiar to Keynes's readers. Through 1919 relief organizations and particularly the American Relief Administration under the direction of Herbert Hoover brought vast amounts of food to Europe to keep the population from starving.

Keynes's argument that the reparation clauses of the Treaty of Versailles would increase the economic dislocation echoed the views not only of the American experts at Paris but also of many in the British and some in the other delegations. As Keynes pointed out, the international trade account of Germany before the war had shown a large deficit of "visible" items, that is, German imports of goods had been much larger than exports. The account had been more than balanced by "invisible exports," that is, payments made by foreigners for the use of German shipping, for interest on German investments abroad, for insurance premiums, etc. The credit surplus in the German account had been invested abroad so that the total account of "visible" and "invisible" items had been in rough balance.

16. Pp. 25, 26.

Now, Keynes said, the capacity of Germany to make payments abroad had been impaired

by the almost total loss of her colonies, her overseas connections, her mercantile marine, and her foreign properties, by the cession of ten per cent of her territory and population, of one third of her coal and of three quarters of her iron ore, by two million casualties amongst men in the prime of life, by the starvation of her people for four years, by the burden of a vast war debt, by the depreciation of her currency to less than one-seventh its former value, by the disruption of her allies and their territories, by Revolution at home and Bolshevism on her borders, and by all the unmeasured ruin in strength and hope of four years of all-swallowing war and final defeat.[17]

Until prosperity and stability had been restored, there was no hope that Germany could make any substantial reparation payments; certainly it was futile to hope that Germany would pay $5 billion before May 1, 1921, as the treaty required. If prosperity and stability did return, Germany might be able to pay as much as $10 billion over a generation, an amount which Keynes estimated was about the sum Germany was obligated to pay under the prearmistice agreement. The popular notion that Germany could pay several times that overlooked two facts: payment must come from the export of German goods, and the goods must find a market. He called on those who expected such sums "to say *in what specific commodities* they intend this payment to be made and *in what markets* the goods are to be sold."[18]

In Keynes's view, the failure of the peacemakers to effect a settlement of the inter-Allied war debts would have consequences as disastrous as the unworkable reparation settlement. The American, British, and French governments had all made loans to other governments. The total of these intergovernmental debts was about $20 billion, of which about $10 billion had been loaned by the United States and nearly $9 billion by Britain. Conceivably, Keynes admitted, these debts *could* be paid. Some almost certainly *would not* be paid. Russia had already repudiated her war debt of nearly $4 billion, and other financially weak allies were unlikely to pay anything. So far as Britain, France, and Italy were concerned, the demand for fantastic sums from Germany was based "not on any reasonable calculation of what Germany can, in fact, pay, but on a well-founded appreciation of the unbearable financial

17. P. 187.
18. P. 202.

situation in which these countries will find themselves unless she pays."[19] In other words, a workable reparation settlement would be possible only in connection with a settlement of war debts. For himself, he did not believe "any of these tributes will continue to be paid, at the best, for more than a very few years. They do not square with human nature or agree with the spirit of the age."[20]

So far, Keynes was saying publicly what many had said privately at Paris. There, however, Americans had argued that, for the present, the linking of war debts and reparation was politically impossible; Lloyd George had argued that British opinion demanded reparation even at the cost, for the present, of an unworkable settlement; and Clemenceau had argued that, for the present, French opinion would say any reparation total was too low, and that therefore the setting of the total must be deferred. None of the Big Three was primarily interested in the economic settlement; all felt that political questions were of greater importance and that the most important political problem was the maintenance of Allied unity. That problem solved, lesser problems, including reparation, could be adjusted when popular passions cooled.

Keynes had no patience with such arguments; for him the Peace of Paris was vicious just because the Allied statesmen did not realize "that the most serious of the problems which claimed their attention were not political or territorial but financial and economic, and that the perils of the future lay not in frontiers or sovereignties but in food, coal, and transport."[21] Keynes professed to speak only as an economist, and he called himself "an immoralist"; yet his indictment of the treaty and its makers was raised from an economic treatise to a landmark in the history of the interwar years by the moral indignation which gave fire to his words. Clemenceau, Lloyd George, and Wilson were for him not merely mistaken, they were worshipers of false gods which must be overthrown if Europe was to have peace.[22]

Moral principle, political expediency, and power politics—all, in Keynes's view, stood condemned. Wilson's promise of a just peace, the

19. P. 277.
20. P. 282.
21. P. 146.
22. Keynes's description of himself as "an immoralist" is in the essay "My Early Beliefs" (*Essays and Sketches in Biography* [N.Y., Meridian Books, 1956], p. 252); this essay and others in the volume are helpful to an understanding of the prophetic fervor which characterizes so much of Keynes's thought about the peace conference.

promise which was the basis of the prearmistice agreement between Germany and the Allies, had led only to "the weaving of that web of sophistry and Jesuitical exegesis that was finally to clothe with insincerity the language and substance of the whole Treaty."[23] Lloyd George's opportunism had not served the interests of his country, which were inseparably linked to the peace and prosperity of the Continent: "An inefficient, unemployed, disorganized Europe faces us, torn by internal strife and international hate, fighting, starving, pillaging, and lying."[24] It was vain for Clemenceau to seek to set the clock back: "You cannot restore Central Europe to 1870 without setting up such strains in the European structure and letting loose such human and spiritual forces as, pushing beyond frontiers and races, will overwhelm not only you and your 'guarantees,' but your institutions, and the existing order of your Society."[25]

These men and these fatal prescriptions must, he argued, give way to a recognition that now as before the war "round Germany as a central support the rest of the European economic system grouped itself, and on the prosperity and enterprise of Germany the prosperity of the rest of the Continent mainly depended."[26] That central support had been broken by the war and by the Treaty of Versailles; it must be rebuilt by a revision of the treaty. Not only must reparation be scaled down and the war debts canceled; inflation must be halted and industry revived by an international loan. Even that would not suffice. Keynes proposed that a great free trade union should be formed under the auspices of the League, and that "Germany, Poland, the new States which formerly composed the Austro-Hungarian and Turkish Empires, and the Mandated States should be compelled to adhere to this Union for ten years."[27] Beyond that, Germany should be encouraged to undertake the economic rebuilding of Russia: "Let us encourage and assist Germany to take up again her place in Europe as a creator and organizer of wealth for her Eastern and Southern neighbors."[28]

It is not strange that Keynes's book was denounced. Before the Treaty of Versailles went into effect he was demanding that it be

23. P. 51.
24. P. 249.
25. P. 37.
26. P. 16.
27. P. 265.
28. P. 294.

scrapped and that Europe be reorganized so that it would be an economic dependency of Germany. Moreover, beyond an occasional passing reference, he ignored what the Allied peoples and statesmen alike had assumed to be the moral justification of the Peace of Paris, the guilt of Germany for the war; instead, his indignation was reserved for the Allied leaders, and his plan for a great customs union of central and eastern Europe was, as even he acknowledged, reminiscent of "the former German dream of Mittel-Europa."[29]

What is startling is not the abuse heaped on Keynes but the respectful hearing accorded his views in the United States, in Britain, and in neutral countries. American opponents of the Treaty of Versailles gleefully quoted not only his castigation of Wilson but his angry statement that "if I had influence at the United States Treasury, I would not lend a penny to a single one of the present governments of Europe."[30] His contemptuous references to Poland, Rumania, and the other countries of the *cordon sanitaire* fortified the British conviction, already evident at the peace conference, that the eastern territorial settlement was both unjust and unworkable, and should not receive British support. His economic proposals came just as the British people were awakening to the uncomfortable realization that the hope of extracting large reparation from Germany was an illusion while the war debts to America were to be a terribly real burden on the British economy, and that the removal of German economic competition was of less importance for British prosperity than the inability of an impoverished Germany and an impoverished Europe to buy the products of British industry.

But other critics had voiced misgivings about the economic clauses of the Treaty of Versailles and about the territorial settlement in central and southeastern Europe. What made Keynes's book, in Maurice Baumont's words, "explode like a bomb"[31] under the Peace of Paris was the apocalyptic fervor with which he attacked the very foundations of the world settlement. Through more than four years of war, the Allied peoples had fought on, hoping that from their sacrifices would come a better, a more decent, and above all a more peaceful world than they had known before 1914. The peacemakers at Paris were able to offer nothing better than hope deferred: by new effort and sacrifice, by

29. P. 267.
30. P. 284.
31. Maurice Baumont, *La faillite de la paix* (3d ed., 2 vols., Paris, 1951), I, 165.

common effort and sacrifice, the Allied peoples could, over time, repair what war had destroyed and slowly build the foundations of a better world. Before the peacemakers had completed their task, rebellion had begun against the assumption of new tasks, rebellion not only in the United States but in Britain and even in France. The hysterical gaiety of the holiday season of 1919 in Paris was symptomatic; the French government was forced to impose a curfew on New Year's Eve to prevent a repetition of the bacchanal of Christmas Eve.

At that moment Keynes's jeremiad appeared. In nostalgic detail he showed that by contrast with the postwar world, and by contrast with earlier centuries, the era which came to an abrupt end in 1914 had been the summit of human history. The war had ended "that happy age."[32] The real task of the peace conference had been "to re-establish life and to heal wounds";[33] instead, the moralism of Wilson, the demagogy of Lloyd George, the vindictive patriotism of Clemenceau, and the greed of a score of little states had resulted in a Carthaginian peace made more odious by "the quality which chiefly distinguishes this transaction from all its historical predecessors—its insincerity."[34]

Keynes found a hearing because he said what many wanted to hear: that the way to secure peace was to repudiate the Peace of Paris. Those parts of his book which called for effort or sacrifice were ignored. In the United States his indictment of Wilson, the League, and the treaty were used to prove that withdrawal from the affairs of Europe was not repudiation of a responsibility but proof of superior virtue; his plea for the cancellation of war debts and the granting of new loans for reconstruction was ignored. Keynes's countrymen found convincing both his economic analysis and his indictment of French preoccupation with security, but even while withdrawing from their responsibility for the defense of the European settlement they clung to the imperial gains obtained by the settlement.

It is partly because it vividly illuminates the mood in which America withdrew completely, and Britain withdrew as far as possible, from the affairs of Europe that Keynes's book merits extended analysis. Beyond that, and of greater importance, the book illuminates the "disenchantment" of the postwar years—to use the title of another British book.[35]

32. Keynes, p. 10.
33. P. 26.
34. P. 65.
35. C. E. Montague, *Disenchantment* (London, 1922).

The moral exaltation of the war years, so admirably expressed in the speeches of Woodrow Wilson, now seemed flat and stale. After years of reading about the heroism of the Allied soldier, and the depravity of the German, there was wry pleasure to be had from reading books with expressive titles such as *Now It Can Be Told*.

It had been far from Keynes's intention to feed the swelling flood of disillusionment and cynicism; but that he did, and here again his book is representative. Some of the most telling blows against the Peace of Paris were delivered by those who, like Keynes, were most concerned to build an international community in which peace would be preserved by concerted action. Wilson, and those who continued to follow his lead, believed that at Paris they had made a beginning with the material available. Only Germany and the other defeated states had been disarmed; but the victors had pledged themselves to disarm, and disarmament had been made one of the tasks of the League. Only the German colonies and parts of Turkey had been made mandates of the League; but it could be hoped that, once started, trusteeship would spread. The principle of self-determination had been repeatedly violated; but the map of Europe was closer to that principle than ever before, and the minorities' treaties provided the means by which, where minorities existed, their rights could be protected by the League. Similarly, means had been provided by which the rights of labor, of women and children, of small nations, could be protected as the League grew to represent the nations of the world. There were grave defects in the treaties, argued their defenders, but the treaties had also created agencies like the League and the reparation commission to cure these defects.

Many besides Keynes believed Wilson had won only words and had sacrificed the substance of his program, and they entered into tacit alliance with those who repudiated any kind of international organization. The result was not to bring about the revision of the Treaty of Versailles which was the purpose of Keynes's book. The unity of the Allies gave way to recrimination and rivalry. The idealism which had given dignity to suffering and death gave way to mockery of all ideals as a fraud found out. Before the first meeting of the League council in January, 1920, it was evident that with the United States absent the covenant did not, in fact, command the allegiance of the remaining members. As for the Treaty of Versailles, France was now determined to enforce even its most onerous provisions, and in the absence of the

United States, France moved into control of the enforcement agencies such as the reparation commission. On the other side, Germany, heartened by the division among the victors, was in full rebellion against the treaty. Others too, such as the Turks, were encouraged to resist. The new or enlarged states of central Europe were conscious that they had attained a new importance for French security and could therefore be more independent and more demanding.

When the peace conference was opened in Paris in January, 1919, the prestige of the Western democracies had been high and their power invincible. When the Treaty of Versailles went into effect a year later the Big Three were no longer united. Their prestige had fallen. Their power and their will to enforce the treaty were alike so uncertain as to invite testing by the rebel and the vanquished.

Already, not only in Britain but in the neutral countries of Europe the ground had been prepared in which, years later, the seeds of appeasement were to grow. Whether this would have been the result had the United States remained a partner in the implementation of the settlement cannot be known. Without the United States and without the full support of Britain, the settlement from the start rested almost entirely on the military power of France. This was too narrow and too weak a foundation.

Chapter Two

THE RUSSIAN AND THE GERMAN REVOLUTIONS

I. THE BOLSHEVIKS AND THE WEST

WHEN the peacemakers met in Paris in January, 1919, the outcome of the revolutions in Russia and Germany was impossible to predict. The revolutionary government in Germany was pledged to the establishment of social democracy, in the sense that these words had been used in western Europe before 1914; in practice, decisive actions of the government were determined by fear that the German revolution would follow the pattern already taken by the revolution in Russia. As a result, the governing classes of imperial Germany kept a strong position in the armed forces, the bureaucracy, and the judiciary. This situation might have been transitory. It is possible that as fear of Communism waned and as parties pledged to social democracy acquired confidence, the old ruling groups which had led Germany to defeat in 1918 would have been pushed aside. The harsh terms of the Treaty of Versailles lessened this possibility. In the intense reaction against the treaty, the blunders of imperial Germany were obscured, and the prestige of the revolutionary government was compromised. Within a few months after the Treaty of Versailles went into effect in January, 1920, events demonstrated that while the German people were not prepared to go back to the old social and political system, neither were they united in support of social democracy. The old Germany was repudiated; the character which the new Germany would assume remained obscure. The victors in the war had wanted, indeed demanded, democratic government in Germany; by the Treaty of Versailles they helped to prevent the growth of social democracy in Germany.

The peacemakers were fully aware that German resistance to the provisions of the Peace of Paris was inevitable, at least for some years. In these circumstances, the attitude of Russia toward the peace settlement was obviously of great and possibly crucial importance. Since the eighteenth century, Russia had been a major element in the European balance of power. In theory, the Peace of Paris substituted a rule of law under the League covenant for the balance of power. But even the strongest adherent of the League had to recognize that with both Germany and Russia out of the League and hostile to the territorial settlement in Europe, the map of central and southeastern Europe could not be secure.

Throughout the Paris conference the shadow of the huge bulk of Russia hung over the discussions. Everyone recognized that the peace settlement would be incomplete and precarious without Russian participation. But what was Russia? When the peace conference began its work in January, 1919, a ferocious, confused civil war was being fought in Russia. When the Paris settlement went into effect a year later, the civil war was still being fought, and although by then it seemed likely that the Bolsheviks would win a military victory, the country was approaching breakdown.

Seen in retrospect, the year 1919 is decisive in Russian history. In that year the new Bolshevik rulers were learning to adapt their ideology to the problems of government, and in that year revolutionary Russia and Europe outside Russia were forming convictions about each other which were to persist through later years.

The break in Russian history came in March, 1917, when almost without bloodshed the parliament, or duma, set up a provisional government and the czar abdicated. This was the February Revolution (the Old Style calendar, thirteen days in arrears, was still in use in Russia). The provisional government never won effective control of the Russian land mass, and in November it was overthrown by the Bolshevik faction of the Russian socialists. This was the October Revolution.[1] Initially, the Bolsheviks did not have the support of most Russians. The closest to a democratic election ever held in Russia was that of November, 1917, for a constituent assembly. The Bolsheviks received much less than half of the popular vote and elected less than a quarter of the delegates. When the assembly met, the Red Guards of the Bolsheviks tried to overawe the delegates; when that failed, the assembly was simply dispersed by force on January 19, 1918.

---

1. A concise account of the events of 1917 in Russia is Isaac Deutscher, "The Russian Revolution," Chap. XIV of Vol. XII (2d ed.) of the *New Cambridge Modern History*, ed. by C. L. Mowat (Cambridge, 1968). *Red October*, by Robert Daniels (N.Y., 1967), is a controversial but brilliant reinterpretation.

Outside Russia, this episode was seen as one of many proofs that the Bolsheviks did not believe in democratic rule, even though they posed as the champions of the masses.

One of the first acts of the new revolutionary government was to appeal for peace. The appeal was issued, not in the usual form of diplomatic notes to the warring governments, but in radio broadcasts to the peoples of the world urging a peace without annexations and without indemnities. To Allied statesmen, this was clear evidence of Bolshevik hostility. In March, 1918, the Bolsheviks accepted the harsh peace of Brest-Litovsk with the Central Powers. To the Allies, this meant that Russia had become a satellite of Germany. Soon there was open enmity leading to armed intervention against the Bolsheviks by small Allied forces in European Russia, and to large-scale Japanese intervention, with some American assistance, in Asiatic Russia.[2]

The government of Bolshevik Russia made a treaty of peace with the government of imperial Germany, but this did not imply either peaceful or friendly relations between the two. When Germany became a republic, there was wild rejoicing in Moscow, now the capital of Russia, but the actions of Bolshevik agents in Germany showed clearly that they regarded the republic as merely the first stage in the transition from an "imperialist" to a "socialist" state. The Bolsheviks, while they might seek temporary "peace" with the governments of other states, regarded all these governments as enemies to be destroyed.

Even Marxists in Europe outside of Russia were, by 1919, coming to recognize that the Bolsheviks were determined to impose their interpretation of the teachings of Marx on all other socialist parties. In 1918 the Bolsheviks renamed their party the Communist party. When preparation began at the end of the war to revive the old Second International of the socialists, a congress was held in Moscow in March, 1919, to organize the Third, or Communist, International. This

2. James W. Morley describes the Japanese decision to intervene in *The Japanese Thrust into Siberia* (N.Y., 1957). For the story behind American intervention see Vol. II of George F. Kennan's *Soviet-American Relations, 1917–1920* (Princeton, 1958). On British intervention, see Richard Ullman, *Intervention and the War,* Vol. I of his *Anglo-Soviet Relations, 1917–1921* (Princeton, 1961). In the second volume (Princeton, 1968), Ullman continues the story to early 1920.

On the Treaty of Brest Litovsk, Werner Hahlweg, *Der Diktatfrieden von Brest-Litovsk und die bolshewistische Weltrevolution* (Münster, 1960), is a good, short introduction. J. Wheeler-Bennett, *The Forgotten Peace: Brest-Litovsk, March, 1918* (N.Y., 1939), is useful.

organization, usually called the Comintern, was headed by leading Russian Communists, and from the outside was seen as the propaganda and subversive arm of Bolshevik Russia; the insistence of the Russian government that the Comintern was a purely private organization was dismissed as hypocrisy.

Next to cruelty, hypocrisy was the charge most often leveled in 1919 against Bolshevik rule in Russia. At the outset, peasants were encouraged to break up the large estates and to farm the land as their own, yet decrees declared that all land was the property of the state and called for the seizure by force of the peasants' "surplus." The city worker was promised social reforms more sweeping than any in effect elsewhere in Europe, but successive decrees imposed military discipline on the worker. Subject nationalities were promised autonomy and, if they wished, independence, but in practice revolts of subject peoples were resisted by force.

Seen from the outside, the inseparable union of hypocrisy and cruelty was glaringly apparent in the contrast between the theoretical and the actual structure of the state in Communist Russia. In July, 1918, a constitution was proclaimed for what was called the Russian Socialist Federal Soviet Republic, that is, all of Russia except territory inhabited by some of the non-Russian peoples. The constitution began with a sweeping bill of rights. Supreme power was to rest in the All-Russian Congress of Soviets, which consisted of representatives of city and provincial councils or soviets, with representation heavily weighted in favor of the cities. When the congress was not in session, its powers were to be exercised by the central executive committee, which in turn appointed the cabinet or council of people's commissars. The vote was denied to those who hired labor or engaged in private trade or lived on capital investments, to members of the clergy, and to some officials of the czarist regime. Voting was to be open; the secret ballot was disdained as middle class.

In practice, supreme power rested in the Communist party, whose structure paralleled the constitutional structure. It was the proclaimed duty of the party to control, at each level, the corresponding political body. At the apex of the party structure was (after March, 1919) the Politburo, where the real discussion and decision took place, with only formal approval reserved for the council of people's commissars. Within the Politburo, and within the central executive committee of the party, discussion was at first relatively free and vigorous. Once an issue had been decided, however, discussion ended and complete obedience to the decision was exacted. This was what Communists called "democratic centralism."

The Soviet regime was not a democracy in the Western sense. And, while there were class enemies to combat, no bill of rights would be permitted to protect these enemies. On December 20, 1917, the All-Russian Extraordinary Commission (the Cheka) was created for "combating counterrevolution and sabotage." Its head was Feliks Dzerzhinski, a selfless lover of humanity with eager willingness to kill. During the comfortable years before 1914, Europeans had read of such altruistic killers with fascinated horror in histories of the French Revolution, but few had expected to see them appear again in the twentieth century. Soon terror was not only an admitted instrument of Soviet policy, but an instrument whose necessity and efficacy were proudly acknowledged by the Bolsheviks.

The silence with which the Cheka acted made an indelible impression. So, too, did the mass flight from Russia of members of the old aristocracy and middle classes. To men of property in the West, these were exactly the men, and their helpless families, who by birth, education, and enterprise were capable of giving leadership to the Russian people, but who, under the terror of Soviet "democratic centralism," were forced to flee to escape extermination. In the years that followed, capacity for horror was to be blunted, as one wave of refugees from terror followed another from one country, then another. However, the Soviet terror was the first, and the flood of Russian refugees was much the largest. Therefore, the identification of Soviet rule with terror and inhumanity was most complete and most lasting, and was to persist even when countries like Italy and Germany came under terrorist rule.

Except for occasional outbursts of rage at the blindness of capitalists to the sufferings of the oppressed masses, the new rulers of Russia were unperturbed by accusations of hypocrisy or cruelty. These new rulers had lived before 1917 in a closed community of revolutionists, whether in Russia or in exile. There they had formed a view of the science of society which had all the clarity and certainty which they attributed to the natural sciences. They were not all in agreement on the laws of social evolution, but they were all confident that Marxism, rightly interpreted, provided the key to historical change, the key which would open the way to the construction of the new, the socialist society.

By the time of the October Revolution, unquestioned leadership in the Bolshevik party had been won by Vladimir Ulyanov, who, like many Russian revolutionists, had adopted a pseudonym, Lenin. From his youth—he was born in 1870—Lenin had only one interest, revolution, in theory the world revolution of which Marxists dreamed, in actuality a Russian revolution, controlled by a revolutionary movement which in organization and leadership was suited to conditions in an absolutist police state.

The most obvious difference between Western Marxism and what came to be known as Marxism-Leninism was the organization of the party. In the West, Marxist parties were pledged to democracy, both in the organization of the party and in the political life of their country. From the outset, the Bolshevik party was a carefully screened group of professional revolutionists. Such an organization could, of course, be justified pragmatically as the only way to escape the vigilant and ruthless czarist police. Lenin, however, did not regard leadership by a highly trained elite as a temporary expedient necessitated by conditions in Russia. He believed that the working classes, living as they did in a capitalist world, could not rise above a trade union mentality which was nonrevolutionary, even antirevolutionary. It was the trained intelligence of the leaders of the workers which must recognize the existence of a revolutionary situation, precipitate the revolution, and keep firm control of the revolutionary government until the hold of bourgeois ideas on men's minds had been broken.

Momentous consequences flowed from Lenin's conviction that understanding was reserved for the party elite. His contempt for "formal democracy," most obviously shown in the armed dispersal of the constituent assembly, carried over to his relations with Marxists outside Russia and was resented even by many who took the lead in organizing communist parties, such as Rosa Luxemburg in Germany. Lenin's conviction that only the elite understood the processes of historical evolution and that all others were blinded by their capitalist mentality quite logically led him to the conclusion that people— whether individually or in the mass—could be treated as objects to be manipulated, if necessary by deception or by force. Finally, leadership within the Communist party became increasingly concentrated, first in the executive committee, then in the handful of members of the

Politburo, and finally in Lenin, a narrowing of authority which, apparently, he came himself to regret.

2. WAR COMMUNISM IN RUSSIA

The elitist mentality of Marxism-Leninism may be explained partly in terms of Lenin's personality, and is in good part a legacy of Russian autocratic traditions. But the sheer pressure of events in the first years of the revolution undoubtedly left a lasting mark.

Sitting in exile in Switzerland during the war, Lenin believed the capitalist world was rapidly moving toward revolution. To fight the war, the belligerent governments were organizing all their resources into a few giant enterprises, with control radiating out from the political and military centers. Meanwhile, he argued, the misery of the masses mounted to the point that a revolt of desperation was becoming inevitable. When the revolt came, Lenin concluded, it would be necessary for the revolutionary leaders merely to step into the positions of control at the center; the bureaucratic organization of government and industry would respond to the orders of the new leaders as it had responded to the old. Seizure of "the commanding heights" gave control over the whole apparatus.

Things proved less simple. In November, 1917, the Bolsheviks took over a country which was exhausted by war and demoralized by civil strife. At first there was only sporadic rebellion against Bolshevik rule, but when vast tracts of Russian territory were surrendered to win the peace of Brest Litovsk with Germany, civil war began, a confused and ferocious civil war against enemies who had little in common with one another except hatred of Bolshevism—against "White" armies, against subject nationalities, against contingents sent by the former allies of Russia, against desperate bands of peasants lumped together as "brigands," against Socialist Revolutionary terrorists. The capital was moved to Moscow in March, 1918, and from this center war radiated in every direction.

Under the pressure of civil war, it became apparent that "seizure of the commanding heights" was not enough. The mechanism of banking and finance began to collapse. Legitimate trade dried up; illegal traders, "bagmen," flourished. The machinery of government slowed; tax receipts fell off; inflation entered on an ever more dizzy spiral as paper currency was printed to meet current expenses.

The most important immediate problem was food. When the peasants seized the big estates they laid rough hands on the segment of agriculture which had earlier produced a surplus. When the estates were divided much equipment was destroyed and large numbers of animals were killed. The new peasant holders were less efficient producers, and what they produced they kept. Soon the provisioning of the Red army and of the cities became the central preoccupation of the government.

"History," Lenin now said, "proceeds by zigzags and crooked paths." Step by step he was driven from his belief that seizure of the commanding heights was enough; he was driven to seize direct control of every segment of the economy, down to the individual city worker and peasant.

The desperate effort of the Soviet government to reverse the trend toward complete collapse came to be called "war communism." In agriculture, war communism dated from decrees of the spring of 1918 calling for forcible seizure of the peasants' "surplus." In industry, war communism dated from a decree of June 28, 1918, nationalizing all major branches of industry; thereafter, the regime progressively moved into direct control not only of the great trusts but of single plants. Trade became a state monopoly in the fall of 1918. In labor relations, a series of decrees progressively approached militarization of the labor force. In December, 1918, industrial conscription was decreed for industries vital for war. As 1919 began, war communism had not been carried to completion, but the outline was becoming clear: for agriculture, the requisition policy; for industry, direct control as well as ownership by the state; for labor, military discipline; for trade, centrally organized allocation of supply to the private consumer as well as to industry and the army.

During the crisis of the Great Civil War in 1919, war communism became an iron dictatorship, political as well as economic. Industry and labor were completely harnessed to production for the Red army; in default of taxes which could not be collected, currency poured from the printing press and prices rose to the point where the currency was scarcely worth the cost of printing; the army was fed, though peasants were not left food for themselves and the cities starved.

The shift to war communism was defended as a holding action until the world revolution came. In May, 1918, Lenin said that Soviet Russia was "for the time being an island in the midst of a raging sea of imperialist depredation."[3] Alone, he said repeatedly, Soviet Russia could not survive; the task of moving this primitive economy, exhausted by war and civil strife, through the stages from a peasant to a socialist economy would be hopeless.[4] Soon, he argued, the people of states with advanced industrial systems would turn on their masters, as the Russians had done. The Russian example would speed the coming of revolution elsewhere. When industrial states like Germany became socialist, the center of Communist power would shift, say, to Berlin.

Lenin and his followers believed with passionate intensity in the world revolution as something which would soon flare up with irresistible force. Three times during the Great Civil War the world revolution seemed about to become a reality. The first was just after the October Revolution in 1917. When Lenin then launched his appeal for a peace without annexations or indemnities, he expected the war-weary masses to rise against their "imperialist" oppressors. That first example of what Communists called "demonstrative diplomacy" failed. Recognizing his failure, Lenin forced his unwilling colleagues to sign away parts of Russia in the treaty of Brest Litovsk; what remained of the Soviet island must be preserved until the "raging sea of imperialist depredation" subsided.

After the overthrow of the Hohenzollerns in Germany in November, 1918, the "iron tramp" of the world revolution was heard once more. In the months following, Communist agents sought to precipitate revolution not only in Germany but throughout central Europe, and the Comintern was organized as the high command of the revolutionary forces. There were a few Communist successes, in Bavaria and in Hungary, but these were quickly suppressed, and the German revolution stubbornly refused to advance. For the next year, from the spring of 1919 to the spring of 1920, the Bolsheviks were absorbed in battles against enemies at home and almost lost contact with the world outside.

The great achievement of that year was the building of the Red army by Leon Trotsky, whose real name was Lev Bronstein. Trotsky had earlier been an opponent of Lenin; now the talents of the two complemented each other. Lenin overwhelmed all opposition by the power of

3. V. I. Lenin, *Collected Works*, XXIII (N.Y., 1945), 16.
4. E. H. Carr, *The Bolshevist Revolution, 1917–1923*, III (London, 1953), 53.

his mind and will, by the persuasiveness of his theoretical writings, and by his ability to adjust theory to intractable circumstance. Trotsky also had a powerful mind, shown not least in his building of the Red army from nothing, shown also in the writings which place him among the literary giants of the century. But he could accept the leadership of another, which Lenin could not do, and he had the warmth and passion invaluable to a man who must win the loyalty of men in battle.

While they were in opposition to the ruling power, the Bolsheviks had worked effectively to destroy the military spirit of the Russian armed forces. Now, in power and under attack from all sides, they had to rebuild an army and inculcate military discipline. Probably the most important single decision of Trotsky, and certainly the decision most hated by other Communists, was the employment of nearly 50,000 czarist officers and about 250,000 czarist noncommissioned officers. Trotsky regarded the families of these officers as hostages, and in every military unit there was a political commissar who knew he would be shot if his unit was not successful. These harsh tactics would not, in themselves, have brought success. Trotsky managed to make the Red army an embodiment of Russian patriotism as well as of revolutionary spirit—after all, few of the czarist officers and noncommissioned officers were fighting for a Bolshevik victory. He also made the peasant believe he was fighting for his land, even though Communists recognized that the "petty bourgeois" mentality of the peasant would someday be one of their toughest obstacles. Finally, Trotsky had the ability to win the love and loyalty of men. This gift made other Communists fear and resent him, except Lenin, to whom Trotsky gave unswerving loyalty.

By the end of 1918, Trotsky from nothing had built a "Workers' and Peasants' Red Army" of half a million. In 1919 the total jumped to 3 million, and by the spring of 1920 he was in a position to wipe out the White armies, one by one.

Victory in Russia was postponed while the Red army was diverted to the pursuit of world revolution, which again seemed imminent in 1920. The Poles had advanced deep into the Ukraine, seeking to regain the frontiers of eighteenth-century Poland. In June, 1920, the Red army seized the offensive and moved from victory to victory, rolling the Poles back to the outskirts of Warsaw. The Communists saw the road into Europe open before them, once they had broken through the "crust" of the Polish bourgeoisie. Ignorant of conditions in the West, indeed forgetful of their debt to the peasant and the nationalist in Russia, the Communists were convinced that the masses of Europe would turn against their bourgeois masters as soon as vigorous Communist leadership was provided.

Lenin's renewed confidence was reflected in the Comintern. When the Comintern was founded in March, 1919, Lenin had been willing to allow almost any sympathetic group to call itself a member of the Third International. Now he demanded that Communist parties abroad conform to the Soviet pattern in doctrine, organization, and tactics. In preparation for the second congress of the Comintern, he spoke out against Communists who refused to participate in bourgeois parliaments or trade unions. This "left-wing" Communism, he said, was an "infantile disorder." With particular reference to cooperation with the British Labour party leader, Arthur Henderson, he maintained that Communists, so long as they could not "disperse the bourgeois parliament," must work within it, must learn to "make all the practical necessary compromises, to 'tack,' to make agreements, zigzags, retreats and so on, in order to accelerate the coming into, and subsequent loss, of political power of the Hendersons." He would, he said, "support Henderson with my vote in the same way as a rope supports the hanged." Similarly, to break the old trade union leaders, Communists must join the unions and then "resort to all sorts of stratagems, manoeuvres, and illegal methods, to evasion and subterfuges, in order to penetrate the trade unions, to remain in them, and to carry out Communist work in them at all costs."[5]

The brutal frankness with which Lenin wrote is itself an indication of his confidence that victory was both inevitable and near. He could not expect the Hendersons to accept the support of the hangman's rope if they had any alternative, nor would labor leaders welcome allies pledged to destroy them, if there was any alternative. Lenin was rallying his forces on the eve of the final battle; if the enemy was listening, no matter.

The same confident peremptory tone pervaded the twenty-one conditions for admission to the Third International adopted at the second congress of the Comintern, which was meeting as the Red army advanced into Poland in July and August, 1920. All parties must adopt the name Communist; all must be organized, like the Russian, "on the

5. " 'Left-Wing' Communism, an Infantile Disorder," in Lenin, *Selected Works*, X (London, 1938), 95, 100, 101, 130, 138.

principle of democratic *centralism*"; within each there must be "iron discipline"; all "must periodically purge" unreliable members; all must "in every way serve Soviet republics," must obtain Comintern approval for the party program, and must accept every Comintern decision. Communist cells were to be established in existing trade unions, and these cells were to be "entirely subordinated" to the party; conversely, all Communist parties must support a new international federation of Red trade unions.[6]

Hard on the meeting of the Comintern, the first (and last) congress of peoples of the East met at Baku on September 1, 1920. When this congress was announced, the enemies to be denounced had included the native rulers of Asian countries. At the congress, however, abuse of native rulers was omitted; attention was concentrated on the wickedness of European, and particularly British, imperialism.

The shift reflected the sudden collapse of hope for revolution in Europe. The Red army fought well when it was repelling the Polish invader, but before Warsaw the stimulus of nationalism passed from the Russians to the Poles, and the retreat of the Red army began on August 16, 1920. Already, to lessen the number of enemies, the Soviet government had recognized the independence of Estonia, Lithuania, and Latvia. On October 12 a preliminary peace was made with Poland at Riga, leaving large parts of the Ukraine and White Russia in Polish hands. A few days later, the independence of Finland was recognized. The bourgeois crust had held along the western frontiers of Russia.

The proletariat of western and central Europe also refused to exchange its old "social chauvinist" leaders for new Communist leaders as Lenin had expected. The twenty-one conditions were rigorously enforced on all groups debating admission to the Comintern. In France a majority of the Socialist party voted to accept the conditions; so the new Communist party took over the party organization and assets, including the newspaper *L'Humanité*.[7] But the minority kept the Socialist party name and soon won recruits, including many who

6. Lenin, *Selected Works*, X, 200–6.
7. On France, see Robert Wohl, *French Communism in the Making, 1914–1924* (Stanford, 1966), and Annie Kriegel, *Aux Origines du communisme français, 1914–1920* (2 vols., Paris, 1964). On Italy, see John Cammett, *Antonio Gramsci and the Origins of Italian Communism* (Stanford, 1967); Giuseppe Fiori, *Vita di Antonio Gramsci* (Bari, 1966); and Paolo Spriano, *Storia del partito comunista italiana*, Vol. I (Turin, 1967).

found the discipline of the Communist party too rigorous. Only by tacitly tolerating many infractions of the twenty-one conditions was still further splitting avoided in the French party. In Italy a majority voted against the conditions; there, as in several other countries, it was the minority which split off to form the Communist party. Britain was, to Moscow, the most baffling problem. There, sympathy for the Soviet government was widespread, so strong that the British government had been held back from full support of the Poles. But the Communist party was tiny, and the Labour party and even the more radical Independent Labour party rebuffed Communist party attempts at union.

Only in Germany did hope of immediate success linger. The German Independent Socialists voted in October, 1920, to accept the twenty-one conditions. Although here too a minority split off, and eventually joined the Social Democrats, the Communist party now claimed a membership of close to half a million and showed far greater strength in local elections. This was something, but not the immediate triumph of world revolution so often expected from 1917 to 1920.

3. THE REVOLUTION IN GERMANY

When Lenin, driven by circumstances he could not control, was moving toward war communism, he spoke of Germany and Russia as twins. In the formless peasant economy of Russia, seizure of the "commanding heights" was not enough. In Germany, however, military necessity had by 1918 clamped a tight and efficient dictatorship on the economy of one of the most advanced industrial countries of the world. In Lenin's view, when the men who directed this dictatorship were replaced by Communists, then Germany would become the center, the driving force, of a federation of soviet republics spreading first over Europe and soon over the world. The delirious relief with which the overthrow of the imperial German government was greeted in Moscow reflected the confidence of the Bolsheviks that Communism would soon expand from the inadequate base of peasant Russia to Germany, where capitalism had reached its completed development. Germany had passed its "czarist" phase; the "Kerensky" phase of Social Democratic rule would soon, as in Russia, be followed by the Communist seizure of power.

The optimism of the Bolsheviks was natural. In the weeks before the collapse of the imperial government, workers' and soldiers' councils had sprung up in Germany. The first successful revolutionary move was the rising of the workers' and soldiers' councils of Kiel on November 3, 1918; in Bavaria councils of workers, soldiers, and peasants led by Kurt Eisner overthrew the royal government on November 8; on November 10 the workers' and soldiers' councils of Berlin accepted the six-man Council of Peoples' Commissars, formed the day before, as the new government of Germany and elected an executive committee to guide the new government. All this, to the Bolsheviks, was reminiscent of 1917 in Russia.

Communist theory and Russian history proved treacherous guides through the crooked paths of German history.[8] Very quickly the determination of the new rulers of Germany not to repeat the Russian experience became evident. The decisive political and social shift had come in Germany not when the emperor abdicated and the republic was proclaimed on November 9, 1918, but more than a month earlier when control was shifted from the aristocracy and upper middle class to parties in the Reichstag representing the skilled workmen and the segments of the middle classes with which they were allied. The formation of the Council of People's Commissars was, outwardly, a shift to the left, an alliance between two of three factions into which the Social Democratic party had split during the war. One faction, the Majority Socialists, would have preferred a limited monarchy to a republic, at least temporarily. Chancellor Friedrich Ebert was their leader, and he made no secret of his hatred for Bolshevism. Three of the commissars were Independent Socialists. This faction had no acknowledged leader and no coherent program. The Independents had split off from the Majority Socialists over the issue of support for the war, and a large proportion of the faction differed from the Majority only in their hatred of war.

The left wing of the Independents was the third faction, the Spartacus League. The Spartacists alone were united in advocating thoroughgoing social revolution and also in demanding close alliance

8. Both as a summary of latest findings and as a guide to recent scholarship, Reinhard Rürup's article "Problems of the German Revolution, 1918–19," *Journal of Contemporary History,* III (1968), 109–35, is valuable. An excellent local study is Richard Comfort's *Revolutionary Hamburg* (Stanford, 1966). Georges Castellan, "La Révolution allemande de novembre 1918," *Revue d'histoire moderne et contemporaine* (Jan.–March, 1969), pp. 40–51, brings into focus some of the important problems of interpretation connected with the German revolution.

with Soviet Russia. Even among the Spartacists, however, there was little desire to repeat what the Bolsheviks had done in Russia. The keenest mind in the Spartacist faction was Rosa Luxemburg. She hailed the Bolsheviks as the initiators of the world revolution, but she castigated Lenin's conception of the revolutionary party as a small elite group of professional revolutionists, condemned his overthrow of the constituent assembly and his suppression of democracy and free speech, and repudiated terror as an instrument of the revolution.[9]

In terms of popular support, the Majority Socialists were in a much stronger position than the Independents. Just because fear was so great that the stages of the Russian revolution would be repeated in Germany, the middle and upper classes, even the more sober military leaders, were eager for alliance with the Majority Socialists. The Independent Socialists and the Spartacists had some trade union and middle-class support, but their mass base was in the half-organized or unorganized city workmen, and some of the enlisted men in the armed forces.

The initial acts of the republican government showed both the preponderant influence of the Majority Socialists and the fear that the German revolution might follow in the steps of the Russian revolution. In Russia the fate of the provisional government had been sealed when the military leader, Lavr Kornilov, broke with the socialist leader, Aleksandr Kerenski. In Germany, during the first night of the revolution, General Wilhelm Groener and Chancellor Ebert agreed that there must be no such conflict: Groener put the army at the service of the government; Ebert promised to combat Bolshevism.[10] In Russia production had been paralyzed by the attempt of the workers to run the factories. In Germany representatives of the employers met with trade union leaders: the employers promised to end company unions and to recognize the independent trade unions in collective bargaining; the

9. J. P. Nettl, *Rosa Luxemburg* (London, 1966), and Rosa Luxemburg, *The Russian Revolution,* ed. by Bertram Wolfe (N.Y., 1940).

10. Only the first volume of Georg Kotowski's biography of Ebert has appeared: *Friedrich Ebert: Eine politische Biographie;* 1. *Der Aufstieg eines deutschen Arbeiterführers 1871–1917* (Wiesbaden, 1963). See also Waldemar Besson, *Friedrich Ebert* (Frankfurt, 1963).

There is a biography of Groener by his daughter: Dorothea Groener-Geyer, *General Groener, Soldat und Staatsmann* (Frankfurt, 1955); and Wilhelm Groener, *Lebenserinerungen: Jugend; Generalstab; Weltkrieg* (Göttingen, 1957).

trade union leaders promised to maintain production and to enforce discipline on the workers. In Russia public administration had broken down as the revolutionary leaders and the bureaucracy fell to quarreling. In Germany civil servants were urged to remain at their posts, and the functions of government went on without interruption.

Even within the workers' and soldiers' councils determination not to follow the Russian example was obvious. In Russia, after the February Revolution the soldiers' councils had worked to undermine military discipline and to break the power of the officers; in Germany, with some exceptions, the councils worked with the officers to maintain discipline on the dispiriting march back to Germany and in demobilization. When a national conference of workers' and soldiers' councils met in Berlin on December 16, 1918, there were scenes reminiscent of the attempt to overawe the Russian constituent assembly: threatening crowds called on the councils to repudiate the governmental decision to hold elections for a constituent assembly on February 16 and demanded that the councils assume supreme executive and legislative power. At first, it seemed that the councils would turn against the government when a resolution was passed calling for the creation of a people's army; but the temper soon changed, and to the disgust of the radicals, by an overwhelming vote the councils refused to sanction a soviet government. Instead, the councils advanced the date for the election to January 19.

So far, that is, through the first three weeks of December, 1918, the alliance had held between the predominantly middle-class and trade union supporters of the Majority Socialists and the city workmen and the soldiers who supported the Independent Socialists. An incident, trivial in itself, precipitated a break. When the government stopped the pay of members of the People's Naval Division, who had rejected an order to give up their headquarters in the royal palace in Berlin, the sailors seized control of some governmental and newspaper offices. On the next day, December 24, there was inconclusive fighting, ended by agreement of the government to pay the sailors.

The fighting on Christmas Eve set two opposing currents in motion. Those who feared that the alliance between Ebert and the military leaders would destroy the revolution moved into opposition to the government. The Independent Socialist commissars resigned; but their faction was paralyzed by reluctance to use force. Disgusted by the inaction of the Independents, the Spartacus League severed its ties with that faction and on January 1, 1919, created the German Communist party. The leaders of the party, Karl Liebknecht and Rosa Luxemburg, urged that the party participate in the impending elections and concentrate its energies on the building of mass support for Communism. They were overruled by those who shared Lenin's contempt for "formal" democracy and Lenin's faith in violence; the party congress voted not to participate in the elections. The advocates of direct action now carried their program into the streets. The Independents and the Communists organized a mass meeting on January 5, in protest against the dismissal of the Berlin chief of police. Impressed by the size of the crowd, the activists demanded the overthrow of the Ebert government, and disregarding Luxemburg's warnings, Liebknecht threw in his lot with the insurrection. Almost immediately the other Independent and Communist leaders realized that the temper of public opinion, even in Berlin, was hostile. By then, however, it was too late to retreat; the insurrectionary current was overwhelmed by the force which the Majority Socialists had been mobilizing.

The fighting on Christmas Eve had demonstrated that what was left of the regular army was not dependable for use against insurgents. Immediately, volunteers were recruited and trained for service in what came to be called the Free Corps.[11] Most of the Free Corps members were veterans or students. Many were lovers of violence who hated the drabness and privation of civilian life in postwar Germany. All thought of themselves as defenders of the fatherland. To direct this new force, Gustav Noske was made minister for war after the resignation of the Independent commissars. On January 11, 1919, Noske moved into action against the rebels in Berlin, and Spartacus Week was brought to a violent end. Among those taken prisoner were Karl Liebknecht and Rosa Luxemburg. On January 15 they were killed "while trying to escape"—possibly the first use of an expression with which Europe was soon to become very familiar.

The Spartacist rising in Berlin precipitated risings in other cities; each in turn was ruthlessly suppressed by the Free Corps. In Bavaria the events of the winter and spring left a lasting imprint. There, elections were held in January, and Kurt Eisner's Independent Socialists

11. Robert Waite, *Vanguard of Nazism: the Free Corps Movement in Post-War Germany, 1918–1923* (Cambridge, Mass., 1952).

were defeated. In February, as he was about to resign, he was murdered by an antirevolutionary student. A confused struggle for power followed. On April 7, left-wing Independent Socialists proclaimed a soviet republic. They were speedily ousted by Communists, who earned the fear and hatred even of those who had initially supported soviet rule. The Communists were easily overthrown by the Free Corps on May 1 and 2. Thereafter Bavaria was the center not merely of anti-Communism but of opposition to everything connected with the republic in Germany. It was in this sour soil that National Socialism grew.[12]

Amid the sporadic violence of the winter of 1918–19, preparations were made for the election of the constituent assembly. Old political parties were revised to take account of changed conditions. The Communist party presented no candidates. The Majority and Independent Socialists nominated separate slates, each claiming to represent true socialism and true support of the revolution. The Center party continued to be, in large part, the representative of the Catholic population; it also continued to advocate social reform and a federal structure for the state. The Center was the one party which included both conservatives and liberals, all united by belief that religion should play a leading part in political life. Until 1918 the Center had favored monarchical government; now the party favored republicanism. The old Progressive party took the name Democratic. Its sponsors were the leaders of German professional, intellectual, and artistic life, united for the first time—if only briefly—in urging the democratic reconstruction of German political and social life. The party which had represented commerce and industry, the National Liberals, was renamed the People's party; it continued to oppose socialism and to advocate free enterprise. The old Conservatives were now the Nationalists; they were the only major political party which frankly denounced the revolution and urged monarchical restoration; the People's party was ambiguous in its attitude toward the republic.[13]

12. Georg Franz, "Munich: Birthplace and Center of the National Socialist German Workers' Party," *Journal of Modern History*, XXIX (Dec., 1957), 319–34.

13. On the political parties of the Weimar Republic, see Ossip K. Fleichtheim, *Die Kommunistische Partei Deutschlands in der Weimarer Republik* (Offenbach am Main, 1948); Richard Hunt, *German Social Democracy, 1918–1933* (New Haven, 1964); Rudolf Morsey, *Die deutsche Zentrumspartei, 1917–1923* (Düsseldorf, 1966); Bruce Frye, "The German Democratic Party, 1918–1930," *Western Political Quarterly*, XVI (1963),

For the election, the suffrage was widened to include all men and women over twenty. Every effort was made both to bring out the vote and to ensure an honest expression of opinion. The result was a sweeping victory for the three parties—Majority Socialist, Center, and Democratic—which not only supported the republic but endorsed the conduct of the government since the revolution. Together, they received more than three-quarters of the vote. The Independent Socialists received less than 8 per cent, in contrast to the Majority Socialists, who received nearly 38 per cent. The Nationalists and the People's party together received less than 15 per cent.

The assembly met on February 6, 1919, not in turbulent Berlin, but in the quiet of Weimar, a town traditionally associated with humanism. Ebert was elected president of the republic. Another Social Democrat, Philipp Scheidemann, was made chancellor, and he chose a cabinet from his own party, from the Center, and from the Democrats—the parties known thereafter as the Weimar coalition. The three parties were united in support of democratic government and social reform as these words were then used in Western political thought; these common convictions overrode differences such as Center support of, and Majority Socialist opposition to, religious instruction in schools.

The constitution made at Weimar was emphatically republican and democratic; on social questions it left the future open. Suffrage was universal; there was proportional representation; there was provision both for popular initiation of legislation and for the submission of proposed legislation to popular referendum. Germany continued to be a federal state, but the center of power was now in the federal government, not the states. There was to be a popularly elected president. By Article 48 he was given great power in emergencies, but his decrees required the signature of the appropriate member of the cabinet, and the cabinet was responsible to the lower house, the Reichstag. So long as there was a united majority in the Reichstag, therefore, the Reichstag ruled. The individual German was protected by a detailed bill of rights. Private property was placed below public welfare. Provision was made for the limitation by law of property rights and for the nationalization of property, but with compensation to the owners. The right of

167–79; Wolfgang Hartenstein, *Die Anfänge der Deutschen Volkspartei 1918–1920* (Düsseldorf, 1962); Lewis Hertzman, *DNVP: Right-Wing Opposition in the Weimar Republic, 1918–1924* (Lincoln, Nebr., 1963).

workers to organize was guaranteed, and the way was opened for the participation of workers in the management of industry. In other words, the constitution made it possible for Germany to move toward, or away from, socialism; but effort was made to ensure that individual and group rights would be protected in the course of either move.

On July 31, 1919, the Weimar constitution was accepted by an overwhelming majority of the assembly, and on August 11 it went into effect. By then, however, unity within and between the parties of the Weimar coalition had been undermined, and the German people had lost interest in the constitutional structure shaped at Weimar. Through the winter, the continuation of the Allied "hunger blockade" and the exclusion of Germany from the peace conference had built up rage among the German people. Now, to the Germans, it seemed that their future would be determined not by this or that constitutional provision but by the Treaty of Versailles.

4. THE WEIMAR REPUBLIC AND THE TREATY OF VERSAILLES

The draft of the Treaty of Versailles was presented to the Germans on May 7, 1919.[14] The national assembly was called into special session in Berlin on May 12. The Socialist chancellor denounced the treaty as a violation of the prearmistice agreement; Germany, he said, had been promised a peace of reconciliation and was now confronted with a peace of spoliation which would reduce the country to slavery. "What hand would not wither," Scheidemann asked, "that binds itself and us in these fetters?" All agreed that the treaty was a breach of contract and that the terms were so harsh that they could not be fulfilled. All—with the exception of the Independent Socialists—demanded that the treaty be rejected. At the end, the chairman of the assembly warned the Allies that the result of the treaty would be a generation of Germans animated by "the will to break the chains of slavery."

Hopefully, the German government asked for a revision of the draft treaty. When it became evident that only minor changes would be made, the consequences of refusal to sign were explored, and in particular the military were asked whether an Allied invasion could be successfully resisted. The military opposed acceptance of the treaty, but they also acknowledged that the German people were unwilling to

14. Alma Luckau, *The German Delegation at the Paris Peace Conference* (N.Y., 1941), is a collection of documents with an excellent introduction and bibliography.

fight and were turning toward the Independent Socialists and Communists because these parties were the only ones urging acceptance of the treaty. General Groener forced his fellow officers to face the alternatives: Germany must capitulate, he said, or the name of Germany would disappear from the map. Reluctantly, Field Marshal Hindenburg agreed there was no alternative to capitulation, and the decision of the military determined the decision of Ebert.[15] Scheidemann resigned and the new cabinet agreed to sign if the so-called honor clauses were eliminated from the treaty. These were Article 231, which, in the German view, "requires Germany to admit herself to be the sole and only author of the war," and Articles 227 to 230, which required the surrender for trial by the Allies of Germans accused of war crimes. When these reservations were rejected, there were new consultations, followed by unconditional acceptance of the treaty.

The treaty was accepted in form but not in spirit. The conviction was almost universal that the treaty was both unjust and unworkable, and that evasion of its terms was therefore legitimate and unavoidable. So far there was unity.

Even before the Treaty of Versailles was drafted, the German government had begun a flank attack on the moral foundation of the treaty, the conviction of the Allies that Germany was responsible for the war. Veteran socialist Karl Kautsky was asked to assemble the documents in the German foreign ministry which related to the crisis of 1914. These documents were published late in 1919, and taken in conjunction with a similar publication by the Austrian government and isolated documents published by the Bolsheviks, they did—in the words of the first scholarly American examination of the evidence—"clear the German government of the charge that it deliberately plotted or wanted the war."[16]

The German government had already embarked on a more ambitious project. In the summer of 1919 German scholars were set the gigantic task of publishing documents from the foreign ministry archives covering the entire history of the German Empire. From that

15. On Hindenburg, see J. W. Wheeler-Bennett's thoughtful biography, *The Wooden Titan* (N.Y., 1936; reissued N.Y., 1967), and Andreas Dorpalen's scholarly *Hindenburg and the Weimar Republic* (Princeton, 1964).

16. *Outbreak of the World War: German Documents Collected by Karl Kautsky* (N.Y., 1924). Sidney B. Fay, "New Light on the Origins of the World War," *American Historical Review*, XXV (July, 1920), and XXVI (Oct., 1920).

decision resulted the forty volumes famous as *Die Grosse Politik,* published between 1922 and 1926. These tactics were effective. Since the German documents were the first to appear, they inevitably colored the views of non-German students of the origins of the war. The French and British governments were put on the defensive because they were slow to undertake similar documentary publications. The Germans had scored a victory in what was soon known as the *Kriegsschuldfrage,* the battle of books and documents on the question of war guilt which raged furiously until it was silenced by war in 1939.

The campaign to destroy the moral justification for the treaty could bring results only over years. On the other "honor clauses," relating to violations of the laws and customs of war by individuals, the German government could not wait. To avoid a renewal of the war, the government had agreed to hand over to the Allies for trial all accused persons. When the Allies submitted a list of some nine hundred persons to be tried, including nearly all the high political and military officials of Germany during the war, the violence of the popular reaction in Germany convinced even the Allies that armed force would be needed to compel extradition. Tacitly, the Allies agreed to allow the German supreme court at Leipzig to try a selected list of forty-five persons. Only a few of these were actually tried, and still fewer convicted; the sentences of those convicted were light. Despite a finding by Allied jurists that the Leipzig trials had not fulfilled the treaty obligations of Germany, no further effort was made to compel extradition. In substance if not in form the Germans had successfully defied the most hated clauses of the treaty. As for the former emperor, William II, he had found sanctuary in the Netherlands, whose government rejected Allied requests for his surrender. He lived on in what the Netherlands government proudly called this "land of refuge for vanquished in international conflicts" to see, before his death in 1941, his refuge overrun by the troops of Nazi Germany.

Ultimately, the success of the German government in attacking the moral foundations of the Treaty of Versailles was to prove of decisive importance. As years passed, there was a shift from moral condemnation of Germany for the origin and conduct of war to moral condemnation of Allied statesmen for the Peace of Paris; by the thirties, appeasement of German ambitions was to be justified by the contention that Germany had a good moral case for violating the Treaty of Versailles.

All that lay in the future. What obsessed the Germans in 1919 was the conviction that they had been tricked. In the summer of 1918, victory had seemed certain. The Treaty of Brest Litovsk gave Germany supremacy in eastern Europe; in France, by a series of hammer blows, the German armies had advanced once more to the Marne. A year later, the Treaty of Versailles despoiled Germany of provinces, placed colossal burdens on the German economy, and put limits on German military strength to prevent any revolt against servitude. What had happened? In their angry impotence, the German people sought scapegoats. There was agreement that the Allies, headed by Wilson, had laid a trap, promising a peace of reconciliation but imposing what even Englishmen like Keynes called a Carthaginian peace. But how had Germany fallen into this trap? The military, headed by the revered Marshal Hindenburg, claimed that the German armies had not been defeated; they had been stabbed in the back by traitors and cowards. This myth found increasing acceptance, and as it spread, the confidence of opponents of the revolution revived. At the other extreme, radicals denounced the Weimar coalition because it had not carried to completion the revolution against militarists and capitalists, the true authors of Germany's misfortunes.

The radicals were, for the moment, powerless to strike out against the national assembly; Noske's suppression of the Spartacist uprisings had been thorough. The right opposition did, for the moment, have organized military power, but that power was threatened. Through the winter of 1918 the Allies had allowed large formations of German troops to remain in the Baltic states which were seeking to break away from Bolshevik Russia. In the summer of 1919, the Allies pressed with increasing vigor for the withdrawal of these troops. By the end of the year the troops were back in Germany. There they found the government busied with plans to reduce the strength of the armed forces in compliance with the Treaty of Versailles. Like the Free Corps and the officers of the Reichswehr, the troops who returned from the Baltic were in a rebellious mood. General Groener had retired after the signature of the treaty, and the titular chief of the army, General Walther Reinhardt, did not have Groener's ability to compel obedience. The "stab in the back" explanation naturally appealed to the officers more than the plain fact that German military strength had been broken in 1918, and hotheads among the officers easily convinced themselves that the German people would welcome the overthrow of the national assembly. The military commander in the Berlin area, General Lüttwitz, joined forces with a conservative politician, Wolfgang Kapp, in a plot to seize power. When Noske called a military council he found that most of the officers, led by General Seeckt, while refusing to join the rebels, were unwilling to fight. The rebels seized control of the government offices in Berlin on March 13, 1920. The members of the government escaped to Stuttgart and proclaimed a general strike.[17]

The result was an impressive demonstration that the mass of the German people, disillusioned though they were with the achievements of the revolution, were not prepared to accept a return to the past. Even in Berlin, despite threats of the death penalty for strikers, all public services halted, and the Reichswehr troops in the city were mutinous. On March 17, the rebel leaders fled and the Kapp putsch collapsed.

Most of the regular officers of the Reichswehr had followed Seeckt's lead in maintaining neutrality during the uprising, and momentarily there was a strong popular movement to retaliate by abolishing the old officers' corps. Soon, however, fear of the military was once more overshadowed by fear of Bolshevism. The German Communists had at first refused to support either Kapp or the government. Once the putsch had failed, some Communists tried to prolong the general strike and to move on to a Communist seizure of power. There were uprisings in several cities, and particularly in the Ruhr. To restore order, the government used the Reichswehr and the Free Corps. By the time order was restored, anger against the officers' corps had subsided.[18]

Moreover, within the German government there was a growing conviction that the Treaty of Versailles could be repudiated only when German military strength revived. This conviction was strengthened when, in reply to the sending of troops to the demilitarized Ruhr area to suppress the Communist revolt, the French occupied several German cities; the French continued the occupation until the troops left the Ruhr. Unless Germany was to abandon all hope of reversing the verdict of Versailles, it seemed, German military strength must be

17. Johannes Erger, *Der Kapp-Lüttwitz-Putsch: Ein Beitrag zur deutschen Innenpolitik 1919/20* (Düsseldorf, 1967).

18. Werner T. Angress, "Weimar Coalition and Ruhr Insurrection, March–April, 1920, A Study of Government Policy," *Journal of Modern History*, XXIX (March, 1957), 1–20.

rebuilt, and the only men who were willing to undertake the task were the officers of the imperial army; Noske's efforts to recruit military formations from supporters of the revolution had met with no success.

So the final result of the Kapp putsch was to confirm the power of the officers' corps. In the initial reaction against the military, Noske and General Reinhardt had been forced to resign. Their successors were, as minister of war, Otto Gessler, and as chief of the army command, General Hans von Seeckt. Seeckt promised that there would be no repetition of the Kapp putsch, and he did insist that the Reichswehr remain aloof from political activity. However, he also insisted that the government must protect the Reichswehr from parliamentary criticism while he was building a strong military machine despite the limitations imposed by the treaty. Gessler proved a willing shield between the military and the Reichstag.[19]

What Seeckt and Gessler did was to put deceit at the service of honor. By steady insistence that the German army was the embodiment of German honor, an atmosphere was created in which parliamentary criticism of illegal military activities could be condemned as dishonorable, even though these activities were illegal under German law as well as under the treaty.

In one important particular, the Allies facilitated Seeckt's task. To the Allies, the Free Corps were an obvious violation of the treaty and, because they were irresponsible, were likely to precipitate dangerous clashes with Germany's neighbors. Therefore, in the summer of 1920 the Allies demanded that they be disbanded. To enable the German government to maintain domestic order while the Free Corps were being suppressed, the Allies agreed to extend the time within which the regular army was to be reduced to the 100,000 men permitted by the treaty. Seeckt was willing to eliminate the Free Corps: they had served their purpose in the early turbulent days of the republic; now their headstrong leaders were not the kind of silent, obedient instruments he needed. The Free Corps put up resistance, backed by a minority of the German people. However, they were smashed, except for those which continued a shadowy existence in Bavaria, where the Reichswehr left

---

19. *The Reichswehr and Politics, 1918–1933*, by F. Carsten (Oxford, 1966), is the most recent and most comprehensive of the many studies of the German army during the Weimar Republic. It has a good bibliography. See also Hans Meier-Welcker's biography, *Seeckt* (Frankfurt, 1967).

them, unable to decide whether they might not some day again be useful. Many of their members were to appear again as Hitler's Storm Troopers.

The extension of the time limit on the reduction of the German army enabled Seeckt to perform his task with care. He could have only a total of 100,000 men. Of these, the 4,000 officers were to be enlisted for twenty-five years, while the enlisted men must serve twelve years. There was no lack of candidates in impoverished Germany. Seeckt picked for the future. Nothing could be done directly with so small a force, particularly since it had no offensive armament, including aircraft. But Seeckt—"the sphinx"—was thinking of the time when Germany would be needed as an ally, and when the treaty limits on German strength would have rusted away. Then the men he was choosing would be the nucleus of a new army. Meanwhile, there were tasks aplenty. It would take years to find the answers to the military problems raised by the war just past, and the immediate problem was to find and train alert and discreet minds.

Only one problem escaped Seeckt's clairvoyant intelligence: was it possible to put deceit in the service of honor without permitting deceit to corrupt honor? The army which he created was to be at once the most perfect and the most terrible expression of German genius.

Seeckt's work, like the sapping of the moral foundations of the Treaty of Versailles, could bear fruit only in years to come. Seeckt was patient, and so were the scholars who slowly pieced together the German version of the origins of the war. The German people, however, were weary and hungry, bewildered by this new age in which nothing fitted old standards of value. Slowly still, but inexorably, inflation made life harder. The present was cheerless, and the burden of reparation, still of undetermined magnitude, loomed ahead.

The verdict of the German people on the work of the Weimar coalition was given in the election of June 6, 1920. The verdict was unfavorable: the Weimar coalition won less than half the seats. The Democrats, the party most completely wedded to Western ideas of democracy, lost most heavily. The Center lost because the Bavarian branch had split off, and the parent party could never count on the votes of the reactionary Bavarian People's party. The Social Democrats were still the largest single party, but some of their strength had been drained off to the Independent Socialists. If the Independent Socialists had been willing to join the coalition, a secure majority would have been possible, but the Independents refused. On the right, both the Nationalists and the People's party greatly increased in strength, but together they controlled less than one-third of the seats. The Communists did badly. They received fewer than half a million votes.

Proportional representation had enabled the German people to give exact expression to their views, and the results showed that no one view, and no possible combination of views, had a majority. A government was organized from representatives of the Center, the Democrats, and the People's party, but it was inevitably a weak government, weak because its members were divided on fundamental issues and weak because it could continue only so long as the Social Democrats refused to join the Nationalists, the Independent Socialists, and the Communists in voting for its overthrow.

The divisions revealed in the election of 1920 were to persist through the life of the Weimar Republic, and the really fatal division was that on the left. The upsurge of votes for the Independent Socialists did not cure the divisions within that party, and very soon it went to pieces, some members returning to the Social Democratic fold, most joining the Communists. The Communist deputies always voted against the government, and their votes, added to the parties of the right, always outnumbered the votes of the Weimar coalition. The cabinets after 1920 represented either a majority without unity or a minority which governed on sufferance. In either case a strong, consistent internal policy was impossible.

On internal questions, a strong policy meant collapse of the cabinet; on foreign policy, a strong policy of opposition to the Treaty of Versailles was essential for survival. Only those Germans who wished to destroy the old social as well as political order would admit that Germany was responsible for all the misery piled on the world by the war. Most Germans repudiated the accusation with horror and indignation. Similarly, Allied strictures against German brutality during the war seemed a desecration of their dead sons to most Germans. Finally, love of country, pride in its past, and confidence that Germany would recover from defeat remained strong. Few recognized any moral basis for the Allied contention that their country, that they and their children, deserved to suffer and should be made to suffer.

The German people were increasingly disposed to blame their woes not on the strain of the war, and not on their own inability to agree upon any domestic course of action, but on the peace treaty. From the day it was presented to them, the Germans agreed that the Treaty of Versailles was intolerable. The cabinets which clung precariously and briefly to power after the elections of 1920 could not hope to survive if they tried to convince the German people that after pouring all their energies and their resources into war for more than four years, the war had been lost, and that reconstruction required disciplined united effort comparable to that expended on the war. It was easier to say that the war had not been lost, that Allied deceit and domestic treason had deprived Germany of the fruits of victory, and that the disunity of Germany's enemies would open the way to freedom. Tentatively and timidly at first, then with mingled confidence and desperation, the German government turned from domestic reconstruction to defiance of the victors, even at the price of completing the ruin of the German economy.

Chapter Three

THE EBBING OF THE REVOLUTIONARY TIDE

In November, 1918, Lenin had been confident that the defeat of imperial Germany would open the way for the triumph of Communism in central Europe. By 1920 it was evident that in Germany, as in Russia itself, Marxism had failed as the infallible guide to an understanding of history. The German people had lost confidence in the revolution as well as in the old monarchy. The future of Germany was obscure, but only a small minority wished to take the road Russia was traveling.

By 1920 Communism had also failed in the band of states, extending from the Arctic to the Mediterranean, which emerged from the ruins of the Russian, German, Austrian, and Turkish empires. In 1917 Lenin had hoped to win converts in eastern Europe by repudiating czarist imperialism and embracing the principle of self-determination even for the nationalities which had been part of Russia. Representatives of almost every nationality were participating in the Russian revolution, learning the techniques of revolutionary activity and the discipline of Communist party leadership. When the war ended in November, 1918, these Communists were ready to return home to lead their people.

Uniformly, failure followed. In only one eastern European country, Hungary, was there even momentary success. On the collapse of the Hapsburg monarchy in November, 1918, advocates of democracy and socialism had taken over the government of Hungary. Then the neighbors of Hungary began to stake out their claims. When the Allies in Paris decided that the whole Transylvanian plain was to go to Rumania, the outraged moderates in the Hungarian government resigned on March 21, 1919, leaving an unstable coalition of socialists and communists in control. Soon the Russian-trained Béla Kun had pushed aside the socialists, set up a Communist dictatorship, and embarked on hostilities with both the Rumanians and the Czechs. The Rumanians advanced with little difficulty and occupied Budapest on August 4. By then Béla Kun had fled.[1] When the Rumanians evacuated Budapest in November, conservatives led by Admiral Horthy assumed control and began a White terror which surpassed the earlier Red terror in thoroughness and ferocity. The new Hungary was organized as a monarchy with Horthy as regent, and on June 4, 1920, the Treaty of Trianon was signed, the harshest of all the peace treaties except the abortive Treaty of Sèvres with Turkey.

The Hungarians were powerless to resist the Allies or their neighbors. They were unable even to fill their vacant throne: twice the fallen Hapsburg ruler, Charles, appeared in Hungary seeking recognition as king; he was turned back when the neighbors of Hungary threatened military intervention. The Hungarians were powerless, but completely confident that their plight was temporary. The Kingdom of St. Stephen had endured for almost a thousand years; Hungarians refused to believe that a state of such antiquity and, as they believed, of such importance as a bulwark of Western civilization on the frontier of the barbarous East could be permanently dismembered. For their present condition they blamed their despised neighbors, the false promises of the Allies—and the short-lived Communist government of Hungary. The prewar leaders of Hungary, repudiated in 1918 as the authors of catastrophic defeat, were now securely in power again. In 1921 Count Bethlen began a decade of rule for and by the old agrarian aristocracy, behind the forms of popular rule. All forms of dissent from aristocratic rule were suppressed; since many of the Communist leaders had been Jews, anti-Semitism was encouraged.

In Hungary, it could be argued that Communism succumbed to the military force of the old conservative leaders. In Austria, where defeat brought terms almost as harsh and where the misery of the people was even greater, Communism received negligible support in the free elections of February, 1919. The Socialists of the cities and the Christian Socialists of the countryside won almost equal representation, with the small German Nationalist party holding the balance of power. In succeeding elections, when hope of uniting with Germany had been dashed by the Treaty of St. Germain, the Christian Socialists held a narrow majority in national elections and, in or out of office, the dominant personality of the twenties was the clerical statesman Monsignor

---

1. *Béla Kun and the Hungarian Soviet Republic,* by Rudolf Tökés (N.Y., 1967), is a scholarly study of these events.

Ignaz Seipel. He succeeded in winning international sympathy for the economic misery of Austria; by 1922 the reparation obligations of the treaty were tacitly abandoned and a large loan, administered by the League of Nations, was floated in the hope that independent existence would become tolerable for the Austrians. A year later the League undertook the reconstruction of Hungary also, and again the hope of reparation was abandoned.

Vienna and the other Austrian cities continued to be strongholds of a socialism which was more dogmatically Marxian than that of Germany or France. To the city workers, it seemed that the federal government was the agent of clerical reaction; to the Austrian peasant, as to the upper classes in the cities, it seemed that the municipal government of Vienna was controlled by godless, and Jewish, despoilers of property. Tension ran high between the rivals and resulted in the formation of private armies—the Heimwehr, unruly allies of the Christian Socialists, and the Schutzbund of the Socialists. But hatred of the Christian Socialists did not result in alliance of Socialism with Communism, even though the Christian Socialists maintained that there was no real difference between the two. In Austria, as in Hungary, Communism made little headway.

In the third of the defeated countries of eastern Europe, Bulgaria, the situation was more obscure. Power at the outset was in the hands of Alexandr Stamboliski, the leader of the Peasant party, who jailed members of earlier governments, curbed the press and the university, levied heavy income taxes, and broke up the big estates to provide land for the peasants. In foreign affairs, he showed less interest in winning back the territory lost in the Second Balkan War and the world war than in promoting a "Green International" of peasant states, opposed equally to Communism and capitalism. In 1923 he was overthrown by conspirators drawn from the Macedonian exiles, the military, and those pinched by his heavy taxes; a few days later he was killed—"attempting to escape." Through the next decade Bulgarian politics pursued a violent course of assassination, revolt, and repression, in which Communists played an active part. The party was outlawed in 1925 after attempts to assassinate King Boris III and to blow up the ministers in the cathedral at Sofia; it continued an underground existence, dreaded but ineffectual.

Communist efforts to seize power were ended even earlier in the new states along the Baltic which emerged during the distracted days of the Russian revolution. In one sense, failure was acknowledged when the Soviet government recognized the independence of Finland, Latvia, Estonia, and Lithuania in 1920. Poland, which bit most deeply into former Russian territory, won favorable peace terms with Russia by the preliminary Treaty of Riga, signed on October 12, 1920; the final treaty, fixing the eastern boundaries of Poland, was signed in March, 1921. Rumania, which seized Bessarabia after the war, did not secure a treaty settlement with Russia, although an armistice was signed on March 2, 1920.

By the time these agreements were signed, the failure of Communism not only to expand but even to maintain Russian rule over formerly subject nationalities was obvious. From an outside point of view, Lenin was a poor prophet. From the Communist point of view, the appearance of unexpected obstacles had compelled, for a time, the acceptance of "compromises."

Equally in doubt was the validity of Woodrow Wilson's faith that self-determination and democracy would bring peace and prosperity to eastern Europe. Certainly the ideal of self-determination was much tarnished in application and frequently led only to new discord. The Lithuanians were outraged by the Polish seizure of Vilna in 1920; but the Lithuanians ensured German enmity by seizing the free city of Memel in 1923. The Poles, backed by France, used military force to extend their frontiers against Lithuania in the Vilna region, against Russia in the eastern regions inhabited by White Russians and Ukrainians, and against Germany in Upper Silesia; still unsatisfied, the Poles lamented that they had, in the dark days of their war with Russia in 1920, been forced to yield part of Teschen to Czechoslovakia. The Czechs, for their part, were acutely conscious of the 3 million Germans within their mountain frontiers, of the Magyars, close to a million, who resented their separation from Hungary, and of the Ruthenians, nearly half a million, who were closely related to the Ukrainians of Russia and Poland; only slowly did the Czechs come to realize that their 2 million Slovak brethren were also far from content with a government dominated by Czechs. In all, possibly one-third of the Magyars were now outside Hungary, for in addition to those given Czechoslovakia, well over a million and a half were in Rumania and nearly half a million in what was at first called the Kingdom of the Serbs, Croats, and Slovenes, and later Yugoslavia. The name Yugoslavia implied that there existed a common South Slav nationality overriding the differences built up over centuries of divergent tradition and political allegiance; events soon showed that the Croats, at least, were unwilling to accept the leadership which the Serbs asserted in the new kingdom.

Obviously, self-determination had found only imperfect expression in eastern Europe, and from this situation it was possible to draw divergent conclusions. Germans regarded the principle of self-determination as a pious fraud, used to despoil the defeated but denied when the defeated would profit, as in the projected union of Austria with Germany. Others drew more optimistic conclusions from the rise of the thirteen states of eastern Europe, with their population totaling more than 100 million. Arnold Toynbee, writing in 1924, was inclined to believe that the age of the great powers was over, and that the small and medium-sized states of eastern Europe, in union with the new states rising in the Middle East and the states of Latin America, would ensure the triumph of world organization through the League of Nations.[2]

With determination hardened by fear, the French government sought to ensure the permanence of the eastern settlement. For France, the new or enlarged states which had profited from the Peace of Paris were insurance against a new German bid for supremacy in Europe and against the spread of Bolshevism to the west. Poland in particular was prized as a barrier separating Germany from Russia. After providing the military leadership for the repulse of the Red army in 1920, France concluded a firm military alliance with Poland in 1921 and assisted in the conclusion of an alliance of Poland and Rumania against Russia. Again, in the division of Upper Silesia between Germany and Poland, France sought to place as much of the industrial resources of the disputed area as possible under Polish sovereignty.

In 1924 Czechoslovakia, which had inherited the bulk of the industrial resources of the Dual Monarchy and which occupied a geographical position vital for the defense of the Danube basin, also concluded an alliance with France. Earlier, in 1920 and 1921, France had supported Czech agreements with Yugoslavia and Rumania to prevent a

---

2. Arnold J. Toynbee, *The World After the Peace Conference* (London, 1925), pp. 25, 32, 35–37, 40, 61, 63. This small volume has value as an illustration of the optimism reviving in western Europe in 1924.

return of the Hapsburgs; it was the French hope that these three states, linked in what came to be known as the Little Entente, would form with Poland a firm barrier against any resurgence of German or Russian power.[3]

If the application of the ideal of self-determination to eastern Europe was a confused story from which it was possible to draw divergent conclusions, the fate of the ideal of democratic government was, on the whole, disillusioning. Nearly all the thirteen states started off with constitutions which provided for universal suffrage, for protection of civil and political liberties, and in many cases for even the most extreme democratic devices such as proportional representation. Partly to destroy the appeal of Communism, and sometimes also to despoil the formerly dominant nationalities, provision was made for the breaking up of large estates and for the giving of land to peasant proprietors.

Even under the best of circumstances, the results fell behind expectations. Czechoslovakia, for instance, was the most highly favored of the states of the area. Bohemia was one of the great industrial centers of Europe, while Moravia, Slovakia, and Ruthenia produced almost enough agricultural goods for national self-sufficiency. A well-trained Czech bureaucracy was inherited from the Dual Monarchy. In Tomáš Masaryk and Eduard Beneš, the Czechs had two of the most respected statesmen of Europe. In the prosperous first decade of the country's existence, all these advantages made Czechoslovakia seem the ideal multinational democratic state. Already, however, the multiplicity of parties made for repeated cabinet crises and weak coalition governments; already, the Slovaks grumbled because they were governed from Prague, because their bureaucrats and teachers were Czechs, and because their economic life was controlled by Czechs; already it was evident that the Sudeten Germans, despite the scrupulous efforts of the Czechs to avoid offense, never forgot that Germans once were dominant in Bohemia and Moravia, and never accepted the position of a favored minority. Still, on the surface, all went well, and this bred in the Czechs a sense of complacent optimism which was poor preparation for the second, and disastrous, decade of the country's existence.

Far to the north, the Finns were from the outset compelled to discipline themselves to live in the face of mortal peril. Both in the Baltic and in the Arctic, Finland was a potential danger to the communica-

---

3. Piotr S. Wandycz, *France and Her Eastern Allies, 1919–1925* (Minneapolis, 1962).

tions of the Soviet Union. The Bolsheviks had reluctantly abandoned their efforts to subjugate Finland by force; but Communist agents ceaselessly sought to win the loyalty of the Finnish workers. However, during the century when the Finns had worked to maintain autonomy within czarist Russia, the aristocracy, for the most part Swedish in origin, had learned to lead rather than dominate the mass of Finnish people. Now aristocrats continued to lead, but as representatives of a political and social democracy in which the condition of the lower classes was steadily improved, at the expense of the possessing classes. Here land reform was carried through, here the cooperative movement flourished, and here agricultural development absorbed the best brains of the country.

To a lesser extent, danger was a spur to national solidarity in the other small Baltic states, Estonia, Latvia, and Lithuania: in all, the small farmer was favored, and the cooperative movement received governmental support. In these countries, however, steady political direction was lacking, possibly because there had been few native leaders during the period of Russian rule. Parties multiplied, and cabinets were short-lived. In the end, all three fell under dictatorial rule without great popular dissent.

Poland began with a constitution which contained almost every conceivable guarantee of democratic government and almost every promise of social reform. Soon the strife of factions and personalities made Polish politics as violent, and as paralyzing, as in the eighteenth century. Increasingly, whether he was in or out of office, the political scene was dominated by the passionate personality of the national hero, Marshal Józef Piłsudski, who had virtual dictatorial power at least from 1926 until his death in 1935.

Everywhere the pattern of personal leadership and authoritarian rule emerged, if not in the relatively prosperous twenties, certainly in the economic depression of the thirties. Some of the leaders were aristocrats who worked within a democratic system, like Mannerheim in Finland; some were aristocrats who tried to revive as much as possible of the feudal past, like Horthy and Bethlen in Hungary. Some were kings with a deep sense of responsibility for the welfare of their divided kingdoms, like Boris in Bulgaria or Alexander in Yugoslavia; but rule by a creature like King Carol of Rumania and his hated mistress Magda Lupescu seemed preferable to the weakness of a regency in a divided country. Even in Czechoslovakia, it is hard to believe that democratic government would have flourished without the patriarchal figure of Masaryk, supplemented by Beneš' capacity for compromise.

In eastern Europe the seed of democracy had fallen on stony soil. Much of the region had been terribly devastated during the war. Everywhere, old political and social habits had been disrupted, whether by victory or by defeat. Land reform, pushed with more or less vigor except in Poland and Hungary, usually meant less efficient agricultural production, and the rapidly increasing population pressed ever heavier on the soil now that migration to America was cut off by immigration restrictions. The bureaucracies were likely to be harsh, capricious, and corrupt. Tariff barriers were pushed higher under the stimulus of aroused nationalism, usually in the interest of pressure groups with political power. Education was regarded as a way to enter the privileged classes, not as a means to render service to society. Over all hung the uneasy consciousness that the triumph of national aspirations had been made possible by the collapse of German, Russian, and Austrian power. Only fear that the Hapsburgs would return held the Little Entente together. Germany was in chains, and Russia was an outcast; but was this permanent?

Something of the atmosphere of eastern Europe in the early twenties emerges in the novels of the Czech writer Franz Kafka: the sense of groping through a world without fixed values, where everything was uncertain, where the individual was moved by forces beyond his control or even understanding, and in the end destroyed. In 1930, when depression was lowering over eastern Europe, the Viennese founder of psychoanalysis, Sigmund Freud, generalized the results of his research, and the experiences of his life, in a single sentence: *"Homo homini lupus*; who has the courage to dispute it in the face of all the evidence in his own life and in history?" When held within the restraints of a firmly based cultural structure, Freud continued, man's "aggressive cruelty" found only indirect expression, but when these restraints were relaxed "it also manifests itself spontaneously and reveals men as savage beasts to whom the thought of sparing their own kind is alien." The evolution of culture was for Freud a struggle "between the instincts of life and the instincts of destruction." He concluded sardonically: "And it is this battle of the Titans that our nurses and governesses try to compose with their lullaby-song of Heaven!"[4]

4. Sigmund Freud, *Civilization and Its Discontents* (N.Y., 1958 [Anchor edition]), pp. 61, 75.

Kafka and Freud were Jews, and their vision was both sharpened and distorted by the anti-Semitism which spread over eastern Europe in the interwar years, not the sporadic anti-Semitism which had appeared earlier when a scapegoat was needed, but an anti-Semitism into which was poured the frustrations, disappointments, and fears of peoples forced to live where all was precarious and contingent. To be sure, it is possible to relate eastern anti-Semitism to the fact that in some places the Jew was the moneylender or the trader who, to a miserable peasantry, seemed to drain off all cash resources. Or, in Vienna, the argument might be made that before the war Jews obtained a monopoly on jobs which gentlemen shunned, but which gentlemen now wanted because there were no other jobs. Or, in Budapest, recalling Béla Kun and the Red terror, the Jew and Communism might be called synonymous. Or, in some countries, anti-Semitism among university students might be dismissed as a mere financial transaction by which students earned money in the service of rabble-rousing politicians. But none of these explanations explains the increasingly pervasive, almost palpable, atmosphere of anti-Semitism, which can be explained only in terms of a mass delusion, shared by high and low alike, in a region where life had lost security and stability, even agreed meaning and purpose.

2. LENIN AND THE NEW ECONOMIC POLICY

After the retreat of the Red army from Warsaw in August, 1920, hope for the coming of the world revolution was kept alive in Russia by the final victory of Trotsky's forces over the divided and demoralized White armies. The large vote for the Communist party in local German elections also was interpreted in Moscow as an indication that resolute leadership would topple the Weimar Republic, as Lenin had overturned the provisional government of Russia in November, 1917. The Comintern pressed the German Communists to seize power. Reluctantly, a rising was attempted in March, 1921. German workers refused to heed the call for a general strike, and the scattered Communist uprisings were quickly and easily put down by the German government. Membership in the German Communist party fell by more than half, to fewer than 200,000, and the party leadership was now divided and demoralized.

Even before this failure, opposition to the Communist regime within Russia began to assume new and more menacing forms. Most peasants had remained quiet while there was danger that the Whites might win and bring back the landlord. After the White armies were wiped out, peasants began to resist the Communist agents sent to requisition "surplus" grain: reports of "banditry" in the countryside multiplied from the fall of 1920. Grain collections fell off, partly because of peasant resistance, partly because peasants had planted less, and partly because of drought, particularly in the Volga area. What grain was collected could not be moved efficiently because the overworked transportation system was collapsing; a large part of the railroad rolling stock was unusable. During 1920, the workers in the cities also began to protest against their increasingly militarized and miserable existence. With the coming of winter the half-deserted cities froze and starved. Strikes increased in number and violence. The violence culminated in February, 1921, in a mutiny of the sailors of Kronstadt, the heroes of the October Revolution, but now rebels calling for soviets without Communists. The rebels were shot down by Trotsky's Red army, just as the Kronstadt sailors had shot down the defenders of the provisional government.

Even before the mutiny, Lenin had decided to retreat. Publicly, retreat was not admitted. According to Communist doctrine, Marxism-Leninism was a science. Therefore, each shift in Communist practice must be a logical development, a stage in the scientifically determined advance toward socialism. What, from an outside point of view, had been desperate expedients to shore up the collapsing economy of Russia was, for Communists, "war communism," the stage of socialist evolution appropriate while waiting for the world revolution. Similarly, when the Russian economy collapsed in 1921, and the world revolution seemed more remote than ever, the retreat from war communism was called the New Economic Policy (NEP) and described as another stage in the evolution of socialism.

The method of retreat showed clearly the seat of power in Soviet Russia. First there were discussions in the Politburo and the central committee of the Communist party, from which emerged a decision to abandon the requisitioning of the peasants' "surplus" and to substitute a fixed tax—in grain because money was now worthless. Next came newspaper articles which gradually revealed the shift. Then the decision was submitted to the tenth party congress, on March 15, 1921. After acceptance by the party, further changes were made by the

Politburo. Only then, on March 20, was the proposal laid before the council of people's commissars; it was approved on March 21.

These concessions kept the peasant quiet while starvation struck the countryside as it had already struck the cities. Russia was engulfed in a famine of unprecedented proportions. Momentarily the regime turned to its enemies for support. Non-Communist Russians offered to form a committee which would seek aid from abroad and organize the distribution of supplies in the famine areas. The offer was accepted. The Soviet government also made agreements with the American Relief Administration (ARA), headed by Herbert Hoover, and with the Norwegian explorer Fridtjof Nansen, the representative of the Red Cross, even though the receipt of aid from "bourgeois" sources was thought humiliating and the presence of "bourgeois" relief workers in Russia was thought dangerous. The Russian committee was soon dissolved and some of its leaders arrested, but the ARA and the Red Cross were permitted to work through the winter; Soviet leaders even expressed gratitude for the aid furnished by the non-Communist world, while admitting inability to understand the motive for this generosity.

The famine passed, and 1922 brought the promise of a bumper harvest, but the substitution of a fixed tax for requisition necessitated a whole series of further retreats. If the peasant was to dispose of his surplus, trade must revive; so private trade was permitted. In practice, this meant that the "bagman" who had illegally brought buyer and seller together now came into the open. If there was to be trade, the peasant must be provided with things to buy: the consumer goods industries, hitherto neglected, were now encouraged by loans and by turning back small industries to private producers on lease. If factories were to produce, there must be managers free to make decisions: the bureaucrat's hand was lifted from the factory, and factory workers found themselves dealing with bosses who acted like capitalists and who indeed often were the old employers, now admitted to membership in the Communist party. If the cumbersome barter of war communism days was to be speeded, there must be currency in which traders had confidence. Hesitantly the government moved toward the devices familiar to capitalist economies—restriction of credit, slashing of budgets, limitations on the printing of currency, and accumulation of gold reserves.

One change led to another, and each pinched some group. In part, these strains had been anticipated by the tenth party congress which initiated the New Economic Policy. The congress, while admitting the desirability of discussion before the adoption of policy, prohibited the formation of factions within the party; individuals could urge a course of action, but they could not form a pressure group. The congress also ordered a purge of the party, to eliminate all who had not been reliable party workers. The ban on group activity and the fear of being purged did much to hold down criticism within the party. The city workers, who felt themselves squeezed between the favored peasant and the favored factory manager, were restive, but the party had moved into control of the unions: all union officials were now to be party members, and the higher the union office the longer the years of membership in the party required of candidates for office. The unions served NEP by preventing strikes and raising the productivity of labor.

On April 4, 1922, a change was made which attracted little attention at the time, but which later proved of decisive importance. Joseph Stalin (real name Iosif Dzhugashvili) was made general secretary of the central committee of the Communist party, with Vyacheslav Molotov and Valerian Kuibyshev as his assistants. Now the party secretariat began to manipulate all appointments to posts in the party and, through the party, in the government. Troublemakers were transferred to obscure posts far from the centers of power or, if they were too prominent for demotion, to posts abroad which were important in themselves but cut off from influence at home. In the turbulent early years of NEP the dominant faction in the party rejoiced that the opposition found so little support in the docile assemblies and congresses which emerged from Stalin's quiet manipulation of appointments and elections. One by one his colleagues were to learn that the general secretary could turn these docile delegates against them as well as against their opponents.

At the end of 1922 another labor of Stalin reached a well-publicized conclusion. From the early days of the revolution, as People's Commissar of Nationalities, he had guided Soviet policy through the tortuous path which began with the right of nationalities to autonomy or independence, proceeded through the turbulent years of the civil war when independent or autonomous republics rose and fell, and then in 1920 led to the consolidation of most of the empire in the Russian Socialist Federal Soviet Republic (R.S.F.S.R.), which contained eight autonomous republics and thirteen autonomous regions. For a time the regions outside Great Russia were linked to the R.S.F.S.R. only by treaty. At the end of 1922 all were brought together in the Union of Soviet Socialist Republics (U.S.S.R.), a union of the R.S.F.S.R. and the Ukrainian, White Russian, and Transcaucasian republics. Each republic had a constitution modeled on that of the R.S.F.S.R., and in 1923 a constitution was drafted for the whole union, again practically a copy of the 1918 constitution of the R.S.F.S.R., with the addition of a council of nationalities as one part of the central executive committee of the union.[5]

It would be almost correct to say that all these republics, constitutions, congresses, and councils were meaningless because all were controlled by the Communist party, and the party was controlled by the Politburo. So far as power was concerned, this was true. By 1923 all power had been drained into the Politburo, not only from the political structure but from the party itself. The U.S.S.R. was a dictatorship such as Europe had never before seen, because no earlier dictatorship had so perfected the means of controlling every detail of every individual's life.

Yet the government and party apparatus had importance. The thousands of individuals who came to meetings of committees and congresses were only dimly conscious that they were not really members of deliberative bodies, but were puppets. When there was complaint against the centralization of power it was heeded, in form. For instance, the Cheka had become thoroughly hated during the police terror of the civil war. So, in February, 1922, it was abolished. Its functions, however, were transferred to a section of the Commissariat of Internal Affairs called the "state political administration" (GPU). After the formation of the U.S.S.R. the name shifted again; now it was OGPU. Whatever the name or the initials, however, the reality of the all-pervasive secret police continued. Indeed, the GPU soon policed the party itself; the Cheka had kept clear of the party. Again, while the council of nationalities had no power, and Stalin's suppression of the nationalities went too far for Lenin's taste, the nationalities were allowed some self-expression so long as the reality of power was not touched.

The New Economic Policy could succeed only if there was a relaxation of control over the individual Russian and over economic and

5. Richard Pipes, *The Formation of the Soviet Union: Communism and Nationalism, 1917–1923* (rev. ed., Cambridge, Mass., 1964).

social groups. After March, 1921, once he had paid his tax, the peasant was free to sell his surplus, free to hire laborers, free to buy and sell land. Soon the more enterprising peasants were adding to their holdings, accumulating stock and equipment, living in relative luxury; they were rich peasants, the kulaks, a name hateful to Communists. Concessions to the peasant entailed concessions to the trader and the businessman. Soon some accumulated profits and began to indulge their taste for luxuries, doubly enjoyable after the lean years of the revolution; these were the nepmen, another name hateful to Communists.

Lenin and his colleagues in the Politburo were confident of the future: they had retained control over the "commanding heights," and particularly over heavy industry. But heavy industry did not share in the buoyant rise in the production of consumer goods and needed a vast infusion of capital, capital which was not available in Russia. Therefore, Lenin looked abroad for help. He had only contempt for kulaks, for nepmen, and for foreign capitalists eager for trade and investments in Russia: these fellows, he said, would even sell the rope for hanging them. But foreign capitalists and foreign governments could be useful while Communists waited for the next revolutionary wave to rise.[6]

In March, 1921—the month of the inauguration of NEP—a trade agreement was made with Britain. The agreement contained stringent provisions against subversive propaganda. This meant some curb on the activities of the Comintern. Almost at the same time, friendly relations were established by treaties with Persia, Afghanistan, and the Turkish nationalist leader Mustafa Kemal. These treaties meant a revision of Communist propaganda to the peoples of parts of Asia, and even silence while Mustafa Kemal killed off the leaders of the Turkish Communist party. In East Asia, despite the renunciation of czarist imperialism, control was slowly and quietly regained over the Chinese border provinces of Outer Mongolia and Sinkiang. In October, 1922, the Japanese withdrew their last troops from Vladivostok, and Soviet rule over the mainland of Asiatic Russia was now complete. Communist parties were established in Japan and China, but they were very small: there, Marxism appealed chiefly to intellectuals. A Soviet emis-

6. T. H. Von Laue's essay, "Soviet Diplomacy: G. V. Chicherin, People's Commissar for Foreign Affairs, 1918–1933," in Gordon Craig and Felix Gilbert (eds.), *The Diplomats, 1919–1939* (Princeton, 1953), is a thoughtful analysis of Soviet policy in the 1920's.

sary, Adolf Joffe, arrived in Peking in August, 1922, and remained in the Far East for a year. His advances were rebuffed by the Japanese and Chinese governments, but he had more success in south China with the rebel Kuomintang and its leader, Sun Yat-sen. In August, 1923, the young military leader of the Kuomintang, Chiang Kai-shek, arrived in Moscow, and in October a Soviet political adviser, Michael Borodin, came to Canton at the invitation of Sun Yat-sen. Just as there seemed more to be gained in central and west Asia by cooperation with native rulers against the British, so there seemed more profit in East Asia from cooperation with "national-revolutionary" movements against the established governments.

Germany occupied a peculiarly important position in the Soviet efforts to escape from isolation, and the ambiguous dualism of Soviet foreign policy could there be seen most clearly. Soon after the failure of the Communist effort to overthrow the Weimar Republic in March, 1921, conversations began between representatives of the Soviet and German governments. The German military leaders, and particularly General Seeckt, were anxious to experiment with the making and use in Russia of weapons prohibited in Germany; the Russians were eager to take advantage of German technological and military skill.[7] More generally, both governments were searching for an escape from political and economic isolation. The economic discussions came to fruition in April, 1922, when in the midst of an international conference at Genoa the Soviet and German delegates withdrew to nearby Rapallo. There they agreed to resume diplomatic relations, and each promised to consult the other before making any international economic agreement affecting its partner. At the time, it was generally believed that the Rapallo agreement contained secret political clauses. Apparently this was not true. However, the military collaboration was intensified after Rapallo, and the first German ambassador, Count Brockdorff-Rantzau, soon established close relations with Foreign Commissar Chicherin.[8]

7. See Hans Gatzke, "Russo-German Military Cooperation during the Weimar Republic," *American Historical Review*, LXIII (April, 1958), 565–97. Informal relations between the two countries had begun earlier. See O. E. Schüddekopf, *Karl Radek in Berlin: Ein Kapitel deutsch-russischer Beziehungen im Jahre 1919* (Hannover, 1962).

8. Herbert Helbeg studies the origins of the Treaty of Rapallo in the first essay in his book *Die Träger der Rapallo-Politik* (Göttingen, 1958). Walter Rathenau, one of those who formulated Germany's "Rapallo policy," is the subject of a study by James Joll:

While economic, military, and political intimacy between the two governments deepened, the Politburo was debating the possibility of exploiting the growing weakness of the Weimar Republic for revolutionary purposes. By the summer of 1923 the Franco-German conflict over reparation had brought the German economy close to total collapse, and the Politburo decided that the moment for revolution had come at last. German Communists were ordered to build secret military formations called the "Red hundreds," to seek a united front with socialists in Saxony, and to seize power in November, 1923. The German government struck first, on October 20; the Communist appeal for a general strike was unheeded; the few Communist risings were crushed. The German government mildly protested against the activities of the Comintern in Germany, and the Soviet government, as usual, replied that the Comintern was not a part of the Soviet government. Then the military conversations were resumed as if nothing had happened. The two governments needed each other, and the German government had lost its fear of Communist revolution.[9]

Other governments also were losing their fear of Communist contagion. The British Labour party would have no dealings with the British Communist party, but the first British Labour government recognized the U.S.S.R. on February 1, 1924. The new Fascist government of Italy jailed all the Communist leaders it could find, but extended diplomatic recognition to the U.S.S.R. on February 7, 1924. France fell in line on October 28. On January 21, 1925, Japan agreed to resume relations and to evacuate northern Sakhalin.

Of the Great Powers, only the United States refused recognition. Even the United States, however, tolerated a Soviet trading mission, organized as an American corporation (Amtorg), and permitted loans by impeccably capitalist banks to finance trade with the U.S.S.R. Similar missions operated in other countries, Arcos in Britain, for instance. And everyone knew these trading missions included the usual Comintern and OGPU agents. Trade, like diplomacy, was acquiring a new dimension in these years; or, more accurately, what had earlier been

---

"Walter Rathenau: Prophet without a Cause," in *Intellectuals in Politics* (London, 1960).

9. The story of Communist revolutionary activity in Germany during this period is told by W. T. Angress in *Stillborn Revolution: The Communist Bid for Power in Germany 1921–1923* (Princeton, 1963).

peripheral and incidental to diplomacy and trade was now becoming an essential characteristic of both.

At the time, outside Russia it was hoped that these characteristics were transitory. As NEP developed with what seemed relentless logic, the Western visitor to Russia felt increasingly at home among the new men of commerce and industry who lived and acted like shabby counterparts of the businessmen of non-Communist countries. Here, too, the façade of Soviet institutions had importance. Western liberals were much impressed by Soviet emphasis on national autonomy, by the sweeping guarantees of political, social, and economic equality in the Soviet constitution, and by the educational and cultural program of the regime. Here again the hard facts of economic misery and the omnipresent secret police stood in sharp contrast to paper promises, but the economy, though still far behind that of czarist days, was improving, and the dictatorship seemed to be disintegrating as rumors spread of the struggle for power in the Kremlin.

On May 26, 1922, shortly after Stalin was appointed general secretary, Lenin suffered a stroke. After a few months he recovered and resumed control over the Politburo. On December 16 another stroke paralyzed his right side. His mind remained clear, but thereafter he communicated with his colleagues through his wife or by letter. He seemed to recognize that he would never return to power, and on Christmas Day he composed the main part of what came to be called his "testament." He warned against a struggle for power within the small group at the top and seemed to regret that all power had been drained to that group. Above all, he feared a quarrel between Trotsky and Stalin. On January 4, 1923, he dictated a "postscript" which was a bitter attack on Stalin; he asked that Stalin be removed from the office of general secretary. For the moment these documents were known only to his wife and his secretary, but on March 5, in a note to Stalin, he broke off "comradely relations." Four days later another stroke silenced Lenin's voice permanently.[10]

After Lenin's first stroke, his colleagues expected him to recover. After the stroke of December 16, 1922, all eyes turned to Trotsky, the one man who, after Lenin, had emerged as a figure of heroic mold

10. This paragraph, and the paragraphs which follow, are largely based on E. H. Carr, *The Interregnum, 1923–1924* (London, 1954), Chaps. XI–XIV, a masterly analysis of fragmentary, contradictory, and tendentious evidence.

during the civil war. Within the central committee, however, Trotsky had few friends and in the Politburo he had only rivals. More important, Trotsky showed no appetite for a fight to the finish. The "triumvirate"—Zinoviev, Kamenev, and Stalin—took over; Grigori Zinoviev, the old companion of Lenin, was accorded priority. The three were eager to avert a showdown with Trotsky while Lenin's return to power remained possible and while the party was shaken by the strains of implementing and extending the New Economic Policy. A truce was arranged, and thanks to Stalin's manipulation of delegates, the twelfth party congress in April, 1923, was a relatively tranquil affair. During the summer and autumn the truce continued on the surface, but more and more those who regarded the New Economic Policy as a betrayal of socialism turned to Trotsky for leadership. Hesitantly and half-heartedly he resolved to do battle with the triumvirate. Soon the dissension broke out of the inner circles of the party. As Lenin lay dying in January, 1924, the triumvirate forced the issue at the thirteenth party conference and won. Trotsky remained a nominal member of the inner circle, but he had been isolated and defeated.

Immediately after the victory of the triumvirate came news of Lenin's death. Already his deification had begun: every speaker at the party conference had appealed to this or that text from Lenin as the final authority. Now, in death, his body was to be perpetually on display in a public shrine. Stalin's funeral oration had the form and cadence of a litany in which the responses of the faithful promised obedience to the commands of their god. Bolshevism, bit by bit, was appropriating the symbols and the liturgy of the Orthodox Christianity it was pledged to destroy.

Fresh from these scenes of adulation, the party leaders were confronted by the demand of Lenin's widow, Krupskaya, that Lenin's testament, with its postscript calling for the removal of Stalin as general secretary, be read at the thirteenth party congress in May, 1924. Stalin characteristically took the offensive by offering to resign. The congress, composed of delegates who owed their position to Stalin, gave him a unanimous vote of confidence. Thereafter, the testament was ignored, until it was read by Khrushchev, together with Lenin's angry letter to Stalin, at the twentieth party congress on February 25, 1956, three years after Stalin's death.

The thirteenth party congress shielded Stalin but launched new

attacks on Trotsky. The delegates reflected the results of a much publi-
cized "Lenin enrollment" of new party members and of an unpubli-
cized purge of old members, both manipulated by Stalin. He still
modestly stood in the background of the triumvirate, but within two
years Zinoviev and Kamenev were to reach out desperately to Trotsky
for support, only to be crushed by the apparatus Stalin had created; in
1927 all three were expelled from the party. By then, Soviet economic
production had reached the prewar level, and Soviet life was being
propelled by NEP ever closer toward that of Europe. Observers abroad
were confident that once the old leaders had exterminated one another,
Russia would emerge from its self-imposed isolation and rejoin the
family of nations.

3. THE RISE OF FASCISM IN ITALY

To most, even of those few Europeans who paid close attention to
what was happening outside their own country, it seemed by 1922 that
the revolution in Russia had been an expensive failure, expensive in the
dissipation of Russian resources, expensive in human suffering and
death; now, it seemed, the Russians must painfully work their way
back to the abiding traditions of European political, social, and economic development.

Most Europeans, even well-informed Europeans, were equally complacent about what was happening in Italy. By the autumn of 1922, the
parliamentary confusion and the social strife which had been endemic
since 1918 were coming to a climax in threats by armed bands of the
Fascist party to march on Rome and seize power by force.[11] Then, on
October 31, the leader of the Fascists, Benito Mussolini, became prime
minister in a government made up largely of representatives of other
parties. The threat of civil war passed, and with its passing European
interest waned. During the few days when Fascism commanded wide
interest, the news stories gave confused and contradictory reports of the
movement and its leader; when interest faded, there was little recognition that anything of profound significance had happened in Italy.

It is not strange that foreigners had so little understanding of the
nature of Fascism; most influential Italians, those who wrote for publication or who talked in parliament, interpreted events in the light of

11. See A. Rossi (pseud. of A. Tasca), *The Rise of Italian Fascism 1918–1922* (London, 1938), and Vivarelli's bibliographical article cited above, Chap. I, fn. 11.

Italian political traditions, modified somewhat by the harsh events of the postwar years. These traditions revolved around two untranslatable words—*combinazione* and *trasformismo*. Italian political parties had always been numerous, and they had never been clearly marked off from one another. They had been more concerned with local or group issues than with national issues, and loyalty had always been given more to party leaders than to the parties themselves. Cabinet building had been a process of negotiation on terms of agreement between politicians who could "deliver" deputies—in American slang, the political chieftains made a "deal," in Italian, *combinazione*. The partners to the deal might have been opponents, but as favors were dispensed *trasformismo* took place, opponents became allies. When the March on Rome took place, Giovanni Giolitti, the old master of *trasformismo*, was waiting patiently for another chance to apply his art. To most politically minded Italians, Mussolini's new cabinet was another *combinazione;* now the old process of *trasformismo* would change unruly Fascists into an accepted and acceptable part of the parliamentary system.

It seemed high time. Since the war, the game of politics had broken down. The elections of 1919 had resulted in a chamber in which more than 150 Socialists and about 100 of Don Sturzo's *popolari* had together a majority of the seats. The Popular party was Catholic in orientation and therefore anti-Marxian. The Socialists were badly split on most issues, with the right-wing leaders content to win concessions by parliamentary bargains and the left-wing leaders committed to the Third International even before they broke off to form the Communist party in January, 1921. Most of the rank and file, in the parliament and in the party, supported a maximalist policy, that is, a "pure" Marxism without regard to either party discipline or political reality. The Socialists and *popolari* could not cooperate with each other; the Socialists could not cooperate with the various liberal groups who had long dominated Italian politics; the *popolari* were drawn to the liberals by fear of Marxism, but repelled by the anticlericalism of the liberals. In this new situation any *combinazione* was unstable, and *trasformismo* was impossible. The result was a series of short-lived cabinets without strength to curb either the inflation which drove prices up or the social unrest which was fed both by inflation and by disillusionment with politicians who could not govern.

At first, the weakness of the government favored the Socialists, whose creed sanctioned violence against the capitalist political and social order. During 1919 and 1920 strikes increased in number and in violence, culminating in the seizure of a large number of factories in September, 1920. Momentarily the syndicalist dream of social revolution through the takeover of industry by the workers seemed imminent. Giolitti was then prime minister. He refused to meet force with force. Instead he waited, confident that the Socialists would not move from seizure of the factories to seizure of the government, confident also that the experiment of factory operation by workers without managerial training would fail. He was correct. Very quickly the workers were forced to make terms for the return of the factories to the managers. When violence spread to the countryside, and the farm workers took over farms, Giolitti waited again, and again the workers made terms with the owners. In Giolitti's judgment the maximalism of the Socialists concealed a lack of real unity or leadership, and his judgment was vindicated by events. After 1920, Italian Marxism was weakened by dissension. The danger of a Communist seizure of power, if it had ever existed, was gone.

Violence continued both in the cities and in the countryside. Now that the unity of the laboring masses was broken, the government abandoned its passive role and met force with force. Moreover, the Socialists and Communists were increasingly harassed by armed bands which progressed from attacks on strikers, to attacks on party meetings and newspaper offices, to attacks on towns with Socialist governments. At first, many of the bands were recruited by local leaders to put down local strikes. Others were led by supporters or imitators of the nationalist freebooter, D'Annunzio. Only slowly was command assumed by Mussolini and his Fascists.

When he first began to gain popular attention, Mussolini seemed just another national Bolshevist of the type which was appearing in many countries. From the prewar days when he had been a Socialist editor, he retained hatred of capitalism, of religion, and of the monarchy; he was marked off from his former comrades only by the nationalism which had made him an interventionist during the war. With this program he was able to recruit plenty of veterans who were bored with civilian life, and also plenty of youngsters who had a taste for violence. His squads were content with the pleasure of beating or killing Social-

ists, with the delight of watching the torments of Socialists who had
been forced to take massive doses of castor oil, and with the satisfaction
of feeling themselves patriots while thus indulging themselves. But
these social misfits could not, by themselves, make Mussolini more
than another freebooter, without the glamour D'Annunzio had won,
first as a writer, then as the "redeemer" of Fiume. Certainly the
workers, to whom Mussolini first addressed himself, refused to listen to
appeals for a national socialism. He won a mass audience only when he
began to praise the Church and the monarchy as vital elements in
Italian national traditions and when he began to discourse eloquently,
if confusedly and vaguely, on a syndicalism and on a corporate state
within which the middle classes would have a leading and honored
place.

If war, depression, and inflation had pressed hard on the city worker
and the farm laborer in Italy, they had pressed even harder on the
salaried man, the professional man, the shopkeeper, who had no union
to protect his interests and who, above everything else, dreaded being
pushed down to the level of the manual worker. Moreover, the middle
classes had always regarded themselves as the peculiar guardians of
Italian nationalism against the internationalism of the Socialists and
the cosmopolitanism of the big businessman and the aristocrat. Italian
nationalism had been affronted by the other victorious powers at Paris,
and the economic position of the middle classes was being eroded by
inflation and by the demands of organized labor. Inevitably, the middle
classes listened when they were told that they would win their rightful
place in Italy, and Italy would win its rightful place in the world, when
the mean-spirited cabinet in Rome, always in retreat before enemies at
home and abroad, was replaced by the courageous Fascists who would
do to foreign foes what they were doing to Socialists.

The fury with which Mussolini attacked parliamentary government
did not greatly alarm the parliamentary leaders, and above all Giolitti,
who had seen many tribunes of the people yield to the subtle attrac-
tions of *trasformismo*. The cudgels and the castor oil of the Fascist
squads were not altogether unwelcome to a government which hesitated to suppress the Communists by force; when Mussolini had put
on the morning coat of the parliamentarian, these things would be
discarded like the black shirt. So, when the *popolari* proved difficult,
Giolitti made the traditional *combinazione* with the Fascists for the

elections of May, 1921. The combined seats of the warring Socialists and Communists in the new chamber were fewer than the Socialist party had held before; the *popolari* won a few additional seats. The Fascists, although they won only a score of seats, held the balance of power. When they ignored their electoral bargains and voted in the opposition, Giolitti resigned in disgust. Untaught by Giolitti's experience, the parliamentary leaders continued confident that, sooner or later, Mussolini must enter some coalition government, and they all wanted to hold the way open for membership in that coalition; no one was willing to take a firm stand against Fascist violence. Therefore, the squads operated with increasing confidence, throwing out Socialist or Communist local governments in metropolitan centers like Bologna and Milan with little or no interference from the police or the army. In August, 1922, the Socialists tried to stem the tide by a general strike which failed dismally and only gave an opportunity for the Fascists to beat, shoot, and kill with new assurance of popular support.

Paradoxically, the more Italy was convulsed by Fascist violence, the more certain the traditional defenders of order became that only the entrance of Mussolini into the government could restore order in Italy. Now that he talked of religion as a vital part of Italian culture, powerful churchmen deserted the *popolari* and in many instances openly supported the Fascists who drove Communist governments from episcopal cities. Military leaders began to hope that Fascism would awaken the martial virtues which had not been conspicuous in Italian national life since the Risorgimento. Capitalists had not forgotten Mussolini's earlier demands for social revolution, but money did flow into the party treasury to support the squads in their war against Communism. Meanwhile, the liberal politicians still sought to hold the way open for alliance with the rising leader. Only at the last moment, when the Fascists assembled their forces and announced that they would march on Rome itself, only then did the vacillating Luigi Facta, a prime minister without a majority, ask the king to proclaim martial law. Victor Emmanuel, after consulting with military leaders, refused to sign the decree. Instead, Mussolini was invited to form a government. He arrived in Rome on October 30, 1922, and formed a coalition cabinet in which only four of the fourteen ministers were Fascists. Then he ordered the Fascist squads to leave the city.

The old *trasformismo,* it seemed, was about to begin. Mussolini was prime minister, but the Fascists were a small minority in the chamber and in the cabinet. To facilitate the restoration of order, the chamber voted full powers for a year to the new government. There was some muttering that the March on Rome was an unnecessary show of force, just as there had earlier been some muttering about the violence of the squads. But these excesses seemed transient to the traditional leaders of Italy, to the businessmen and aristocrats, the churchmen and military commanders, the intellectuals and the artists, the king and the politicians, who by action or inaction had made it possible for Mussolini to take over the state. It could plausibly be argued that the end was good, bringing order to a divided country and a distracted people. For the first time since the war, indeed for the first time since the war with Turkey in 1911, it seemed that Italians could relax and lead quiet lives again.

Even those Italians to whom educated Europeans looked for guidance, the liberals and particularly the great philosopher Benedetto Croce, were slow to understand. As late as the elections of 1924, when it had become hard not to see that terror was essential to Fascism, the liberals allied with the Fascists against what Croce called "the antinational socialists and the demagogic popular Christian party." Fascism, he argued, had been necessary, and had done much good. Italy must not "return to the weakness and inconclusiveness" of the pre-Fascist period. Only in 1925 did Croce recognize that Fascism was the implacable foe of the liberty he prized.[12]

Croce's slow awakening deserves emphasis because it so well catches the contemporary view of Fascism and of the spread of dictatorship in Europe. Over and over, one meets the argument: "We could not live forever under the fear of revolution." In this view, Mussolini was not a revolutionary, and Fascism was not a revolution; Fascism was an escape from revolution. This was not the view of many intellectuals and trade union leaders, but these were not the rulers of Europe. To the British Foreign Secretary Austen Chamberlain, Mussolini was "the simplest and sincerest of men when he is not posing as the Dictator," and Chamberlain freely admitted that "if I ever had to choose in my own country between anarchy and dictatorship I expect I should be on

12. D. Mack Smith, "Croce and Fascism," *The Cambridge Journal*, II (March, 1949), 343–56. See also D. Mack Smith, "The Politics of Senator Croce," *The Cambridge Journal*, I (Oct., 1947), 28–42, and I (Feb., 1948), 279–91.

the side of the dictator." Winston Churchill, in his review of the post-war decade, had much to say about Communism, none of it favorable, but he ignored Fascism except for a passing reference to Mussolini's foresight and realism.[13]

13. Sir Charles Petrie, *The Life and Letters of the Right Hon. Sir Austen Chamberlain* (2 vols., London, 1939–40), II, 290, 295. Winston S. Churchill, *The Aftermath* (N.Y., 1929), p. 487.

Chapter Four

NATIONALISM AND IMPERIALISM AFTER THE WAR

I. THE LEAGUE OF NATIONS, 1920–1922

On January 10, 1920, the Treaty of Versailles at last went into effect. The delay resulted from hope that the United States would, after all, participate in the implementing of the treaty and the organization of the League of Nations. That hope lingered during 1920. The council of the League was set up, and met frequently, but the assembly did not meet until November. By then it was obvious not only that the United States would not be a member but that the newly elected Republican administration in Washington would be happy if the League, as Woodrow Wilson's handiwork, languished and died.

At the meeting of the assembly, two apparently opposing points of view emerged from the speeches of representatives of the smaller states. On the one hand, these states made clear their refusal to accept the provisions of the covenant which might involve them in a war to resist aggression. This became evident in the debate on proposals to amend Article X and Article XVI. The amendments were not accepted, but after the debate it was certain that most members did not, in fact, acknowledge an obligation to "preserve as against external aggression the territorial integrity and existing political independence of all Members of the League," or to resort to sanctions against an aggressor. In other words, each member reserved the right *not* to go to war in case of aggression.

On the other hand, the smaller states showed great eagerness not only to bring all existing international agencies under the control of the League but, much more important, to insist that all international controversies be submitted to the League for settlement. On the first of these objectives progress had already begun, and continued. Despite the sullen attitude of the United States government, many of the prewar international agencies were placed under direction of the secretariat of the League. Some functions had been set for the League in the peace treaties, such as the protection of minorities, and administration of the

Saar and Danzig. Other tasks quickly appeared. In supervising the exchange of prisoners of war and in arranging for the resettlement of refugees, the towering personality of Fridtjof Nansen achieved results which redounded to the credit of the League. Again, in attempts to control the epidemics of typhus, cholera, and other diseases which were spreading westward from starving Russia, the League was not content to establish a *cordon sanitaire* but, after repeated rebuffs, succeeded in winning the cooperation of the Soviet government for an attack on the sources of the epidemic diseases within Russia. By 1923 the spread of epidemics which, beginning with the influenza of 1918, had taken a toll of life far greater than the great war itself at last was halted. The resettlement of refugees, however, which was at first regarded as a short-term activity, was to outlast not only that last decade of the intrepid Norwegian scientist's life, but the life of the League itself.

One could go on. In innumerable fields, representatives of the League worked with selfless zeal setting in high relief the nobility mankind could aspire to achieve. Less selflessly, but with great results, that autonomous agency of the League, the International Labor Organization, worked for the improvement of conditions of work throughout the world.

It was the hope of those who looked to the League for the development of a world community free from war that the growth of League functions would, in time, give the League the character of a world government. At the same time, only an enthusiast could ignore the fact that the larger issues of world politics were decided with scant regard for the League. Two great powers, the United States and the Soviet Union, were not only outside the League but hostile to it. A third great power, Germany, was kept out by the blunt French threat to quit the League if Germany were admitted; inevitably, Germans regarded the League as an instrument for the perpetuation of French supremacy on the continent, although this was not the intent of most members. So far as problems arising from the peace treaties were concerned, the League had no jurisdiction; the supreme council and the conference of ambassadors of the victors continued to meet for consideration of these questions.

The League was invited to intervene in only one major question, for which an immediate settlement was imperative and on which the conference of ambassadors could not agree—the question of Upper Silesia.

EUROPE

AFTER THE PEACE TREATIES

Areas lost by Germany

Areas lost by Russia

Austria-Hungary, 1914

Areas lost by the Ottoman Empire

ARCTIC

ICELAND
(Den.)

Reykjavik

Narvik

FAEROE IS.
(Den.)

NORWAY

SWEDEN

Oslo

Stockholm

BALTIC SEA

AALAND
(Fin.)

NORTH
SEA

DENMARK

Copenhagen

Memel

Edinburgh

POLISH
CORRIDOR

ULSTER

EAST
PRUSSIA

IRISH
FREE
STATE

Dublin

GREAT

Amsterdam

Hamburg

Bremen

Berlin

Warsaw

BRITAIN

London

RUHR

GERMANY
(WEIMAR REPUBLIC)

Dresden

P O

ATLANTIC

OCEAN

Brussels

BELG.

Cologne

Weimar

Prague

Teschen

Paris

LUX.

Frankfurt

CZECHOSLOVAKIA

Versailles

Metz

SAAR

Stuttgart

Strasbourg

Munich

Vienna

FRANCE

SWITZ.

AUSTRIA

Budapest

Bordeaux

Geneva

Locarno

Trent

HUNG.

Bilbao

Trieste

Fiume

PORTUGAL

Marseilles

Zara
(It.)

YUGOSLAVI

Lisbon

Madrid

Florence

CORSICA
(Fr.)

Belgrade

SERB

SPAIN

Rome

ITALY

ALBANIA

Seville

BALEARIC ISLANDS
(Sp.)

Naples

ADRIATIC SEA

Cadiz

SARDINIA
(It.)

Tangier

GIBRALTAR
(Br.)

SP. MOROCCO

Algiers

MEDITERRANEAN

SICILY
(It.)

MOROCCO
(Fr.)

ALGERIA
(Fr.)

TUNISIA
(Fr.)

MALTA
(Br.)

0   100   200   300   400

Scale of Miles

Map by Harry Scott

The peace treaty had called for a plebiscite. The plebiscite was held on March 20, 1921, and almost three-fifths of the voters and well over half of the voting districts voted to remain in Germany, but election officials were unable to agree on a settlement. The conference of ambassadors was also divided and asked the council of the League to recommend a frontier line. On October 12, 1921, the council not only submitted a frontier line but also proposals for the economic administration of the area and for the protection of minorities. The ambassadors next asked the council to take charge of the negotiations between Poland and Germany; in June, 1922, the German-Polish convention for the administration of the area went into effect. In one sense, the problem of Upper Silesia strengthened the League: the League commission moved with dispatch and produced a settlement which worked, despite the animosity between Germans and Poles. On the other hand, because a majority of the residents had voted for union with Germany, the Germans saw in the division of Upper Silesia only another illustration of French domination over the League.

On other questions, even when they were themselves divided, the victorious Great Powers were united in refusing jurisdiction to the League. Therefore, to obtain perspective on the evolution of Europe, it was still necessary to look out from the capitals of the Great Powers. Just as the League was meeting in improvised quarters in Geneva, so Geneva had none of the prestige of the traditional national centers of power.

2. THE REVOLT AGAINST IMPERIALISM

When the armistice was signed in 1918, Lord Curzon, who was to be British foreign secretary from 1919 to 1924, boasted that the British Empire had never been more strong or more united, and that the power of Britain to shape the destinies of the world had never been so great. When the Treaty of Versailles was signed in 1919, British Prime Minister David Lloyd George boasted that the peace treaty had further strengthened the position of Britain in the world.

For the moment these boasts seemed justified. Russia was paralyzed by civil war, and the pressure of Russia on British interests all the way from the Aegean and the Persian Gulf across the land mass of Asia to the Pacific was at least temporarily lessened. The German colonial empire was gone, the strategically important parts of it in British possession; the German battle fleet, interned after the armistice in Scapa Flow, had been sunk by its own crews to escape transfer to the victors. France was for the moment supreme on the continent. Given the greater natural strength of Germany, however, the British were convinced that since French supremacy in Europe was dependent on British support, France could not afford imperial rivalry with Britain. In the Mediterranean the dependence of weak Italy on British favor was expected to continue. To fill the vacuum left by the collapse of Russian and Turkish power in the region of the Straits, Lloyd George had encouraged the Greeks to land troops at Smyrna in May, 1919; if both the European and the Asiatic shores of the Aegean could be put securely in Greek possession, the short route to India through the Mediterranean would be protected. In the Far East, friction between the United States and Japan seemed to ensure the continued loyalty of Japan to the alliance with Britain. The one obvious threat to the security of the British Empire seemed the naval building program of the United States, which, if carried to completion, would jeopardize the naval supremacy of Britain. The initial inclination of Lloyd George was to accept the challenge. Britain would, he said, spend her last guinea to preserve the naval supremacy which, he was convinced, had just saved the freedom not only of Britain but of the world.

There was the same confidence bordering on arrogance in imperial affairs. Unrest in India early in 1919 was met by the Rowlatt Acts permitting the summary conviction of persons accused of sedition, by the arrest of the Indian nationalist leader Mohandas Gandhi, and, as a climax, by what Indians and Englishmen alike came to call the Amritsar Massacre, the killing of some hundreds of Indians who were attending a political meeting, by soldiers under the command of General Reginald Dyer. Again, in Egypt, Saad Zaghlul and the other nationalist leaders, who tried to bring the cause of Egyptian independence to the attention of the peacemakers in Paris, were arrested and deported to Malta. Close to home, in Ireland, the nationalist Sinn Fein representatives who had been elected to Parliament in the election of December, 1918, refused to proceed to Westminster and instead declared the independence of the Irish Republic on January 21, 1919, and also declared war on the British in Ireland. After some hesitation, the reaction of the British was to take up the challenge.

Very quickly this mood of confident willingness to meet with force every challenge to British power gave way to a willingness not only to negotiate but to retreat. In large part the shift resulted from recognition of weakness. The first weakness was military. The wish of the British government to retain a large army was overborne by popular pressure; in 1919 the vast imperial armies were demobilized. The second weakness was financial. At the end of 1918, Britain was pouring money into Persia alone at the rate of about $100 million a year. After the drain of the war years, continued expenditure at this rate was impossible.

Beyond these tangible weaknesses, there was a shift in popular feeling which some have called a failure of nerve, but which others have attributed to a changed morality. The shift, and the cleavage, in British opinion was evident after the Amritsar Massacre. Indignation was great enough to force the recall and censure of General Dyer; on the other hand, his supporters at home presented him with a sizable fortune as thanks for his services to Britain. Similarly, the arrest of Zaghlul and Gandhi brought cries that Britain was hypocritical in its defense of self-determination, and both were released.

Possibly the supporters of General Dyer were right in maintaining that force, steadily and ruthlessly used, could have brought peace and strength to the Empire: when, in the general colonial unrest after the war, the Koreans revolted against Japan, there was such use of force, and thereafter Korea was quiet until Japanese power was broken in the Second World War. But Japan had only one Korea, and Korea was small, isolated, and relatively leaderless. In any case, the British people were obviously in no mood to be intransigent, as Lloyd George was quick to recognize. Once the intoxication of victory had passed, he saw that the British Empire had entered not a more spacious but a straitened age. With the same ingenuity he had shown in winning the war, and the same willingness to abandon courses of action once shown they could not bring success, he set out to save as much as could be saved.

In imperial problems he set a course which was followed by his successors. It was not a heroic course, and it had little appeal either to those who regarded the Empire as sacred or to those who regarded self-determination as an inalienable right. Instead it was a zigzag course of concession and resistance, seeking to save what was essential for the security of the Empire without resort to wholesale violence and repression, and without any great concern either for moral principle or for consistency. Where there was slight pressure for change, as in the African and other colonies under the Colonial Office, things went along much as they had in the nineteenth century. Where dominion status had already been won—in Canada, South Africa, New Zealand, Australia—there was ambiguity which could be very irritating to other states. On the one hand the British insisted that these were free states, entitled to all the rights and privileges of independent nations; on the other hand the British insisted that the dominions and the mother country could grant each other special privileges, on tariffs for instance, without extending these privileges to others, because all were parts of what had come to be called during the war the British Commonwealth. To outsiders, this kind of logic was not far removed from the Russian argument that there was no connection between the Soviet government and the Comintern.

India was in an even more ambiguous position. India was a charter member of the League of Nations, but the reality of British power in India and the lack of native control over the Indian government were clear. In December, 1919, the Government of India Act set up a complicated series of mixed governmental councils, sometimes called dyarchy, with Indian representation but ultimate British control. The new government was launched at an inauspicious time. The privations of the war years, climaxed by crop failures and the great influenza epidemic of 1918 which took possibly 5 million lives in India, had led the Hindus and the Moslems to lay aside for the moment their hatred for each other and to combine forces against their British masters. Moreover, in India as elsewhere in the colonial world, the wartime slogan of self-determination had aroused the hope of independence. Finally, in Gandhi the Indian nationalists had a leader, an astute politician seasoned by legal education in England and apprenticeship as defender of the Indian minority in South Africa, but above all a leader with moral stature who won the respect of the British no less than the Indians. Under his guidance, in jail or out of jail, the nationalist movement attained massive strength.

The struggle in India, begun in 1919, continued to and beyond 1939; it was sometimes marked by violence, bloodshed, and repression, sometimes broken by truces and efforts to find a basis for agreement. Taking the period as a whole, the British could be said to be in retreat; on the other hand, British rule was maintained, and the stated objective of the British—to prepare the Indians for self-government—was advanced. Above all, at no time did the British government abandon its search for accommodation, and throughout mutual respect was maintained. Therefore the British could believe that their faith in compromise was justified.

With more difficulty they could believe themselves vindicated in Egypt. Here again, inflation and the other privations of the war years had pressed hard on peasants who lived at best on the margin of subsistence. Here also talk of self-determination had raised hopes. And here there was a peasant leader, Zaghlul, without Gandhi's appeal to the outside world but with great ability to influence the Egyptian masses. As in India, the British alternated between repression and conciliation, seeking a ground for accommodation. Egypt, however, had only peripheral importance for Britain—as a possible threat to communication with the east through Suez and the Red Sea, and because of the Sudan. So the British, in February, 1922, simply proclaimed the independence of Egypt, reserving for future settlement the security of communications, defense, the protection of foreigners, and the Sudan; meanwhile, British troops remained in Egypt. The results were satisfactory, in that British imperial interests were protected. But to the Egyptians, to foreign observers, and to many Englishmen, "independence with safeguards" was merely "an attempt to shirk the responsibilities of Empire, and at the same time to take the profits."[1]

The greatest test of Lloyd George's faith in agreement through negotiation was Ireland.[2] There, on both sides, passion seemed to ensure failure. Even before the war the battle over home rule had threatened civil war in Ireland and revolt against the government in Great Britain. To the British, the Easter Rebellion of 1916 was final proof of Irish perfidy; to the Irish, the execution of the rebel leaders was final proof of British inhumanity. Through 1919, Sinn Fein and the Irish Republican army were busy undermining British rule, terrorizing all those who participated in any way in the British administration of Ireland, and building a framework of illegal republican

---

1. Lord Lloyd, *Egypt Since Cromer* (2 vols., London, 1933-34), I, 359. Lord Lloyd was British High Commissioner in Egypt and the Sudan from 1924 to 1930; *Egypt Since Cromer* is an excellent presentation of the imperialist point of view.

2. See Desmond Williams (ed.), *The Irish Struggles 1916-1928* (London, 1966), an excellent collection of essays on Ireland and on British policy.

government. The British government was slow to respond, partly because opinion at home was divided, partly because American opinion had taken up the Irish cause. In 1920, however, the ranks of the Royal Irish constabulary, decimated by resignations forced by terrorism, were filled by demobilized British soldiers who, from their uniforms, came to be called the Black and Tans. Under the impact of Irish republican terror, discipline declined in the Black and Tans. By the end of the year the tale of reprisals sickened the most fanatical. In December, a new Government of Ireland Act was passed, separating the predominantly Protestant counties of the north from the predominantly Catholic south. The organization of Northern Ireland, however, merely produced a new wave of terror as Protestants sought to drive Catholics out of these counties.

In June, 1921, Lloyd George invited the Irish leader Eamon De Valera to a conference in London to discuss a settlement. A truce was declared by both sides in July, and through the remainder of the year conversations went on between members of the British government and two of De Valera's lieutenants, Michael Collins and Arthur Griffith. Out of these negotiations came an agreement by which the south would become the Irish Free State with complete self-government but within the Empire; Britain would retain naval bases in Irish ports; northern Ireland could choose between joining the Free State and remaining part of the United Kingdom. Collins and Griffith signed because they were convinced no better terms could be had, and the Irish parliament, the Dail, ratified the agreement in January, 1922. De Valera, however, resigned and organized a republican party. By spring there was civil war, more deadly than the terror of the preceding years. The armed resistance of the republicans was put down in 1924, and in 1925 the frontier between the Free State and Northern Ireland was fixed. De Valera continued to be a power, however, and in 1932 when the depression had hit Ireland, he was elected president. Soon he was involved in a tariff war with Britain, and, one by one, he cut all political ties. At last, in 1938, there was a new agreement with Britain which ended the tariff war, surrendered control over the Irish ports to what was now called Eire (Ireland), and was silent on any connection between Eire and Northern Ireland, or between Eire and Great Britain. In fact the majority in Northern Ireland was by now united in opposing union with the south, and in fact Eire was independent.

As in his dealings with Egypt and India, it could be said that Lloyd George had, by the Irish negotiations of 1921, set Britain on a path of retreat, with Chamberlain's surrender of the Irish ports and acceptance of Irish independence as the inevitable conclusion. It could also be said, however, and most of Lloyd George's countrymen believed, that since British rule could be maintained only by terror, it was far better to bring the enmity between Britain and Ireland to an end, to have the Irish as friendly neutrals rather than as rebellious subjects. Beyond that, the truce of 1921 and the creation of the Irish Free State removed a formidable barrier to the improvement of relations between Britain and the United States.

3. THE WASHINGTON CONFERENCE, 1921–1922

In 1919, when business was booming, most Englishmen did not seem greatly bothered either by the withdrawal of the United States from Europe or by French determination to hold Germany to compliance with every clause of the Treaty of Versailles. The general opinion seemed to be that, if necessary, Britain could go it alone. In the summer of 1920, however, the boom ended; economic depression spread rapidly over the country. By 1921 the world, and the position of Britain in the world, looked very different. Relations with the United States were bad; pessimists were saying that the Anglo-American naval rivalry must end, as the rivalry with Germany had ended, in war. Relations with France were bad; pessimists were saying that the French were building airplanes and submarines to extend French hegemony from the continent to the British Isles. With his usual respect for facts, however unpleasant, Lloyd George set out to improve relations with the United States and France by compromises which would preserve the essential, the security of Britain. With the Americans he succeeded; with the French he failed.

The depression of 1920 brought home to the British for the first time the magnitude of American economic power. Now the British government would have been happy to end the naval race, to settle for parity. Many Americans were unwilling to accept parity. The emotional argument of those urging American naval supremacy centered on the idea that, at least since the days of George III, the British had been foes of freedom. The effectiveness of this argument, not just with Irish-Americans, was blunted by the truce of July, 1921, and by the creation of the Irish Free State. The other telling argument of those urging American naval supremacy was the existence of the Anglo-Japanese alliance. During the war years the Japanese had extended their influence in China. At the peace conference Japan had won the succession to German rights in the Shantung peninsula, as well as a mandate over German islands in the Pacific north of the equator. Japanese troops were occupying eastern Siberia, ostensibly to oppose the spread of Bolshevism. Advocates of American naval supremacy maintained that the Japanese persisted in designs for control over China and Asian Russia only because they believed the Anglo-Japanese alliance prevented American opposition. In order to implement the traditional American policy of the "open door" in the Far East, the argument concluded, it was necessary for the United States to build a fleet capable of defeating the combined fleets of Britain and Japan.

There was economic depression in the United States as elsewhere, however, and the new Republican administration was willing to halt the naval race if the Anglo-Japanese alliance could be ended. Like the British, the Japanese had come to respect American economic power and were willing to compromise.

With the three great naval powers in tacit agreement, the American government issued invitations to a conference to be held in Washington to discuss reduction of armaments and problems of the Pacific. Germany was not invited, and this was interpreted by Germans as new evidence of determination to keep their country in a permanently inferior position. Russia was not invited; the Soviet government protested vigorously but without success against exclusion.

The Washington conference met from November 12, 1921, until February 6, 1922. It seemed, at the time, almost a model of what a successful international congress should be. The Anglo-Japanese alliance was widened into what was called the Four-Power Pact by the inclusion of France and the United States, and changed from a military alliance into an agreement to consult in case of controversy over any Pacific question. Three documents dealt with mainland Asia: an agreement between China and Japan gave assurance of the return of Shantung to China; a Japanese declaration promised evacuation of Russian territory; a Nine-Power Treaty gave assurances against new incursions on Chinese territory or independence.

The Treaty for the Limitation of Armament which emerged from the conference put limits only on capital ships; no limitation was placed on smaller vessels such as destroyers and submarines. At the opening of the conference Secretary of State Charles Evans Hughes proposed specific reductions in capital ships which would leave the British and American navies with about 500,000 tons each in this category and Japan with 300,000. This ratio of 5:5:3, he proposed, should also be used in determining tonnage in smaller categories. The Japanese agreed, in return for a promise by Britain and the United States not to fortify their possessions within striking distance of the home islands of Japan. The British also agreed, on condition that the British fleet was larger than the combined fleets of the next two naval powers, that is, Japan and France. This seemed reasonable to the Americans and the Japanese, who also, like the British, thought it reasonable that the Italian fleet should be as large as the French; therefore, the ratios of the five powers would be 5:5:3:1.75:1.75. The Italians eagerly concurred; they said they would accept any ratio, so long as their fleet was as large as the French.

The French objected. They had come to Washington expecting to mediate between the old mistress of the seas and the American upstart. Instead, the British and Americans cooperated so smoothly that the French suspected a prior secret agreement between the two governments. The French had also expected that when reduction of land armaments was discussed—and the invitation to the conference had called for such a discussion—they would be able to force acceptance of some security arrangement to replace the unratified Anglo-American treaty of guarantee. However, to avoid discussion of a security guarantee, the Americans decided not to press the question of reduction of land armaments; again the British followed the American lead, and again the French suspected an Anglo-American secret agreement.

The French were in no mood to accept relegation to the position of a minor naval power or equality with the Italians. In their own estimation, the French were seeking only security for themselves and for Europe. To them, it was obvious that since they must defend both their Atlantic and their Mediterranean coasts, they needed a fleet larger than Italy, a Mediterranean power. Again, if there was to be a consultative pact for the Pacific, why should there not be one for the Atlantic? These arguments were brushed aside by the British and Americans, who began to talk about French militarism and about France as the obstacle to the peace desired by the world. When the discussion turned to air power, the British, already uneasy about what this new weapon meant for the security of the British Isles, questioned the need for the growing French air fleet; since there was no other air power on the continent, it was hard for the British to see why this growth was needed for defense. Again, France seemed a militarist, aggressive power. Finally, there was the submarine. To the French, the submarine was a defensive weapon. A country burdened with the necessity for a large army, argued the French, needed many inexpensive submarines for defense. To the British, the submarine was an offensive weapon which had struck at helpless passenger ships during the war and had nearly starved Britain into surrender. From the British delegation came "leaks" to the press; in English and American newspapers there were new denunciations of French militarism; there were even prayers that God might turn the French from their love of war. Furious, the French premier, Aristide Briand, asked if British battleships were less a menace to France than French submarines were to Britain. He won no hearing in Washington and returned to France to face a people outraged by the accusations of the British. Under heavy American pressure, he agreed to accept the proposed ratio for capital ships and thus permitted the completion of the naval treaty. But the treaty set no limit on building in the smaller naval craft, and through this gap naval rivalry was to revive very quickly.

The Washington treaties did not, as Secretary Hughes promised, end competition in naval armament. Neither did they prove "the greatest forward step in history to establish the reign of peace."[3] In large part this was because the American people, and their government, convinced themselves that the one step was enough. After the repudiation of the League, and the separate peace with Germany, many Americans had an uneasy conscience about their refusal to accept any responsibility for the world settlement. The Washington conference, for most, ended these twinges of conscience. America, it was thought, had shown the way to peace in the field of disarmament and in settlement of the problems of the Pacific. If Europe continued in turmoil, that was because the European states refused to take the large and generous view shown by the United States at the Washington conference, and instead continued the old secret diplomacy, the old balance-of-power

3. Harold and Margaret Sprout, *Toward a New Order of Sea Power* (Princeton, 1940), p. 252.

politics, the old militarism which Woodrow Wilson had sought in vain to end. Through the years of returning prosperity after 1922, most Americans, if they thought of Europe at all, were content to thank God that they were not as other men.

4. THE MIDDLE EAST AND THE TURKISH REVIVAL

The British shared the pharisaical attitude of the United States toward the quarrels of the distracted continent of Europe, but they could not, like the Americans, stand disdainfully aloof. On the continent there was wild currency inflation. In countries with debased currencies the manufactures of countries with stable currencies found no market, while products priced in terms of falling currencies were flooding the market in "hard currency" countries. The Americans had a continental market of their own; therefore they were content to keep out foreign competition by the Fordney-McCumber tariff, the most protectionist in American history, passed in September, 1922, a few months after the end of the Washington conference. Even earlier, in 1921, the British had passed the Safeguarding of Industries Act to protect the British market from invasion by the products of countries with debased currencies. For Britain, however, it was not sufficient to exclude foreign products. British goods must be exported. From the summer of 1920, when the postwar boom collapsed, whole industries such as coal languished and unemployment grew. Since, during the war, old British markets in North and South America and in the Far East had been invaded by the Americans and the Japanese, or lost through the growth of native industries, continental European markets were more important than ever. With Russia starving, with the new or enlarged states of central and southeastern Europe racked by problems of adjustment to changed frontiers, with Italy almost paralyzed by social strife, and with the German inflation increasing daily, there was no possibility of increasing exports to the continent.

Moreover, there was growing fear in Britain that the continuation of economic misery on the continent would produce social convulsions which must, in the end, shake the social structure of Britain. To placate labor, the Lloyd George government had passed two measures of great importance. One, the Housing and Town Planning Act of 1919, gave support to the building of the "council houses" which were to revolutionize living conditions in England. The other, the Unemployment

Insurance Act of 1920, was intended to put payments to the unemployed and, by later amendments, to their families on a self-supporting basis. Almost immediately, the appearance of mass unemployment wrecked the solvency of the insurance plan; but the principle of support for the unemployed had been accepted, and the "dole" became a permanent burden on the state. Support both of housing and of the unemployed was expensive and intensified the need to bring about economic revival. Moreover, these social reforms did not produce social peace. There were new waves of strikes as the depression deepened, and much talk of a general strike to force social and political change. Fear of revolution in Britain gave heightened impetus to the demand for economic revival in Europe.

France now seemed the enemy of European reconstruction. Earlier, on April 27, 1921, the British representative on the reparation commission had concurred in the decision to fix German reparation at 132 billion gold marks (about $33 billion), in the demand that Germany pay a quarter billion dollars immediately, and in the ultimatum which forced German acceptance of these terms. When, however, acceptance of the terms was followed by a drastic and continuing decline in the value of the mark, the British began to urge the necessity for a moratorium on reparation payments until the German economy could be stabilized. Now it seemed to the British that the French were defeating their own interests by insisting on impossible reparation payments which threatened to end the possibility of any payments by Germany. Moreover, the incessant clamor of the French for military and political guarantees of their security seemed ridiculous at a time when France was the only real military power in Europe and when there seemed more danger of the collapse of all continental states except France in common ruin than of any attempt to overturn the Peace of Paris. In these circumstances, the insistence of France on unrestricted air and submarine strength suggested a sinister motive: did France intend to dominate not only the continent but Britain also? This motive, attributed to France at the Washington conference, was advanced in more or less veiled form by sections of the British press to explain the otherwise incomprehensible conduct of France.

Lloyd George permitted the chorus of abuse of France, but he was convinced that his next task was to do with France what he had so successfully done with Japan and the United States: to arrange a settlement by personal diplomacy. The alternative was rivalry which Britain, no less than France, could not afford. The French had repeatedly demonstrated both their determination and their ability to prevent any action to revive the European economy until their demand for British participation in defense of the Paris settlement was met. No less important, British refusal to give any guarantee of French security was resulting in effective French opposition to British policy in Asia Minor.

The treaty settlement with Turkey had been delayed both by the conflicting ambitions of the victors and by the distracted condition of Turkey. During the war there had been several attempts to arrange the partition of Turkey by secret agreements between the European Allies and also between Britain and Arab chieftains.[4] In addition, the British had promised support for the creation of a Jewish national home in Palestine. The Russian revolution simplified the situation to some extent by removing one very hungry claimant, but there were enough conflicts remaining to delay the conclusion of the Treaty of Sèvres with Turkey until August 10, 1920. By the treaty, Turkey lost all territory in Europe except in the immediate vicinity of Istanbul (Constantinople). The Straits connecting the Black Sea and the Mediterranean were to be administered by an international commission and were to be open to shipping in war and peace. Armenia was to be independent and Kurdistan autonomous. All the Arab lands were taken from Turkey, but only the territory then called the Hejaz and later called Saudi Arabia was to be independent. The other Arab territories were to be mandates of the League of Nations—Syria under French rule, and Mesopotamia (later named Iraq) and Palestine under British rule. Greece was to get eastern Thrace and Turkish islands in the Aegean, and was to administer Smyrna and the surrounding territory at least for five years. Italy received islands in the Aegean. Turkey, then, would consist only of the interior of Anatolia and Istanbul.

By the time the Treaty of Sèvres was signed by the sultan's government in 1920, it was doubtful whether the treaty could be carried into effect. In central Anatolia, beyond the reach of Allied warships, a Turkish nationalist movement was developing under the leadership of Mustafa Kemal. At first, Kemal had sought to work through the

4. See Elie Kedourie, *England and the Middle East: the Destruction of the Ottoman Empire, 1914–1921* (London, 1956).

sultan, but when Istanbul was occupied by the Allies, in March, 1920, a separate government was set up at Ankara. Kemal now showed himself one of the most astute diplomats of the century. Turkey and Russia had long been enemies; they were divided by territorial rivalry in the region of the Caucasus and by the efforts of the Comintern to create a Communist party in Turkey. However, they had a common interest in opposing the Allies, and particularly Britain. So, even while military clashes continued in the Caucasus and while Turkish Communists were being exterminated, negotiations proceeded. On March 16, 1921, a treaty was concluded fixing frontiers in the Caucasus, ending all Russian rights which impaired Turkish sovereignty, and affirming that the states bordering on the Black Sea should determine the status of the Straits. More important than the terms of the treaty were the arms and supplies now received from Moscow and the knowledge that the Turkish frontier with Russia was secure. The Italians also were eager to make terms with the ascendant Turkish nationalists; conscious of their own weakness and angry because neither Britain nor France showed interest in Italian ambitions for empire, the Italians withdrew their troops from Asia Minor in June, 1921. Next, the French sought an agreement, in part to show that if Britain would not support France in Europe, France could hurt British imperial interests. On October 21, 1921, a Franco-Turkish treaty fixed the frontier between Turkey and Syria, and thereafter Kemal received military supplies from France also. Meanwhile, Greek armies remained deep in Anatolia, too weak to advance, and the discontent of the Greek people was shown in December, 1920, by the return to power of King Constantine, who had been deposed during the war because of his friendliness toward Germany. With the military strength of the Turkish nationalists growing, Greek resolution faltering, and the other powers aloof or hostile, Lloyd George saw his Turkish policy facing collapse. In these circumstances, he made his bid to reknit the entente with France.

While debate was proceeding at the Washington conference, there was a meeting of the supreme council at Cannes. On January 4, 1922, before the meeting opened, Lloyd George laid proposals for a general settlement of Anglo-French differences before the French premier, Briand. As published, the proposals centered on the convocation of an economic conference at Genoa in the spring, to which both Germany and Russia would be invited. The conference would attempt a settlement of the economic ills of Europe, including reparation and the defaulted debts of czarist Russia. In return for consent to the calling of this conference, Britain would agree to give France full military assistance in case of an unprovoked attack by Germany. Lloyd George also had hopes of reviving Anglo-French cooperation in Turkey and of a settlement of the submarine issue then under debate in Washington.

In Briand he had a sympathetic partner. Briand had been premier in 1916, during the battle of Verdun, and from that experience had come both a determination that France should not again be subjected to such a test and a recognition of the need for allies. He was premier through 1921, and his policy was directed toward ending Franco-German enmity and toward regaining the alliance with America and Britain. At Washington he learned the impossibility of drawing the United States back into defense of European security, but this setback only intensified his desire for alliance with Britain. He agreed, therefore, to the calling of an economic conference and to a suspension of reparation payments for the next few months. As for the British guarantee, he sought vainly to broaden its provisions to include the demilitarized Rhineland; he sought also to win a British promise to consult with France if the treaty settlement on Germany's eastern frontiers was threatened. If he had succeeded, he might have been able to hold French opinion in line, but Lloyd George was convinced that British opinion would support nothing beyond guarantee of the Franco-German frontier. As Briand's failure became clear, there was rebellion in the French Chamber of Deputies. Briand resigned, and Raymond Poincaré became premier, pledged to enforce all the rights of France under the Treaty of Versailles.

In Briand's mind, the memory of the appalling casualties of Verdun was central. Poincaré's view of Europe had been formed in his childhood, when France was the great nation of Europe and there was no German Empire. From his point of view, the war had restored France to its old, its natural, preeminence, and he believed it was his duty to beat down all rebellion against this restored political order. In his view, Britain was encouraging the rebellion of Germany against the Treaty of Versailles and also, by the commercial agreement of 1921 with Russia, prolonging the life of the Bolshevik regime which had taken Russia out of the war, had repudiated the loans made by France to Russia, and had ceaselessly proclaimed its determination to overthrow the Peace of Paris.

In addition, by refusing once more at Cannes to accept any responsibility for the eastern frontiers of Germany, Lloyd George had made clear British indifference to the new states upon which France counted for aid in maintaining the peace settlement. France must, Poincaré believed, not merely defend its own frontiers, but be prepared to march beyond those frontiers if the security of the eastern states was threatened. A British guarantee against a German invasion of France was useless; if resurgent Germany and Russia demolished the eastern settlement, the position of France would be hopeless. Since the British had refused to give effective support, France must enforce the treaty settlement. It was with this view of Europe that Poincaré took office in January, 1922.

The French delegation at Cannes had agreed to the calling of an economic conference, so the conference duly assembled at Genoa on April 10, 1922. Poincaré refused to attend and refused to allow discussion of political questions at the conference; the instructions to the French delegation precluded any possible settlement of either the czarist debts or reparation. From the first, therefore, the conference was in confusion, and it threatened to break down completely when, on Easter Sunday, April 16, the German and Russian delegations went off secretly to Rapallo and concluded a treaty settling their economic claims against each other.[5] To the French, the Rapallo treaty was clear evidence that the two powers opposed to the Peace of Paris were uniting; to Lloyd George, the Rapallo treaty showed the need for the general agreement on the economic problems of Europe which he had advocated. The conference limped on for another month, until May 19, and failure was faintly disguised at the end by a public statement that discussions would continue. But the breakdown of the Anglo-French entente was obvious.

At Genoa, Poincaré had demonstrated that without French cooperation Britain could not bring about the economic revival of Europe. In Turkey, he made it clear that if Britain would not support France in Europe, France could strike at the imperial interests of Britain. In August, 1922, the Turkish nationalists took the offensive against the Greeks, who fell back in disorder. Early in September the Greek base at Smyrna was taken, and a few days later the city was practically destroyed by fire. The triumphant Turks now turned north, and Lloyd

5. See above, p. 75.

George appealed to the British Dominions and to France for aid in defending the Straits. The replies from the Dominions promised little military aid. As for the French, their troops stationed at the Straits took ship and departed, leaving the British to face the Turks unaided. Lloyd George, his policy in ruins, agreed to an armistice on October 11 and to the drafting of a new peace treaty satisfying the claims of Turkish nationalism.

Not because he had agreed to make a new treaty, but because he had been prepared to fight to protect his Turkish policy, Lloyd George's ministry collapsed immediately after the signing of the armistice of Mudanya. The ministry had begun as a wartime coalition. In 1918 Labour had withdrawn, and a fraction of the Liberal party, led by Asquith, was also in the opposition. In the years following, a division had grown within the Conservatives: should the party end the coalition with the Lloyd George Liberals or should the two parties unite in opposition to socialism? The Conservative leaders had long defended the coalition and leaned toward fusion; some defended this course to the end. However, at a meeting on October 19, 1922, a majority of the Conservatives voted to end the coalition. The view of the majority was clearly expressed by the new prime minister, Bonar Law, in his election manifesto. He called for "the minimum of interference at home and of disturbance abroad"; in his view "tranquillity and stability both at home and abroad" was "the crying need of the nation." That he had correctly divined the popular mood was shown by the eagerness with which the other parties imitated these electoral slogans. A cynical critic commented that the St. Vitus's dance of the Lloyd George years had been replaced by the sleeping sickness of the Bonar Law government. The public was satisfied; the elections of November 15 returned a Conservative majority.[6]

5. THE LAUSANNE CONFERENCE, 1922–1923

The Lausanne conference to draft a new Turkish treaty opened on November 20, 1922; the Treaty of Lausanne was not completed until July 24, 1923. From the opening session the conference was a duel between the British foreign secretary, Lord Curzon, and the Turkish delegate, Ismet Pasha.[7] Curzon was ending a lifetime of diplomatic

---

6. Robert Blake, *Unrepentant Tory* (N.Y., 1956), pp. 466, 467.
7. See Harold Nicolson, *Curzon: The Last Phase 1919–1925* (Boston and N.Y., 1934).

service to an empire which he considered sacred. Ismet was a soldier who later took his surname, Inönü, from one of his military victories. It was a strange duel, not only because of contrast between the undiplomatic arrogance of Curzon and the gentle, tireless diplomatic skill of the warrior, but also because both antagonists were resolved that the conference must close the gap between their countries. The Turks had profited from their alliance with Russia, but now British friendship was needed to avert dependence on the Soviet Union. To the disgust of the Soviet delegate, Ismet did not insist that passage through the Straits be regulated by states bordering on the Black Sea. Instead, the Straits were demilitarized and the right of passage in peace and war was detailed in the treaty. When dispute over the ownership of the Mosul region between Turkey and Iraq threatened to become a quarrel between Britain and Turkey, the dispute was left for settlement later; the region was eventually awarded to Iraq. The Turks did, however, insist on complete sovereignty within their frontiers, including eastern Thrace. They also demanded not only the end of reparation but the end of capitulations, the special rights of foreigners in Turkey. Finally, the Turks insisted that there be an exchange of minorities with Greece. On all these points the Turks won.

By the end of the conference, resurgent Turkey attracted the attention not just of Europe but of the colonial world. Mustafa Kemal had taken hold of a defeated, decadent empire, long the prey of other states. Within a few years he had built an army, aroused fanatic nationalism among the Turkish people, defeated the Greeks, and forced the Great Powers to conclude a new peace treaty which accepted the program of the National Pact of 1920. Already he had begun the internal transformation of Turkey. Just as he had made a clean break with the imperial traditions of Turkish history and built his state on nationalism, so he ruthlessly suppressed religious, cultural, and social tradition which impeded the development of the science, technology, and bureaucratic efficiency of the West. The results were impressive: in education, sanitation, and commerce, in all material aspects of civilization, Turkey leaped in years across centuries, and this appropriation of Western technology was sustained by nationalism, another import from the West. To be sure, much that Westerners valued was sacrificed. Western schools in Turkey, like Robert College, which to the West were symbols of humanistic ideals far higher than nationalism, now were harassed because they diluted the nationalism of Turkish youth. The rights of individuals disappeared as all Turks were forced into a common mold. There was no room for opposition parties which really opposed: their leaders were silenced, if necessary by death. Yet, to a remarkable degree, Western observers concluded that the end justified the means. The American ambassador to Turkey, Joseph Grew, was the embodiment of the ideals of individualism, democracy, and cosmopolitanism so ruthlessly suppressed in nationalist Turkey, yet Grew concluded that

the Nationalists will have to follow their autocratic and ultrachauvinistic policy for some time to come, until the present show has crystallized and a new generation has sprung up, and much as all the deification in the press and elsewhere rubs one the wrong way, it is certain that for this particular people and situation it is the only wise course to follow.[8]

If the achievements of the dictatorial government of nationalist Turkey seemed so impressive to Westerners as to make palatable the means by which they were attained, it is not strange that Turkey seemed a model to be imitated by other peoples struggling against alien imperialism and against the legacy of history. That success in the struggle required obedience to a leader seemed demonstrated not only by the example of Mustafa Kemal. The importance of Sun Yat-sen in China, of Gandhi in India, and of Zaghlul in Egypt could also be cited. Imitation of Kemal's ruthless determination was easy. Too rarely perceived were the peculiarities of the Turkish story. Kemal built on a national consciousness which had long been growing, and the collapse of the Ottoman Empire made it easier for the Turks to cut loose from historical tradition. Moreover, the rivalry between the Great Powers had a unique intensity at the Straits and in Asia Minor; these rivalries were exploited with skill by Kemal, but their existence was a great help. Above all, Kemal was unique among the leaders of colonial peoples in his superb ability both to set limits on his own ambition and to curb those who would pass those limits. In success, he refused to take the road to conquest suggested by the history of the caliphate; instead, he

8. Joseph C. Grew, *Turbulent Era* (2 vols., N.Y., 1952), II, 793–94. Grew was an American observer at Lausanne, and his diary gives an interesting and valuable account of the conference (*ibid.*, Vol. I, Chaps. XVIII–XX). Cf. also Roderic H. Davison, "Middle East Nationalism: Lausanne Thirty Years After," *Middle East Journal*, VII (Summer, 1953), 324–48.

suppressed the caliphate to eliminate the center of such aspirations; he was even willing to buy support by giving up territory claimed by Turkish nationalists, Batum to Russia, Mosul to the British mandate of Iraq, and Alexandretta to France. Ismet at Lausanne confronting Curzon, the last of the British proconsuls, goading him to paroxysms of impotent rage and compelling his surrender, was an inspiring spectacle for other opponents of imperialism, but Ismet was solicitous not to lose the support of other Great Powers and not to insist on a settlement which would permanently alienate Britain.

6. THE BALDWIN ERA

Before the conference at Lausanne had completed its work, Bonar Law was forced by illness to resign, in May, 1923. His successor was Stanley Baldwin, who was to dominate British public life until 1937. Even more than Bonar Law, Baldwin prized tranquillity. He was the delight of cartoonists, who portrayed him contentedly sucking his pipe as he leaned, portly and relaxed, against a fence and contemplated his equally relaxed pigs. He strengthened this caricature by repeatedly affirming that he was not a clever man and that he knew nothing about politics. Neither of these claims was true. When aroused, he was a master politician, and he had intelligence, courage, and eloquence. His whole program could be found in the prayer with which he ended his greatest speech: "Give peace in our time, O Lord." That speech in the House of Commons, on March 6, 1925, was recalled in 1939, when Britain was again at war, by David Kirkwood, who had been one of the violent Labour "Clydesiders." Kirkwood contrasted the bitterness between capital and labor in Britain in 1914 with the social harmony of 1939. He explained this in terms of Baldwin's influence: "In your speech you made flesh the feelings of us all, that the antagonism, the bitterness, the class rivalry were unworthy, and that understanding and amity were possible."[9] Baldwin by 1939 had many more critics than supporters, and his critics then and since have claimed that his one prescription for social peace was a massive dose of sedatives. This much, however, is true: between 1914 and 1939 social unrest produced

9. G. M. Young, *Stanley Baldwin* (London, 1952), p. 95. Young's is the "official" biography. There is additional material and a more sympathetic view in A. W. Baldwin, *My Father: The True Story* (London, 1956). The most detailed study is Keith Middlemas and John Barnes, *Baldwin* (London, 1969).

revolution or paralysis in all the Great Powers of Europe except Britain; in Britain, the possibility of violent social strife was often present, and with the possibility a determination among some on both sides to push the fight to a conclusion. That the fight between classes always ended inconclusively and without destroying the possibility of reconciliation must, in some measure, be attributed to Baldwin's hold not only on his own party but on the respect and affection of the Labour opposition.

Baldwin confessed, almost boasted, that he did not like foreigners, that he knew little about foreign countries, and that foreign affairs bored him. These weaknesses did not bother most of his countrymen, who, since they shared the weaknesses, counted them virtues. There is tragic irony in the fact that, hard on the repudiation of Lloyd George by his countrymen, the leadership in Europe which he had vainly sought passed by default to a Britain uninterested in leadership. From the wreckage of Lloyd George's attempt to strengthen imperial communications by building a screen of Greek power in the Aegean there emerged a strong Turkey no less determined than Lloyd George to prevent Russian control over the Straits and eager for British backing in that task. In Italy, a few days after the fall of Lloyd George, power fell to Mussolini and his Fascist party; soon Mussolini embarked on rivalry with France in the Mediterranean and in central Europe, inviting, almost necessitating, British resumption of her old role of balance wheel. In 1923 German passive resistance to the French occupation of the Ruhr ended in the exhaustion of both antagonists, opening the way for Britain to take the lead in settling the problems of reparation and security. For Baldwin, these were not challenges, opportunities; they were burdens. The unity with which Britain faced up to the fact of war in 1939 must in some measure be credited to Stanley Baldwin, but the fact that Britain, and Europe, faced war in 1939 is in part the result of Baldwin's refusal to give more than grudging and sporadic leadership to Europe.

Chapter Five

FRANCE: THE SEARCH FOR STABILITY, 1923–1931

1. THE OCCUPATION OF THE RUHR, 1923

AT the close of the war in 1918, the most common view of France in western Europe and America was that of valorous France, invaded, deprived of rich provinces, sacrificing a generation of young Frenchmen, fighting to save French freedom and Western civilization. That picture faded rapidly during the recriminations of the Paris peace conference. Keynes's central argument in his *Economic Consequences of the Peace* was that the attempt to weaken Germany, economically and politically, and the attempt to reestablish French primacy in the continent were bound to impoverish Europe, to lead to social upheaval, and in the end to engulf France and Britain in the common ruin of Western civilization.

In 1919 Keynes's view was thought extreme, but it rapidly gained acceptance. By the end of the Washington conference the picture of an incorrigibly militarist France was emerging in Britain and America. In the spring of 1922, after the failure of the Genoa conference, it did indeed seem that to hold Germany in subjection France was prepared to block economic revival in Europe, even at the cost of a German default on reparation payments. Before the year was over, the conviction grew that Poincaré intended to use the German default on reparation as an excuse to seize the Rhineland and the Ruhr.

Briand had vainly sought to change the British and American view of France by yielding to the American position on battleships at the Washington conference, and by his willingness to accept the limited security agreement offered by Lloyd George at Cannes in January, 1922. Poincaré abandoned conciliation. He repeatedly demonstrated that since Britain would not support French efforts to attain security in Europe, France would thwart British policy in, for instance, Turkey, and would, unaided, force Germany to comply with the Treaty of Versailles.[1]

1. P. Miquel, *Poincaré* (Paris, 1961), is excellent.

Seen from London, as from Paris, the drift of events in Germany was ominous, but from the same events the two governments drew opposed conclusions. Violence was spreading in Germany. On August 26, 1921, a leader of the Center party, Matthias Erzberger, was assassinated. On June 24, 1922, Walther Rathenau, the foreign minister, was assassinated.[2] These were only the most prominent of those killed by armed bands, mostly made up of youngsters. The vilification heaped on their victims by nationalist leaders had in each case made it easy for the murderers to believe they were serving their country, and when the assassins were caught, the courts showed more sympathy for the murderers than for their victims.[3]

There was clear evidence that the violence was becoming organized. From Munich, British representatives reported on the activities of the National Socialist German Workers' party of Anton Drexler and Adolf Hitler. The party name was adopted in April, 1920; earlier the organization had been called the German Workers' party.[4] The party program was contained in a confused and contradictory list of twenty-five points, but the central themes of the party meetings were hatred of the Treaty of Versailles and hatred of the Weimar Republic. The British reporter stressed that the party had financial resources far exceeding what the members could contribute; there must be powerful support back of the two demagogues who led the party. From Cologne, another British representative reported a conversation with the mayor, Konrad Adenauer, who feared that hunger was driving the masses in Germany to a combination of nationalism and Bolshevism directed against France and Britain; the reporter regarded Adenauer as a reliable if pessimistic observer.[5]

2. Count Harry Kessler, *Walther Rathenau, His Life and Work* (London, 1929; a revision of the German edition of 1928), evokes both the man and the age. The best study of Erzberger is Klaus Epstein, *Matthias Erzberger and the Dilemma of German Democracy* (Princeton, 1959).

3. This was not unusual judicial behavior during the Weimar era: see H. Hannover and E. Hannover-Drück, *Politische Justiz* (Frankfurt, 1966), and Hugo Sinzheimer and Ernst Fraenkel, *Die Justiz in der Weimarer Republik: Eine Chronik* (Neuwied, 1968).

4. See W. Maser, *Die Frühgeschichte der NSDAP: Hitlers Weg bis 1924* (Frankfurt, 1965).

5. A brief, interesting study of Adenauer and the movement for Rheinish autonomy in 1919–20 and 1923 is K. D. Erdmann's *Adenauer in der Rheinland Politik nach dem ersten Weltkrieg* (Stuttgart, 1960). For a detailed study of ideas and movements seeking to combine nationalism and Bolshevism, see O.-E. Schüddekopf's *Linke Leute von rechts: Die national-revolutionären Minderheiten und der Kommunismus in der Weimarer Republik* (Stuttgart, 1960).

As such reports accumulated, the British government concluded that to avert the gathering crisis it would be necessary not only to reduce the reparation burden on Germany (Bonar Law was consulting with Keynes on German capacity to pay), but also to assist Germany in ending inflation and getting back to a healthy economic life. From the same symptoms, Poincaré drew opposing conclusions. The nationalism of the Free Corps assassins and of leagues like Hitler's Nazis, the drift of the German government from a policy of fulfillment to stubborn insistence that the total reparation bill must be reduced, all these to Poincaré meant that the German people refused to recognize defeat. In Bavaria nationalist parties like the Nazis and illegal armed military formations flourished under the protection of the reactionary Bavarian People's party government. In Berlin in November, 1922, a new cabinet was formed by the head of the Hamburg-American Line, Wilhelm Cuno. Cuno's allies were the businessmen who were profiting from inflation, extending their business empire in Germany, increasing their holdings abroad—and refusing to pay taxes for reparation. To Poincaré, the remedy was to convince these German nationalists and these German profiteers that France had the strength and the will to compel respect for the Treaty of Versailles.

In December, 1922, and in early January, 1923, there were meetings in London and Paris, but neither the British nor the French would give way. The reparation commission declared Germany in default; on January 11, 1923, French and Belgian troops entered the Ruhr. The British protested. The Americans, to show their disapproval, withdrew the last of their troops from the Occupied Rhineland. The German government, heartened by the division among the former allies and encouraged by the Russians, ordered the people of the Ruhr to lay down their tools and resort to passive resistance.

In a great outburst of patriotic fervor Germans drew together, from the nationalists and racialists to the Communists, all united in determination to show that, alone, France could not conquer even a disarmed Germany. General Seeckt momentarily forgot his cold respect for unpleasant facts and agreed to the mobilization of the remnants of the Free Corps into a Black Reichswehr which may have totaled as many as 50,000, but which could have been of little use against disciplined troops. Isolated acts of sabotage in the Ruhr were hailed by the German people as great national victories, and hotheads, like Leo Schlageter, who were executed by the French were extolled as martyrs.

The dream of a great campaign with Russia against the Versailles settlement made the strange amalgam of "national Bolshevism" seem politically possible, and Bolshevists like the journalist Karl Radek were happy to feed this delusion by words of praise for Schlageter and other Free Corps terrorists, "the wanderers into the void." Berlin restaurants did their part by posting large signs: "No Frenchmen or Belgians served here." Every American and British speech or writing which opposed the occupation of the Ruhr, criticized the Treaty of Versailles, or suggested that Germany had not been exclusively responsible for the war was seized as evidence that Britain and America would soon compel the French to retreat.

The French did not retreat. Instead, they sealed off not only the Ruhr but the occupied Rhineland from the rest of Germany. They revived the plans for separating the Rhineland from the Reich; separatists were openly supported by the French military, while the local police were forcibly prevented from interfering with the separatists' activities.

Meanwhile, cut off from both the products and the revenues of the richest parts of the country, and burdened with the necessity of supporting the idle workers of the Ruhr, the German government paid its bills by printing currency. Earlier, businessmen had profited from the inflation by prompt conversion of currency into goods or foreign exchange; now all Germans knew that they must spend their money immediately, before its value disappeared. So there was, on the one hand, a frantic rush to buy property or clothes or furniture or anything tangible; on the other hand, there was extravagant indulgence in food, in drink, in any amusement. Berlin presented harsh contrasts, of women with their bags of currency queuing up for groceries which might triple in price before the purchase could be made, of hotels and night clubs crowded with the momentarily rich and the permanently depraved, of children with faces pressed to the windows of restaurants simply for the pleasure of looking at food, of the omnipresent peddlers of marks offering many times the official rate in exchange for the dollars which could be kept until the mark plunged again.

By summer the end was in sight. The harvest was good, but the farmers refused to sell. The workman's wage became worthless before it could be spent. The old had no more furniture or family silver to exchange for food. Even the manufacturer could no longer estimate the number of zeros necessary for a profitable selling price. Something must happen. Daily the half-expectant, half-hopeless crowds grew larger before the government buildings on the Wilhelmstrasse, crowds passively waiting, for what they did not know.

On August 12, 1923, Cuno resigned. A new coalition government, backed by the parties of the Weimar coalition and the People's party and headed by Gustav Stresemann, took office. Negotiations were attempted: Germany would abandon passive resistance if France would evacuate the Ruhr. Despite American and British pressure, Poincaré refused to negotiate until passive resistance ceased. As the days passed without action, strikes and hunger riots spread. Once more revolution seemed at hand; the German Communist leaders were summoned to Moscow to lay plans for the seizure of power. At last, on September 26, Stresemann ended passive resistance. At the same time he proclaimed a state of emergency. The Reichswehr was made responsible for the preservation of order.

For the next six weeks it seemed doubtful whether the Weimar Republic could survive this new defeat at the hands of France. The German Communist leaders returned from Russia with orders to precipitate a revolution within the next four to six weeks, and they seemed to acquire a base for operations, when, early in October, Communists entered the governments of Saxony and Thuringia. On October 10 the Berlin Communist newspaper, *Rote Fahne,* printed a letter from Stalin, who boasted:

The approaching revolution in Germany is the most important world event in our time. The victory of the revolution in Germany will have a greater importance for the proletariat of Europe and America than the victory of the Russian revolution six years ago. The victory of the German proletariat will undoubtedly shift the center of world revolution from Moscow to Berlin.[6]

The Communist threat in central Germany provided an excuse for intervention by reactionary forces in Bavaria. When Stresemann proclaimed the state of emergency on September 26, the Bavarian government proclaimed a state of siege and assumed control over the Reichswehr units in Bavaria. In October, using as an excuse the presence of Communists in the cabinets of Thuringia and Saxony,

6. Quoted in W. T. Angress, *Stillborn Revolution* (Princeton, 1963), p. 428.

Black Reichswehr formations gathered along the northern borders of Bavaria; a march on Berlin, in imitation of the Fascist coup a year earlier in Italy, seemed imminent.

Stresemann moved against both enemies on October 20, with very different results. The commander of the Reichswehr in Bavaria was ordered to surrender his command, but the Bavarian government refused to recognize the order and instead ordered the Reichswehr to take an oath of allegiance to Bavaria. To the Socialist premier of Saxony, Stresemann sent notice of the dispatch of troops to prevent attacks "by right-radical Bavarian forces." The Communists recognized that once the troops arrived, revolution would be impossible. When the trade unions and the Socialists rebuffed a Communist proposal for a general strike, plans for the national uprising were abandoned. Through an error, the Communists in Hamburg tried to take over the city on October 23, but the workers did not rise and the Communists were easily defeated. In Saxony, as soon as the Reichswehr was in control, Stresemann demanded the eviction of the Communists from the state government. The contrast between his passivity in face of Bavarian defiance and his use of the military to overthrow the Socialist-Communist coalition in Saxony was too much for the Socialists in the national government; on November 2 they withdrew from the coalition.

In Bavaria, the state government recognized the futility of an attack on the Reich government now that the border was lined by troops loyal to Berlin. On November 8, Hitler tried to force a revolution by seizing the leaders of the Bavarian People's party while they were meeting in a beer hall. The next day, when he, Ludendorff, and the Nazi Storm Troopers marched through the streets of Munich, they were ignominiously dispersed by the Bavarian police and the Bavarian Reichswehr units. For a few weeks more the Bavarian government held out against Berlin, but in February, 1924, a new government was set up, the rebellious Reichswehr leader resigned, and the Nazi rebels were brought to trial. Ludendorff was acquitted; Hitler received a short prison sentence. The dreams, either of a separate Bavarian kingdom under the Wittelsbachs or of a Germany dominated by Bavaria, were ended. Revolt from the right, like revolt from the left, had failed.

The Reichswehr could not enter the Rhineland, but there too the separatist movement failed. A Rhineland republic was proclaimed on

October 21, 1923, but it had no roots among the people, and the leaders whom the French were forced to use were a sorry lot. By 1924 even the French military recognized defeat and allowed the puppet regime to collapse.

As soon as the revolutionary danger had been ended in Saxony, Thuringia, and Bavaria, Stresemann embarked on the difficult task of currency stabilization. A new unit of currency, the Rentenmark, with the value of the prewar mark, was issued on November 15, 1923. In theory, the currency was backed by a mortgage on all the land and industry in Germany, but since there was no way to foreclose such a mortgage, the only real support was the eagerness of the German people to believe that inflation was ended. To confirm that belief, taxes were raised and expenses of government were slashed by cutting salaries and dismissing hundreds of thousands of civil servants. Overnight the wild prosperity which had fed on inflation gave way to depression. Unemployment soared. The remedy was effective in that the Rentenmark circulated at face value. But the government was faced by the wrath of all those who were ruined, whether by the inflation or the deflation, of all the unemployed, and of all whose hopes of revolutionary change had been thwarted. Stresemann accepted the role of scapegoat. He resigned on November 23, and a new cabinet was organized with a chancellor drawn from the Center. Stresemann remained in the government as foreign minister, a post he was to retain in one cabinet after another until his death in 1929.

Even Stresemann's enemies recognized that he was indispensable in the post of foreign minister. The Rentenmark was bound to collapse unless the reparation burden was lightened, and German commerce and industry could revive only with the assistance of foreign capital. By his courage in abandoning 'passive resistance, and by his repeated public declarations that, having lost the war, Germany must accept the penalties of defeat, Stresemann had won the respect of the governments of the West. Negotiations for a restudy of the reparation problem had been proceeding through the weeks before the fall of his ministry. For the success of these negotiations it was essential that he, the advocate of the policy of "understanding," remain.

By the end of November, an international committee of experts had been appointed, with the American banker Charles G. Dawes as chairman. From the deliberations of the committee came, in April,

1924, the Dawes Plan, a series of interdependent proposals for the evacuation of the Ruhr, an international loan to Germany, and a temporary schedule of reparation payments; if this temporary plan worked, then a permanent settlement could be made later.

By recognizing defeat, Stresemann had achieved victory. For five years, from the armistice of November 11, 1918, to the abandonment of passive resistance on September 26, 1923, Europe had been distracted by the deadly Franco-German feud. Germany was unwilling to accept the consequences or even the fact of defeat. France was torn between determination to secure the reparation which only a strong and prosperous Germany could pay, and determination to keep Germany weak and impoverished. Poincaré had invaded the Ruhr to force from Germany an acceptance of defeat and to enforce the payment of reparation. He achieved his first objective, but not the second. Instead, surveying the prostrate Germany of September, 1923, and recalling that for years the French government had been borrowing money in the expectation that the loans would be redeemed by reparation payments, the creditors of the French government, at home and abroad, lost confidence in French credit and the franc fell rapidly. By November, Poincaré was forced to accept the review of the reparation problem he had earlier rejected, and by the Dawes Plan France was forced to cooperate in the rebuilding of German economic strength. Forced at last to choose between a weak Germany and a Germany strong enough to pay reparation, the French chose reparation.

2. STRESEMANN, BRIAND, AND THE LOCARNO PACT

Even while France and Germany were fighting their bloodless war in the Ruhr, the search for some solution to the problems of security and disarmament continued. In the Treaty of Versailles the disarmament of Germany had, at least by implication, been justified as the first step in "a general limitation of the armaments of all nations," and as soon as the League was organized there was pressure, particularly from the small member states, to initiate general reduction of armaments. The partial success of the Washington conference in limiting naval armament intensified the demand for a reduction of land armament.

At Geneva, as at Washington, the French insisted that arms reduction could come only after a security system had been devised to supplement the general provisions of the League covenant, and at Geneva the influence of France and its eastern allies was sufficient to force action. During the League assembly meeting of September, 1923, a draft treaty of mutual assistance was discussed and referred to the member states. Under the treaty, the League council was required to designate the aggressor in any controversy, and every signatory was obligated to give armed assistance to the victim of aggression, if the aggression took place on the continent of the signatory.

The draft treaty did give assurance that every aggressive act would be countered not simply by an economic boycott but by military force. The treaty also gave assurance of arms reduction, since under the terms of the treaty help was to be given only to those signatories who had agreed to reduce their armed forces in accordance with a schedule to be devised by the League council. But to the British in particular, the cost was too high: since the British Empire included territory in all continents, Britain would be compelled to give armed assistance to repel aggression anywhere in the world. Moreover, since the United States and the Soviet Union refused even to consider the treaty, and therefore could not be expected to accept the jurisdiction of the League council in any dispute, these powers were likely to oppose military action or economic sanctions under the treaty; Britain had no intention of risking war with these formidable antagonists over issues not vital to the Empire.

It fell to Ramsay MacDonald, the prime minister in the first Labour government, to report in 1924 the British refusal to accept the draft treaty. Since support of both the League and disarmament was strong within the Labour party, he coupled his rejection of the treaty with a promise to cooperate in a new effort to solve the related problems of security and arms reduction. By now, the *cartel des gauches,* a loose alliance of the center and socialist parties, was governing France. The French premier, Edouard Herriot, gladly cooperated with MacDonald in the drafting of another equally ambitious agreement, the Geneva protocol. The protocol made the test of aggression the refusal to agree to settlement of any dispute by action of the League council, by judicial settlement, or by arbitration; every signatory promised assistance in resisting the aggressor. The protocol was to go into effect only when a plan for the general reduction of armaments had been adopted.

It is doubtful whether MacDonald, had he continued in office, could have secured parliamentary approval of the protocol. Indeed, it is difficult to see that the obligations of Britain under the protocol were less than under the draft treaty. Certainly the risk of dispute or even war with the United States had not been reduced: the American government stated firmly that it would resist efforts to interfere with American trade in case an aggressor was subjected to economic sanctions. In May, 1925, the foreign secretary in the new Conservative government, Sir Austen Chamberlain, announced that Britain would not ratify the protocol.

Chamberlain was already working on a less ambitious plan to satisfy the French demand for security, what was to be known as the Locarno Pact. At the outset, Chamberlain had been disposed merely to revive and strengthen the old entente with France, but it seemed doubtful whether France would accept anything less than a general military alliance for the defense of the Versailles settlement, and neither Chamberlain nor British opinion was ready to go that far. He turned, therefore, to a proposal which Stresemann put forward as a means of blocking the formation of an Anglo-French alliance, a proposal that the existing frontier between France and Germany be guaranteed by Britain and Italy. That far Chamberlain was willing to go. He believed the western frontier of Germany, the frontier with Belgium as well as France, was an area "on which, as our history shows, our national existence depends." The frontiers in the east, such as the Polish Corridor, lay in a region "for which no British government ever will or ever can risk the bones of a British grenadier."[7] In 1939 Austen Chamberlain's brother Neville was to risk much more than the bones of a British grenadier for that region; but while there were some in Britain who urged in 1925 that if the states to the east of Germany fell, "the whole of Europe would at once be in chaos," they found no hearing.[8]

Briand, who returned to the French foreign office in April, 1925, was reluctant to accept a proposal so like the one which Lloyd George had made at Cannes in 1922 and which had then precipitated Briand's fall from the premiership. Moreover, the temper of the German people was such that a Frenchman was bound to look into the future with uneasi-

7. Sir C. Petrie, *The Life and Letters of the Rt. Hon. Sir Austen Chamberlain* (2 vols., London, 1939–40), II, 259.
8. Sir James Headlam-Morley, *Studies in Diplomatic History* (London, 1930), p. 184. The quotation is from a memorandum written in February, 1925, when Headlam-Morley was historical adviser to the foreign office.

ness. The disarmament clauses of the Treaty of Versailles were being evaded, as the Allied control commission pointed out, but when the British and French refused to evacuate the first zone of the Rhineland until the violations ceased, there was an outburst of indignation in Germany. In April, 1925, the wartime commander of the German army, Hindenburg, was elected president of Germany. The election produced new outbursts against the Treaty of Versailles, and although the old general showed himself a supporter of the republican constitution and of Stresemann's foreign policy, many of those who had elected him obviously supported neither.

Still Briand agreed to negotiate on the terms set by the British and the Germans. It is impossible to say with complete confidence why he agreed: statesmen who must win and hold public opinion and a majority in parliament inevitably suit their argument to the group they are addressing at the moment and rarely feel free to express themselves with complete frankness. Therefore, with Briand as with Stresemann, it is possible to draw very different conclusions from what he said, each conclusion solidly buttressed by quotations from his writings and speeches, but each susceptible to demolition by equally pertinent evidence. Taking Briand's whole career after 1918 into account, his policy seemed based on the conviction that the restraints laid on Germany at Versailles must inevitably be transitory. In time, the natural strength of Germany in population, in industrial development, and in military skill would erode the restraints of Versailles. Timely concession might temper the determination of resurgent Germany to overthrow the territorial settlement of 1919, might make Germans reluctant to accept the suicidal risks war would entail. Whatever the temper of Germany, in Briand's view French security depended on alliance with Britain and on the good will of the United States. Conciliation would bring to the side of France allies who might persuade Germany of the folly of war, and certainly would ensure the victory of France in war.[9]

The bases of Stresemann's policy are harder to probe, partly because his own descriptions of his policy are more widely at variance with one another, but partly also, one suspects, because he envisaged his immedi-

---

9. G. Suarez, *Briand: Sa vie, son oeuvre, avec son journal et de nombreux documents inédits* (6 vols., Paris, 1938–52). There is an excellent brief analysis of "Briandism" in Gordon Wright, *France in Modern Times* (Chicago, 1960), pp. 443–46.

ate objectives much more clearly than his ultimate objectives.[10] He saw very clearly that no matter how successfully this or that restriction on German armament was evaded, Germany could not build military force sufficient to overthrow the Versailles settlement. That was impossible, not only because open rearmament would unite the old enemies of Germany and precipitate an invasion more costly than that of the Ruhr. Much more important, the rebuilding of German economic strength required large and continuing infusions of foreign capital, and this capital could come only from these same former enemies of Germany. He was impatient with those who dreamed of regaining German power in Europe by alliance with Soviet Russia: Russia, he argued, was poor, poorer than Germany; and the Red army, if it entered Germany, would be far more interested in making Germany a Communist state than in fighting the enemies of Germany. The tie with Russia effected at Rapallo was useful, and he would make no agreement with the West which entailed separation from Russia; but he never forgot the experience of the Ruhr, when the Soviet leaders, even while they were promising support to the German government, sought to precipitate Communist revolution against the German government. The freeing of German power from the restraints of Versailles, Stresemann argued, could be effected only with the acquiescence of Britain and France, and the rebuilding of German power could be effected only with the aid of Western capital. This freeing and this rebuilding required a policy of "understanding" with the victors of 1918. The Treaty of Versailles was to be destroyed not by German defiance but by "understandings" between Germany and the victors.

What would happen when Germany was free and strong? Certain complaints Stresemann made: the frontiers in the east were unacceptable; there were Germans living under alien rule; Germany should not be the only great power without colonies. Did this mean that Germany would take the Polish Corridor and Upper Silesia, would make the defense of Czechoslovakia impossible by vaulting the mountain barrier, and would open the way to domination of the Danube basin by the

---

10. Hans Gatzke, "Gustav Stresemann: A Bibliographical Article," *Journal of Modern History*, XXXVI (March, 1964), 1–13; Hans Gatzke, *Stresemann and the Rearmament of Germany* (Baltimore, 1954); Annelise Thimme, *Stresemann: Eine politische Biographie zur geschichte der Weimarer Republik* (Hannover, 1957); Henry L. Bretton, *Stresemann and the Revision of Versailles* (Stanford, 1953); Henry A. Turner, Jr., *Stresemann and the Politics of the Weimar Republic* (Princeton, 1963).

union of Austria with Germany? And, having achieved hegemony in Europe by these conquests, would Germany then take the path to world power?

Almost certainly Stresemann never aspired to such sweeping objectives. When he said his aspiration was to serve as a bridge between the old Germany and the new, what he probably meant was that given the nature of war in the twentieth century, and given the shaken foundations of Western civilization after the great war, the fate of the peoples of non-Communist Europe was inextricably joined. Germany had been wronged by Versailles, and these wrongs would be ended when, with the acquiescence of Britain and France, the natural strength of Germany had been rebuilt. Changes there then would be, in the eastern frontiers of Germany and in the world position of Germany. But the exact shape and extent of these changes would be determined within the context of a Europe of which Germany was a great but not the supreme part; to aspire to hegemony would invite the war of all against Germany, and common ruin.

It is impossible to say with certainty that this was the limit of Stresemann's objective because his speech often suggests German supremacy. His policy of "understanding" was accepted by most of the left (except the Communists) and by the center parties. His enemies were within his own People's party, among the Nationalists who, when the fanatical Alfred Hugenberg became their leader, had the services of Hugenberg's great press and cinema empire, and among the small, even more violently nationalist parties, including the discredited Nazis. Given the fact that about 10 per cent of the seats in the Reichstag were held by the Communist party, which always voted against Stresemann, he required for success the support or the abstention of the People's party and at least some of the Nationalists. Therefore he stressed his hatred of Versailles and the gains to German power which would ultimately accrue from his policy. Probably, but not certainly, this was a tactical maneuver to win the acquiescence of the extremist opinion which would, he believed, shift to more moderate courses as Germany prospered and the restraints on Germany lightened.

Despite the eagerness of Briand and Stresemann to achieve agreement, and despite Austen Chamberlain's willingness to guarantee the frontiers in the west, the negotiations were prolonged and vigorous. In the end, Briand abandoned hope of securing a guarantee of the eastern frontiers of Germany, but, reversing the earlier policy of France, he insisted that Germany must join the League of Nations. The League guarantees against aggression offered at least some protection for Poland and Czechoslovakia. Stresemann was willing to accept the League limitations on German freedom to change the eastern frontiers, but he was determined to maintain the Rapallo tie with Russia, and the Soviet government insisted that the League was a capitalist conspiracy to overthrow the U.S.S.R. Turning German disarmament to his advantage, Stresemann argued that without an army large enough to repel an invader Germany could not invite attack by taking part in sanctions imposed by the League. After a hard argument he won veiled exemption from the obligation to take part in military or economic sanctions and thereby disarmed Soviet suspicion that Germany was joining the enemies of the U.S.S.R.

The results of the negotiations between Germany and her former enemies were made public in a carefully dramatized meeting at Locarno in October, 1925. There was, first, the guarantee of Germany's western frontier, usually called the Locarno Pact. By this treaty France, Belgium, and Germany accepted their frontiers and the permanent demilitarization of the Rhineland as inviolable; Britain and Italy guaranteed the frontiers and the demilitarization of the Rhineland and promised full assistance to repel armed aggression across this frontier. In the East, while there was no guarantee of the frontiers, arbitration agreements between Germany and Poland, and between Germany and Czechoslovakia, pledged the settlement of all disputes by peaceful means. By separate treaties, not part of the Locarno agreements but concluded at the same time, France and Poland, and France and Czechoslovakia, promised military assistance to each other in case of attack. Finally, the Locarno treaties were to come into force only when Germany was admitted to the League of Nations, with a permanent seat on the council. As an indication that Locarno marked the end of the war period and the beginning of a new era of peace, in November the Germans were told that the first zone of the occupied Rhineland would be evacuated.

The German admission to the League was delayed almost a year by the effort of other states to win permanent seats in the council. During the interval, Stresemann worked out the terms of a neutrality pact with Russia. By this agreement, signed in Berlin in April 24, 1926, each promised neutrality in case the other was attacked; neither would join a political combination or an economic boycott directed against the other.

When it was signed, the Berlin treaty was regarded in western Europe as a disturbing interruption of the reconciliation between Germany and her former enemies. In fact, however, the Russo-German treaty brought no change in the relations between the two countries. Cooperation between the Reichswehr and the Red army continued, and military leaders on both sides thought the cooperation profitable. Economic relations became closer after the Soviet five-year plans created a demand for capital goods which was limited only by German willingness to grant credits. Politically, after 1926 relations followed an erratic course, but the long-term curve was down. When Germany and Russia had come together at Rapallo in 1922, both were isolated, and each feared the other would make a deal with Britain and France. After Locarno, Russia was still fearful of isolation, but for the moment Germany felt able to balance between east and west. This situation soon changed. By 1929 German relations with France were deteriorating, and German nationalists were fulminating against the Soviet Union as the home of Communism. The Treaty of Berlin was renewed in 1931, but by then all cordiality had gone out of political relations. Almost immediately after the renewal, the Soviet Union made similar neutrality agreements with France and Poland, the countries against which the Treaty of Berlin was implicitly directed.[11]

It is not strange that the Berlin treaty proved without sequel; the alignment had from the first been regarded on both sides as a temporary necessity. On the other hand, the Locarno treaties were intended as a first step, not only by Briand and Stresemann, but by the peoples of the West. When the German delegates took their seats in the League on September 10, 1926, there was a general expectation of new moves which would strengthen security and make disarmament possible. A week later, Briand and Stresemann slipped away from the glare of publicity in Geneva for a quiet lunch at the village inn at Thoiry. They explored the problems separating their countries and the possibility of changing the temper of European politics by a dramatic settlement. If

11. Harvey Leonard Dyck's *Weimar Germany and Soviet Russia, 1926–1933* (N.Y., 1956) is a thoughtful evaluation of the evidence and of the scholarly writing on Soviet-German relations.

France agreed to the evacuation of the Rhineland and the Saar in exchange for a final reparation payment, a payment to be financed by an international loan guaranteed by a mortgage on German assets—might this not stabilize the franc, the Weimar Republic, indeed the whole structure of Europe? There was exploration of a less grandiose project. Stresemann urged that by abolishing the inter-Allied control commission on German disarmament and transferring the supervision of disarmament to the League, nationalist criticism of his policy of understanding would lose much of its effectiveness. Briand pointed out that he also had to consider public opinion and that French opinion was uneasy about semimilitary activities, particularly of the German veterans' organization, the Stahlhelm; however, he was prepared to explore this possibility and the larger issues opened in their discussion.

Momentarily, the journalists who swarmed around Briand and Stresemann on their return from Thoiry were convinced that this was "the beginning of a new era." Then came disillusionment. Poincaré was now premier, and while he had changed enough to accept Locarno, he was not prepared to give up the protection to French frontiers afforded by the presence of French troops in the Rhineland; moreover, he was confident that the franc could be stabilized without surrendering the control over Germany which the long-term reparation payments permitted. Austen Chamberlain also felt that Briand and Stresemann "dreamed dreams and saw visions" at Thoiry; certainly Locarno was as far as Britain would go.[12]

Possibly an opportunity to effect the lasting pacification of Europe was lost when the enthusiasm aroused by Locarno was not exploited to achieve a more general settlement. Or, possibly, the concessions made to Germany and the massive infusions of capital which the German economy received during and after the negotiation of the Locarno treaties merely served to strengthen the German will and capacity to overthrow Versailles. These are questions on which no worthwhile judgment is possible. All that can be said is that, here as elsewhere in these years, a course was set and then, in midcourse, courage failed. Locarno, intended as a beginning, proved an end point. In the West, statesmen and peoples were satisfied. Briand, Chamberlain, and Stresemann received the Nobel peace prize; over western Europe hovered the comforting, warming Spirit of Locarno. In Ger-

12. Petrie, *op. cit.*, II, 306, 307.

many, however, it became the fashion to pun on the double meaning of the word *Geist,* to speak of the "ghost" of Locarno.

3. THE YEARS OF HOPE, 1924–1929

Even before the Dawes Plan was accepted, economic revival began in Europe, and hope rose for peace within and between nations.

For a time, fear of social revolution persisted, and indeed was intensified in 1924 by the advent of the Labour government in Britain in January, by the victory of the *cartel des gauches,* a coalition of the center and non-Communist left parties, in the French elections of May, and also in May, by a sharp rise in the Communist vote in German elections. In Britain, however, the Labour government of Ramsay MacDonald had a minority of the seats in the House of Commons and survived only so long as it had Liberal support.[13] When, after extending diplomatic recognition to Soviet Russia, the Labour government negotiated a trade treaty, the Liberals moved into opposition. In the election of October, 1924, the Conservatives made much of the Communist peril, and the publication of a letter supposedly from the Comintern leader, Zinoviev, to British Communists intensified the drift of opinion against Labour; the Conservatives won by an overwhelming majority.[14] Belief that the election had been decided by fraud (and the Zinoviev letter almost certainly was a fraud) intensified the conviction in the rank and file of British labor that social change could be won only by direct action, a conviction which led in 1926 to a general strike in support of workers in the depressed coal industry.[15] However, public opinion swung decisively against the strikers, and within a few days the general strike collapsed. Thereafter, the fear of revolution subsided. When the elections of 1929 brought Labour to office again, the change was received calmly; Labour was accepted as a parliamentary, not a revolutionary, party.

In France also the rule of the *cartel des gauches* was short and troubled. The premier, Herriot, was an old-fashioned radical with no desire for drastic social reform, and the inability of the cartel to halt the fall of the franc or to cope with native uprisings in Syria and Morocco

13. R. W. Lyman, *The First Labour Government, 1924* (London, 1957).
14. Lewis Chester, Stephen Fay, and Hugo Young, *The Zinoviev Letter* (London, 1967).
15. J. Symons, *The General Strike* (London, 1957), is a lively account.

led to a succession of cabinet crises which ended in July, 1926, when Poincaré returned to power pledged to stabilize the franc.[16] He retired three years later; then France was prosperous and untroubled by fear of revolution.

In Germany there was consternation because the Communist vote rose from half a million in 1920 to more than 3½ million in the elections of 1924, but this proved the high-water mark of Communist strength in the twenties. The Communists continued to hold enough seats in the Reichstag to be a nuisance, but with about 10 per cent of the seats they were not dangerous.

Communist strength was obviously declining in Europe. As for Russia, few in the West even tried to understand the controversies raging within the ruling group of the Communist party. There was a general disposition to believe that as the years passed, Communist Russia was becoming increasingly like czarist Russia. The subversive activities of the Comintern still evoked protests, but when the Conservative government in Britain raided the premises of the Russian trade mission, Arcos, and broke off relations with Russia in 1927, many Englishmen who had no love for Communism felt this a meaningless and rather foolish political gesture.

The threat on the left diminished after 1924. Some intellectuals and some labor leaders warned that democratic government was more threatened from the right. However, intellectuals reached a narrow and ineffectual audience, while most labor leaders were too preoccupied with the task of halting the decline of the trade union movement to concentrate on less immediate dangers. It was hard, in the older democracies, to take reaction very seriously. In Britain, Stanley Baldwin successfully resisted those in his own party who, after the general strike, sought to smash the political power of organized labor. Even Poincaré moved to a middle position in both domestic and foreign policy during his long rule; in 1928 a social insurance law was passed which, while far less generous than those of most western European countries, was at least a beginning. Similarly, in Belgium, the Netherlands, and the Scandinavian countries there was relative peace, social as well as political.

Elsewhere in Europe dictatorship was spreading almost unnoticed.

16. Michel Soulié, *La vie politique d'Edouard Herriot* (Paris, 1962).

In 1923, Primo de Rivera seized power in Spain, with the support of the king; in 1926 General Pilsudski overthrew the Polish government by force, and General Pangalos set aside the constitution in Greece; in 1929, King Alexander of Yugoslavia assumed dictatorial power, and by then, in Portugal, the austere Professor Salazar was rising to leadership within the dictatorial regime of General Carmona. These were only the more obvious examples of the decay of parliamentary institutions in Europe. They were ignored, just as the increasingly ominous evolution of Italian Fascism was largely ignored.

In these prosperous years after 1923, France seemed to attain the primacy Clemenceau had sought, seemed also the embodiment of all that was best in European culture. As Gertrude Stein said, "Paris was where the 20th century was."[17] Gertrude Stein, of course, was thinking of the bright youngsters, and those neither so bright nor so young, who came to the Paris of arts and letters, study and play. Beyond that, however, once the devastated areas had been rebuilt, there was the France which seemed so perfectly and harmoniously to combine the best of the past and the present. There were the family farms, the family shops, and the family industries left over from earlier, simpler generations. There were the luxury trades, exporting the products of skilled French hands to the whole world. There were the new industries which could compete successfully with American trusts and German cartels, and still leave scope and profit for the small family business. There were the banks, serving alike the individual, the great industry, and international finance. Here, it seemed, the idea was realized: an organism which retained all that was best from the past but kept fully abreast of the present.

On the surface, French political life was relatively tranquil. It was hard for most Frenchmen to take seriously issues like royalism and clericalism which had seemed so important before 1914. With the cascade of crowns at the end of the world war, the royalist cause in France seemed not only hopeless but slightly comic. Maurras' journal *Action Française* continued to be royalist in theory. In practice, Maurras' appeal was to those who were attracted by attacks on the inefficiency and corruption of the parliamentary system of the Third Republic; the response to his virulent campaign rose when there was

17. Quoted in Justin O'Brien (ed.), *From the N.R.F.: An Image of the Twentieth Century from the Pages of the Nouvelle Revue Française* (N.Y., 1958), p. xi.

reason to be discontented with conditions in France and fell when times were prosperous.

The other burning issue of the prewar period, anticlericalism, had also lost its appeal. For one thing, French Catholics like Marshal Foch had so obviously demonstrated their patriotism during the war that it was impossible for most to believe that the Church was "the enemy." More important, the clerical issue was dead because the Church so obviously had neither the capacity nor the desire to continue the fight against the Third Republic. What was worrying most Catholics now was not the decline in their political power but the decline of religion in France. Only a small minority of the workmen in the cities had any religious life, and even in the countryside, church attendance was declining. Those members of the upper classes who scorned the republic continued to make much of the Church as a precious part of the cultural heritage of France, but this devotion was so obviously political rather than religious that churchmen were coming to regard it as a liability. At the end of 1926, Maurras' writings and his journal were placed on the index of prohibited writing by the Vatican; some earnest Catholics were shocked by this action, but most were relieved by the break with the moribund royalist cause.

What was harder to break, indeed in these years impossible to break, was the identification of the Church with middle-class culture. Through most of France, clergy and laity were united in a tacit determination to make the parish a center of middle-class morality, middle-class respectability, middle-class sentiment. If the attendance dwindled, that did not matter, so long as the priest and what remained of his flock were untroubled by the discordant voices of those who did not possess middle-class decorum. Catholic novelists like François Mauriac and Georges Bernanos and Catholic thinkers like Jacques Maritain sought to break out of this suffocating embrace; a few Catholics organized Young Christian Farmers, Young Christian Students, and other youth groups; there was a small Catholic trade union movement; there was a small Popular Democratic political party. Many of these ideas and organizations were to be important after the second war; between the wars they attracted little attention. Rather, the Church in France seemed to have become a harmless, a dwindling, appendage of a middle class which was itself on the defensive.

In these circumstances, the old anticlerical slogans had little appeal.

Religious orders, even those prized enemies of the anticlericals, the Jesuits, returned to France; little effort was made to use against them the laws against religious congregations which remained in the statute books. At the time of the victory of the *cartel des gauches* in 1924, the Radical premier Edouard Herriot sought to unite the left by reviving the issue of clericalism: diplomatic relations with the Vatican were severed, and an effort was made to enforce the legislation against the teaching of religion in the schools in Alsace. But the response in France as a whole was negligible, while the result in Alsace was the rapid growth of resistance; so the issue of anticlericalism was quietly dropped.

The new and pressing issues of political life were, for most Frenchmen, bewilderingly complex. In an age of rapidly expanding budgets taxation became a very live issue. As everyone knew, the French tax structure was defective. The income tax was widely evaded by those who could conceal their income, that is, by everyone except those who worked for a fixed salary or wage, and in any case the income tax bore more heavily on those with small or moderate incomes than on the rich. During the early postwar years, when French budgets were chronically unbalanced, the Socialists tried to shift the incidence of taxation to the rich by a capital levy, but their partners in the *cartel des gauches,* the Radicals, resisted and transferred their support to the parties of the center and right; thereafter, the Socialists firmly believed that the will of the electorate in the elections of 1924 had been thwarted by a bankers' plot.

In the years after 1926 Poincaré pulled France out of the financial morass of inflation by first allowing the dollar value of the franc to sink, and then by stabilizing the franc at one-fifth its prewar value. In disguised form, the financial ills of France were temporarily cured by what amounted to a capital levy on those who were not sophisticated enough to get rid of their francs before they depreciated, and not poor enough to have no francs to depreciate. Roughly speaking, it was the middle and lower segments of the middle class which found themselves much poorer; the wealthy and the wage earner largely escaped the consequences of inflation and devaluation. Poincaré was hailed as the "savior" of the franc, but in France, as in Germany, the costs of inflation were indelibly printed in the memory of the vast middle classes.

Later, when economic depression came, Frenchmen were to realize that the relative tranquillity of their political life under Poincaré had not been the result of domestic harmony, but rather had resulted from the determination, and for the moment the ability, not to press too hard on any of the many jealously suspicious social and economic groups in France. Similarly, after 1929 it became apparent that the tranquil international scene over which Briand presided so benignly had been makeshift and temporary.

4. DISARMAMENT AND SECURITY, 1925–1931

While the search for security proceeded from the draft treaty in 1923, to the Geneva protocol in 1924, to end with Locarno in 1925, the League discussions of disarmament had been in abeyance. Now they were resumed with the appointment of the preparatory commission for the disarmament conference on December 8, 1925. Germany was represented for the first time, and the German representative reminded his colleagues that Germany had been disarmed to make possible general disarmament.[18] He eloquently argued that the burden of armaments not only drained the strength of the world but, as all history showed, must lead to war. The German argument was persuasive, because so many wished to be persuaded. Petitions descended on the preparatory commission from churches, schools, clubs, and individuals, all with one theme: give us peace through disarmament.

No one could deny that Germany was disarmed, in the sense that Germany did not have the forces in being, trained and equipped, to fight a major war. But Germany did have an industrial plant of surpassing size and efficiency which could be quickly converted to war production, and Germany did have manpower which could be quickly converted into the kind of fighting force which was painfully fresh in the memory of those who had suffered invasion by Germany in the war. Finally, Germany was rearming, in the sense that German minds were keeping abreast of the latest developments in military science. The German military men who worked in the U.S.S.R., in countries like Sweden and Portugal, and in Latin America, and who then applied what they had learned in the exercises of the Reichswehr, were

18. J. W. Wheeler-Bennett's useful account, *Disarmament and Security since Locarno 1925–1931* (London, 1932), was written to provide information for the disarmament conference of 1932. It is one of a series of "information" books by Wheeler-Bennett on related topics.

fully abreast of the best military thinking. While Briand and Strese-mann were lunching at Thoiry, Hindenburg was reviewing the Reichswehr maneuvers. "I have seen today," concluded the old general, "that the German army's traditional standard of spirit and skill has been preserved."[19]

The French and their eastern allies were convinced that to disarm in face of Germany's military potential and her obvious determination to overthrow the Versailles settlement would be to court disaster. After Locarno as before, the French insisted that disarmament could come only when sufficient force was mobilized in defense of the Versailles settlement to deter even a rearmed Germany from war; since Britain refused to guarantee the eastern settlement and the United States would guarantee none of the settlement, France would not disarm.

From harsh experience, Briand had learned that to put the French position that baldly was to invite denunciation of French militarism and love of war. Therefore he proceeded by indirection. Within the preparatory commission, discussion revealed the difficulties of balancing potential strength against present strength, trained reserves against men under arms, one weapon against another, etc., etc.; all the discussion led to the conclusion that there really was no yardstick for accurately comparing the military strength of countries. Outside the commission, in January, 1927, an effort was made to placate the Germans by abolishing the Allied control commission for supervising German disarmament; its functions were turned over to the less vigilant auspices of the League.

This concession did placate the Germans, temporarily, but the French were not successful in convincing opinion in Britain, in America, and in the neutral states of the justice of their position. Rather, the conviction hardened that France blocked disarmament. The situation was not helped when Russia joined the preparatory commission in 1927 and the Russian representative, Litvinov, argued in speech after speech that the way to disarm was to disarm, disarm completely and at once; who, he asked, needed arms unless he had ambitions which could be achieved only by force?

With the encouragement of American leaders of the movement to "outlaw" war, in June, 1927, Briand submitted to the American gov-

19. *New York Times*, Sept. 19, 1926, p. 7.

ernment a draft treaty by which the two governments renounced war in their relations with each other and promised to settle all disputes by peaceful means.[20] At first the suggestion was greeted with embarrassed silence by the Department of State. Early in 1928 (there would be a presidential election in 1928, and "peace" was popular), Secretary Kellogg proposed that the treaty be made among as many states as would sign, not just between France and the United States. In the ensuing negotiations he made it clear that every nation reserved the right of self-defense and was to be the sole judge of what constituted self-defense. With this interpretation, every government felt free to promise to "outlaw" war. The Kellogg-Briand Pact for the renunciation of war was signed in Paris on August 27, 1928. Popular enthusiasm was great. To those who had been vainly preaching disarmament it seemed clear that since war had now been abolished, armaments were no longer necessary—except for those who had not honestly renounced war. Briand's attempt to escape the onus of militarism had merely intensified the clamor against French "militarism."

He had no greater luck in his effort to replace the provisional Dawes Plan with a permanent settlement freely accepted by Germany. Here again the auspices seemed favorable. Germany was prosperous in 1928 and was carrying the reparation payments easily. Payments under the Dawes Plan would mount to their maximum in 1929 and would continue at that level indefinitely; lower annual payments, with a definite terminal date, should be more attractive to the Germans. Moreover, under the Treaty of Versailles, the Rhineland was to be occupied until 1935; an offer of immediate evacuation should be attractive to the Germans. These considerations appealed to Stresemann, and early in 1929 a committee of experts, headed by an American, Owen D. Young, began deliberations. In June the committee completed what became known as the Young Plan, with a graduated scale of payments averaging about $500 million a year, payments which were to continue until 1988.

The Young Plan was ratified, but only after debate which set in naked relief the isolation of France. In August, 1929, there was a conference at The Hague to consider the experts' report. Since June, Britain had had a Labour government, and the Labour party had long

---

20. Robert H. Ferrell, *Peace in Their Time: The Origins of the Kellogg-Briand Pact* (New Haven, 1952).

been impatient with the French demand for security before disarmament.[21] To most of the Labour leaders, it was disarmament which would give security, because it was the armaments race which led to war. Earlier, MacDonald had scoffed at sanctions as "a harmless drug to soothe nerves." He denied, however, that he had no interest in security. "It is the thing I am most interested in. I want you to feel perfectly secure that no son of yours, no grandson of yours, will ever be asked to go through what I see by your badges many of you have gone through." Security, he maintained, must be sought "not by military, but by moral means." As Noel Baker, another Labour leader, said in November, 1929, the prevention of another war depended on disarmament and "upon the spread throughout the world of the spirit of peace." Strangely, or perhaps significantly, such circular logic found wide acceptance in the homeland of the philosophy of analysis.[22]

When Labour returned to office in June, 1929, every effort was made to demonstrate British love of the spirit of peace. Construction on the naval base at Singapore was stopped, and also work on new submarines and cruisers. Agreements to refer disputes to the International Court or to arbitration were accepted. Relations were resumed with Soviet Russia and a new trade agreement was signed. Negotiations for a new conference on naval disarmament were begun with the new American President, Herbert Hoover.

It was France which felt the displeasure of Labour, first at The Hague. In the view of the Labour party, France was rich and was forcing the burden of arms on the world; yet France was to receive favorable consideration in distributing the payments received under the Young Plan. The British objected and forced a change in the

21. On the second Labour government, see Robert Skidelsky, *Politicians and the Slump, the Labour Government of 1929–1931* (London, 1967). David Marquand's "The Politics of Deprivation: Reconsidering the Failures of Utopianism," *Encounter*, XXXII (April, 1969), 36–44, reviews recent literature on the failure of the Labour party either to deal effectively with the depression after 1929 or to win the loyalty of the large proportion of workingmen who voted Conservative. There are several good studies of the Labour party's views on foreign policy: William Tucker, *The Attitude of the British Labour Party Towards European Collective Security Problems, 1920–1939* (Geneva, 1950); H. R. Winkler, "The Emergence of a Labour Foreign Policy in Great Britain, 1918–1929," *Journal of Modern History*, XXVIII (Sept., 1956), 247–58; and John Naylor, *Labour's International Policy: the Labour Party in the 1930's* (London, 1969).

22. J. R. MacDonald, "Protocol and Pact," *Labour Magazine*, III (April, 1925), 531–34; Mary Agnes Hamilton, *J. Ramsay MacDonald* (London, 1929), p. 210; Parliamentary Debates, Commons, 5th Series, Vol. CCXXXI, p. 920.

distribution. The amount involved was small; what counted was the demonstration of British irritation with France at a moment when rebellion not only against the Young Plan but against Versailles was mounting in Germany. There, an alliance was struck between Hugenberg, with his newspapers and his cinema, and Hitler, with his iron-lunged agitators. They were unable to prevent ratification of the Young Plan, but they did demonstrate that the German people were not reconciled to a burden extending to 1988, and they did wear out their enemy Stresemann. He died in October, 1929.

The isolation of France was revealed once more when after agreeing with each other about the size and number of cruisers, but not consulting others, the British and Americans summoned a new naval conference to meet in London in January, 1930. There, the Japanese went along with the Anglo-American proposals for limitation of the smaller naval categories such as cruisers, destroyers, and submarines, but once more the French refused to accept equality with Italy. As at Washington in 1921, the French argument was that since France had to defend her Atlantic coast against Germany and her Mediterranean coast against Italy, equality with Italy meant, in practice, inferiority. France, therefore, would accept inferiority only if Britain and America would agree to a consultative pact, that is, would agree to discuss ways of avoiding war when aggression threatened. In the end, agreement on naval construction was confined to the Americans, British, and Japanese; if Italian or French construction mounted, an "escalator clause" in the treaty permitted further building by the three principal naval powers. Again disarmament had been prevented, and again it was the French who were blamed.

In the autumn of 1930 the theme of French "militarism" was reiterated when the preparatory commission for the disarmament conference met to prepare its final report to the League. The commission had prepared a draft treaty which set forth in elaborate detail everything which must be considered by the forthcoming disarmament conference without attempting to say how, or to what levels, arms reduction was actually to be made. The German delegate lamented that after five years of labor nothing had been accomplished, and his strictures were echoed by the Soviet and Italian delegates. As the commission disbanded, and the League set the opening of the long-awaited disarmament conference for February, 1932, a great movement spread over the world to bring the pressure of public opinion to bear on the forthcoming conference, so that governments, and above all the French government, would no longer thwart the craving of the world for peace.

The final and crowning blow to the position of France also grew, at least in form, from an effort of Briand to strengthen the existing political and social structure of Europe. With the acceptance of the Young Plan, he began to look ahead to the day when, with the Rhineland evacuated and reparation settled, German power would be free to grow, relatively unfettered. At the meeting of the League assembly in September, 1929, he suggested the advisability of some sort of federal union for Europe.[23] Negatively, the moment was well chosen. In Europe there was uneasiness concerning the debates in the American Congress on the Hawley-Smoot tariff bill, debates which pointed toward much higher import duties. There were suggestions that the logical answer was a European customs union so that Europe could bargain as an equal with America on tariffs. Briand's proposal was, therefore, discussed with some enthusiasm until he presented a detailed outline for union, which included guarantees of the existing territorial frontiers of Europe. Now the "United States of Europe" seemed only a new effort to win support for the old French definition of security. Thereafter discussion languished until March, 1931, when the German and Austrian governments suddenly announced that they were taking the first step toward European union by a customs union, which other countries were free to join.

Immediately, France and the Little Entente powers denounced the Austro-German customs union as a violation of Austrian pledges not to unite with Germany. In May, the International Court was asked to decide whether the customs union was legal; in September the court, by a vote of eight to seven, declared the union illegal. France, however, did not wait for the decision of the court, but demanded that Germany and Austria abandon the customs union. Fearing a crisis, investors began to withdraw their short-term deposits in Austrian and German banks.[24] The credit of both countries had already been shaken by

23. W. Lipgens, "Europäische Einigungsidee, 1923–1930 und Briands Europaplan im Urteil der deutschen Akten," *Historische Zeitschrift*, CCIII (Aug. and Oct., 1966), 46–89 and 316–63.

24. On this crisis, see Karl Erich Born, *Die deutsche Bankenkrise, 1931: Finanzen und Politik* (Munich, 1967), and Edward Bennett, *Germany and the Diplomacy of the Financial Crisis, 1931* (Cambridge, Mass., 1962).

economic depression, and during May, after the collapse of the leading bank of Austria, the Kredit Anstalt, panic spread through central Europe. On June 20, to avert financial collapse, President Hoover proposed a one-year moratorium on reparation and war debt payments. Like other American proposals, this was made after consultation with the British, but not with the French, which was a serious mistake. Relatively, France was as yet untouched by depression; the French financial position was strong; and while France had a vital political stake in Germany, relatively little French capital was invested there. Therefore the French government withheld its consent to the Hoover moratorium until satisfied that the French legal claim to reparation was not impaired. By then it was obvious that the financial collapse of central Europe could be averted only by a moratorium on private loans also. The French refused to agree until Germany and Austria abandoned their customs union. In mid-September the "standstill agreement" went into effect, but by then the panic had spread to Britain, bringing down the Labour government in August and forcing the new National government to abandon the gold standard in September.

France had blocked the union of Germany and Austria, but at terrible cost. German reparation payments never really resumed; at a conference in Lausanne in 1932 the German obligation to pay was buried under a flood of words. Similarly, payments on war debts to the United States dwindled practically to nothing. The warnings of the American economic experts at Paris in 1919 and of writers like Keynes had been vindicated by events.

Similarly, the French search for security had failed. Germany was in rebellion against the Treaty of Versailles, and in face of this rebellion France was isolated from Britain and America. The victorious Western democracies were separated, and the road lay open before those who would destroy the world settlement created by the Peace of Paris and by the Washington and Locarno treaties.

1. The Big Four at the Paris Peace Conference, 1919: Vittorio Emanuele Orlando, David Lloyd George, Georges Clemenceau and Woodrow Wilson. (*Brown Brothers*)

2. American Relief Administration kitchen in Vienna. (*The Hoover Institution, Stanford*)

3. Weimar Germany. Lithograph by the expressionist artist Oskar Kokoschka: "Down with Bolshevism; Bolshevism brings war and ruin, hunger and death," 1919. (*The Museum of Modern Art, New York*)

4. Drawing by George Grosz, *Café*, 1928. (*The Museum of Modern Art*)

5. Lithograph by Kathe Kollwitz: "Vienna is dying! Save Her children," 1920. *(The Museum of Modern Art)*

6. Russian poster of 1930 with inscription: "Imperialists cannot stop the triumphal success of the Five Year Plan." (*University of California Library, Berkeley*)

7. Five Year Plan poster, on the superiority of mechanized agriculture, and on the need to increase production so that the tools for mechanization and electrification could be procured. (*The Hoover Institution, Stanford*)

8. Poster of Lenin with inscription by the futurist poet Vladimir Maiakovsky: "Lenin lived; Lenin lives; Lenin will live!" *(Prof. Herschel Chipp, University of California, Berkeley)*

9. The People's Commissar for War, Leon Trotsky, reviewing troops. In the rear, on left, foreign delegates, including Chinese. *(U.P.I.)*

10. Signers of the Locarno Pact at a dinner given by the British Foreign Secretary, Austen Chamberlain in London, Dec. 1, 1925. From left, Scialoja of Italy; Luther and Stresemann of Germany; Baldwin, Chamberlain and Lady Chamberlain of Great Britain; Beneš of Czechoslovakia; Briand of France; Skrzynski of Poland; and Vandervelde of Belgium. *(U.P.I.)*

11. The League of Nations meeting, March 18, 1926, at which the admission of Germany was postponed. Briand and Stresemann are at right. *(Brown Brothers)*

12. Mao Tse-tung, the leader of the Chinese Communist Party, and Chu Teh, the military commander, in Yenan, 1937. *(The Hoover Institution, Stanford)*

13. Chiang Kai-shek in March 1927, on the eve of his break with the representatives of the Comintern. *(U.P.I.)*

14. Nationalist Rulers. Riza Shah Pahlevi of Persia (saluting) at Ankara with Mustafa Kemal, the President of the Turkish Republic (center), and Ismet Pasha, the Premier (right), June 26, 1934. Riza Khan had led a successful nationalist revolt in 1921 and was proclaimed Shah in 1925. *(U.P.I.)*

15. Charles A. Lindbergh in Paris in May 1927 after his flight, alone, from New York to Paris in the monoplane *Spirit of St. Louis. (U.P.I.)*

16. Mohandas K. Gandhi seated beside Charles Chaplin in the East End of London, September 22, 1931. Gandhi, who had been released from prison early in the year, was in Britain from September to December for the Second Round Table Conference on India. *(Wide World)*

17. Crowds in Paddington Station, London, waiting for a train during the railroad strike which continued after the end of the general strike, 1926. *(Brown Brothers)*

18. Jacob Epstein, *Head of Albert Einstein*, c. 1933. (*Joseph H. Hirshhorn Collection*)

19. Jacob Epstein, *The Visitation*, 1926. (*Joseph H. Hirshhorn Collection*)

20. Pierre Bonnard, *Woman and Dog,* 1922. As with Matisse, much of Bonnard's painting is lost in a black and white reproduction; in this case the composition, at least, is preserved. *(The Phillips Collection, Washington)*

21. Bonnard's *Girl Bathing,* c. 1923. *(Joseph H. Hirshhorn Collection)*

22. Henry Moore, *Mother and Child,* 1931. Moore defined his work as an effort to represent subjects like the human figure in forms natural to the materials in which he was working; power, vitality of expression, not beauty was his objective. *(Joseph H. Hirshhorn Collection)*

23. Henri Matisse, *Reclining Nude No. 3,* c. 1929. *(Joseph H. Hirshhorn Collection)*

24. Henri Matisse, *White Plumes*, 1919. (*The Minneapolis Institute of Arts*)

25. Constantin Brancusi, *Bird in Space*, 1928? According to Henry Moore, it was above all Brancusi who stripped away the surface "excrescences" of sculpture and restored a consciousness of shape as the essential of sculpture. (*The Museum of Modern Art*)

26. Georges Rouault, *Christ and the High Priest*, before 1937. Rouault is set apart from most professed expressionists by his concentration on the sufferings of others rather than on himself. (*The Phillips Collection, Washington*)

27. Piet Mondrian, *Composition 2*, 1922. Mondrian, with Kandinsky, one of the first "abstract" artists, sought by the use of primary colors and planes marked off by broad vertical and horizontal lines to eliminate the feelings and concepts of the artist and attain a "vision of true reality." *The Solomon R. Guggenheim Museum)*

28. Fernand Léger, *Woman Holding a Vase*, 1927. The black and white print conveys the architectural character of his painting, with his use of forms which tend toward geometric patterns. *(The Solomon R. Guggenheim Museum)*

29. Marc Chagall, *The Dream*, 1939. (*The Phillips Collection, Washington*)

30. Alberto Giacometti, *The Palace at 4 A.M.*, 1932-33. Construction in wood, glass, wire, string. His early works are surrealist dream constructions; in these, the qualities of loneliness, isolation and spiritual emptiness are already strong; in his later works, they become overpowering. *(The Museum of Modern Art)*

31. Walter Gropius, *The Bauhaus,* Dessau, Germany, 1926. The airview (lower left) shows how "the parts of the building are sharply defined according to use and arranged in a free, pinwheel-like composition": the classrooms are in the foreground; the studio dormitories are on the left; the craft workshops are in the rear; between are the auditorium-dining hall, offices, etc. In the view from the southeast, (above left) are the studio dormitories and the workshops. The photograph of the workshops, (above) shows how the floor and roof are "cantilevered out beyond the reinforced concrete supporting frame....The walls become curtains, defined at the top and bottom by apparently floating bands of white stucco. The effect of weightless transparency is one possible only in modern architecture." From *What Is Modern Architecture?* edited by Margaret Miller, copyright 1942, 1946, The Museum of Modern Art, New York, and reprinted by permission of the publisher. The photographs are also used courtesy The Museum of Modern Art.

32. Lazlo Moholy-Nagy, "A-II," 1924. In 1922, Moholy-Nagy became a professor in the Bauhaus; he left when Gropius resigned in 1928. *(The Solomon R. Guggenheim Museum)*

33. Ludwig Mies van der Rohe, director of the Bauhaus, 1930-33; Barcelona Chair, 1929. Mies' furniture achieves its machine-made appearance only through painstaking handcraftsmanship. *(The Museum of Modern Art gift of the manufacturer, Knoll Associates, Inc.)*

34. Marcel Breuer, at the Bauhaus, 1925-28; Side Chair, 1928. This cantilevered tubular steel chair is the prototype of innumerable later variations. *(The Museum of Modern Art)*

35. Lyonel Feininger, *Viaduct,* 1920. *(The Museum of Modern Art)*

36. Ernst Barlach, *Two Monks Reading,* 1932. Barlach's art, like that of most of the artists illustrated here, was declared "degenerate" under Hitler, and some pieces were destroyed. *(Joseph H. Hirshhorn Collection)*

37. Georges Braque, *The Round Table*, 1929. From derogatory comments on his paintings came the word "cubism." (*The Phillips Collection, Washington*)

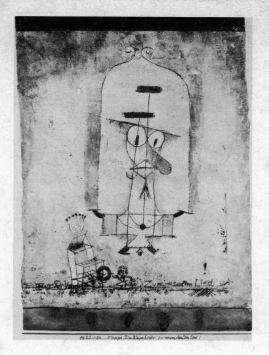

38. Paul Klee, *Dance, Monster, To My Soft Song, 54, 1922.* (*The Solomon R. Guggenheim Museum*)

39. Vasily Kandinsky, *No. 259, In the Black Square,* 1923. (*The Solomon R. Guggenheim Museum*)

40. Oskar Kokoschka, *Courmayeur*, 1927. (*The Phillips Collection, Washington*)

41. Max Beckmann, *The Departure*, 1932-33. (*Museum of Modern Art*)

42. President Hindenburg and Chancellor Hitler, May 1, 1933. This was The Day of German Labor, in which employers and trade union leaders marched; the next day the trade union offices were occupied by the government and a new Nazi labor front was formed. (*Brown Brothers*)

43. On his visit to Germany in September 1937, Mussolini was given a whirlwind demonstration of German organization and power which left a permanent impression on Italian policy. (*Brown Brothers*)

44. Mussolini reviewing the new boys' organization, The Sons of the Wolf, on the twentieth anniversary of Italy's entrance into the World War, 1935. (*Brown Brothers*)

45. Peter Blume, *The Eternal City*, 1937. This painting effectively portrays the view of Fascist Italy dominant among Western liberals by 1937. (*The Museum of Modern Art*)

46. French poster equating a vote for the Communist Party in the 1936 election with a vote against Nazism. *(University of California Library, Berkeley)*

47. Another 1936 poster equating a Popular Front victory with inflation, the burning of churches as in Spain, and Soviet dominance in France. *(University of California Library, Berkeley)*

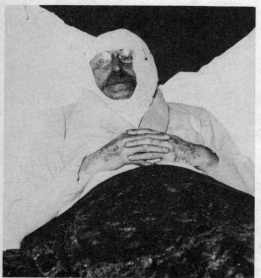

48. This widely printed photograph, dated February 21, 1936, had the heading: "Léon Blum, French Socialist leader and deputy is shown in bed in his home in Paris, recovering from a brutal attack, by alleged members of the Camelots du Roi, division of the Action Française, militant Royalist group. Following the attack the French Government took immediate measures to disband the Royalists." *(U.P.I.)*

49. General Franco (right) congratulating the defender of the Alcazar, Colonel Jose Moscardó (left), after the siege by the Loyalists had been broken, September 30, 1936. (*Wide World*)

50. Pablo Picasso, *Guernica, 1937*. Picasso's most famous masterpiece was painted between the destruction of Guernica by German planes on April 26, 1937 and early June. (*On extended loan from the artist; The Museum of Modern Art*)

51. The Spanish Civil War. Soldiers of the newly formed People's Army on their way to the front in Aragon, 1936. One of Robert Capa's "Death in the Making" photographs. (*Magnum Photos*)

52. Defeated Loyalist troops entering France, 1939. One of Robert Capa's "Images of War." (*Magnum photos*)

53. The Munich Conference, 1938. Mussolini, Hitler, the interpreter (Schmidt), and Chamberlain. (*Brown Brothers*)

УРОКИ ХАСАНА ПОВИННІ БУТИ ПАМ'ЯТНІ НЕ ОДНИМ ТІЛЬКИ ЯПОНСЬКИМ ГЕНЕРАЛАМ, АЛЕ И УСІМ АГРЕСОРАМ З ТАК ЗВАНОГО АНТИ-КОМІНТЕРНІВСЬКОГО БЛОКУ. (з промови тов Берія на XVIII з'їзді ВКП)

54. A 1939 Soviet poster portraying the ejection of Japan from Soviet soil by the Red Army, while Hitler and Mussolini look on, apprehensive. (*The Hoover Institution, Stanford*)

55. Molotov signing the Nazi-Soviet Pact of August 23, 1939; behind him is Ribbentrop and, on his left, Stalin. (*The Hoover Institution, Stanford*)

Chapter Six

THE RISE OF TOTALITARIANISM

I. THE EVOLUTION OF ITALIAN FASCISM, 1922–1933

THE changed international climate could be felt in the changed conduct of Italy, for two generations the weather vane of Europe. At the Washington conference in 1921, while Italy had claimed naval parity with France, the claim had been coupled with professions of anxiety for drastic reduction of armaments. In 1923, when France occupied the Ruhr, Italy had given support to France, and at Locarno Italy had been happy to appear as a guarantor of the Franco-German frontier. To be sure, Mussolini had struck a belligerent pose at Lausanne in 1922 when the peace treaty with Turkey was being prepared, but in the end, as Harold Nicolson reported, " 'Je suis d'accord' was the most important thing that he said."[1] Again in 1923 Mussolini had awakened uneasiness when, to avenge the killing of Italians who were delimiting the frontier between Greece and Albania, Italian warships bombarded defenseless Corfu, and when Mussolini insisted that the dispute be handled by the council of ambassadors rather than the League of Nations.[2] But this disquieting resort to force was forgotten when, early in 1924, an agreement between Italy and Yugoslavia settled the troublesome Fiume question, giving the city to Italy but giving the countryside and port facilities to Yugoslavia. Under Fascism, it seemed, Italy moved with moderation as well as decision.

The council of the League of Nations met at Rome in December, 1924—unwittingly throwing a mantle of international approval over Mussolini at a moment when, at home, the murderous brutality of his rule had been exposed. Thereafter, admirers of the Duce, such as the British foreign secretary, Austen Chamberlain, ignored repeated evidence that in Albania and Bulgaria, in Austria and in Hungary, Mussolini was seeking to build a counterforce to the Little Entente: the

---

1. Harold Nicolson, *Curzon, the Last Phase, 1919–1925* (Boston, 1934), p. 290.
2. James Barros, *The Corfu Incident of 1923: Mussolini and the League of Nations* (Princeton, 1965).

strength of France and the French alliance system seemed to make pathetically obvious the futility of these Italian schemes to win recognition as a great power. As for Fascism, Mussolini himself said repeatedly that it was not an article for export, and indeed where could his vain posturings be taken seriously except in Italy, against the operatic backdrop of the ruins of ancient Rome?

In May, 1930, a few days after the end of the London naval conference, Mussolini again struck a bellicose pose. He proclaimed the need for a great fleet so that Italians would not "remain prisoners in the sea which once belonged to Rome." If others attempted to interfere with "our future" he would raise to "fever-heat" the Italian nation. "Words are very beautiful, but rifles, machine-guns, ships and aeroplanes are still more beautiful. A powerfully-armed fascist Italy would offer two simple alternatives: either a precious friendship or an adamantine hostility."

There was a flurry of alarm. The British ambassador consulted the Italian foreign minister, who explained that these violent words were only intended for domestic consumption and who reported the light-hearted comment of Mussolini: "What does it matter what I say to my crowds?" The ambassador sought an interview with Mussolini and came away convinced that the Duce was "under an obsession of a French menace. . . . He expects aggression from France and does not, for a moment, contemplate it on his own account."[3] The British were reassured, since France obviously did not contemplate aggression. In any case, unless Mussolini was completely mad—as the French were beginning to suspect—there was nothing he could do. Alone, Italy could not hope to defeat France; Germany was disarmed, and in any case fear of German designs on Austria and South Tyrol barred Italy from alliance with Germany; Russia was weak, and alliance between Bolshevik Russia and Fascist Italy was too unnatural to contemplate: therefore, what Mussolini said to his crowds really did not matter. It would be enough to soothe the nerves of the impetuous dictator by the friendly words and the inconsequential concessions which Britain and France, in their calm strength, could easily afford. So there was no real alarm when, ever more stridently, Mussolini proclaimed the imperative necessity for imperial expansion or when, with characteristic disregard

3. *Documents on British Foreign Policy, 1919–1939*, Second Series, Vol. I (London, 1946), pp. 368, 381.

for truth, he denied he had ever said Fascism was not for export and boasted instead that the twentieth would be the Fascist century, the century when for the third time Italy and Italian culture would dominate Europe.

What few saw was that, in Mussolini's eyes, deepening division between the Great Powers was creating the opportunity, while deepening economic depression was creating the necessity, for imperialist expansion. In the decade since the March on Rome, Fascism had moved first through a brief period of personal dictatorship covered by the forms of parliamentary government, and then through years when, without clear plan and driven by determination to maintain and consolidate their hold over Italy, the Fascists had reached out to control, or to destroy, one activity or interest or organization after another until everything and everyone was in their grasp and they could dignify the whole formless structure with the resounding name of the corporate state.

In his comments on Fascism, after as well as before Mussolini became premier, Croce had stressed the absence of any program, any coherent body of ideas, uniting the Fascist movement. Mussolini talked largely and vehemently of his love for Italy, but so did most politicians; on almost everything else he swung violently from one side to the other or even espoused contradictory positions at the same time. To Croce, and to Italian politicians, who were emphatically not philosophers, it seemed that lack of settled convictions had been an asset to Mussolini while he was the irresponsible leader of a mass movement recruited from those who, for whatever reason, were in rebellion against conditions in postwar Italy; once saddled with the responsibility for governing Italy, Mussolini must either accept the limitations imposed by the economic weakness and the political divisions of Italy or be overwhelmed by inexorable fact.

At first, events bore out the hopes of the politicians who argued that responsibility would chasten the Fascists and end the era of violence. Since Mussolini had no economic program of his own, he followed the advice of economists trained in the classical tradition. To halt inflation, governmental expenses were cut and taxes were raised. A new spirit of efficiency spread through the government, and public order was restored. Even the Fascist gangs were brought under control by transforming them into militia controlled from above, that is, by

Mussolini and his close advisers, and by making the militia a part of the defense forces of the state. The results were gratifying. Inflation was halted. The budget was balanced. To the delight of tourists, trains ran on time, or almost. Economic conditions improved. Businessmen, who had been suspicious of Mussolini's socialist past, were reassured. Ecclesiastics, impressed by gestures such as the placing of crucifixes in classrooms, forgot Mussolini's sneers at religion and turned against the *popolari,* forcing Don Sturzo to resign his leadership of the party. The Italian parliament passed a law designed to end the paralysis of the past by giving two-thirds of the seats in the lower house to any party which won more than a quarter of the popular vote. In the election of April, 1924, Mussolini had the support of the parties of the center and right, and he won an overwhelming majority.

The electoral campaign had been, on the surface, relatively calm. But even during the campaign there had been disquieting signs of what was happening in Italy. In one way or another, the Fascists had, since the March on Rome, put their people into provincial and local offices. During the campaign these officials had "influenced" the voters, discreetly where possible, by torture or murder where necessary.

When parliament met after the election, one of the most respected Socialist deputies, Giacomo Matteotti, rose to denounce these excesses. He ended by accusing the Fascists of determination to maintain their power by force; the Fascist deputies shouted back "yes!" A few days later, on June 10, Matteotti was murdered by Fascists. A wave of disgust rolled over Italy. Mussolini was shaken and tried to disavow the act. A group of deputies, still not including some of the liberal leaders, withdrew from the chamber. As always, ancient Rome was the model: since the plebs had once withdrawn to the Aventine hill, this was known as the Aventine secession. It included noble characters and famous names, but they were leaders without followers and without a program. Like Croce, most Italians recoiled before the prospect of the violence and confusion which must accompany, and follow, the overthrow of the Fascists.

It was the new year before Mussolini recovered his courage. Then, not suddenly or systematically, but piecemeal and over the course of several years, he set out to paralyze or destroy all institutions or groups which might oppose his will, and to bring every part of the national life under the control of the Fascist party. One by one, other political parties were abolished. When the deputies of the Aventine secession tried to return to the chamber they were refused admission. In elections, the voters were presented with a single list of candidates, all approved by the Fascist grand council, which also was given the responsibility for choosing the head of the government. A safe majority in the upper house was assured by the creation of new senators. The docile parliament gave Mussolini the right to issue decrees with the force of law. The law courts were little changed, but the law they enforced was now Fascist law. In local government, elected officials gave way to appointees of the central government, actually appointees of the party. The prestige of the party militia was enhanced by the incorporation of the militia into the army—to the disgust of career officers who must now accept the gang leaders as equals or superiors. The air force became a party stronghold. Only the navy managed to resist penetration by party favorites. In every public place, members of the militia stood watching. A secret police, known as OVRA, was created to ferret out opponents.

All means of communication, beginning with the press and radio, came under party control. For the most part, the old teachers, professors, and journalists were retained, so long as they followed every shift of the party line. There was much talk of Fascist culture, but the artists and architects, the writers and actors, were, again with some exceptions, those who had painted or built or acted before.

The Socialist and Catholic trade unions languished and died as it became impossible for anyone to find a job unless he belonged to the Fascist trade unions. Strikes and lockouts were prohibited. Labor contracts were made between employers' organizations and the Fascist union, and were binding on all parts of an industry or trade; disputes concerning the contracts were settled in special courts. Since the trade unions were headed by Fascists, while the employers' organizations often were not, party control was more complete over labor. However, capital was hard to secure in the years of economic stagnation after the stabilization of the lira, and the government could reward or punish by granting or withholding capital; so the men of property, who at first viewed the Fascists with suspicion, became accustomed to accepting or even seeking party guidance.

The network of Fascist control over labor and capital was invested with dignity by use of the words "syndicate" and "corporative state."

The first, of course, was taken over from its earlier usage in the trade union movement, and it was taken over because the words "syndicate" and "syndicalism" evoked memory of the men who had fought to raise the position of the laboring man. Similarly, "corporation" and "the corporate state" evoked the memory of those who, like Pope Leo XIII, had hoped for social peace by cooperation between labor and capital. The words were used, but the Fascist syndicate was not the free, fighting organization of the syndicalist's dream, and the Fascist corporative state was a façade for Fascist dictatorship over both capital and labor.

This was typical. Mussolini's years as a journalist had given him a keen sense for the value of words as a means of evoking desired responses: since "democracy" had been the aspiration of a century, he ceaselessly described Fascist Italy as a democracy, even while he was destroying everything democratic. Similarly, he was at pains to claim a distinguished ancestry for Fascism: the Frenchmen Sorel and Bergson, Germans like Nietzsche, Italians like Mosca and Pareto, all these and many other thinkers were said to have shaped the man of action, Mussolini, and the Fascism which was the product of his action. This claim was not as preposterous as the claim that Fascism was the highest form of democracy. Undoubtedly the devastating critique of nineteenth-century rationalism and liberalism common to all these thinkers had helped to undermine confidence in parliamentary government and in the possibility of attaining truth by reasonable discussion, helped also to prepare men for the acceptance of violence and of faith in irrational "myth" as essential to successful government. But, in what he destroyed as in what he constructed, Mussolini was following no higher guide than the determination to rule, and he had no higher faith than the conviction that most men could be kept in line by force.

The fact that Fascism had no creed did not, as Croce prophesied, mean that Fascism could not govern. But important consequences did flow from the absence of dogmatism, and above all the paradoxical consequence that, as compared with German Nazism or Russian Communism, Italian Fascism gave the appearance of tolerance and moderation. Because the king had surrendered before the threat of force, the monarchy seemed harmless and was continued as a useful link with the past. Similarly, it was useful to preserve the façade of an impartial judicial system, so long as judges were willing to enforce Fascist laws. Even opponents like Croce and the non-Fascist senators could be useful, so long as they merely talked and wrote: the outside world and even many Italians were placated by this harmless concession to traditional European values. In general, criticism was permitted so long as it did not lead to action against the regime. Foreign tourists who came to Italy were amazed and delighted to hear Italians complaining of their government much like the citizens of a democratic state. The black-shirted militiamen lounging in the railroad stations seemed a picturesque part of the landscape, and the secret police, like the ferociously scowling countenance of Mussolini stenciled on walls, seemed bogeymen to frighten the simple.

The traditions of Italian life made the task of the regime both easier and harder. The centuries when Italians were governed by foreign or native despots were a living memory, and had bred an attitude of detachment from government. The government was like the weather, something about which nothing could really be done but to which a sensible man accommodated himself. Like all governments, and like the weather, Fascism could be harsh or gentle. The workman and the peasant felt the harshness in a lowered standard of living, but also received the festivals and the favors of the workman's recreation organization, Dopolavoro, and received also the vicarious self-importance of the enhanced position of Italy in the world. That position meant even more to members of the middle classes and compensated for the loss of independence in private as well as public life. All Italians thrilled to reports of victory in the "battle of wheat," which would, it was hoped, make Italian agriculture self-sufficient. There were great ships launched, marshes drained, hydroelectric plants dedicated, and, above all, marks of foreign esteem, such as the knighthood conferred on Mussolini by the king of England. Something like the golden days of the Risorgimento seemed returning; the excitement was the more welcome after the wrangling frustration of the years after the war.

Indeed, by the Lateran accords of 1929 Mussolini seemed to close the wound left by the Risorgimento, the quarrel between the Italian national state and the Italian national church. By the Lateran treaty, the papacy abandoned its claim to the old estates of the church in return for a financial indemnity and recognition of the independence of the tiny Vatican state, with the pope as its ruler. By the accompanying concordat, Catholicism was recognized as the national religion, and the rights of Catholic ecclesiastics and lay organizations and the place of religion in education were defined. Liberals like Croce were outraged by the concessions to the Church, but most Italians rejoiced that peace had been made between their church and their state; adulation of Mussolini rose to new heights, with ecclesiastics leading the chorus of praise. The gain abroad was great too. Not only did many Catholics now see Mussolini as a great Christian statesman; many non-Catholics saw Mussolini as a man of moderation and high ideals.

Very quickly new disputes arose between church and state. Mussolini valued the Church, just as he valued the monarchy, as an august institution which could dignify Fascism. He had no intention of permitting the existence of independent Catholic organizations. In religion, as in any organized action, independence held the possibility of opposition. The conflict flared first and most persistently over Catholic Action, the collective name for the activities of Catholic laymen. Each conflict was ended by an uneasy truce because neither side wanted an open breach: the Vatican did not want to reopen the conflict between loyalty to their church and loyalty to their state among Italian Catholics; Mussolini cherished the approbation of distinguished prelates who were Italian nationalists as well as churchmen. Over the long run, what was to prove of most importance was the fact that, aside from the underground Communist organization, the only alternative to Fascist rule which continued to exist within Italy was that of the Christian Democrats. The old leader of the *popolari,* Don Sturzo, was driven into exile, but his deputy, Alcide de Gasperi, found haven in the Vatican. Other leaders of the disbanded party lived quietly in Italy, avoiding open opposition, regarded with suspicion by the regime and by Fascist ecclesiastics, but still inside the country and inside the life of the country, keeping alive the possibility of ridding Italy of Fascism without throwing the nation into chaos.

That possibility seemed increasingly remote during the first decade of Fascist rule. The near-unanimity of election results meant nothing, of course, but there is little doubt that most Italians, despite their grumbling, thought the color and excitement of Fascism a great improvement over the drab, wrangling parliamentary government which it had supplanted; no doubt also that Mussolini had won the admiration of most of his countrymen. Above all, there was a general expectation of great things to come when, as a result of the sacrifices more or less cheerfully accepted in the present, Italy forged ahead of decadent France in the councils of Europe and mounted to equality with Britain as an imperial power. As Mussolini repeatedly stressed during the ceremonies marking ten years of Fascist rule, the first decade had been preparation; the second decade would bring achievement.

The second decade must bring achievement. It was all very well to dedicate new highways, to launch new luxury liners, or to give a splendid setting to newly discovered ruins of ancient Rome. None of these could long conceal the fact that depression was slowing economic life or that graft was spreading like a fungus through the corporative state. For a decade Italians had cheered expectantly; these expectations could not, much longer, be deferred. Mussolini had come to power with no purpose but to rule. To rule, he had haphazardly created a ramshackle totalitarian state, for which verbal artists like Croce's former disciple, Gentile, obligingly furnished a philosophical façade. Now, to hold the loyalty of a people made skeptical if not cynical by long experience with corrupt and tyrannical government, he must win the glory of empire. The need was imperative. The division between the Great Powers would, as so often in the past, give Italy the opportunity.

2. THE SOVIET UNION FROM NEP TO FIVE-YEAR PLAN, 1924–1933

While the Italian Fascists were inventing an intellectual ancestry and a body of doctrine to dignify their rule, the Russian Communists—all professing allegiance to the doctrinal legacy of Marx and Engels as interpreted by Lenin—were divided on the best means to maintain and strengthen their rule. All agreed that Marxism was a science which, rightly interpreted, showed the direction in which history was moving and also showed the way to hasten and guide historical change. They believed Lenin had, through his mastery of Marxism, been able to make a few thousand Bolsheviks the rulers of Russia, a sixth of the land surface of the globe; if his successors showed equal mastery of Marxism-Leninism, they could rule the entire globe. If they did not understand Marxism, or if they blundered, they could not only postpone the world revolution, they could lose Russia, lose the socialist fatherland.

Marxism-Leninism was held to be a science with which history could be predicted and manipulated, but only by those with understanding of the science. In the years after Lenin, Soviet leaders suspected each other not only of deficient understanding of the science but of willingness to sacrifice the revolution in the selfish pursuit of personal power. If the Communist leaders were quick to accuse each other of acting from no higher motive than lust for power, outside observers, at the time and later, were likely to conclude that power was the goal of all the Communist leaders, and that the wordy battles, in which fragments from Marx or Lenin were flung at the heads of antagonists, were meaningless.

Undoubtedly each of the antagonists did tend to identify the triumph of the revolution with his own triumph. At the same time it is difficult to believe that men who had accepted privation or gone into exile or prison in order to further the revolutionary cause would in middle life foresake the ideals for which they had been willing to give their lives in their youth. It is hard also to understand how men who had shown themselves strong-willed and courageous could bring themselves, as defeated Soviet leaders did repeatedly, to make craven confessions of error or guilt and to beg abjectly for forgiveness unless the Communist party was the center of their existence and exclusion from the party an intolerable privation. Western Communists—British, French, Hungarian, and the rest—could break with the party and rejoin the national life of their country; for most Russian Communists, life apart from the party was empty of meaning. Finally, except in terms of belief in the sacredness of the party, the survival of the regime in face of the horrors of the thirties becomes incomprehensible. Within the party, to the very top, even within Stalin's family, there was revulsion against the human sacrifice exacted by Stalin to achieve the success of the five-year plan. Only fear that the revolution would be lost, and with the revolution all that gave meaning to life, can explain the passivity, indeed the participation in the holocaust.

Controversy was inevitable in the years after Lenin's death. He himself had regarded the New Economic Policy as a temporary retreat, as a "compromise" with the still strong capitalistic spirit of the Russian people, particularly of the peasant, a retreat necessitated by economic collapse at home and by the stabilization of capitalism abroad. From the outset, the NEP compromise was detested by many Communists, but they hesitated to oppose Lenin's will, until it became evident that he was dying, and until Trotsky proclaimed that Communism must choose between permanent revolution and decay. At home, Trotsky demanded an end to private trade and production, and a resumption of collectivization, including the collectivization of agriculture. Abroad, Trotsky denounced not only the efforts to win diplomatic recognition from capitalist governments and the efforts to form tactical alliances with trade unions and with socialist and labor parties; he denounced also the alliance with nationalist movements in "backward" countries, such as the alliance with Mustafa Kemal in Turkey and with Sun Yat-sen in China.

Trotsky was a formidable antagonist. He was the only Communist leader with Lenin's ability to arouse and hold mass enthusiasm. Moreover, he was head of the Red army, which, after its victories in the civil war, regarded itself as the savior of the revolution. To be sure, the Communist party had its agent beside every military commander, but it was an open question whether these agents were coming to feel themselves more a part of the army than of the party. With the end of the civil war, the Red army was a school in which millions of young Russians were indoctrinated with the glorious past and future of the revolution. Their leader was Trotsky.

Finally, what was happening abroad and at home gave ammunition to Trotsky. In Europe, the NEP compromise seemed to work only in favor of the hated capitalist. With humiliating ease, in 1923 the German government put an end to the hope of revolution through alliance of Communists with socialists in Saxony and Thuringia. The swift collapse of the British general strike of 1926 and the decision of British unions in 1927 to end the short-lived Anglo-Russian trade union committee showed clearly, to Trotsky, the futility of efforts to advance the revolution by cooperation with capitalist trade unions. Similarly, the futility of trying to advance the cause of Communism by securing diplomatic recognition and making trade agreements seemed demonstrated in 1927 when, after a raid on the premises of the Soviet trade delegation (Arcos Ltd.), the British government terminated the trade agreement and broke off diplomatic relations. Closer to home, the cooperation of Polish Communists with the socialists in establishing Pilsudski's dictatorship ended ignominiously in 1927 when the Soviet ambassador was murdered.

No less disastrous, in Trotsky's eyes, was the result of cooperation with nationalist movements in Asia. Mustafa Kemal had exploited the Soviet alliance to win concessions from the capitalist West, but he exterminated Turkish Communists, and at Lausanne in 1923 he disregarded the wishes of his Soviet ally. Similarly, Persia and Afghanistan were happy to secure Soviet support against Britain, but vigilant in suppressing Communism.

Failure was most obvious and most complete in China. For a time the Soviet government managed very successfully to play between the Peking government, the war lord in Manchuria, and Sun Yat-sen's Kuomintang in Canton. By 1924 railroad and other special concessions in Manchuria had been regained, Sinkiang was again coming under Russian influence, and a puppet "People's Republic" had been set up in Outer Mongolia. More promising than the recovery of these czarist privileges on the periphery of China was the deepening intimacy between the Soviet Union and the Kuomintang which followed the agreement of 1923.[4] The contact with Canton was maintained through the Comintern, since the Soviet Union had a treaty with the Peking government promising not to aid enemies of that government. In 1923 young Chiang Kai-shek came to Moscow to study and to seek arms, while Michael Borodin went to Canton as political adviser. By 1924, Chiang was back in Canton organizing the Kuomintang army under the guidance of Soviet army officers led by General Galen, a marshal of the Red army. When Sun Yat-sen died early in 1925, Chiang Kai-shek assumed control of the Kuomintang, and by 1926 he was ready to begin the conquest of China.

In March, 1927, Shanghai and Nanking fell, and with their fall came the crisis in the relations between the Kuomintang and the Comintern.[5] As soon as the cities were captured, the Communists sought to turn Chinese nationalism against "imperialist" foreigners. Promptly Chiang moved to suppress the Communists, and soon there was civil war within the Kuomintang. By early summer Chiang was victorious, and Borodin, Galen, and the other Russians were expelled. In December there was a Communist rising in Canton. It was suppressed, and in 1928 every trace of Communism was exterminated in areas held by the Kuomintang. A remnant, led by Mao Tse-tung and Chu Teh, retreated

4. Cf. above, p. 74.
5. See Conrad Brandt, *Stalin's Failure in China, 1924–1927* (Cambridge, Mass., 1958).

into the interior of China and waited. Meanwhile, Chiang pushed north. In July, 1928, Peking fell. The Kuomintang was now recognized as the government of China, with Nanking as the new capital of the country.

On the surface, the antagonists in Shanghai and Nanking and Canton had been the right and left wings of the Kuomintang. In a very real sense, however, the antagonists were Britain and Russia. Chinese nationalists were united in the determination to be masters in their own house; they were divided on almost everything else. By turning the force of Chinese nationalism against the "imperialist" powers, particularly Britain, the Comintern hoped to ensure the dependence of China on the Soviet Union. The Communists failed, in part because the British government understood their objective, in part because the British recognized their own lack of effective power. When Chinese mobs attacked foreigners and foreign property in Shanghai and Canton, the British urged patience: the Communists should be given enough rope "to hang themselves." The signatories of the Nine-Power Treaty of Washington were asked to show "sympathy and understanding" for Chinese nationalism and to support the Kuomintang against the decadent Peking regime.[6] The forebearance of the British strengthened the hand of Chiang Kai-shek, who recognized that he could obtain capital for the development of China only from the West and from Japan. Therefore he not only resisted the efforts of the left wing of the Kuomintang to force a break with the "imperialist" powers, he also tried to channel Chinese nationalism into a campaign against Communism and Russia. He was successful in 1927, while the enemy was native Communism and the agents of the Comintern.

Failure in China reinforced the argument of Trotsky and his supporters that the bureaucrats who controlled the U.S.S.R. were retreating in face of the capitalist world, were betraying the revolution by compromising with the enemies of the revolution. At home also, they contended, there was betrayal. With the love for historical analogy so dear to believers in historical materialism, Trotsky said the bureaucrats were "Thermidorians," were betraying the revolution as the French revolution had been betrayed after 1793.

Here again a strong case could be made. The evolution of the New

6. Sir Charles Petrie, *The Life and Letters of the Right Hon. Sir Austen Chamberlain* (London, 1939–40), II, 363–65.

Economic Policy was disquieting. By 1927 Soviet industrial production was back about to the level of 1913, and agriculture also was reviving. In the cities the trade unions were regaining some of their old independence, and their efforts were now, as in the West, devoted to improving wages, hours, and conditions of work. In the countryside competitive agriculture was producing a revival of large farms owned by kulaks, and also a vast number of "middle peasants" who, if they did not produce much of a surplus for export, were at least able to lead comfortable lives. Many Russians, possibly most Russians, were content with this slow improvement in their lot and looked back with horror to the violence and the hunger of the revolutionary years. Within the Communist party, the right wing wanted nothing better than the indefinite continuance of the New Economic Policy, and the right included powerful leaders like Rykov, the chairman of the council of people's commissars; Tomski, the head of the trade unions; and Bukharin, the protector of the peasant proprietors. For a time, Stalin allied himself with the right, and his program of "socialism in one country" seemed more in harmony with the New Economic Policy than with Trotsky's "permanent revolution." With Stalin on their side, the right was sure to win, since he controlled the party organization, the "apparatus."[7]

Through his control over the apparatus, Stalin was able to break his opponents on the left, beginning with Trotsky and including his old allies Zinoviev and Kamenev; at the fifteenth party congress in December, 1927, they and their supporters were excluded from the party. Trotsky refused to submit and was first exiled to central Asia and then driven from Russia; he continued his opposition to Stalin until his assassination in Mexico in 1940. The others submitted and, upon confession of their errors, were taken back into the party.

Stalin silenced his critics, but there remained the problem of arresting the inexorable drift of the New Economic Policy away from the revolution. In solving that problem Stalin borrowed much from his defeated rivals. His view of the nature of the problem was not too different from theirs. Abroad, the road to revolution was blocked by the revival of the advanced capitalist states and by the persistent refusal of states like Turkey and China to allow their nationalist revolution to

7. Robert V. Daniels, *The Conscience of the Revolution: Communist Opposition in Soviet Russia* (Cambridge, Mass., 1960), is a thorough study of the conflict between Stalin and his opponents before 1929.

be taken over by the Communists. At home, there was general agreement on the need to expand the industrial plant and general recognition that industrial expansion required a "shift of means of production towards producing means of production."[8] Since 1921 the state planning commission (Gosplan) had, with increasing efficiency, been studying just what this shift would involve. It meant, first of all, an increase in the industrial labor force. By the late twenties the decline in the Russian population through war, civil war, and famine had been repaired. There was plenty of manpower in Russia, but it was in the countryside, eating up the produce of an inefficient agriculture. As things stood, Russia was barely producing enough food to feed the peasants and the small urban population; whenever the cities failed to produce enough goods which the peasants wanted, the peasants stopped producing, or ate what they produced, and the cities went hungry. The delicate balance between agricultural production and consumption was dramatically shown early in 1928. In January deliveries of foodstuffs slumped; energetic efforts by the government brought in enough to feed the cities. In the spring, however, deliveries fell drastically; if what he had was going to be taken, the peasant simply ate what he had.

The solution was clear. Instead of sitting on the land, large numbers of peasants must come to the cities and build factories, or must go dig in mines, or must build roads and railroads. To feed these workers, a much smaller agricultural population must produce much more than in the past. And, most important, for many years both the enlarged industrial population and the diminished agricultural population must accept a much lower standard of living because the "shift of means of production towards producing means of production" meant neglect of production of consumer goods. The problem was obvious and the solution was obvious. But fresh in memory was what had happened in the early years of the revolution, in the days of war communism—sabotage, famine, rebellion. Courage failed before that memory.

Yet the problem must be solved. Russian production was back to

8. For the arguments which preceded and accompanied the five-year plan, see Alexander Erlich, *The Soviet Industrialization Debate* (Cambridge, Mass., 1960). On collectivization, see M. Lewin: *Russian Peasants and Soviet Power: A Study of Collectivization* (London, 1968; the French original edition was published in 1966); and E. H. Carr, "Revolution from Above: Some Notes on the Decision to Collectivize Soviet Agriculture," in *The Critical Spirit: Essays in Honor of Herbert Marcuse*, ed. by Kurt Wolff and Barrington Moore, Jr. (Boston, 1967).

what it had been in 1913. Further advance, as things stood, would be slow and uncertain. The Russia of 1914-17, even with strong allies, had collapsed in war. New wars there would be: Communist dogma held that the revolution could win only by war and that the "imperialist" powers would attempt to avert revolution by attack on the Soviet homeland of revolution. Common sense reinforced dogma: since the Soviet Union was determined to destroy the "imperialist" governments, they must be under constant temptation to avert destruction by destroying the Soviet Union. Communists believed Lenin had posed the question around which the history of the twentieth century must turn: "Who, whom?" If the question was to be answered in favor of the revolution, the Soviet Union must be vigilant and strong.

Even while he was breaking the party leaders of the left, Stalin was searching for an escape from the impasse of the New Economic Policy. The fifteenth party congress of December, 1927, which expelled the left opposition, called for the formulation of a five-year plan, with emphasis on industrialization. The economists of the Gosplan and the more politically minded experts of the supreme economic council presented a succession of rival drafts during 1928. The leaders of the right became alarmed; promptly they were condemned, first by the Politburo, then by the central committee of the party. In April, 1929, the sixteenth party conference declared the first five-year plan already in effect and set its beginning from October 1, 1928. The plan was not a detailed blueprint. It was a set of goals to be attained by various branches of industry and agriculture, and as originally adopted it called for a vast increase in consumer goods as well as producer goods—everything was to spurt forward.

Through the remainder of 1929 wave after wave of propaganda beat over the Russian people, calling for support of this second Bolshevik revolution, which under Stalin's leadership would transform the country, blast the hopes of the "imperialists" for an easy conquest of the Soviet fatherland, and prepare the way for world revolution. The campaign found a ready response among Russian youth, for whom the revolution of 1917 was the beginning of a new age, and prosaic existence under the New Economic Policy a postponement of the millennium. The enthusiasm came to a climax in the celebration of Stalin's fiftieth birthday on December 21, when he was deified as "Stalin the Lenin of Today." As the adulation mounted he suddenly, on December

27, gave a focus for enthusiasm by calling for the "liquidation of the kulaks as a class."

Immediately, the resources of the party, the police, and the army, backed by millions of young zealots, were turned against Lenin's land settlement. In theory, a kulak was a peasant with enough capital to be a usurer. In practice, any peasant who resisted collectivization became a kulak to be liquidated. Villages were shelled and stormed as in war. Individuals who resisted were killed or packed into boxcars and dumped without resources in areas where they were strangers. The peasants retaliated as in the past by destroying their crops and killing their animals. The number of horses on Russian farms fell by half, throwing the burden of increased tractor production on the five-year plan. The slaughter of cows and goats was almost as great, and this loss of meat and milk could not be repaired. By the beginning of March, 1930, more than half the peasant families had been forced into some form of state or collective farm, but the countryside was in a state of confusion verging on civil war. On March 2, Stalin called a temporary halt, denouncing the "dizziness from success" of those who would "establish collective farms by force." Immediately, the number in collective farms fell by more than half, and planting went forward. Soon the drive was stepped up again; within another two years well over half the peasants were again on collective farms. The cost was terrible. In 1932–33 there was famine, and agricultural production was lowered for several years; the loss in farm animals was never repaired. Possibly 2 or 3 million people had perished; other millions were herded into forced labor camps in areas where free labor was scarce and used for the construction of dams, the building of factories, or the digging of mines.

But peasant resistance was broken. By 1936 about nine out of ten peasants were in collective farms. On these farms hundreds of thousands of tractors were working. Productivity was increased by the work of an ever growing number of technicians. By 1939 a harvest a fifth larger than 1929 was produced by many fewer people.

The excess rural population was drained off to the cities, where a revolution of comparable magnitude was in progress. Here again there was resistance, from the trade unions. Tomski, the head of the unions, was dismissed; at every level party zealots were given control. The function of the unions changed from protection of worker interests to promotion of production. The right of workers to choose their place of employment ended; instead they were sent where they were needed. Absence from work, tardiness, or any other infraction of rules could lead to dismissal, without possibility of finding other employment except in a forced labor camp. Hours of work and the pace of work were increased. Payment was, where possible, by the piece and not by the day. With the spread of piece rates the old ideal of equality of income disappeared; the skilled worker made vastly more than the unskilled. The resistance of the city workers was not comparable to that of the peasants, but for several years industrial conditions were as chaotic as those in agriculture because the planners were unable to keep labor, materials, construction, machinery, and transportation moving to the right place at the right time.

For all, in the cities and on the land, the standard of living fell drastically. Rationing returned in 1929, and the rations were meager. For those who could afford more than the basic ration, the regime provided the equivalent of the "bagman" in government stores where goods could be bought without ration cards but at fantastically high prices. In large part, the fall in the standard of living was an inevitable consequence of the decision to industrialize rapidly, to force a "shift of means of production towards producing means of production." In part also the fall in living standards resulted from resistance to agricultural collectivization, from the resistance of the trade unions, and from the inefficiency of the planners. Finally, the fall was increased by the decline in the world price of grain after 1929. Fulfillment of the plan required the import of machinery, and to pay for the machines, grain was dumped on the already depressed world market. While Russians starved in the famine years, export of grain mounted to the highest level since the revolution. The plan, at the outset, had promised an increase in consumer goods as well as increased industrialization. Very quickly the first promise was forgotten.

Repeatedly, between 1929 and 1933, it seemed that the plan must collapse, and with it the Soviet regime. This fear silenced party leaders who were appalled by the human sacrifice Stalin was offering on the altar of industrialization. To party zealots, particularly the young, the plan demonstrated that Stalin's rule was not, as Trotsky had claimed, the Thermidor of the revolution, but rather a return to the mood of 1793. At the center, remote and implacable, was Stalin, convinced that industrialization was worth the accumulating price in human misery and hate.

By 1933 the worst was over. Agricultural production was still below 1929, but most of the peasants were in collective farms, farms not only managed by Stalin's agents but dependent for power on the Machine Tractor Stations (MTS) over which Stalin exercised close control. Peasant resistance was broken. Now agricultural production and distribution could be planned and would not depend on millions of independent peasant farmers. Industrial production was up, spectacularly. Between 1929 and 1933, the industrial production of the United States fell by nearly half; Soviet industrial production almost doubled. In face of that achievement, the human cost seemed slight, to Stalinists. What the peasant or the city worker thought, no one could say. The only voices audible in the Soviet Union were those acclaiming the victory of Stalin. All others had been stilled. During the tumultuous years of the plan, the leaders of the right opposition were broken, and both the danger and the futility of opposition was dramatized by a series of mass trials of "wreckers," supposedly in the service of "imperialist" states, who were blamed for all the failures of the plan. By the time of the seventeenth party congress in January, 1934, Stalin could say there was no one left to fight. The apparatus of the party functioned from one end of Russia to the other and from the Politburo down to every individual Russian, the apparatus held in the steel hand of Stalin. For the first time in history there existed a truly totalitarian state.

Before the twentieth century, the creation of such a state was impossible. All the technological triumphs of the century—the electricity of the great dam at Dneprostroi, the radios which ceaselessly dinned the party line into every Russian, the MTS which made the collective farms both possible and possible to control, the mechanized efficiency of bureaucracy and police—all these and all the other marvels of the age of technology were needed to build Stalin's totalitarianism on Lenin's dictatorship. Essential also, however, was zeal for the revolution. This was not, of course, a dictatorship of the proletariat: even if the peasants, the overwhelming majority of the Russian people, be excluded from the proletariat, there is every evidence that the city worker cooperated because he was forced to cooperate. Still, the revolution concealed behind the words "first five-year plan" was possible only because of the fanatical devotion of millions of Russians, and particularly young Russians.

Finally, the creation of the totalitarian state required Stalin. He was not the only Soviet leader to recognize that continuation of the New Economic Policy would erode the power of the regime and blast all hope of world revolution. Neither was he alone in urging industrialization and collectivization as the solution. However, others drew back, as Lenin had drawn back, from enforced industrialization and collectivization, because they feared the wrath of the peasant and the city worker. Stalin had confidence that the party apparatus, backed by revolutionary fanaticism, could break the resistance of the peasant and the worker. Repeatedly, failure seemed certain, but in the end relentless terror brought victory, or rather the beginnings of victory. When, amid new propaganda blasts, the announcement was made in January, 1933, that the first five-year plan had been achieved in four years, the industrial and agricultural plant was a rickety structure. But worker and peasant resistance had been broken, broken by Stalin's implacable will.

Even a generation after the event, it is impossible to see Stalin's achievement in clear historical perspective. The most obvious connection is with the efforts of Russian rulers of the nineteenth century, and even since the seventeenth century, to bring Russia up to the West by a "revolution from above." All, from Peter the Great to Lenin, had failed. Armed with instruments of control provided by twentieth-century technology, and sustained by fanaticism for the revolution among young Russians, Stalin succeeded. By 1933 he had laid the foundation for the rapid industrial growth which was to enable Russia to survive a second war with Germany and then was to raise Russian power far above that of any European state.

Seen in the perspective of Russian history the cost must be set against the achievement. The cost was not simply the millions who died resisting or the further millions who were uprooted and dumped into forced labor camps or into areas where they were harmless. Whether or not Stalin really believed there was no one to oppose in 1934, he soon found many to oppose. It was not enough, he discovered, to end the resistance of peasants and city workers by terror; terror soon pervaded all Soviet life.

The shift in Comintern policy, effected when the first five-year plan was being formulated, is also most easily understood as a triumph of Russian tradition over the internationalist tradition of Communism. At the sixth Comintern congress of July, 1928, a halt was called to the united front policy of seeking alliance with Western socialists. Social democrats were now branded "social Fascists." As the organ of the Comintern put it: "In order to grasp the bourgeoisie by the throat, it is necessary to step across the corpse of social democracy."[9] Communist parties outside Russia, purged of all who questioned orders from Moscow, were given one overriding task: to protect and further the interests of the U.S.S.R. The Comintern continued to talk of world revolution, but it was now in fact an instrument of Soviet foreign policy, just as each national Communist party was an expendable instrument of Soviet policy.

The cost to international Communism was great. The years of the first five-year plan were also the years of the Great Depression. With the decline of indices of production in the West, faith in capitalism sank; and the contrasting rise in Soviet production suggested the superiority of Communism. Particularly among Western intellectuals there grew the conviction that, as Harold Laski said, "whatever its defects and errors, the mood of the Russian experiment was one of exhilaration." Conservatives like Winston Churchill might warn that "hellish things are being done in Russia today"; most liberal writers and teachers saw only the "exhilaration" of the "experiment." If they admitted the fact of coercion, they dismissed it as part of the Russian tradition or called it "social engineering." For the most part, the fact of terror was simply ignored, and attention was focused on "the large human goals" of "the greatest social experiment of history."[10]

The Soviet government did little to take advantage of this mood to advance the cause of world revolution. To be sure, visitors from the West like George Bernard Shaw were taken to visit model factories and model collective farms, even model "corrective" labor camps, and foreign correspondents in Russia were kept from reporting unpleasant facts, less by the deletions of the censor than by fear of exclusion from

9. Quoted in Barrington Moore, Jr., *Soviet Politics: The Dilemma of Power* (Cambridge, Mass., 1950), p. 107.

10. Herbert A. Deane, *The Political Ideas of Harold J. Laski* (New York, 1955), p. 213; London *Times*, Feb. 3, 1931, for Churchill's judgment; George S. Counts, introduction to M. Ilin, *New Russia's Primer: The Story of the Five-Year Plan* (Boston, 1931), pp. vii, x.

Russia. But Communist parties in the West did little to turn the widespread discontent into revolutionary channels, and the Soviet government often seemed more fearful that needed machine tools could not be imported than solicitous that revolution be exported. There was in Stalinist policy of those years a curious split. Internally, stress was placed on the capacity of the party, and of Stalin, to force the pace of history. Abroad, stress was laid on the inevitability of capitalist collapse. At most, Communist parties encouraged what was thought the rush of capitalism to self-destruction. Undoubtedly the tacit cooperation of the German Communist party with the Nazis helped to ensure the destruction of the Weimar Republic. That was the objective. To Communists, Fascism was merely the last stage of dying capitalism, a stage which would very quickly be followed by the Communist revolution. Therefore German Communists stepped with the Nazis across the corpse of German social democracy, confident that this was necessary "in order to grasp the bourgeoisie by the throat."

3. GERMANY: FROM DEMOCRACY TO NAZISM

The Soviet government was not alone in failing to see, until too late, that Hitler could do in Germany what Stalin was doing in Russia.[11] When Croce was in Germany in October, 1931, and talked with intellectual leaders like Albert Einstein and Thomas Mann, he "did not hear anywhere an expectation, or even a timorous suspicion, of the triumph of Hitler."[12] This blindness continued to the end. A few days before Hitler became chancellor on January 30, 1933, the chief permanent official of the German foreign office, Bernhard von Bülow, wrote: "The National Socialists are not getting along well at all; the party structure has been badly shaken and the financial situation is rather

11. For the coming to power of the Nazis and the subsequent transformation of the German state and nation, see Karl D. Bracher, *Die Auflösung der Weimarer Republik: Eine Studie zum Problem des Machtverfalls in der Demokratie* (3d ed., Villingen/Schwarzwald, 1960); the sequel by Bracher, Wolfgang Sauer, and Gerhard Schulz, *Die nationalsozialistische Machtergreifung: Studien zur Errichtung des totalitären Herrschaftssystems in Deutschland, 1933–1934* (2d ed., Cologne, 1962); the collection of essays *Das Ende der Parteien 1933* (Düsseldorf, 1960), ed. by E. Matthias and R. Morsey; and the excellent summary by K. D. Bracher, "The Technique of the National Socialist Seizure of Power," in *The Path to Dictatorship, 1918–1933* (Garden City, N.Y., 1966), by T. Eschenburg and others.

12. Benedetto Croce, *Germany and Europe: A Spiritual Dissension* (New York, 1944), p. 38.

hopeless. Some people are even concerned lest a collapse of the party might possibly come too quickly, so quickly that it will not be possible to absorb the voters and many of them will be delivered up to the Communists." After Hitler became chancellor, Bülow admitted he had been a bad prophet, "but in this I share the fate of the vast majority of even well-informed persons." Undaunted by his mistake, Bülow now proceeded to a new prophecy. "When they have the responsibility, the National Socialists are naturally different people and pursue a different policy than they proclaimed before. It was always like this, and it is the same with all parties." He ended, "Things are boiled in water here like everywhere else."[13] Very quickly it became clear that the Nazis were not like all parties; by July, not merely the Communist but all other political parties had been abolished; in a rush, the Nazis had broken all opposition and could now build a new totalitarian state.

All this is reminiscent of the Italian experience of a decade earlier, and indeed there were many similarities. Above all, in Germany as in Italy, there was a breakdown of parliamentary rule. Even while Stresemann lived and while Germany was prosperous, it had been impossible to find a stable majority in the Reichstag. Prosperity was waning before Stresemann died in October, 1929, and thereafter depression spread and deepened. On March 30, 1930, President Hindenburg chose as chancellor a leader of the Center party, Heinrich Brüning. When the Reichstag refused to follow Brüning's lead, it was dissolved. In the elections of September, two out of five German voters gave their votes to parties pledged to overthrow the Weimar Republic; the Communists, with more than 13 per cent, and the Nazis, with more than 18 per cent, received nearly a third of the total vote. The big surprise was the growth in Nazi strength: in 1928 they received 800,000 votes; in 1930 they received nearly 6½ million.

Thereafter, any measure proposed by any cabinet was sure to be opposed by two out of every five members of the Reichstag; the Nazis, the Nationalists, and the Communists always voted against the government. In this situation, the slim majority of Republican deputies was forced, not to work together, but to refrain from open opposition to Brüning. Since there was no majority for any legislative program,

13. *Documents on German Foreign Policy*, Series C, Vol. I (Washington, 1957), pp. 21, 22.

Brüning governed through presidential decrees. Under Article 48 of the Weimar constitution, such decrees could be set aside by the Reichstag; to avoid a crisis, the Republican parties refused to override the decrees.

The next test of German public opinion was the presidential election of 1932. No candidate received a majority in the first election, on March 13. In the second election, on April 10, Hindenburg received 53 per cent of the votes; Hitler received nearly 37 per cent; and the candidate of the Communists, Ernst Thälmann, just over 10 per cent. Two interpretations of this result were possible. Brüning was encouraged. The Nazi threat had, he believed, been turned back; it would now be possible to take the offensive against the violence of the Nazi squads— the brown-shirted Storm Troopers (SA) and the black-shirted Schutz-staffel (SS). No sooner had the squads been banned, however, than Hindenburg forced Brüning's resignation, on May 30. Back of his action lay the conviction of the army officers and other conservatives who were his trusted advisers that the results of the presidential election showed, not that a majority of the German people stood firmly behind the republic, but that in a critical hour German patriots were divided. To Hindenburg, Hitler was a vulgar fellow, and the Storm Troop leaders were ruffians. But in Hindenburg's eyes, the 13 million Germans who voted for Hitler were, most of them, lovers of Germany, while a large proportion of the 19 millions who voted for Hindenburg were socialists, closer to the Communists than to the fatherland.[14]

Hindenburg's advisers convinced him that the division between patriotic Germans could be healed by another Centerist leader, Franz von Papen. As chancellor, Papen did not even have the support of his own party. Unperturbed, he ordered new elections on July 31, 1932. In unprecedented numbers Germans went to the polls. The Nazis received 37.5 per cent of the vote. Since the Communist party polled more than 14.5 per cent, the enemies of the Weimar Republic had over half the vote. Confident now of victory, Hitler showed no gratitude for favors such as the lifting of the ban on the Nazi squads, and he refused to join in a coalition government headed by Papen. Papen now set out to discipline the Nazis: the flow of contributions from industrialists and other nationalists was checked; the courts showed a new harshness

14. Theodor Eschenburg, "Die Rolle der Persönlichkeit in der Krise der Weimarer Republik," *Vierteljahrshefte für Zeitgeschichte* (Jan., 1961), pp. 1–29.

in punishing Nazi excesses. When the Nazis joined in a vote of no-confidence, Papen ordered new elections, on November 6. His tactics worked, in that the Nazi vote fell by 2 million, below a third of the total. But the Communist vote was up, creating the fear that a collapse of Nazism would strengthen the left.

A new and desperate maneuver was now attempted by General Kurt von Schleicher, who replaced Papen on December 3: to bring about what might be called a Prussian socialism by uniting the trade unions with the left wing of the Nazis, under the leadership of the Reichswehr. The project failed. Like the Italian Facta at the time of the March on Rome, Schleicher now called for a military dictatorship. Like the Italian king, Hindenburg recoiled before the prospect of using force against a "nationalist" movement. Following the Italian precedent, he appointed Hitler chancellor in a coalition cabinet, only three of whose members were Nazis.

Just as Mussolini, although he came prosaically in a sleeping car, liked later to talk of his "March on Rome," so the Nazis spoke later of "the seizure of power" (*Machtergreifung*), although Hitler was appointed chancellor on January 30, 1933, by President Hindenburg, who thought he was healing the schism between German patriots. To secure a Reichstag majority, new elections were ordered for March 5. The elections were, in appearance, free; only the Communists were directly attacked. Their headquarters in Berlin was raided and plans for a revolution were supposedly seized, although no evidence was given. An opportune fire destroyed the Reichstag building, and the Communists were blamed.[15] Under cover of the alarm and indignation aroused by the fire, emergency decrees were issued on February 28, decrees giving a covering of legality to the terrorism which cowed all opponents. For the rest, there was much denunciation of the "November criminals" of 1918, much talk of the evils of the republic, and large promises of "freedom" for Germany. The electorate was moderately impressed. The Nazis and Nationalists together won slightly more than half the seats, but this was not the real story. The Nazis, although still a minority, were confident and eager for a fight. The other parties were confused, frightened. To symbolize the break with the Weimar tradition, the new Reichstag met first in the garrison church at Pots-

15. See Fritz Tobias, *The Reichstag Fire* (New York, 1964).

dam, the center of the Prussian military tradition, with the surviving
military commanders of the war as honored guests and the Communist
deputies excluded as traitors. At the first business session on March 23,
Hitler demanded the right to rule by decree for four years. This Enabling Act changed the constitution and therefore required a two-
thirds majority. The Socialists, still the second largest party, voted
against the act. The other parties, including the Catholic Center, fell in
line and provided the needed votes.

Now events moved rapidly. In April, Hitler took control over the
government of all the states of Germany, thereby removing one of the
traditional brakes on action by the national government. On May 1
there was a great celebration honoring German labor; even employers
marched. The next day, the police seized the headquarters of every
trade union and arrested the leaders; a new labor front, headed by a
Nazi, was set up to replace the independent unions. Another brake on
government action had been removed. Next it was the turn of the
political parties. The Communist party had already been banned and
its leaders arrested. In May, the assets of the Socialist party were seized
and the party was abolished. The other parties, under pressure, disbanded. In July, the National Socialist party was declared for all time
the only legal party in Germany.

In all these actions, the Nazis showed one marked divergence from
Bolshevik theory and practice of control. In Bolshevik theory a hostile
group as a whole was dangerous; when Stalin set out to collectivize
agriculture, he called for "the liquidation of the kulaks as a class," just
as earlier Lenin had attacked all members of the middle and upper
classes. In Nazi theory, the individuals in a group were harmless; only
the leaders were dangerous. Germany could contain any number of
people who were not Nazis, who were even opposed to the Nazis, so
long as the opposition had no leadership and no organization. Hitler's
contempt for the masses, for people taken one by one, left millions who
had voted Communist, left trade unionists free and used them in the
labor front, left at their posts bureaucrats and diplomats without sympathy for Nazism. Like the Bolsheviks, the Nazis immediately opened
slave labor camps, but the Nazi concentration camps in the thirties
held relatively few political prisoners, most of them leaders or potential
leaders around whom, if free, others might gather. Since Hitler believed in the "leadership principle," he contemptuously allowed op-

ponents their physical freedom as long as they were insulated from effective action with others.

There was one conspicuous exception, the Jews. Since he held fanatically to the "racial principle," every Jew, including everyone with a Jewish grandparent, was in his eyes a menace to Germany. Therefore, even during his first months of power, when he was feeling his way cautiously, Hitler struck at the Jews, as a group. One of the first laws enacted under the Enabling Act provided for the elimination of Jews from government service; boycotts, beatings, and arrests gave a faint foretaste of what was to come later.

During the first months of Nazi rule the German trade union movement, so recently the model for all labor organizers, the bulwark of the republic in the dark days of the Kapp putsch, was broken without resistance. The Socialist party, nurtured by Bismarckian oppression, the leader of the revolution in 1918, the dominant force in the government of Prussia as late as 1932, was suppressed, again without resistance. The Center party, victorious over Bismarck in the Kulturkampf, the balance wheel of successive republican governments, simply collapsed, like the Nationalist party, which regarded itself as the custodian of German patriotism and which had confidently expected to guide and discipline the Nazi rabble. The states of Germany, with traditions far older than the Reich, and the strongholds of particularism, were taken over, unresisting. Germany, the land where centered so much that was great in science and art, in thought and feeling, where love of learning was most obviously exemplified by the recognition accorded Jewish genius, that Germany was now the land where, on May 10, 1933, the students of Humboldt's University of Berlin burned books written by men of world renown, where gangs of Storm Troopers demonstrated their bravery by beating, stabbing, and shooting defenseless victims, where teachers showed their patriotism by humiliating Jewish children. How could this be?

The question still defies answer. Some answers are obviously inadequate. It is not enough to say that the depression plunged Germany into a crisis which had been surmounted when the senile Hindenburg, surrounded by schemers who were seeking either to protect their selfish interests or to further their own careers, put Hitler in power. Similarly, to lay the blame on the workings of proportional representation leaves too much out of account. Superficially more satisfying, but in reality no less inadequate, are attempts to show that the Nazi regime was the logical conclusion of German history, whether from the days of the romantic movement, from Luther, or for that matter since Tacitus.

A partial answer is the cumulative effect of the successive crises through which the German people lived, stretching back two decades or more. Even before 1914 tension had been mounting, tension in political, social, and moral life. Outwardly Germany was, as the saying went, a well-tended garden, but from the garden came discordant voices. Some were lamenting that a faint-hearted government was shirking the task of pushing out into the world to win a position worthy of German power and German genius: in the early nineties, it was the harsh strangled voice of the deaf Treitschke; in the years before 1914, it was the mutterings of the "Crown Prince's circle." Some were lamenting the dominance of property in society and politics. Socialists, Centerists, and Progressives orated in the Reichstag against the vagaries of imperial rule, impotently. Some lamented the spread of crass material values. "Wherever I turn, I see shadows before me," wrote Walther Ranthenau in 1911. "I see them every evening as I make my way through the shrill noise of the Berlin streets: I see them when I consider the insane way we flaunt our wealth; when I hear the empty, sabre-rattling speeches."[16] Some lamented that Germany's greatest writers and artists were alienated from state and society alike. Finally, ever more pervasively, there rose the sound of young voices to the accompaniment of lute or guitar, the voices of the Wandervögel and other youth groups, young men and women retreating from cities to mountains and forests, singing, always with that note of yearning to escape from the well-tended garden of middle-class life.

With the coming of war, lament ceased; for a time the joy of communion was greater even than fear and suffering. Time eroded the unity, dug a gulf between those at the front and those at home, separated those who suffered from those who prospered, made taut the nerves of a people living as in a beleaguered fortress. All this was only faintly realized until, in the full expectation of victory, the German people were suddenly told the war was lost. A new fantastic hope replaced the old: that Woodrow Wilson would bring a peace of reconciliation, that German strength and German skill would help repair the

16. Count Harry Kessler, *Walther Rathenau: His Life and Works* (London, 1929), p. 143.

waste of war and build a new and better world of free peoples. This hope was blasted by the Treaty of Versailles and gave way to rebellion which culminated in passive resistance to the Ruhr occupation. Resistance failed, and Stresemann forced acceptance of the policy of "understanding." Then came a few years of almost miraculous revival, followed by swift descent into economic depression. All of these a German who was fifteen in 1914 would have experienced before he was thirty-five; each left an imprint, varying with social position, temperament, and luck.[17]

The war left much the same legacy as in other countries. As elsewhere, some Germans became habituated to violence, while others came to loathe not only war but all physical force. Reverence or even respect for authority, law, religion, and morality fell away as the war dragged on despite all promises of victory, as death became a commonplace, as some were taken and others spared, some prospered and others sank, all without any discernible relation to merit or motive. Some took refuge in the cynicism, the disgust, the fantasy, or the mordant satire expressed in so much German art and literature in the war and postwar years. Others cherished the memory of brotherhood in suffering and death in the trenches and carried this comradeship over to the postwar world in the Free Corps or in literary groups like the circle of Stefan George, wherever an island of intimates could be built in a sea of uncomprehending humanity. Some, beginning as profiteers in the war, continued to live predatory lives, battening on inflation, deflation, or depression.

With the revolution began the tale of the disinherited, symbolized by the substitution of the saddler President Ebert for the Hohenzollern Emperor. The rich and well-born came off very well in the German revolution, and they continued to enjoy respect and influence. But they did not rule, and they regarded the plebians who did rule as usurpers. Furthermore, few members of the old ruling groups could aspire to the traditional career of their class, military service, now that the German armed forces were restricted by Versailles. Some became reconciled to the new regime, but most held disdainfully aloof, waiting for the return of what was to them the right ordering of political and social life.

17. There is a masterly description of German hopes and disappointments in Albrecht Mendelssohn Bartholdy, *The War and German Society: The Testament of a Liberal* (New Haven, 1927).

The years of inflation, culminating in 1923, brought more disinherited. At one extreme were those who regarded the trade unions and the socialists as the enemies of the workers, the fluctuating mass who supported the Communist party. At the other extreme were those who were proletarianized, but who scorned the proletariat, the middle-class pensioners, shopkeepers, and others ruined by inflation. These unfortunates refused to make common cause either with the socialists or with the parties representing successful businessmen; in the prosperous late twenties some voted for the splinter racist parties, but most simply refused to vote, except to put Hindenburg in the presidency. Even the years of prosperity added to the toll. On the one hand, there were the farmers who, like farmers everywhere, were bewildered to find themselves sinking into debt while others grew rich. On the other hand, as big business expanded in the "rationalization" era, the small businessman was squeezed out, and he, like the other members of the middle classes ruined earlier, stood aside, scorning the republic, nursing his wounded pride.[18]

All these were as nothing compared with the toll of the depression years. The Brüning government sought to cure the depression by cutting costs and government expenses. Again the middle classes were hit as salaries were slashed and employees were dropped by business and government. The trade unions were able to protect their members, to the extent that those with seniority kept their jobs. But this bore hard on the young. Whether skilled or unskilled, educated or uneducated, young people were simply barred from a place in society; by 1932 the roll of young men and women of working age who had never found work was mounting fast, fed from below as children grew to maturity but losing few of those who after years of waiting still waited.

This was the really dangerous group, the young with their vigor, their impatience, their conviction that there must be a way out, their thwarted idealism. It was to these youngsters, the counterparts of the young Communists who pushed through Stalin's collectivization drive, that the German Communists looked hopefully, now that the bankruptcy of the trade unions had been so obviously demonstrated.

These young Germans were, most of them, socialists, in that they had no respect for property or the propertied; penniless themselves, they made a virtue of poverty and scorned those with money, fine

18. Robert A. Brady, *The Rationalization Movement in German Industry* (Berkeley, 1933).

clothes, fine houses—everything they did not have and had no prospect of gaining, everything possessed by those, from aristocrats and businessmen to trade unionists, who had tried their hand at ruling Germany and had brought Germany to defeat and depression. These youngsters rejected the property and security they did not have; to that extent they were socialists. But they refused allegiance to the dictatorship of the proletariat or to world revolution; they were Germans who, in the words of the Nazi song, intended to rule Germany today and the world tomorrow. Communists and conservatives insisted on fitting them into the traditional categories of "left" or "right," but they were neither; they and what they stood for were something new.

New too, in the West, was their fanaticism, although fanaticism was growing in other Western countries. It was the American Ernest Hemingway who gave the best ironical statement of the creed of the "lost generation" everywhere. "After one comes, through contact with its administrators, no longer to cherish greatly the law as a remedy in abuses, then the bottle becomes a sovereign means of direct action," he wrote in 1932. "If you cannot throw it at least you can always drink out of it."[19] In 1932 the cult of violence preached by Hemingway had more devotees in defeated Germany than in the Paris of Hemingway; in Germany also, Hemingway's rebellion against traditional social and private morality was more in evidence. In every country, depression heightened violence: British sailors demonstrated when their pay was cut; American farmers violently prevented the foreclosure of mortgages. In the West, however, hope continued, and most young Englishmen rallied behind the national government in 1931, just as most young Americans rallied behind the New Deal in 1933. Two decades of blasted hopes, climaxed by the depression years when young people sought vainly to find their place in society, had given Germany a younger generation which was "hard-boiled" beyond anything known in the Western democracies, young nationalists, young socialists, whose physical strength and idealism could, if captured and exploited, give power over Germany.

The Communists tried, but they were too obviously agents of the feared and despised Russians. The Socialists tried, but while they could enroll young workers at least passively for defense of the republic in their Reichsbanner organization, they had little to offer the proletarianized children of the middle classes. The Steel Helmets of the National-

19. Ernest Hemingway, *Death in the Afternoon* (New York, 1932), p. 189.

ist party were too obviously in the service of the discredited rich and well-born, just as Catholic youth organizations were too close to traditional middle-class life. The Nazis promised both nationalism and socialism, they promised action, they were uncontaminated by the failures of imperial or republican rule. Few young Nazis had made close study of the "immutable" twenty-five points of the party, still fewer had absorbed more than the usual excerpts from Hitler's interminable *Mein Kampf,* and even if attention did not wander during the endless speeches at Nazi rallies, there was little to be learned from them except that Germany had been, and was being, betrayed and that in the New Germany there would be unity, peace, and prosperity at home and success abroad. From the turgid flood of Nazi words, what emerged was the conviction that the time for words was past; it was time to act.

Possibly, as the "vast majority of even well-informed persons" maintained, the Nazi party would have disintegrated if the government had continued the pressure begun by Brüning and resumed by Papen, although there was so much sympathy for the Nazis within the Reichswehr that a military dictatorship, which Schleicher thought the alternative, would have been a hazardous venture. The issue was decided by the fears and the illusions of men of property. The fear was partly of a swing to Communism by disillusioned Nazis, but more immediately it was fear for the safety of property. The republican government had sought to cure the depression by cutting wages, salaries, and prices, but had drawn back when the deflationary policy threatened bankruptcy for German commerce, industry, and agriculture; to prevent collapse, loans were made, secured by stock ownership or mortgage. By 1932, if the government had chosen to do so, it could have taken over much of the business and landed property of Germany simply by foreclosure. One reason for Brüning's fall was Hindenburg's fear that he would move against the great landed estates, and fear for property rose again when Schleicher tried to ally with the trade unions.

The illusion of men of property was that they were strong enough and clever enough to manage Hitler. In part this was contempt for Hitler as an ignorant rabble-rouser, in part it was arrogant confidence in the power of money and social position. When Hitler agreed to become chancellor in a cabinet containing only three Nazis, a cabinet which Hindenburg could dismiss at any time, it seemed that now the

Nazis would have to become just another political party. Here, of course, the parallel to Italy in 1922 is complete. The German men of property learned nothing from the Italian experience; rather, like the Italians, they argued that to end violence it was necessary to give the violent the burden of responsibility.

By July, 1933, in a paroxysm of violence, the Nazis had consolidated their power in Germany. Obviously Hitler could not now be removed from the chancellorship as Brüning, Papen, and Schleicher had been removed. The future, however, remained uncertain. Hitler had promised to free Germany from the "slavery" of Versailles and to effect revolutionary social change at home; the young zealots of the party dominated the Storm Troopers, and they were pressing for action. Across the road to both goals there were formidable obstacles. Before 1933, in foreign affairs Germany could count on support from other "revisionist" powers, and particularly Italy and Russia. Now, however, Mussolini was fearful of Hitler's designs on Austria, and Stalin was coming to realize that Hitler was unwilling to continue the Rapallo friendship with the U.S.S.R. In France and Britain, Nazi attacks on the Jews awakened disgust and also fear; if, as was now evident, Hitler's fantastic anti-Semitism must be taken seriously, should not his determination to tear up the Treaty of Versailles be taken seriously? Germany was more isolated than at any time since 1918, and Germany was still disarmed. There seemed no possibility that the extravagant Nazi promises in foreign policy could be achieved once Europe recognized both Nazi ambition and Nazi ruthlessness.

Internally, revolutionary social change would undoubtedly have encountered resistance from the Reichswehr, but there is no reason to believe Hitler could not have broken the army as he broke other opponents. There is every evidence, however, that he had no desire for sweeping change; he was interested not in social change but in power, and power could most quickly be built by using the existing social and economic structure, and by strengthening the Reichswehr. It seemed that the hopes of exactly his most violent supporters, the Storm Troopers, were doomed to disappointment at home, just as it seemed they were doomed to disappointment abroad. Whether the Nazi regime could survive this double disappointment was doubtful. To nations preoccupied with problems of the depression it seemed that the German problem could, at least for the time being, be ignored.

Chapter Seven

THE HOPE FOR PEACE AND PROSPERITY
THROUGH SCIENCE AND TECHNOLOGY

I. THE DILEMMAS CONFRONTING POSTWAR EUROPE

THE panic which seized Europe west of Russia in 1931 was not simply a financial panic. It was a crisis of confidence. The accepted precepts for directing the life of man in society seemed suddenly not to work. Since 1919, the rulers of Britain, France, and Germany had, for the most part, been trying to guide Europe back to what the American President Harding called "normalcy." They assumed that life before 1914 had been "normal," that the war had introduced distortions which it was the duty of statesmen to correct by measures such as currency stabilization, and that once "normalcy" had been regained, Europe would grow much as it had grown before 1914. In this view, Mussolini's Fascism was a temporary expedient, like the dictatorships in the less stable states of Europe, and Communism was a contagion which ceased to spread as "normalcy" was restored and which, within Russia, would inevitably evolve into something approximating the western European model when prosperity returned.

Immediately, it is necessary to draw back. In the first place, one of the difficulties was exactly the fact that so few precepts went unchallenged after Europe had passed through four years of war. A great deal of the interwar years is compressed into the rough rejoinder of General Wilhelm Groener on November 9, 1918, to the contention that the German army would remain loyal to William II: "Oath to the flag? War Lord! Those are only words—that is a mere concept."[1] Another discerning German, in analyzing the effects of the war on German society, entitled his first chapter, and made the center of his story,

---

1. These are Groener's words as reported by the Crown Prince (*Erinnerungen des Kronprinzen Wilhelm* [Stuttgart, 1922], pp. 283, 284). In his memoirs, Groener gives a slightly different version which does not alter the meaning as interpreted here (Wilhelm Groener, *Lebenserrinerungen* [Göttingen, 1957], p. 461).

"Dispensing with Causality." To Germans, he said, by 1918 everything depended on chance; only a gambler could win; there was no predictable relation between conduct and consequence.[2] Most obviously, this was true of economic life. Stanley Baldwin's remark to Keynes on the House of Commons elected in 1918—"They are a lot of hard-faced men, who look as if they had done very well out of the war"—could have been repeated for most of the belligerent and the neutral nations.[3] The unsavory business ethics which brought quick returns during the war were equally effective in the unstable years of peace; they intensified the instability and spread to poison all ethics, public and private.

All this is true, and yet the old precepts still held in Europe west of Russia and north of Italy, at least in most men's conscious loyalty. The men who seemed most representative of their countries in the twenties —Baldwin in England, Briand in France, Stresemann in Germany— were men who gave a comforting assurance that the old values still governed men's conduct. To many young people, including a large proportion of those who were being educated for positions of leadership, it seemed that the gap between precept and conduct in the life of their elders could be bridged only by hypocrisy, and this had serious consequences, very early in Italy, later in Germany, still later in France.

A more obvious shift was the decline in willingness to compromise. Before 1914, faith in compromise had been central to liberal thought and had been accepted by moderate conservatives. The war, dragging on year after year with mounting ruin and suffering, made fanaticism seem a virtue; there was no other way to bring the cost of the war into any relation with its conceivable rewards.

In Russia, where civil war followed hard on international war, compromise was redefined: for Lenin, compromise was a temporary accommodation to overpowering circumstance, an accommodation to be repudiated at the first opportunity. Within Russia, Communists made "compromises" with other parties until it became possible to

2. Albrecht Mendelssohn Bartholdy, *The War and German Society: The Testament of a Liberal* (New Haven, 1937), pp. 19 ff.

3. The remark is in J. M. Keynes, *The Economic Consequences of the Peace* (New York, 1920), p. 145; Baldwin is identified as the author in R. F. Harrod, *Life of John Maynard Keynes* (London, 1951), p. 266.

wipe out the other parties; abroad, Communists sought "compromises" with trade union and socialist leaders, but the objective was a "united front" of rivals temporarily united against stronger rivals. As the fear of social revolution declined in western Europe with the return of prosperity after 1924, governments became less fearful that diplomatic relations with the Soviet Union would open the way for subversive activities by Soviet agents, but down to and through the crisis which culminated in a second world war in 1939, "normal" relations with the Soviet Union were impossible. This was most obviously true of states on the borders of Russia: in 1939, when subjugation by Nazi Germany impended, the governments of these states feared the U.S.S.R. to the point that they preferred Nazi conquest to the presence of the Red army on their soil. Even in Britain and France, disappointment was mingled with relief when the alliance negotiations of 1939 with Russia failed, and in some of the British Dominions opinion swung to wholehearted support of the mother country only when the alliance negotiations failed. What was true in the crisis of 1939 was true throughout the interwar years. Always there was at least latent fear that friendly relations with Russia would open the way for Communist infiltration and subversion.

In some ways more important was the split on the left. Before 1914, as socialism lost its dogmatically Marxist and revolutionary fervor, cooperation had become usual among middle-class social reformers, socialist parties, and trade unions. This cooperation found its most dramatic expression in Germany during the war, as the union of socialists, middle-class liberals, and the predominantly Catholic Center party hardened into the Weimar coalition which led the German republic in 1919.

Such cooperation became increasingly difficult after the organization of the Comintern in 1919. Thereafter, socialists had to use much of their strength combating the efforts of Communists to win control over socialist parties and trade unions. Thereafter also, middle-class liberals became increasingly wary of cooperation with the socialists who, despite their deadly rivalry with the Communists, seemed somehow contaminated by Bolshevism. Quite naturally, those fearful of social change did their best to identify socialism with Communism in the popular imagination. Much of the history of Europe in the interwar years can be understood only in terms of the split on the left, the history not just of social struggle, but the history of every aspect of national and international history.[4]

Middle-class and peasant leaders explained their heightened reluctance to work out compromises with socialist leaders by stressing their fear of Communist infection. A more plausible explanation is fear of losing their social and economic position. Almost everywhere, farmers found themselves caught in the scissors of rising costs of industrial products and falling prices of farm products. Similarly, the trend was toward big business; the small craftsman, the shopkeeper, and other members of the lower middle class found themselves being pushed down, "proletarianized." In their resentment, the peasant and the "little man" of the cities were quick to identify all city workers with Communism, and slow to recognize that, by compromises with labor, the position of all could be improved. This decay of faith in the efficacy of compromise was exploited by leaders of the right; on the whole, in Europe west of Russia, the drift was toward conservatism.

Very often the surviving faith in compromise aided the enemies of compromise. The triumph of Fascism in Italy was made easier by the conviction of Italian politicians that the Mussolini government of 1922 was in reality a *combinazione,* and that once they had the responsibility of governing, the Fascists would, by *trasformismo,* become just another party. Again, it was faith in the efficacy of compromise which made the word "appeasement" fashionable. When Briand used the word in the twenties, appeasement meant much the same as Stresemann's policy of "understanding": a series of agreed adjustments which would, in the end, give peace. It was only as men learned that Fascists shared Communist disdain for compromise that appeasement became a synonym for weakness, cowardice. It is not surprising that faith in appeasement survived longest in Britain. In Britain, alone of the Great Powers of Europe, compromise continued to demonstrate its efficacy as a means to attain social peace: what Stanley Baldwin did in domestic politics, his successor, Neville Chamberlain, aspired to achieve in international politics.

At first sight, it was exactly in the field of international relations that the collapse of prewar values was most obvious. Before 1914, men had

4. The most comprehensive treatment of the split on the left, written from the point of view of social democracy, is Julius Braunthal, *History of the International,* Vol. II, *1914–1943* (London, 1967).

looked to arms, to alliances, and to the balance of power as means to preserve the peace; looking back, it seemed that in the crisis of 1914 arms, alliances, and balance of power combined to transform an obscure Balkan quarrel into a general European war. Before 1914 war had been thought an acceptable instrument for the defense of national interest; by 1919 it seemed obvious that no interest—except that of munitions makers and other "profiteers"—could be served by such carnage as that of 1914–18. There is no doubt of the intensity, or the sincerity, with which the old justification for war and the old instruments for the preservation of peace were repudiated by a large proportion of those who spoke for the conscience of Europe in the years after 1919. The very idea of nationalism was repudiated by many; national loyalty was attacked as a blind passion or as a cloak for selfish interests.

The temper of the discussion of war among intellectual leaders was admirably displayed in an exchange between Albert Einstein and Sigmund Freud in 1932. Einstein wrote "as one immune from nationalist bias." He could see, he said, that efforts for peace were thwarted by "the craving for power which characterizes the governing class in every country," that this "power-hunger" was aided by munitions makers and others who hoped to profit from war, and that the small ruling class was able to sway the masses because it had "the school and press, usually the Church as well, under its thumb." What he could not understand was the "lust for hatred and destruction" in the nature of man which the ruling class was able to exploit. Surely Freud, the scientist of man, could point the way to control over man's evolution, with the objective of making man "proof against the psychoses of hate and destructiveness."[5]

Freud's reply was Delphic. As befitted the author of *Civilization and Its Discontents,* he could not be optimistic about the possibility of curbing the destructive instinct, and he suggested that all feasible prescriptions "conjure up an ugly picture of mills that grind so slowly that before the flour is ready, men are dead of hunger." However, he concluded, perhaps it was not chimerical to hope that "man's cultural disposition and a well-founded dread of the form that future wars will take" would put an end to war. "But by what ways or by-ways this will come about, we cannot guess."[6]

5. Albert Einstein and Sigmund Freud, *Why War?* (Dijon, 1933), pp. 13, 16–19.
6. *Ibid.,* pp. 51, 56, 57.

Freud's reasoning was too discouraging to obtain wide hearing, but Einstein had said with simple, almost naïve, directness what an increasing number believed: nationalism was an illusion encouraged by the ruling class; the ruling class profited from preparation for war and from war itself; the problem of men "immune from nationalist bias" was to find ways of foiling the plots of munitions makers and, more generally, of the men of property who profited from war. Communists gave a twist to this argument which many thought plausible: war for the defense and spread of capitalism was evil; military preparation or even war for the defense and spread of the revolution was good. Even labor leaders who refused alliance with Communists were impressed by this logic. In 1920 when the British Labour party was rebuffing requests of the British Communist party for affiliation, labor leaders opposed aid to the Poles in their war with Russia. Intellectuals, who were less impressed by the fate of the trade union movement in Russia than were workmen, found Lenin's arguments even more appealing. The Comintern was more successful in its efforts to recruit what Trotsky called "fellow travelers" for service in the Communist version of the fight against war than in its attempts to dominate trade unions and labor parties.

By many paths, men were led to the one simple conclusion that war was the worst of all possible evils and that nationalism was evil because it led to war. This faith was held not only by men who belonged to the non-Communist left, men like Ramsay MacDonald and Léon Blum, but by conservatives who by any definition belonged to the supposedly bellicose ruling class. Neville Chamberlain's Guild Hall address of 1937 was a most persuasive demonstration that the road to armaments and war was the road to the end of civilization. In the collapse of ideal values, one value remained, human life, and Chamberlain believed that war destroyed not only life but all that made life worth living.

The difficulty was the lack of acceptable alternatives open to the governors of states. To restrain aggression, Woodrow Wilson put his faith in collective action exercised through the League of Nations, but the American people preferred to isolate themselves from the quarrels of Europe behind their ocean barriers. By the time the League was organized it was evident that France alone of the Great Powers was prepared to defend the new map of Europe by collective action. Many of the smaller European states professed devotion to collective security;

the British were prepared to enter into limited agreements such as the Locarno Pact and more generally preached the necessity of settling all disputes by peaceful means; the Germans ceaselessly reminded the world that German disarmament had, by implication, been justified as the first step in general disarmament; the Italian Fascists proclaimed their willingness to throw away their arms, so long as France was no more heavily armed; the Russians boldly called for total disarmament, immediately.

Behind this babel lay tragic choices men were not prepared to make. In the twenties, outside Communist Russia and Fascist Italy, most informed observers, backed by popular opinion, believed Europe simply could not afford another war. Here, as so often, Stanley Baldwin spoke for his generation when he asked, "Who in Europe does not know that one more war in the West, and the civilization of the ages will fall with as great a shock as that of Rome?"[7] The difficulty was that the only way to prevent war seemed the threat of war, and the threat of war would carry conviction only if aggressors were convinced of the sincerity of the pledge to wage war. In other words, resort to "sanctions" might precipitate what was believed to be the worst of all evils—war. Pacifists like Ramsay MacDonald turned and twisted to avoid their dilemma. Politicians who were not pacifists but who knew the intensity of the popular aversion to war talked grandly of the irresistible force of public opinion as the "sanction" behind the Kellogg-Briand Pact. Such talk seemed cant when men observed the armies of two signatories—China and Russia—battling in Manchuria on the eve of the ratification of the pact, or when the opening session of the disarmament conference in 1932 was delayed because the security council of the League was discussing the bombardment of Shanghai by Japanese planes. Again, contrasting the words and the actions of their elders, the young were likely to speak of hypocrisy.

Hypocrisy was too strong a word. Confusion, or muddle, is more accurate. The conviction was strong that war was an evil to be avoided at almost any cost. Equally strong was the conviction that the arms race, alliances, and balance-of-power diplomacy had precipitated war in 1914 and would have the same result again. Yet there seemed no other acceptable way to avoid war. Few who understood what was

---

7. Stanley Baldwin, *On England* (London, 1926), p. 106.

involved were willing to allow questions of peace and war to be determined by "foreigners" in the League's council. In practice, statesmen continued to arm, if half-heartedly; they continued to seek "friends" if not allies; they were concerned with, in disguised forms, the balance of power. At the same time, they did count on popular fear of the consequences of another war to restrain aggressors: no pacifist ever described the consequences of another war with more apocalyptic fervor than Winston Churchill at the conclusion of his survey of the decade after 1918.[8]

Beyond fear, observers of the European scene were sustained by hope, the hope that technology, now closely allied to science, would bring an increase of well-being so great as to buttress firmly the peace of the world. Here again, we are back at the search for normalcy. Looking back to the years before 1914, it seemed that Europe had found the path to progress. Progress had been interrupted by the war and the dislocation following the war. If time could be had, science and technology would again restore prosperity and create a well-being so widespread and so great that the most ambitious aggressor would be restrained by public opinion from again offering up progress on the altar of war.

2. SCIENCE AS LIBERATOR, AND AS MENACE TO FREEDOM

It was a commonplace for most of "the reading public" that science was the glory of the twentieth century. In one form or another, the cliché was repeated: what Plato and the Parthenon were to ancient Greece, and what Thomas Aquinas and Chartres cathedral were to the Middle Ages, Albert Einstein and the New York skyline were to the twentieth century.

Here, as through all this story, it is immediately necessary to enter a couple of caveats. In the first place, Einstein and the other giants of science were products of the world before 1914, and most of their revolutionary insights antedated 1919, just as, for that matter, the architecture symbolized by the New York skyline had been developed earlier. Between 1919 and 1939 science advanced ever more rapidly and

---

8. Winston Churchill, *The Aftermath* (N.Y., 1929), pp. 482–83. Cf. William E. Scott, "Balance of Power as a Perennial Factor: French Motives in the Franco-Soviet Pact," in *Foreign Policy in the Sixties,* ed. by Roger Hilsman and Robert C. Good (Baltimore, 1965), pp. 207–28.

in ever more close union with technology, but the impetus and the direction had been given earlier. A more sweeping caveat was entered by a large proportion of the artistic and cultural leaders of Europe; indeed, much of their work can be understood only in terms of their estrangement from an age dominated by science and technology.

In retrospect, the diatribes of the alienated and the extravagant hopes of those who looked to science for salvation seem equally wide of the mark. Instead, the history of science and technology in the years between the wars, and more especially the history of atomic physics, epitomizes the tragedy of those years, when the mightiest efforts of even the most devoted servants of truth seemed to contribute to the disaster which, at the end, fell on Europe.

The new world of science suddenly became visible, if not understandable, after the solar eclipse of May 29, 1919, a date which surely ranks in importance with the other crucial events of that spring—the drafting of the League covenant and the Treaty of Versailles, the establishment of the Third International, and the formation of the Fascist party in Italy. The eclipse was important because it gave experimental proof of Einstein's general theory of relativity, which had been completed in 1916 and which had followed his special theory of 1905. The special and general theories had, like Max Planck's quantum theory of 1900, been devised to take account of phenomena which could not be brought within Newtonian physics. In turn, these perplexing phenomena had come to light as technology had provided the instruments necessary to "see" further and further into space, and deeper and deeper into energy and mass. Energy and mass? These terms, which had earlier seemed so distinct, so separate, now began to appear intimately related, even interchangeable: light, which had seemed to move in waves, was shown by Planck to behave like particles, quanta; the atom, long accepted as the solid, indestructible building block of matter, was shown by Rutherford and others to be a complex structure and a furnace of energy, capable of disintegration, as in the radioactivity described by the Curies.

Before 1919, all of this rethinking of old theories expressed in equations unintelligible even to those who prided themselves on their mastery of Euclid's geometry made little impact on a culture which had become accustomed to thinking in terms of a neat machine-like universe and which accepted the infallible authority of Newton and his descendants.

During the war Einstein patiently perfected his theory, ignoring the news from the battlefront; in neutral Holland another scientist, Willem de Sitter, grasped the importance of the theory and sent on Einstein's paper, together with papers of his own, to England; there, the Cambridge scientist Arthur S. Eddington resolved to test the theory experimentally during the eclipse of 1919. In November the results of the experiment were described at a meeting of the Royal Society: there could be "little doubt that a deflection of light takes place in the neighborhood of the sun and that it is of the amount demanded by Einstein's generalized theory of relativity as attributable to the sun's gravitational field."

The philosopher Alfred N. Whitehead, who was present at the meeting, wrote that "the whole atmosphere of tense interest was exactly that of the Greek drama." The London *Times* the next day reported the meeting under sweeping headlines: "Revolution in Science: Newtonian Ideas Overthrown." But just what had been overthrown, and just what was the revolution, few could say; even the president of the Royal Society said during the meeting that "no one has yet succeeded in stating in clear language what the theory of Einstein really is." Eddington himself retreated into a parody of the *Rubáiyát*, concluding:

> Oh leave the Wise our measures to collate
> One thing at least is certain, LIGHT has WEIGHT
> One thing is certain, and the rest debate—
> Light-rays, when near the Sun, DO NOT GO STRAIGHT.

Popular interest was intense: by 1924 it was possible to list 3,775 books on Einstein and on relativity; the periodical and newspaper articles were far greater in number. Since few could understand what the excitement was about, and these few were rarely willing even to attempt the task of translating Einstein's equations into language understood by those without training in mathematics, the field was open for conjecture and suspicion. It was easy enough to talk about "space-time," about a "four-dimensional universe," and about "curved space," but what did these mean? The same obscurity surrounded, for most, the quantum theory: possibly it was necessary to stop speaking of the wave motion of light and go back to what had seemed the exploded corpuscular theory, but how could one be expected to believe that one must speak, now of waves, and now of quanta of light? When a Soviet scientist tried to treat the matter as a joke—"So, Comrades, you can believe in the particles on Mondays, Wednesdays and Fridays and in the waves on Tuesdays, Thursdays and Saturdays"—he was denounced as "bourgeois" and "reactionary." Einstein was suspected of being a Bolshevik atheist in the West and accused of being a bourgeois idealist in the Soviet Union.

On top of this confusion there came in 1927 the Heisenberg principle of uncertainty to explain, among other phenomena, that while it was possible to predict, as in actuarial tables, how many atoms would disintegrate in a given time, it was not possible to predict which atoms would disintegrate. To the uninitiated, this meant that the universe was no longer an orderly place where cause and effect ruled. When, to halt the questioning, scientists said that for all purposes except those involving the almost infinitely large or the almost infinitesimally small, nothing had been changed, that Newton still ruled, and every effect had a discernible cause, then the bewildered newspaper editor, and reader, asked why, then, all the commotion? The clamor provoked Einstein to write to the *Times:* "By an application of the theory of relativity to the taste of the reader, today in Germany I am called a German man of science and in England I am represented as a Swiss Jew. If I come to be regarded as a *bête noir* the description will be reversed, and I shall become a Swiss Jew for the German and a German for the English." The jest proved a prediction as accurate as his calculation of the deflection of light by gravitation, but his joking identification of relativity with relativism was exactly that which many were coming to make. Relativity, one of the greatest intellectual achievements of the century, an achievement possible only because science was dominated by passionate devotion to truth, was equated with a vulgarized relativism which made truth, and all values, a matter of time, place, circumstance—and convenience. In this mood, *Punch* could link Einstein, the iconoclast of science, with Jacob Epstein, the iconoclast of traditional values in sculpture:

> Einstein and Epstein are wonderful men,
> Bringing new miracles into our ken.
> Einstein upset the Newtonian rule;
> Epstein demolished the Pheidian School.
> Einstein gave fits to the Royal Society;
> Epstein delighted in loud notoriety.

Einstein made parallels meet in infinity;
Epstein remodelled the form of Divinity.[9]

The intense interest in the generally incomprehensible theory of relativity showed the popular reverence for science and the scientists, a reverence which was to deepen as the wonders of electronics such as radio and as synthetic fibers and "miracle" drugs moved from the laboratory into mass production. Bewilderment about the meaning of the theory showed the gap which was widening between the world of the senses and the "real" world of the scientist.

Over generations, men had become accustomed to the idea that the sun did not "rise" in the morning and "set" in the evening; it was possible, by an effort of the imagination, aided by fairly simple mechanical models, to envisage the motion of the sun and the planets, including our earth. Again, after the first shock, men's minds had become accustomed to the idea of evolution over not thousands but millions of years. But now it was necessary to envisage, first of all, a cosmos within which our sun was merely a minor star among millions, within a galaxy which was merely one of millions, stretching out into a space which could be measured only in light-years, so that the star "seen" through the telescope was, so to speak, a ghost—light which had started through space millions of years ago, light from a star which by now was in a different position, in a different stage of its existence, if indeed it still existed. At the other extreme, again "seeing" through instruments which sought to compensate for man's weak senses, it was necessary to envisage "matter," whether a chair, a building, a plant, or a galaxy, as composed of atoms which were not "solid," but miniature solar systems of varying stability, packed with energy of such incredible magnitude that, as one scientist put it, we walk on guncotton. Galaxies rushing through space, restless atoms, and man whose technology was devising ever more sensitive means of observation, all had a history stretching, not through the few thousands of years of recorded history, but back possibly a million or more years to the appearance of

9. A. N. Whitehead, *Science and the Modern World* (Lowell Lectures, 1925; N.Y., Mentor Books, 1948), p. 11; A. Vibert Douglas, *The Life of Arthur Stanley Eddington* (London, 1956), pp. 37–45; Philipp Frank, *Einstein, His Life and Times* (N.Y., 1947), pp. 133–47; Robert Jungk, *Brighter than a Thousand Suns* (London, 1958), p. 41, for the Soviet scientist; *New York Times*, Sept. 28, 1924, Sec. VIII, p. 10, for books on Einstein and relativity.

man, back possibly 2 billion years to the appearance of life on our earth, back possibly 5 billion years to the beginning of the universe. All that, to be comprehended by man.

And what was man? The weakness of his sense perception was made obvious by his own instruments. What he learned with the aid of these instruments could no longer be expressed in words, but only in equations at which most stared, uncomprehending. Even those who did comprehend—and who could demonstrate their comprehension either by drawing new technological achievements from their knowledge or by predicting what was not yet perceived, as Einstein predicted the deflection of light—were not agreed on the meaning of it all. Granted that it all started with an explosion lasting possibly half an hour, some 5 billion years ago; what was before that? Was God brooding over the void? Eddington, a Quaker, and Georges Lemaître, a Catholic, said he was, and both were great scientists. Others, equally great, scoffed at the idea. Still others gave no answer. Did Heisenberg's principle of uncertainty bring free will back into what had seemed a rigidly determinist universe? Again, some said yes; some said no; some were silent.

An increasing number of scientists were beset by a deeper doubt: whether man, for all his unique gift of reflective intelligence and for all his technological skill, could understand what he called "reality." Less and less did the scientist profess to explain, he merely described relations. Less and less did the scientist speak of "laws" of nature; he might use the word "policy," as suggesting something more tentative, less pontifical, something which suggested that what the mind "saw" might have only a shadowy relation to "reality," whether the reality of interstellar space or the reality of the atom—or of man.

On a more prosaic level, science, like industry and agriculture, was going through a revolution in organization. Germany had shown the way: the close connection between the German lead in the electrical and chemical industries and the German lead in scientific and technical education was obvious. Even before the end of the nineteenth century Germany had gone a step further and formed specialized research centers in the universities and in foundations where a few scientists of great distinction worked with advanced students, as in the Kaiser Wilhelm Institut to which Einstein was called in 1913. Again, the achievements of Germans in pure science and the part played by applied science during the war led to imitation by other countries. After

1919, the tradition of the scholar-teacher who formulated and executed his own projects continued in the western European countries, but in Britain, and especially in the United States, the research center gained increasing importance. Governments and industries began to subsidize research, sometimes in the universities, sometimes in their own laboratories. This seemed an inevitable trend, not only because of the demonstrated practical advantage of group research, but because the instruments provided to the scientists by technology, as they increased in power and delicacy, increased astronomically in cost.

The process was carried furthest in the twenties in the Soviet Union, partly because Communism tended to centralize direction and control, partly because the revolution had depleted the ranks of Russian science. It was a commonplace of science that a few great minds could guide the research of many less original minds, or less mature minds. Every year, Russian scientists found it harder to leave their country for research abroad, until in the thirties such travel almost ceased. In the thirties, too, there came increasing pressure to fit Soviet science into the mold of Communist ideology. Earlier, in their reverence for science, the political rulers of the U.S.S.R. had left the scientist free to follow where his theory and experiment led. The psychologist Pavlov, for instance, continued his experiments on behavior, and particularly on reflex action, despite his detachment from Communism. Even before his death in 1936, however, his followers were under attack, and Soviet students of psychology sought to avoid identification with his theories (later, when the wheel of Communist fortunes turned and Pavlov was made a Hero of the Soviet Union, there was a rush to espouse his ideas).

Pavlov's difficulties were shared by other workers in what were coming to be called the "life sciences," and difficulties were encountered in the West as well as in Russia. Psychologists who insisted that psychology was an experimental science were likely to stress the similarity between the behavior of the animals on whom the experiments were usually performed and the behavior of man; in some schools of psychology the human mind became merely an intricate machine. The Viennese founder of psychoanalysis, Sigmund Freud, and not only his disciples but also those who, like Carl Jung, broke with the master, also insisted that they were scientists, but they stressed the part played in thought and action by unconscious drives. Freud himself placed most emphasis on early, especially infantile, experience, in his explanations of mental illness; Jung stressed the importance of primitive social experience in his explanations of the contrast between what men consciously wanted to do and what they were unconsciously driven to do.

Freud, like most of those who profoundly influenced the intellectual life of Europe in the years after the great war, had made many of his greatest contributions before the war. Moreover, he did not discover the unconscious; he himself accented the age-old quality of his wisdom by giving classical names to what he considered the basic instinctual drives of man—to love (Eros) and to death or destruction (Thanatos)—as well as to that "choice of the mother as love-object" which figures so largely in psychoanalysis, which he called the Oedipus complex. Partly because of his stress on sex, and partly because psychoanalysis seemed to dethrone reason and make man a slave to his unconscious desires, Freud and his followers aroused antagonism in the West, not least in Vienna. On the other hand, he had great influence on central and western European cultural life. Looking back, the French novelist François Mauriac said, "For the last half-century Freud, no matter what we think of him, has compelled us to see everything, beginning with ourselves, through spectacles which we shall never, now, be able to lay aside." With little exaggeration, so far as literature and art are concerned, he concluded that "since the ending of the First War, his has been the dominating influence on everybody."[10]

Mauriac was one of the few great artists who immersed themselves in the thought of the interwar years without losing their faith in Christianity and in the freedom of the individual to shape his destiny. The trend of thinking was against both. In the study of history, outside Russia the trend was strongly toward relativism: men were seen, and judged, in relation to the "climate of opinion" dominant in their generation. In sociology, in western Europe between the wars, the day of giants like Émile Durkheim and Max Weber was over, and the trend was toward description, bolstered by statistical tables; the individual was almost lost from sight. In anthropology there was a movement to apply to advanced cultures the techniques developed in the study of primitive societies; these efforts reinforced the disposition to regard man's reflective intelligence as something like the chorus in a Greek tragedy, capable of commenting on action but unable to influ-

10. François Mauriac, *Mémoires Intérieurs* (N.Y., 1961), p. 9.

ence the action in any significant way. Philosophy, for the most part, abdicated its old search for an understanding of man and nature, and concentrated on logic and language, fields in which few could follow what was being said: even philosophers groped for an understanding of what an acknowledged master like Wittgenstein was saying.

The life sciences, such as genetics, which were developing most rapidly, aroused hope in some, but fear and even despair in others who were aware of what was being done. Genetics had taken form before the war, when three biologists independently verified the results of experiments reported more than a generation earlier by the Austrian monk Gregor Mendel, experiments which set forth the first principles of heredity. The study of the laws of heredity now made startling advances. For centuries, of course, men had been working to improve breeds of animals and plants. Now, with growing knowledge of the laws of inheritance, the improvements were spectacular. According to one calculation, "the costs of research and development in the production of hybrid corn have yielded a return of 689 per cent per year."[11]

From one point of view, discovery of the laws of inheritance completed the theory of evolution. Darwin had taken variation for granted, but he had not explained the variations among individuals. Now it was possible not only to explain variations but to produce desired variations by controlled breeding.

Controlled breeding was used for plants and animals with remarkable success, and the advocates of "eugenics" dreamed of producing a superior breed of men by mating only "the fittest." Most men recoiled from what seemed the ultimate in the dehumanization of science—particularly when the Nazis set out to breed "pure Aryans" and to eliminate the "unfit" by sterilization and death. But to some eminent scientists it seemed that the advances in medicine and sanitation were enabling the "unfit" not only to survive but to reproduce, and that evolution had therefore entered an era in which struggle for existence, with consequent survival of the fittest, was giving way to the multiplication of the unfit and ultimately to the drowning of humanity in a sea of numbers and mediocrity.

11. Zvi Griliches, cited in Paul C. Mangelsdorf, "Genetics, Agriculture, and the World Food Problem," *Proceedings of the American Philosophical Society*, CIX, 4 (Aug. 18, 1965), 245. This issue of the *Proceedings*, entitled "Commemoration of the Publication of Gregor Mendel's Pioneer Experiments in Genetics," contains valuable papers and bibliographies.

For those with an appetite for such horrors, it was not necessary to contemplate the alternatives of socially controlled breeding or degeneration of the species; there were present or impending horrors aplenty. The advances of psychology suggested that advertisers—or dictators—could shape the minds of men at will. The growth of bureaucracy in government and business suggested that the individual was losing that freestanding autonomy of which the Renaissance man had long seemed the model and was instead shrinking until he became, for the most disheartened, no better than an insect—in Kafka's *Metamorphosis* a cockroach. Technology, in one sense, lifted the load of toil from man's back, but in another sense reduced him to a helpless slave, whether of the machine (the "robot" in Karel Čapek's *R.U.R.*), of the state, of the business cycle, or of fashion.

With Kafka and Čapek, of course, we are back with the cultural rebels who stressed what they believed to be the dehumanization resulting both from scientific advance and from middle-class society. In the West such opponents were powerless, except to the extent that they were able to dissuade able young people from scientific and technological study.

In Russia the situation was different. There science was given every possible encouragement, unless the conclusions of the scientist ran counter to the science of Marxism-Leninism. At first, the teachings of Freud and of psychologists like the behavioralists were welcomed. But in the thirties, when the Soviet regime was seeking to force the pace of history by the five-year plans, Freud and the behavioralists lost favor because they did not leave room for such deliberately willed change. And since the Soviet government controlled all research, when the psychologists lost favor they lost their facilities for research. Genetics suffered a similar fate. Marxism-Leninism was disposed to explain the mechanism of evolution by the inheritance of acquired characteristics. Mendelism demonstrated by experiment that heredity is transmitted by what came to be called genes from both parents, and that these genes combined into cells according to statistical rules. Mendelism, therefore, left no room for the inheritance of acquired characteristics. But Mendelism did work, as the production of hybrid corn demonstrated. In the thirties in Russia there was acrimonious dispute between scientists and politicians. Gradually, power shifted to those scientists who adhered to belief in the inheritance of acquired characteristics, led by a favorite of Stalin's, Trofim Lysenko, with crippling effect on Soviet scholarship.[12]

The increasing isolation of science in Russia and the increasing determination that the scientist should further distinctively Soviet science seemed a denial of the very nature of science, of knowledge, which scientists believed could flourish only if ideas and men could circulate freely over the world. In 1932, when he lectured on "The Expanding Universe," Eddington boasted that his was "an international subject" and that his lectures drew on ideas and experiments of scientists of Germany, Holland, and Belgium, of America, Denmark, and France, even of Fascist Italy. "My subject disperses the galaxies, but it unites the earth. May no 'cosmical repulsion' intervene to sunder us!"[13]

By 1932 the free world of science was already contracting. Not only was Russia closing within itself. Reaction, and especially anti-Semitism, had driven many scholars from Hungary and the countries of eastern Europe. These exiles found a ready welcome in the West, and nowhere more warm than in Germany, where a center of atomic physics like Göttingen attracted students from many countries and where the sense of achievement pulsed in the air. But violent nationalism and anti-Semitism were convulsing the German universities, and within a year the Nazis were to begin the dispersion of German science which enriched the science of other nations and wrecked the science of Germany. Some great figures like Heisenberg remained, but the heart went out of their work even though they continued to share ideas in writing with their exiled colleagues.

It is one of the ironies of history that the Nazis, who wished above all to increase German power, destroyed the German centers of research in atomic physics on the eve of that marriage of science and technology which was to produce power "brighter than a thousand suns." The Nazis came to power in 1933; in 1934, in Fascist Italy, Enrico Fermi's experiments hit on the process of disintegrating the atom which was to produce the chain reaction. Fermi himself was slow to realize what he had done. In 1938 he journeyed from Italy to Stockholm to receive the Nobel prize. By then the excesses of the Fascist regime, and particularly Mussolini's imitation of Nazi racism, had filled Fermi with disgust. Instead of returning to Italy, he proceeded to

12. Zhores A. Medvedev, *The Rise and Fall of T. D. Lysenko* (N.Y., 1969).
13. Sir Arthur Eddington, *The Expanding Universe* (Ann Arbor, 1958), p. vii.

New York, where he found welcome at Columbia University. He arrived early in 1939, just as news came of the first deliberate splitting of a uranium atom—in Germany. Soon he and other scientists, many exiles like himself, were discussing the possibility that nuclear fission might produce a weapon of decisive force in the war which was lowering over Europe. Out of their discussions came the idea of interesting the American government in the possibilities and the dangers of atomic weapons. To lend prestige to their appeal, they induced the exiled Einstein—by now a "Swiss Jew" in German eyes—to sign a letter to President Roosevelt. This was on August 2, 1939, the day Ribbentrop, Hitler's foreign minister, proposed a pact between Nazi Germany and the Soviet Union. Alexander Sachs, a Russian-born economist and friend of the President, delivered the letter on October 11. The President was impressed by Einstein's prediction that on the basis of the experiments of the Italian exile Fermi and the Hungarian exile Leo Szilard, it would almost certainly be possible very soon "to set up a nuclear chain reaction in a large mass of uranium, by which vast amounts of power and large quantities of new radium-like elements would be generated."[14]

The road from Einstein's letter of 1939 to the Manhattan Project and the atom bomb was long and rough, but by 1939 the story of science and technology between the wars had drawn to a conclusion which in retrospect is logical, but which few would have expected in 1919. The prestige of the scientist had grown to the point where the predictions of Einstein, based on the experiments of Fermi, Szilard, and others, could command the attention of businessmen and statesmen, and in the end produce action requiring the expenditure of vast capital resources. But such capital could come only from governments; with capital and with support went control, including the right to restrict or even prohibit that free exchange of ideas upon which, scientists were convinced, the very life of science depended.

The exiles who sought to interest the American government in nuclear fission in 1939 had more cause than most to be suspicious of government control over scientific research. From personal experience with totalitarian rule, however, they had learned that against the totali-

14. William L. Laurence, *Men and Atoms* (N.Y., 1959), p. 57. Richard G. Hewlett and Oscar E. Anderson, Jr., *The New World, 1939–1946* (Vol. I of *A History of the United States Atomic Energy Commission*, University Park, Penna., 1962).

tarian state the individual was helpless, just because twentieth-century science and technology enabled dictators for the first time to control the speech and action, even the thought, of men, with no possibility of successful revolt until the instruments of control were broken. If the power promised by nuclear fission came first into the possession of a totalitarian state, then the freedom of the individual would be lost everywhere. Even before Einstein's letter to President Roosevelt, individual scholars had excluded the scientists of totalitarian states from their laboratories and had tried to stop the publication of papers which might assist research in the totalitarian states; inevitably, these efforts had failed. The only way to prevent the extinction of all freedom, it seemed, was to entrust this new power to a national state in which the tradition of individual freedom still lived.

The story of atomic physics, in its inception and development so perfect an example both of the scientist's devotion to truth and of the international character of science, had by 1939 been caught in the political struggle which was dividing the world. When the technological consequences of scientific progress promised the production of power sufficient to dominate or exterminate civilization, scholars devoted to truth recognized that the "cosmical repulsion" of totalitarianism had indeed intervened to sunder science as an "international subject."

3. PROSPERITY REGAINED

Most of those who looked to science for deliverance from the political, social, and economic problems of the postwar world knew little about the philosophic problems which obtruded in the swift advance of knowledge and did not suspect that science itself might jeopardize the hope of mitigating if not ending the horrors of war. What men saw was that, by alliance with science, technology held out the hope of lifting the burden of toil and suffering which had weighed on man from the beginning of time. The alliance of technology with science, like the spurt in scientific knowledge, had come before the great war. As Whitehead said, "The greatest invention of the nineteenth century was the invention of the method of invention."[15] With the methods of investigation and the information, provided by the scientist, the technologist had learned to devise artificial products which were cheaper

15. A. N. Whitehead, *Science and the Modern World* (N.Y., 1948), p. 98.

and often better than natural products and to devise new products and whole new industries.

War needs accelerated technological change. Artificial fertilizers, synthetic foodstuffs, and a variety of substitute products helped blockaded Germany to hold out for so long. The internal combustion engine, fitted into the tank, proved a decisive weapon, while the internal combustion engine in the truck and the airplane showed rapidly mounting importance.

After the war, automobile manufacturing became a major industry which gave great stimulus to other industries like steel and textiles, to the production of raw materials like rubber and petroleum, and then fanned out to stimulate the building of roads, service stations, roadside stores, and housing in the suburbs of cities. On the farm the tractor replaced the horse. In transport the truck and bus competed with the railroad. As the use of petroleum products soared, the geologist roamed the world searching for new supplies, while in the laboratories scientists searched for synthetic rubber and for cheaper ways to extract oil from coal so that transport would not be paralyzed if access to distant sources should be cut.

More slowly, the airplane moved from military to civilian use. Charles Lindbergh's flight, alone, across the Atlantic in 1927 fired the popular imagination as no earlier exploit in aviation had done. Year by year, planes improved in speed, in size, and above all in dependability. With an eye to future military use, commercial airlines were fed by government subsidies. By 1939 the airplane was ready to play the decisive part which the tank had played in the First World War.

No less dramatically than the automobile and the airplane, radio moved into mass production and broadcasting stations multiplied. Politicians, like commercial advertisers, were quick to see the opportunities for molding mass opinion afforded by the radio. The amateur builder of a crystal set and the intent listener with earphones strapped on his head were separated by only a few years from the loudspeakers blaring in every square, from the mammoth assemblies where Hitler could sway an audience of hundreds of thousands with his raucously magnified voice—and from the jamming stations which drowned out unwelcome voices on the airwaves.

Midway through these years, the motion picture, already crowding out other forms of mass entertainment, was wedded to electrical recording and broadcasting, and the "talkies" gave a new dimension to the "movies." Here again, there were political possibilities, exploited systematically first in the Soviet Union, then in Italy and Germany, to mold the mind of the audience.

Other technological advances were less susceptible to political exploitation. From electricity came products like the vacuum cleaner and the electric refrigerator; improved methods of production and transmission brought electric light and power machinery to the village and then to the farm. New drugs banished old terrors like childbed fever and pneumonia; technology, applied to medicine, seemed to offer the prospect of freeing man from his servitude to pain, particularly when, on the eve of 1939, the age of antibiotics dawned. The list of new processes and new products could be extended indefinitely, but all added up to the triumphant conclusion that this was indeed "the century of progress."

The years just before 1914 were boom years, but even then discerning observers were alarmed by the strains produced by the accelerating pace of technological and economic change. Large-scale production was advancing. The independent firm was being absorbed into trusts and cartels. The largely self-sufficient farmer was being pressed by the great industrial farm capable of utilizing the new sources of energy. Within factories, efficiency studies were not only transferring more and more functions from man to machine, but were breaking down complicated operations into a succession of simple tasks, each of which could be performed by a worker with little skill or trained intelligence. Henry Ford's perfection of the assembly line for automobiles in 1909 was only a dramatic spurt in the evolution of this process.

Within Europe, before 1914 German economic power was advancing, particularly in the newer industries based on electricity and chemistry. Even more important, Germany was becoming, as Keynes said, the "central support" of the economy of continental Europe. To the east, Russia was in the throes of a "revolution from above," a spasmodic and haphazard effort of the czar's ministers to build Western technology into the peasant economy of Russia. Earlier, a revolution from above had transformed the economy of Japan, and the success of the revolution, from the point of view of national power, was demonstrated by the triumph of Japan over Russia in 1905. Even this success was dwarfed by the swift growth of industrial power in the

United States; it was clear that the United States would soon tower over other industrial states. As the balance of industrial strength shifted within Europe, and as new industrial states appeared outside Europe, the impact of what was now a world economy was at once shattering old cultures like India and China and arousing opposition to Western rule. Everywhere, particularly after the victory of Oriental Japan over Russia, there was a stirring among the "backward" peoples which was recognized later as the beginning of the revolt of subject peoples against their European masters.[16]

The shifts were not only between countries and continents. The rise of new industries or the transformation of means of production in old industries had widely ramifying effects. The growing use of petroleum and hydroelectric power was menacing the position of the coal industry, and that menace held ominous possibilities not only for the domestic economy of Britain but for the position of Britain in international trade. On the other hand, as the importance of petroleum rose, so rose the importance in international relations of areas rich in oil, such as Persia and the Arab regions. As electricity replaced steam power, states with little coal but much water, like Italy, could hope for industrial development.

Social forces also were shifting; the years before 1914 were marked by strikes and violence in industrial disputes. Many British liberals, like some liberals everywhere in Europe, were coming to recognize that to win and hold power they must abandon the laissez-faire philosophy which had once been central to liberalism, and move instead toward the social service state which first used the power of taxation to narrow the gap between rich and poor, and then used the proceeds of taxation to further the education, the health, and the social security of the poor.

In 1914 Europe was still the center of world trade, and Britain was still the center of world finance. Both goods and capital still moved freely, with only minor political impediments. But new centers of industrial and financial power were rising outside Europe, the increasingly restive "backward" countries were becoming a less attractive field for capital investment, and both the growth and the free movement of capital, upon which the expanding and interdependent world economy depended, were menaced by the demand for social reform, and also by

16. See Elie Halévy, "The World Crisis of 1914–1918: An Interpretation," in *The Era of Tyrannies* (N.Y., 1965), pp. 228–31; these are lectures delivered in 1929.

the demand for expensive armaments in all of the states of Europe. While the curve of the business cycle was going up, these great shifts in the economic face of the world were perceived by few, but some were beginning to ask what would happen when the curve tilted downward as, to judge by the past, it would.

Instead of ebbing prosperity, Europe experienced more than four years of war. At the outset, the interdependent world economy was shattered. Some states—Germany, Austria-Hungary, Russia—were forced to live largely on their own resources. Germany most rapidly and most successfully adapted to the enforced isolation, thanks initially to the foresight of a few individuals like Walther Rathenau and then to the capacity for organization long shown by German finance and industry. By 1917 the resources of Germany were more completely harnessed to war production than those of any of the other belligerents. This triumph of planning strengthened and prolonged the German war effort but, at the end, left the economic structure worn out and badly adapted to peacetime production. Neither Austria-Hungary nor Russia had great success in mobilizing resources for war; in 1917 the czarist regime collapsed, and in 1918 Austria-Hungary broke into fragments; long after hostilities ended in the West, fighting continued between the starving, desperate peoples of eastern Europe.

During the war, except when the submarine was effective, Italy, France, and Britain had access to the resources of the world outside Europe. In Italy enthusiasm for the war was neither universal nor intense and the government did not feel capable of demanding great sacrifices from the people, except from soldiers at the front. Therefore the war economy of Italy was inefficient and corrupt, and Italy's finances were saved from collapse only by loans from allies. The French people were committed to the war, but in France also the government was reluctant to tax mercilessly or to compel the husbanding of resources. At the end, victorious France faced the task of reconstructing its devastated northern provinces with an economy which was in disarray. The British, once they recognized that they could not both conduct "business as usual" and fight the war, settled to the task not only of redirecting their own economy to war production but also of financing their allies. In accomplishing this task, they were forced to liquidate a large proportion of their foreign investments and to devote their industrial resources to war production.

Meanwhile, the rest of the world was, perforce, changing in ways which would make a restoration of the old relation to Europe impossible. On the one hand, the insatiable demand of the European belligerents for food and raw materials led to a vast expansion of production, which continued after hostilities ended in Europe. On the other hand, the preoccupation of Europe with war production meant that the rest of the world must now produce manufactures formerly imported from Europe. The United States and Japan moved into markets formerly supplied from Europe and, once there, were reluctant to leave. New industries took root in Latin America and elsewhere, industries which, after the war, were determined to live and to grow.

Under the best of circumstances the transition to a peacetime economy was bound to be difficult, and the circumstances of 1919 were far from ideal. Very quickly, planning for economic cooperation among the victorious powers was swept aside by the same popular revulsion against continued regimentation and continued sacrifice which negated the hope of Wilson, Lloyd George, and Clemenceau for political cooperation.

As in politics, so in economics, the action of the United States was decisive. Before the war the United States had been a debtor country, and every year American business enterprises and governmental units made large payments to foreigners for money borrowed. During the war many of these securities were sold to Americans to finance purchases in the United States, and the European belligerents borrowed vast sums from America; the United States became a creditor country. Now, Europeans had to make large interest payments to Americans and to the United States government. As Keynes pointed out, international accounts could be settled only by the export of goods or by payments for services such as shipping charges, and not by currency or gold. Before the war, when Britain had been a creditor nation and America a debtor nation, Britain had imported far more goods than she exported and the United States had had a large export surplus. After the war, Britain was still, on balance, a creditor nation and could afford an excess of imports. But, as a creditor nation, it seemed that the United States must become an importer. This did not happen. America continued to be a great exporter, and to check imports the tariff was raised. For a time this anomalous situation could be, and was, concealed by continued large export of American capital, that is, the amount Americans were sending abroad to foreign borrowers was greater than the amount foreigners must pay in interest on old loans. But what would happen when the United States stopped exporting capital? No one knew until this happened, beginning in 1928; then the economy of the debtor countries was shaken.

One import which the United States had formerly welcomed was now severely restricted—people. The immigration restrictions of the 1920's reflected in part the transition from human to machine power in American industry and agriculture which made the import of new labor unnecessary. It also reflected the revulsion against contact with the rest of the world which so swiftly replaced Wilson's hope of American leadership in a world community. The fact that the sudden stoppage of immigration created grave problems for the countries of southern and eastern Europe which had come to count on emigration to ease the pressure on the land, and on remittances from emigrants to ease financial problems, made no difference to the Americans. So great was the determination to exclude the alien that even though the influx of Japanese was of negligible proportions, and even though exclusion gravely complicated the conduct of American foreign relations, California was able to carry through its Japanese exclusion policy.

In more subtle ways, the emergence of the United States as the greatest industrial and financial power complicated the economy of Europe. Before 1914 world finance had centered in London. Now New York was a center of equal or greater importance. The competition between the two centers had an unsettling effect. Moreover, New York and lesser American centers like Chicago were relatively inexperienced in the problems of world finance. In London, from bitter experience, the leaders of finance had at least partly learned the necessity of disciplining the more rash and the less scrupulous members of the financial community. Not so in the United States. There was a more erratic, more irresponsible, character to American finance, which helps to explain the violent swings of the interwar economy.

The British found it hard to adjust to the new economic world. In 1918 they confidently expected to resume their old leadership, ignoring the prewar and wartime shifts in the economic balance of power; indeed, the elimination of their old German competitor was thought to have improved the economic position of Britain. Very quickly, the leaders of industry and finance came to recognize that Britain could not flourish while much of the world was impoverished. In British efforts to revive trade with Russia, the desire for markets conflicted with fear of Communist subversive activity, particularly in the restless colonial countries of Asia; Anglo-Russian economic relations were always at the mercy of political currents in the two countries. In British relations with Japan, political necessity tended to offset economic rivalry. The economic rivalry was intense, particularly in textiles; in other industries also, British exporters lost ground to their Japanese competitors. However, the necessity for political cooperation made the British government reluctant to combat Japan economically, even in the British colonies.

The economic problems which had accumulated in the prosperous years before 1914, and which had been vastly complicated by the distortions of the war years, passed almost unnoticed during 1919. Everywhere there was an apparently insatiable demand for consumer goods and for new construction. Then, midway through 1920, the boom collapsed. Employment fell off, and industrial strife took on a violent, even revolutionary, tinge. Tax receipts also fell off, and government budgets showed mounting deficits; first speculators and then businessmen began to exchange the currency of countries in financial difficulty for the currency of countries with a relatively strong financial structure. The currency of Russia collapsed first, during the years of war communism. The currencies of the smaller states of central and southeastern Europe were almost without value at a time when the purchase of food from abroad was necessary to avert starvation. The Italian currency slipped as social unrest spread and fear grew that the Italian government would never be able to repay the debts incurred during the war. With the beginning of reparation payments the German currency sagged ominously. French, and to a lesser extent British, currency stability was progressively impaired as doubt grew that Germany would pay reparation and as American determination to recover sums loaned to the British and French governments during the war became evident.

The climax came in 1923, after the French invasion of the Ruhr. By September the German mark was worthless, and there seemed real danger that the financial collapse of Germany would drag down the whole of Europe. Then came the abandonment of German passive resistance in the Ruhr, the drastic financial reforms of the Stresemann era, and the appointment of an international commission headed by the American banker Charles G. Dawes to review the reparation problem.

Promptly confidence revived, and even before the acceptance of the Dawes Plan at a conference in London in August, 1924, it seemed that the restoration of the economic life of Europe was at last assured. The lesson drawn by most Europeans, and Americans, was that the restoration must be entrusted not to politicians but to those who thought in terms of economics. The Keynes of 1919 seemed vindicated: the mistake of the peacemakers and of their successors was failure to recognize the necessity of restoring the freely functioning world economy which had brought prosperity before 1914. Revelation of the corruption of politicians by businessmen during the Harding administration in the United States did not disturb the conviction that business must be allowed free rein; the passive economic policy of Calvin Coolidge, who became President on Harding's death in 1923, seemed the height of wisdom. Similarly, the exploitation by businessmen and financiers of the opportunities for profit during the runaway inflation in Germany and other countries was ignored; the central objective of governments became the creation of conditions in which business and finance could operate without political impediment. As a French writer, Francis Delaisi, put it, from 1918 to 1923 Europe had been dominated by "political myths," whether the myth of nationalism dominant in the Western democracies and the new Fascist government in Italy, or the myth of Communism in Russia. The results had been disastrous. "Democracy has solved nothing; Soviet rule is bankrupt; Fascismo is an expedient that can only be provisional; and the whole world a prey to cross purposes, stillborn solutions, hazardous improvisation, indecision and insecurity." All, Delaisi argued, because statesmen, their vision narrowed by a parochial outlook, had refused to recognize that nationalism, like feudalism before it, had become obsolete. The world was now one economic unit, and the real task of governments was "the restoration of the international mechanism of exchanges." The appointment of the Dawes commission, dominated by men who thought in terms of economics, not politics, began the triumph of wisdom over blind folly, Delaisi concluded.[17]

17. Francis Delaisi, *Political Myths and Economic Realities* (N.Y., 1927), pp. xiv, 416, 417. The book was written in 1924 and early 1925.

The initial results justified such optimism. Britain settled to the task of putting its financial house in order in 1923 by an agreement with the United States for the repayment of the war debts of Britain. In 1925 the pound sterling was stabilized at its old parity with the dollar ($4.85). Critics maintained that the terms of the war debt settlement were intolerably hard, and Keynes vehemently argued that prices in Britain were so high that stabilization at the old parity would seriously impair exports; the Conservative government replied that the essential was to reestablish faith in the value of the pound and thereby to make London once more the banker of Europe. The government claimed vindication as funds flowed from all parts of the world for deposit in London and as British investments abroad mounted to the point where, by 1929, the total foreign investment equaled or exceeded that of 1914. Keynes and other critics could claim that the continued stagnation of the export trade and the persistence of unemployment—never under a million in any year—justified their criticism; but their claims found little acceptance among a people rejoicing at the attainment of stability.

In Germany the new mark which replaced the worthless currency in 1923 was fortified on the one hand by the Dawes loan and on the other by a new firmness in taxation policy. Each year the German government turned over to the agent of the creditor powers the mounting sums required by the reparation schedule set by the Dawes commission; each year the agent found it possible to convert the payments into foreign currencies without disturbing the value of the mark. German business revived rapidly and found no difficulty in borrowing abroad the sums needed to reequip and expand the German industrial plant, just as German local governments found it easy to borrow money for public improvements. Each year the process of "rationalization"—the consolidation of industry into bigger units, the meshing of business and finance, the mechanization of production—was speeded under the guidance of trade associations. The spectacular revival seemed to make possible a permanent reparation settlement; the Young Plan went into effect in 1929.[18]

The consequences of the shift to "economic realities" in France were, if anything, more dramatic. The shift was made slowly and reluctantly. In 1928 the value of the franc was fixed at about four cents; for two

18. Cf. above, p. 134.

years it had fluctuated around that point. In effect, the war effort of France and the reconstruction of France had been financed by lenders who had provided francs worth up to twenty cents; they would be repaid in francs worth four cents. The "rentier" lost, but France had been rebuilt. The devastated areas were the most industrialized parts of France. They now had new buildings and equipment, and added to the industrial plant of Alsace-Lorraine, they made France a great industrial nation. At the same time, France kept her lead in the export of luxury goods, and more than ever she attracted tourists, who spent freely and thereby increased French capital. Unemployment disappeared; indeed, every year hundreds of thousands of temporary immigrants found work in France. Once again the French were investing abroad, and the government made sure that much of this investment went to the allies of France in central Europe.

With funds for foreign investment plentiful in France, Britain, and above all the United States, the smaller states found it easy to obtain loans for the stabilization of their currencies. The currency of a few of the states which had remained neutral during the war returned, like the British pound, to the old parity with the dollar. In most countries, however, prices had risen so far that the currency was revalued at a fraction of the old parity, usually a fraction much smaller than the French franc; in some cases the old currency was worthless and a new start was made, as in Germany and Russia. In Italy "political myths" retained their hold. Italian prices had risen more than French, and therefore "economic realities" suggested that the lira be stabilized at a value below that of the franc. The Fascist government was determined, however, to assert at every point the superiority of Italy to France; therefore the lira was stabilized at more than five cents. At this rate, Italian exports found it hard to compete, Italian economic life stagnated, and there was much unemployment or migration to France for work.

By 1925 world trade was back to what it had been in 1913. In the United States a boom of unprecedented proportions was in progress, and Americans with surplus capital were eager to find fields for profitable investment. In a golden stream, the American export of capital floated enterprises all over the world. Nowhere else did prosperity mount so high, but, taken as a whole, Europe prospered mightily. As the benefits of the new technology spread, the economic problems which loomed so large in the early postwar years, and which remained unsolved, faded from the consciousness of most men basking in prosperity.

4. THE GREAT DEPRESSION AND THE CRISIS
OF CONFIDENCE

The boom peaked in the United States in 1928. In that year there was a drastic fall in the export of capital and, with the decline, a slackening of the economy of Germany and other countries dependent on the import of capital. For a time the wild speculation in stocks, especially on the New York Stock Exchange, obscured the symptoms of economic recession. Then, on October 24, 1929, there was a sharp break in the stock market; between September 3 and November 13, when the first wave of selling subsided, the *New York Times* index of stocks traded on the New York exchange fell from 452 to 224, down more than half. This was only the beginning. On July 8, 1932, the average was 58.[19]

Between October, 1929, and July, 1932, the world descended into a depression of unparalleled severity. The indices of industrial production tell part of the story. Taking 1929 as 100, industrial production in 1932 was: for Japan, 98; for Britain, 84; for France, 72; for Italy, 67; for Germany and the United States, 53.[20] The U.S.S.R. was a case apart: on the one hand Russia had been insulated from economic shifts in the rest of the world since 1917, and on the other hand the first rapid spurt of Russian industrial production under the five-year plan was achieved by methods no other state was prepared to adopt. Back of the relatively high Japanese production lay deliberately inflationary measures which kept up industrial production at the expense of the Japanese workman's standard of living. British industry had been relatively stagnant in 1929 and did not suffer a precipitate decline; also, the decision to abandon the gold standard in September, 1931, with the consequent fall in the value of the pound, was beginning to stimulate British exports and production. The depression hit France and Italy late, and these

19. J. K. Galbraith, *The Great Crash, 1929* (N.Y., 1961), pp. 12–27, 70, 103, 104, 114–16, 140, 142, 146.
20. W. Arthur Lewis, *Economic Survey, 1919–1939* (London, 1949), Table, p. 61. Lewis' estimate of Soviet production (183) is probably too high (see below, p. 253).

countries had not yet fallen to the bottom of production. It was in Germany and the United States, where the boom had been greatest, that the decline was most precipitous.

Unemployment also varied greatly. Here again, the United States with close to 15 million unemployed and Germany with 5 or 6 million suffered most. But Britain had nearly 3 million unemployed, and everywhere the magnitude and the persistence of unemployment was the distinguishing and most ominous characteristic of the depression. Bad as conditions were in the industrial countries, however, the raw materials-producing countries fared worse, since the price of most raw materials and foodstuffs fell 50 per cent or more; indeed, the impact of the depression on industrial countries was cushioned by the shift in the "terms of trade," that is, the more rapid and the greater decline in the price of raw materials and food relative to the price of manufactures.

Very quickly, the currency stability so slowly and so painfully achieved since 1924 was disturbed, first in countries producing raw materials, then in countries like Japan and to a lesser degree Britain, which resorted to inflation to keep up production. By 1933 international trade was strangled, in part by fluctuating currencies, in part by stringent controls on foreign exchange transactions imposed by countries like Germany and France which, with the memory of the consequences of inflation still painfully fresh, sought desperately to avoid a new devaluation of the currency; and everywhere tariff barriers mounted.

Europeans were disposed to lay the blame for the depression at the door of American finance, which, it was said, had first stimulated an unhealthy boom in Europe by pouring money into all sorts of schemes in the years after 1924 and then had precipitated the collapse of the European and world economy by suddenly ceasing to lend even to sound enterprises. Americans preferred to stress the sins of Europeans: the stock market crash, it was said, was precipitated by the collapse of the shaky financial empire of the Englishman Clarence Hatry in September, 1929, while the last convulsive financial panic was precipitated by the politically inspired French attacks on the credit of Austria and Germany in 1931, attacks which led to panic in other countries; as for dishonesty, America could show nothing to compare with the fantastic story unfolded after the suicide of Ivar Kreuger, the Swedish "match king," on March 12, 1932.

Less politically motivated analysts stressed that the years of recovery, from 1924 to 1929, had been made possible by the productiveness of the new technology; the dislocations resulting from economic change and war had continued, and eventually they came to the fore again. The Dawes Plan had not really tested German capacity to pay reparation. Payment had been made on reparation and war debts, but all this meant was that with money borrowed from the United States, Germany made reparation payments; and that with the money received from Germany, payments on war debts were made to the United States. When American loans ceased, and Germany was confronted with the task not only of buying the foreign exchange needed for reparation payments but also of buying the foreign exchange needed to pay interest on the loans received since 1924, the German economy was shaken, and the desperate efforts of the German government to prevent a new inflationary cycle merely deepened the depression without improving the financial position of Germany. At the Lausanne conference in 1932 reparation payments were, in effect, ended, and the end of reparation soon led to default on the war debt payments to the United States.

Similarly, economists argued, the prosperity of the industrial countries in the late twenties had obscured, but not cured, the plight of countries producing raw materials, and also of agriculture even in the industrial states. The wartime spurt in production of raw materials and foodstuffs continued after 1918, and all price-fixing expedients merely increased the surpluses hanging over the markets. The surpluses slowly and inexorably forced prices down; as prices fell, the desperate producers produced more and drove prices down still further.

Again, the theoretical return of most countries to the gold standard after 1924 had not in fact restored "the international mechanism of exchanges." Confidence had been an essential ingredient in the working of that mechanism, and even at the height of the boom lack of confidence was evidenced by the magnitude of short-term investment, loans which could be recalled on a few months' or even a few days' notice. Lack of confidence was obvious also in the fact that investment went so largely to economically mature countries like Germany, not to develop "the more untrodden" areas of the world. Above all, in the twenties there had not been a return to the relatively free world economy of the prewar era. Protective tariffs were the most obvious evidence of political intervention in economic life; as international economic conferences stressed, tariffs were high, and rising. At the height of the boom in 1929, the American Congress began debate on the extremely protective Hawley-Smoot tariff bill, which became law in 1930 and touched off a new wave of protective legislation in Europe.

Even in prosperity, all these weaknesses of the world economy had been obvious to close observers and exposed in treatises, learned or popular, usually with the conclusion that in an economically inter-dependent world, economic nationalism must inevitably disrupt "the free movement of people and of goods so necessary to economic welfare."[21]

In theory, most of the statesmen in Europe west of Russia accepted this conclusion. In the depression, as in the international conferences held under League of Nations auspices in the twenties, the conviction was general that a sick international economy could be cured only by international action. The climax, and the turning point, of these endeavors was the economic conference held in London in June and July, 1933, at the depth of the depression. There all efforts to grapple with the depression by international action failed. Thereafter, while lip service continued to be given to the restoration of a free world econ-omy, each nation sought to solve the problems of its own economic life with slight regard to the effect on the rest of the world.

In one sense, this meant merely that the peoples of Europe were grasping the other horn of "the world's economic dilemma." While economists had stressed the interdependence of the world economy, they had also recognized that "economic life is almost of necessity organized along national lines, an organization which to a degree helps in each country to stabilize the local economy."[22] Now, when the world economy was paralyzed by depression, each government sought by isolated action to revive economic activity at home.

The dilemma went much deeper, however, both in time and in the problems confronting the statesman. Even before 1914 there had been recognition that there was a contradiction between the ideal of a world economy, freely functioning without political interference, and the ideal of the social service state, in which the economy was increasingly molded by the state to serve social objectives. During the war there had

21. E. M. Patterson, *The World's Economic Dilemma* (N.Y., 1930), p. 3.
22. *Ibid.*, p. 304.

been recognition that the whole national economy must be directed to serve the purposes of war; where there had not been firm direction, as in Russia, the results had been disastrous. After the war, however, there had been a violent revulsion against economic planning even to achieve recognizably desirable social objectives, and there had also been a strong disposition to trust the wisdom of the leaders of business and finance rather than the political leaders who were blamed for the economic chaos of the early postwar years.

In the depression, reverence for the businessman declined with the indices of production. In the United States "credit for wisdom, foresight, and, unhappily also, for common honesty underwent a convulsive shrinkage."[23] In Germany adulation of the businessman had been, if possible, greater: politicians had led Germany from one defeat to another from 1914 to 1923; then came the miracle of recovery and prosperity, when the businessman was permitted to take command. But after 1929 there appeared in ever more stark and frightening form the contrast between the smokeless chimneys of factories and the millions of workers without work, and between the bankrupt farmer and the hungry nation. The businessman, like the emperor and the republican politician, had failed to make a reality the promise of plenty so tantalizingly held out by technology.

Years earlier, Stalin had adopted what had seemed even to many Communists the desperate remedy of the five-year plan, and by 1932 Mussolini was moving to fasten state control over every aspect of Italian life, and over every Italian. In France the government was beginning a vain effort to keep the depression out of France by import quotas and exchange controls, but was showing itself unwilling to take positive action to bring about economic revival. In Britain and the United States also the governments still believed in theory that little could be done by governmental action to revive the economy: Franklin D. Roosevelt, in the American election of 1932, called for a balanced budget and other austerities dear to twentieth-century disciples of Adam Smith. Once in office, however, Roosevelt showed a willingness to experiment and a confidence in government action which outraged the older economists and delighted the younger. In Britain, Neville Chamberlain became chancellor of the exchequer in 1932; he was, to

23. Galbraith, *op. cit.*, p. 149.

put it mildly, not an advocate of economic experiment. Yet during his five years in office the government did intervene, albeit without coherent plan, to bring about economic revival and also to produce social change. Meanwhile economists in Britain and America were breaking free from the economic orthodoxy which had failed to find an escape from the depression. Some, like John Strachey, looked to planning on the Soviet model as the way out. Most, however, were more influenced by John Maynard Keynes, who in a succession of tracts gave increasingly coherent form to the ideas which found classic expression in his *General Theory of Employment, Interest and Money* (1936).

The *General Theory* was written for economists, and only an economist skilled in mathematics could read the ponderous tome with understanding. In general, the book won immediate acceptance among younger economists of Britain and the United States; in general, older economists were unenthusiastic or hostile. That was not strange. After all, it had taken Keynes many years to break free from the economic theory he had studied and accepted in his youth, and to shape a theory more in accord with the actual working of the economy; and the skeptical could easily find flaws in his generalizations.

Fortunately a grasp of the completed structure of Keynesian theory was unnecessary. It was enough to be willing to try what Keynes called a simple device, government expenditure to put men to work, and to be willing to accept that bogey of conventional thought, deficit spending. In the American New Deal, this was euphemistically called "priming the pump." Back of this willingness to experiment with devices to lessen unemployment, however, there lay something infinitely more important: confidence that men were not caught in a tide they were powerless to resist, confidence that men, by thought and by experiment, could shape their fate. The Russian five-year plan was, in one sense, an assertion of the ability of man to shape his destiny; but this freedom was merely freedom to understand and to implement the science of Marxism-Leninism. Italian Fascism and German Nazism spoke of the triumph of the will, but this was the will of the leader with complete power over people for whom the leaders took little pain to conceal their contempt. In France and in much of western Europe both rulers and thinkers stood paralyzed between a capitalistic economy which obviously did not function even tolerably well and the abhorrent totalitarian systems. Why, in Britain and America, confidence persisted that ways could be found to get the economy moving without sacrificing democratic government and individual freedom, indeed ways which would strengthen both democracy and freedom—why this confidence persisted cannot be explained, but the fact of the confidence is clear, and that confidence was, in the end, to prove of more importance than all the bungling, the wavering, the sordidness of so much of the record of Britain and America in the thirties.

Chapter Eight

THE ARTIST IN A BROKEN WORLD

I. THE ARTIST AND THE MIDDLE CLASS

THE deepening economic crisis gave support to those artists and writers who, since the war, had believed that a return to the "normalcy" of the prewar years was impossible or abhorrent, or both. It was not, usually, a matter of poets or artists suddenly changing; rather, those who earlier had been rebels now became models to be imitated. Virginia Woolf was a sensitive observer of the literary scene in the early 1920's. She dismissed British writers like H. G. Wells, Arnold Bennett, and John Galsworthy as "materialists"; they were, she said, "concerned not with the spirit but the body." On the other hand, "Mr. Joyce is spiritual." The point of interest for the future, she concluded, "lies very likely in the dark places of psychology."[1]

For her, as for many, the war itself was a barrier to continuity. For some artists it was the adaptation of technology to the uses of wholesale destruction which shattered the ideal of progress through science and technology. For others the national state became a mindless monster, devouring a generation of young men to feed the ambitions of scheming statesmen, wooden-headed generals, and greedy industrialists. At the most extreme, the dignity of man was itself called into question as examples of cruelty and depravity multiplied; when the veneer of civilization was stripped away, man appeared to some of the most sensitive and imaginative Europeans not a little lower than the angels, but lower than the animals.[2]

Almost everywhere among artists and intellectuals, the middle class was excoriated, the middle class which ruled before the war and which, its critics maintained, had produced a civilization in which money alone had value and everything in the realm of thought and feeling,

---

1. Virginia Woolf, *The Common Reader* (N.Y., 1925), pp. 208, 209, 213–15.
2. Cf. Brian Gardner (ed.), *Up the Line to Death, The War Poets, 1914–1918* (London, 1964), for the way the war looked at the time; and George A. Panichas (ed.), *Promise of Greatness* (London, 1968), for the way it looked after fifty years.

even humanity itself, was sacrificed. Like Thomas Mann, these older rebels devoted their lives to the task of freeing themselves from the world of the middle class. For younger rebels the title which Robert Graves gave to his account of his life before and during the war— *Goodbye to All That*—could stand as the epitaph of the age and the class. And yet, after the war, west of Russia, the hold of the middle class was unshaken. John Galsworthy might be a materialist to Virginia Woolf, but it was he who received the supposedly highest intellectual recognition of the Order of Merit.

Before the war, many artists had dreamed of escape from what they thought the corrupting moralism of middle-class life by alliance with the worker and the peasant. This hope persisted, and rose in the economic depression of the thirties, but it was increasingly hard to avoid the conclusion that most workers—and peasants too, as they emerged from what Marx had called the idiocy of rural life—wanted nothing better than entrance into the supposed prison of middle-class life and thought. Moreover, in the era of the five-year plans, cultural life in Russia became completely regimented, and it seemed to observers like André Gide that in Marxist Russia exactly those qualities were exalted which they found most repulsive in middle-class culture.[3] Much of the intellectual and spiritual life of Europe west of Russia centered on the effort to find some path to the future other than that of the philistine middle class or that of the equally philistine Soviet Union.

2. THE SYSTEM BUILDERS

Possibly the most direct repudiation of the world being shaped by science and technology was, in form, an emphatic acceptance of that world, that offered by the German Oswald Spengler in his two large volumes of *Decline of the West*. The first volume appeared as the war was ending in 1918, the second in 1922. The timing could not have been better. Just as Germans were being compelled to accept the overwhelming catastrophe of defeat, they were told that not just German power was sinking, but that the whole "West-European-American" culture was doomed. Spengler did not develop his thesis as a tentative hypothesis to be debated; he presented it as a scientific demonstration. "Every culture passes through the age-phases of the individual man," he as-

3. André Gide, *Retour de l'U.R.S.S.* (Paris, 1936).

serted. "Each has its childhood, youth, manhood and old age."[4] This kind of reasoning, in which metaphor became fact, was not new to Germans. Through the nineteenth century, German thinkers had tended to personify peoples and national states until, for many, the state became not a more or less revered device for governing men but a living thing, an organism which sought to live and to grow, with a personality developing in conflict with other living states. Spengler extended this organic view of the state to whole cultures and combined it with the very old idea that history moves in cycles, with the phases of the cycle always repeated through time.

The ideas were not original with Spengler, and they were not very profound ideas, but he clothed them in a wealth of vivid and learned metaphor, and his conclusion that the West had passed from the age of creative Culture into the age of uncreative and technical Civilization fitted the despondent mood of postwar Germany. In this late age, said Spengler, life drained away from the countryside into the world-city. "In place of a type-true people, born of and grown on the soil, there is a new sort of nomad, cohering unstably in fluid masses, the parasitical city dweller, traditionless, utterly matter-of-fact, religionless, clever, unfruitful, deeply contemptuous of the countryman and especially that highest form of countryman, the country gentleman."[5] In this last age, it was vain to hope for great art, great music, great thought. "And I can only hope that men of the new generation may be moved by this book to devote themselves to technics instead of lyrics, the sea instead of the paint-brush, and politics instead of epistemology."[6]

In his second volume, Spengler developed another idea which drew a responsive note from many of his countrymen. As he elaborated what he believed to be the inevitable evolution of the West in the age of Civilization, his narrative became increasingly apocalyptic and concluded with what he called the struggle between money and the heroic, with the strong implication that Germany, where the country gentleman still held out against the world-city, would produce the hero who would give to the West the kind of rule which the Roman Empire had given the ancient world. "For us, however, whom a Destiny has placed in this Culture and at this moment of its development—the moment

4. Oswald Spengler, *The Decline of the West*, Vol. I (N.Y., 1926), p. 107.
5. *Ibid.*, p. 32.
6. *Ibid.*, p. 41.

when money is celebrating its last victories, and the Caesarism that is to succeed approaches with quiet, firm step—our direction, willed and obligatory at once, is set for us within narrow limits, and on any other terms life is not worth the living."[7]

For some years, Spengler was a prophet in his own country, the prophet who had, in language reminiscent at once of Goethe, Nietzsche, and Wagner, foretold a high if tragic future for his countrymen. As, it appeared to many, that future began to take form in Nazism, which used much the same language, Spengler became uneasy: Nazism too obviously was a product of the despised world-city, and Hitler was emphatically not a country gentleman. After Hitler became chancellor, Spengler explored the possibility of cooperating with the new regime and then retired into disapproving silence. In 1936, in Munich, he died. His two volumes survive, not as the way of "predetermining history" but as an illustration of the hold of science even on men who were convinced that the age of science was the age of the decline of the West.[8] Such illustrations abound. Even a poet like W. B. Yeats tried to construct an elaborate mathematical scheme which would give understanding of an age when, as he wrote in his poem "Nineteen Hundred and Nineteen," "Many ingenious lovely things are gone."[9]

A much more lasting impression was left by another German effort to restore unity to European thought and feeling. This was the tangle of activities called the Bauhaus. Its story can be told very simply: the Bauhaus was a school of art, architecture, and handicraft which, just at the end of the war, grew out of an earlier school at Weimar; in 1925, after the Communists had been thrown out of the Thuringian government and conservatives had taken control, the Bauhaus was forced to move to Dessau, where Social Democrats ruled; by 1932, the Nazis had won control in Dessau, and the Bauhaus moved to Berlin, where it was suppressed by the Nazis in 1933. That is the story, but if that were all, the Bauhaus would scarcely be worth mentioning.

As Mies van der Rohe, the last director, said many years later, the Bauhaus was an idea. It was an almost religious faith that art could

7. Spengler, *op. cit.,* Vol. II (N.Y., 1928), p. 507.
8. H. Stuart Hughes, *Oswald Spengler: A Critical Estimate* (N.Y., 1952), esp. pp. 120–65.
9. W. B. Yeats, *The Tower* (Edinburgh, 1928), p. 32.

ally with technology to produce a social revolution from which would follow material plenty, social harmony, and, as a natural consequence, beauty. Within a group, some of whom were touched by genius and nearly all of whom were able and strong-willed, there were some who smiled at these high hopes, and each would insist on his own interpretation of the vision to which the Bauhaus was dedicated; but the vision was there.

The first director, Walter Gropius, had genius not only as architect but as guide to the remarkable group who worked more or less closely with the Bauhaus. Gropius held firmly to the idea of social revolution, although his idea of revolution, or of social change for that matter, did not fit the usual categories. He could enlist the talents of Johannes Itten, whose strange dress, diet, and way of life were reminiscent of Rudolf Steiner's anthroposophic cult, one of the many prewar efforts to wed Western mysticism and Eastern spiritualism. Itten seemed more than slightly insane to those preoccupied with technology, but he did work out the introductory course on the materials provided to the artist and builder by technology, the course which was for some years the one systematic exercise of the Bauhaus. When Itten's mysticism became too extreme for his colleagues, he was replaced in 1923 by Lázló Moholy-Nagy, who looked and acted like the complete technologist but whose prophetic vision saw photographs and motion pictures as the international language of the future, whose art did give even the uninitiated a glimpse of a universe where beauty was wedded to science, and who continued to influence the evolution of design long after the collapse of the Bauhaus. Gropius himself gave concrete form to his vision in the simple grace and strength of the cluster of buildings he designed as the home of the Bauhaus in Dessau. In 1928 Gropius turned over the directorship to Hannes Meyer; but with Meyer Communist ideas became too obtrusive for his colleagues, and in 1930 he was replaced by another great architect, Mies van der Rohe.

Along the way, the connection between technology and social revolution had been a matter of acrimonious dispute, both within the Bauhaus and between the Bauhaus and powerful elements in German society. Despite all the fine words about the artists as members of a guild and about social revolution, the most distinctive Bauhaus productions— whether buildings, chairs, lamps, wallpapers, pictures, or books—were stamped by the personality of an individual, were, if designed for mass production, produced in capitalistic factories, and were sought not by the masses but by members of the middle and upper classes. Looking back, it is hard to see in what way, precisely, the ironic humor of Paul Klee's paintings, the abstractions of Vasili Kandinski, Lyonel Feininger's search for the spirit in color and plane, plus the designs of Moholy, the workers' apartments and the industrial or commercial structures of Gropius and Mies, the tubular chairs of Marcel Breuer— how these had much to do with either medieval guilds or mass democracy. Certainly, organized labor in Weimar was easily turned against the Bauhaus when mass production of housing was advocated, and the "little man" who voted Nazi was quick to identify the Bauhaus with "cultural Bolshevism." Yet in almost every field of artistic endeavor the debt to the Bauhaus is, a generation later, eagerly acknowledged. And somehow that endeavor was linked with the vision of mending the broken world of man through a union of art and technology.[10]

3. THE ARTIST IN TOTALITARIAN SYSTEMS

While the Bauhaus was setting out to build what Feininger called the "Cathedral of Socialism," the Soviet government was attempting to make the artist and the intellectual express, and advance, the ideals of Communism. During the first years of the revolution, partly as a result of the confused but sympathetic efforts of Anatoli Lunacharski, the commissar for education, to protect artists from rigorous advocates of Communist discipline, and partly because cosmopolitans like Lenin and Trotsky had great respect for the cultural achievements of the past and no respect for those who demanded that a Communist culture appear overnight, Russian artists enjoyed freedom approaching anarchy. Ilya Ehrenburg, one of the few Russian intellectuals who survived all the shifts of party doctrine through a half century, looked back with nostalgia to the first of May, 1918: "Moscow was decorated all over with Futurist and Suprematist paintings. Demented squares battled with rhomboids on the peeling facades of colonnaded Empire

---

10. The most comprehensive documentary collection is Hans M. Wingler, *Das Bauhaus* (2d enl. ed., Bramsche, 1968; English ed., Cambridge, Mass., 1969). For a comprehensive if debatable survey of the relation between the Bauhaus and, on the one hand, other schools of architecture and, on the other hand, architecture in Nazi Germany, see Barbara Miller Lane, *Architecture in Germany, 1918–1945* (Cambridge, Mass., 1968).

villas. Faces with triangles for eyes popped up everywhere. (The art now called 'abstract,' which today arouses so much argument both in Russia and in the West, was in those days issued unrationed to all Soviet citizens.)"[11] Even in these early years there was, of course, rivalry and persecution which, combined with the harsh conditions of the time, forced into exile many who had been sympathetic at the outset. Inevitably resentful at the indignities heaped on his fellow Jews in czarist Russia, Marc Chagall welcomed the freedom of the revolutionary days and threw himself into the work of commissar for art and head of the art school in his native Vitebsk. But he soon found himself under attack by party leaders who could not see that green cows and horses flying in the sky had anything to do with Marx and Lenin. On the other hand, powerful painters like Kandinski and Kazimir Malevich disapproved of him, possibly because they equated Marxism with abstract art, and Chagall's horses and cows were recognizably horses and cows. Chagall was soon demoted to the post of art instructor in the obscurity of a school for orphans. He loved the orphans although, because of what they had seen in the civil war, "their eyes would not, or could not, smile," but he and his wife and baby nearly starved; so Chagall went into exile, and his, from the party point of view, unrevolutionary paintings were removed from sight, where they remain.[12] Like most who fled revolutionary Russia, Chagall did not return. Some did, like the composer Sergei Prokofiev and Ehrenburg himself, while some even of those with scant sympathy for Communism, such as the poet Anna Akhmatova, refused to leave their native land. In the days of war communism and of the New Economic Policy, there was much good writing, most by Trotsky's "fellow travelers"— poets like Boris Pasternak, novelists like Isaak Babel and Boris Pilnyak. The twenties saw what promised to be the beginning of a great age in film making; Sergei Eisenstein, in particular, could make convincing the hope that Communism would sweep over the world and would unleash the most noble aspirations of man. In those years, even

11. Ilya Ehrenburg, *First Years of Revolution*, Vol. II of his *Men, Years—Life* (London, 1962), p. 55. Ehrenburg's praise of Soviet cultural life in the 1920's was rebuked in party organs of the 1960's (cf. *New York Times*, Dec. 29, 1965).

12. Marc Chagall, *My Life* (written in Moscow in 1921–22; English edition, N.Y., 1960), pp. 139, 169–73. Franz Meyer, *Marc Chagall, Life and Work* (N.Y., 1964), pp. 217–313.

Akhmatova could be stirred to hope, as in the poem she wrote in 1921:

> All is gnawed away in hungry torment;
> The black wings of death flutter above us,
> All is gnawed away in hungry torment;
> But why do we feel so happy? . . .
> The miraculous comes so near
> To our dirty tumbledown houses,
> Something completely, completely unknown,
> Something promised us by this century. . . .[13]

Even in those early years it proved impossible for most poets to hope for long. Alexander Blok, who welcomed the revolution with religious fervor, apparently lost hope before he died in 1921; others went into exile; some who were filled with enthusiasm at the beginning, like Sergei Esenin and Vladimir Mayakovski, ended by taking their own life. Mikhail Sholokhov was the one distinctively Communist novelist of real power to appear; his many-volumed *Silent Don* continued its unhurried course long after most artists had run afoul of Stalin's demand for a "Soviet realism" which would give moral support to the five-year plan. In the years after 1929 when, as Max Eastman said, artists were put into uniform, some fell silent like Akhmatova and Pasternak, some, like Babel and Pilnyak, disappeared in Stalin's purges, and literature was left to those who could write what Trotsky called assembly-line romances. Motion pictures fell into the same flat, lifeless pattern, as did painting, sculpture, and the theater. Music alone eluded the leveling attacks of the party theorists; both Prokofiev and Shostakovich were censured, and recanted. The quality of their work was unimpaired, but to outsiders that quality did not seem distinctively Communist.

Stalin's campaign to change Russia from an agricultural to an industrial state was sustained by the idealism particularly of young Russians. But this was not the idealism of 1917, when at least some Russian artists and writers had felt themselves suddenly freed from the bonds of materialist culture and had believed that the revolution would produce a democratic, and a beautiful, world. That kind of idealism was forced

---

13. I have used the translation given in the excellent review article on Akhmatova in *The Times Literary Supplement*, June 9, 1966, pp. 505–6.

underground, just as the idealism of the Bauhaus was forced into exile.

The early days of Fascism in Italy evoked the enthusiasm which greeted the revolution in Russia. Indeed some of the Russian poets had, before the war, come under the influence of Filippo Marinetti's Futurism. Futurism was proudly and loudly defiant in its rejection of such supposedly feminine qualities as gentleness and compassion. What Marinetti loved in technology was speed and power, and above all the heightened violence made possible by the steam engine and the internal combustion engine: the automobile, the locomotive, and the airplane were his icons. First the war and then Fascism seemed to embody the masculine brutality revered by the Futurists.

Another strain in Italian culture seemed realized in Fascism: the aspiration to reach back of the years since the Risorgimento when, it was believed, banal middle-class rule reduced Italy to squabbling factions, to reach back to the great periods of Italian history, to the glorious past whose ruins were a perpetual reminder that Italy had been the center of Western civilization. Probably this aspiration was best expressed in the writings of the expatriate American poet Ezra Pound, and it is likely that no Italian steeped in Italian history could have held with such passionate conviction to the possibility of rule by a magnanimous elite.

Finally there was room in Fascist Italy for those who, in their writings, saw only the futility of middle-class culture. In the years before the war Luigi Pirandello had depicted in his plays what was later called the "alienation" of the individual from society with a precision which the interwar generation could accept as valid; but Pirandello was to be an enthusiastic supporter of the Italian conquest of Ethiopia. The much younger Alberto Moravia wrote even more damning descriptions of middle-class corruption. He held aloof from Fascism. Italy was ruled by the middle class under Mussolini no less than earlier; but Mussolini never lost his youthful contempt for the middle class, and he was indulgent toward artists who shared his view.

What Mussolini could never evoke was an art or a literature which gave substance to the Fascist "myth." There was plenty of the "poster art" which satisfied Stalin and, later, Hitler; there were plenty of grandiose literary works and gigantic artistic creations. These satisfied the regime and probably did have propaganda value so far as the

Italian people were concerned. But they were certainly no better than the most conventional prewar works, and certainly also Fascism was not able to inspire Marinetti, or Pirandello, or even Pound to scale new heights.

In retrospect, possibly the finest talent produced by Italy between the wars (that is, leaving aside men like Croce, whose great work was produced earlier) was Ignazio Silone. Silone, as a youth, was in trouble because of his efforts to organize the poorest Italians, and during the early years of the Fascist regime he was the organizer of the Communist underground within the country. As Stalin fastened his grip on the Soviet regime and on the Comintern, Silone came to see Communism as a bureaucracy no less destructive of human freedom than Fascism. Moreover, Silone's compassion was for the laborer, whether in the countryside or in the city, and in his view Communism, no more than Fascism or middle-class rule, and no more than traditional Christianity, had anything to offer the dispossessed except words. In his *Bread and Wine* (1937), Silone groped for a view of life which would liberate the poor and not simply substitute a new form of bureaucracy. He did not find the answer, but he did demonstrate the compassion and the reverence for the human personality which run through the most varied attempts to escape the bureaucratization of life in the interwar years.[14]

4. THE ARTIST IN WEIMAR GERMANY

It was in Germany that the revolt against the bureaucratization of life and thought was most intense, and the failure most fateful—and culturally during the twenties Germany was not simply Berlin, but Prague and Vienna and Budapest also.[15] In fact the sense of a world breaking apart which began to spread in Germany in the years just before the war had taken hold of the cultural life of Austria-Hungary before the new century began. It was in Austria that the great paradox of western European intellectual and artistic life first became apparent: the artist, while in full revolt against middle-class

14. See Silone's contribution to Richard Crossman (ed.), *The God That Failed: Six Studies in Communism* (London, 1950).

15. See the thoughtful essays of Carl E. Schorske in *American Historical Review:* "Politics and the Psyche in fin de siècle Vienna" (LXVI, July, 1961, 930–46), and "The Transformation of the Garden: Ideal and Society in Austrian Literature" (LXX, July, 1967, 1283–1320). The trend of much current research on the cultural life of central Europe is powerfully sketched in Wolfgang Rothe, *Schriftsteller und Totalitäre Welt* (Bern, 1966).

values, was spiritually within the world of the middle class and had
identity only in relation to that world, against which he was rebelling.
In the Hapsburg monarchy, by the end of the nineteenth century, the
more discerning members of the middle class had lost confidence in the
ability of their class to continue what had long been accepted as the
"historic mission" of the monarchy, to defend and advance Western
culture in the East. Instead, writers like Arthur Schnitzler endlessly
portrayed the emptiness of middle-class existence, in the same years
when the political leaders of the empire were coming to doubt whether
the disintegration of the Hapsburg monarchy could be halted. None of
the political leaders rose above the commonplace; culturally, Austria
achieved a brilliance which students are still groping to understand.
That the satire and irony so characteristic of Austrian, and later of
Weimar, culture, and that the preoccupation of men as different as the
composer Arnold Schoenberg and the philosopher Ludwig Wittgenstein with the inadequacy of language to convey meaning, grew out of
a deepening sense of the irrationality of life is now widely accepted.[16]
Still a matter of intense debate is the distinctive, even predominant,
part played by Jews in the cultural life of Austria before the war and of
Germany after the war. Whatever the full explanation of this distinctive phenomenon, the still precarious position of the Jew in these years
of apparent assimilation partly explains the fact that Jews were likely
to be the most mordant critics of the weaknesses of Weimar culture, as
well as the most gifted representatives of that culture. Finally, the
culture of prewar Austria and postwar Germany shares the preoccupation of western European culture with sex. Again, this is easy to establish as a fact, and again there is no agreement on why preoccupation
with sex is possibly the most distinctive quality of art and writing
between the wars. Probably a clue is to be found in I. A. Richards'
passing comment on T. S. Eliot's "persistent concern with sex, the
problem of our generation, as religion was the problem of the last."[17]
Religion had been the problem in the age of Darwin; in the age of
Freud and Jung, the point of interest shifted to Virginia Woolf's "dark
places of psychology."

Looking back, it now seems that the keenest and most gifted ob-

16. Many penetrating suggestions are scattered through George Steiner's *Language and
Silence: Essays on Language, Literature, and the Inhuman* (N.Y., 1967).

17. I. A. Richards, *Principles of Literary Criticism* (N.Y., 1934; a reprint of the 2d
ed. of 1926), p. 292.

server of the disintegration of the Hapsburg monarchy was Franz Kafka, who was almost unknown when he died in 1924. He left instructions that his unpublished writings be destroyed, but Max Brod, convinced of the genius of his young friend (Kafka was born in 1883), published what he called the trilogy of loneliness, *The Trial* in 1925, *The Castle* in 1926, and *Amerika* in 1927; in 1931 he published a volume of Kafka's short stories.

Kafka was a Jew from Prague who spent part of his brief adult life in Berlin and Vienna, who wrote a beautifully spare German, and who was everywhere an alien. He wrote of a world in which the absence of God was the central fact, where love was absorbed into power, and where the individual, at the end, acquiesced in his own destruction by a bureaucracy made irresistible by the wonders of technology. And yet, never completely expressed, and certainly never presented as an attainable objective, there was always the suggestion that if God could be brought into the world, and if men could break free from the meshes of bureaucracy, then love would show itself to be a force imparting both compassion and courage, and men would be worthy of love.

In his insistence on the bleakness of life and in his suggestions of a life in which both love and beauty were possible, Kafka spoke not even to most who read widely, but emphatically he spoke to those who helped mold the mind of a generation. To Auden, for instance, Kafka ranked with Shakespeare; and through Auden's poetry Kafka spoke to countless young people who had only the most vague notion of his work.

The writers and artists who were called expressionists spoke more directly to the young people of central Europe in the harsh years following the collapse of 1918. "Expressionism" is one of those large, vague classifications under which are lumped the most diverse talents; this becomes possible if expressionism is defined as preoccupation with the inner world of the emotions, in opposition to impressionism, defined as an effort to portray the outer world as perceived by the senses.[18] In this way, Kandinski, who confessed to a distaste for letting others know his thoughts, and whose abstract paintings sought less to communicate than to evoke a mood in the beholder, can be linked with Chagall's childlike directness and Klee's whimsical humor, neither of

18. As in Alfred Barr's *What Is Modern Painting?* (N.Y., 1952), pp. 20–24.

which concealed or was intended to conceal consciousness of the horror which for Klee and Chagall always hung over life. It is that horror which looks out from most expressionist art and which suffuses most expressionist writing. That the present was evil and must be replaced by a new world, the expressionists were agreed. They excelled in the description of horror, whether by chilling portrayal of mental derangement in motion pictures such as *The Cabinet of Dr. Caligari* or in Max Beckmann's paintings of torture chambers. But neither with the brush nor with the pen were they able to present a picture of the new world.

That is true of much in the thought and feeling of Weimar Germany. To take an extreme example, the savage drawings of George Grosz stripped the pretense from every aspect of German life, and his caustic wit made his attacks unforgettable, but nearly all his art could be characterized by the title which he gave his autobiography, *A Little Yes and a Big No*. "Hitler served to confirm my old contempt for the masses as a herd of docile sheep directed by the will of their shepherd, with a perverted pleasure in choosing their own butcher," he wrote. "I did not see much good in people."[19]

This outburst was provoked by the memory of two meetings with Thomas Mann, the first in Germany, after Mann had achieved the honor of the Nobel prize, the second in the United States in 1933, when both men were in exile. At the first, Mann was surrounded by younger people who acknowledged his greatness and who admired, yet resented, his seeming ability "to say yes and no at the same time, all with an air of cool grace." At the second, Mann seemed to Grosz incapable of acknowledging the depravity of the world in which their fate was cast.[20]

In some ways, Mann was more obsessed by decay if not depravity than most German artists. Decay is the theme of his great novel of the prewar years, *Buddenbrooks*. Nobility and depravity, beauty and corruption, exist side by side in *The Magic Mountain*, Mann's great novel of the Weimar years in which the only refuge from despair seems irony.

Much more common in writing of the Weimar years was flight, flight from the present into mysticism, or a mythical past, or some

19. George Grosz, *A Little Yes and a Big No* (N.Y., 1946), pp. 318, 319.
20. *Ibid.*, pp. 313–21.

aesthetic refuge—these or, in the later years, flight into one or another of the cults of nationalism. The most impressive of the writers who sought refuge in mysticism was Hermann Hesse. He had great ability as a storyteller. From his childhood in a missionary family, from his travels, and from the needs of his own disturbed personality, he was attracted to "the wisdom of the East"; and from his love for his fellows in an age when the old guideposts were gone, he came to the consoling and immensely popular conclusion that all ways lead to God. Almost at the opposite pole was the aesthetic creed of Stefan George and his disciples, drawing strength from ancient Greece and the medieval empire, disdainful of the Weimar Republic and the plebian masses it sought to serve, themselves in their own eyes an elite preparing the way for a new German empire which would take up once more the world mission of the great Hohenstaufen, Frederick II—an ideal which somehow attracted men with distinction of intellect and character, and youngsters of great promise.[21] For a larger audience, the poet who had achieved fame before the war, Rainer Maria Rilke, wrote of the necessity for those who had preserved the traditions of European culture to hold firmly to those traditions in an age when barbarism threatened, within Europe from the mass culture and overseas from America. Probably this is too definite a reading of Rilke; his last poems are, by general agreement, of great beauty and even greater obscurity. Almost as difficult to understand is the writing of another who won a great following among the young, Ernst Jünger. His novels of soldiers in action in the war exalted courage and comradeship, and accepted violence and war as part of the natural order of things. He also believed in rule by an elite, but he had respect for the worker, and he preached the necessity for the strong to help the worker to achieve a position in which dignity of life was possible.

In some ways the most winning poet and playwright was Bertolt Brecht. He had the humor, at once biting and compassionate, of the city dweller; he admired daring and the joy of living, even in his capitalist gangster Mac the Knife; once he took firm hold of Marxism he had a coherent system with which to oppose capitalist society. Yet the writings which he carefully did not publish during his lifetime show how much misgiving and doubt he suffered as he watched Stalin build totalitarianism on the achievements of technology and on terror; when the time came to flee the Nazi terror, Brecht went west, not east.

These are representatives of Weimar culture, with its obsessive search for wholeness. The story moves out from individuals like Mann and Hesse and Brecht, and also Spengler, to clusters of individuals like the Bauhaus, to institutes such as that at Frankfurt for the building of a social science through a union of the teachings of Marx and Freud, and to the other institutes which sought to break free from the tradition-bound disciplines of the universities. Then there were the many cults of the "homeland," all the way from nostalgic efforts to understand what it meant to be a German by walks in the country, over to the spurious science of Alfred Rosenberg's *Myth of the Twentieth Century*. The discordant clamor died down with the return of prosperity in the mid-twenties, only to rise higher in the depression. Through it all, at night when the noise of the city was stilled, could be heard the song of the young, marching away from the babel of conflicting counsel, out to the peace of the mountains and the forests, there to strengthen the idealism which, in the end, Hitler and Goebbels twisted to the service of Nazism by appropriating the verbal symbols of Stefan George's myth, and Ernst Jünger's aristocracy of service, and Rilke's tradition, and Hesse's mysticism. After 1933 nearly all the leaders left or became silent; their followers mistook the words for the ideals.

5. THE ARTIST IN WESTERN EUROPE

Among intellectuals and artists in France and throughout western Europe, no less than in defeated Germany and in the fragments of the Austrian empire, there was recognition that the Europe of earlier centuries was broken, possibly beyond repair. There was substantial agreement also that while the war separated the present from the past, the war itself had attained unparalleled ferocity because of the achievements of technology. Finally, there was belief that technology would, unless subjected to strong moral purpose, reduce Europe to an ant heap—or as Paul Valéry said, send European culture crashing into the abyss of history which had swallowed so many high cultures.

Paris and the other capitals of western Europe did not, of course, show a despondent face corresponding to these convictions. Rather, after the horrors of the war, still visible in the twenties in the devastated areas not far from Paris, life had a beauty which looks out, undiminished or even enhanced, from the canvases of Bonnard or Matisse. The School of Paris had been at its most brilliant in the years before 1914, and the character of most of the artists of the interwar years had been formed long before the war—both Bonnard and Matisse were born under Napoleon III, and even revolutionists like Picasso and Braque were in their late thirties when the Paris peace conference met. How closely the work of these revolutionists is related to the revolution in science which was taking place in the first years of the century, when cubism and abstract art were attempting to give new answers to the old problems of representation, was a matter of debate. There was some agreement that the rapidly changing fashions in art and music were in some ways connected with the fact that on the one hand technology almost overwhelmed the artist with photographs of the art of all ages, and, on the other hand technology threatened to paralyze the artist by the excellence of the photograph. It was agreed that the revolutionary gestures were related to the sense of isolation in artists who felt themselves cut off from city masses which had lost contact with folk art and seemed quite content with gangster movies and pictures with photographic accuracy, cut off also from the middle-class collector who was willing to pay large sums for a picture so long as the artist always painted variations of the same easily identified picture. Finally, the revolutionary movements in art and literature alike were obviously connected with the absorbing interest in unconscious thought and feeling, with the depth psychology of Freud and Jung. But while critics like Ortega y Gasset were conscious of the forces pressing on the artists, these were not forces of which most artists were conscious. As Gide noted in his journal in 1922: "Freudianism. . . . For the last ten years, or fifteen, I have been indulging in it without knowing it."[22]

The most impressive, and devastating, account of the passing of prewar culture was contained in the many volumes of Marcel Proust's *Remembrance of Things Past*. Proust's overall theme was the impossibility of escaping time, which changed, and in the end demolished, not only all things but love and life itself; art alone could cheat remorseless time, but even art was overborne in the end. Within that larger theme,

22. *The Journals of André Gide* (N.Y., 1951), II, 298.

not uncommon in French literature before the war, Proust described in minute detail the moral evolution of the propertied classes in France during his lifetime, since 1871. In the first volume, published in 1913 and almost unnoticed, the vanished past was recalled with nostalgia. He worked on the later volumes during and after the war, until his death in 1922. In these the emphasis was on decay and degeneration; by the end, the only value respected by the creatures whose sorry existence was played out against the background of the war was social position. The second volume, published in 1918, received the Goncourt Prize the following year, which assured success. By the time the final volume appeared in 1927, Proust was acclaimed as the historian, in Edmund Wilson's phrase, "of the Heartbreak House of capitalist culture."[23]

A much more widely read book, and one which probably affected the life of many more people in the postwar years, had been published in 1897, André Gide's *Fruits of the Earth*. Its message—that the young should enjoy their natural impulses to the full, undeterred by the commands of religion or society—found little hearing at the time, particularly since Gide's style was then almost embarrassingly lush. After the war, when the book became the evangel of a generation determined to shake off restraint, Gide was greatly changed. He still held almost fanatically to the belief that all sexual desires, emphatically including those called unnatural, were good and should be given free expression. But, on the one hand, he had become an acknowledged master of the art of letters, and through his position with the *Nouvelle Revue Française* he had great influence on French literature.[24]

He had also become a moralist, although he never succeeded in bringing the parts of his thought and feeling into a coherent structure. These parts included deep love of the Gospels, and particularly for the figure of Jesus, carried over from the religious training of his youth. They also included a sense of guilt surviving from that youth, when his actions ran counter to the beliefs of his beloved Protestant mother. Add to these a love for beauty and for mankind, and an oppressive sense that the upper-middle-class life into which he was born was the enemy of both beauty and love. The result was restless search and blasted enthusiasms, all recorded in prose now endowed with serenity

23. Edmund Wilson, *Axel's Castle* (N.Y., 1950), p. 190.
24. On Gide and his circle, see Justin O'Brien's introduction to the anthology he edited, *From the N.R.F.* (N.Y., 1958).

and strength. Particularly for the young who mistrusted old guides, Gide was a guide who gave confidence and who did not threaten. In a very real sense, the twenties were Gide's decade in France. Therefore, when Gide, after a journey through central Africa, denounced the inhumanity of French colonialism, his words found a hearing among the young, although within the political structure he occasioned no more than the usual questions in the Chamber. His adherence to Communism, and still more his repudiation of Communism after visiting Russia in 1936, caused a stir, although by 1936 Gide was beginning to lose his audience; the problems which preoccupied the aging moralist, and particularly his unceasing war against restraints on sexual freedom, no longer seemed so important to a generation menaced by the loss of all freedom.

One of the most telling tributes to Gide's stature was his friendship with the remarkable group of French Catholic artists and intellectuals, remarkable because in France alone was there such a group of Christian artists. It Germany, Karl Barth's call for a return to Pauline faith, and more generally in European Protestantism the rediscovery of Sören Kierkegaard's call for a faith built out from the individual, had a profound effect on religious life and thought. But it is hard to see an active Christian faith working in German literature and art in the years between the wars; in some ways the impact of Kierkegaard's thought was more obvious on the non-Christian existentialists of Europe. Similarly, it is hard to see, in those years, the impact of Martin Buber on the thought or feeling of Jews, despite the prominence of Jews in the intellectual and artistic life of Europe. In France there were Catholic thinkers like Jacques Maritain and Gabriel Marcel; there was a great Catholic artist, Rouault; there were major Catholic men of letters like Mauriac, Bernanos, and Claudel. Why, it is not clear. Like other intellectuals and artists, these men had a sense of living in a broken world, broken, as Marcel put it in a play of 1933, like a watch with a broken spring; in appearance nothing was changed and everything was in place, but put the watch to the ear, and one heard nothing.[25] Or as Julian Green, then a skeptic, noted in his diary at the climax of the tranquil Locarno era, in the spring of 1929, "Descriptions of factory stacks and women with bobbed hair are not what date a 1928 book, but

---

25. Gabriel Marcel, *Le Monde Cassé* (Paris, 1933), pp. 44, 45.

all that lies at the bottom of the book, uneasiness, a need to rebel, etc." A few weeks later he noted: "Any plan for the future seems to me more and more futile"; the feeling that all would change "gives an extraordinary flavor to the present hour."[26]

It was probably the recognition that they were, though in opposing ways, aware of the need to remake the broken world, and working to build anew, which cemented the friendship of Gide and Claudel and Green.

For the rest, in the twenties the cultural life of western Europe seemed not too different from that of central Europe. Corresponding to the expressionists there was first dada and then surrealism. Dada—a nonsense word to flout a nonsensical world—began during the war among exiles in Zurich as a revolt against the society, the culture, and the morality of the age which had culminated in the war; to the dadaists, the only effective protest against an insane world was desperately irrational protest.[27]

After the war, the dadaists scattered to spread their message that everything—not just art, but society also—had become worthy of destruction. The most successful new center of dada was Paris, where the master showman Tristan Tzara, a Rumanian, and the ebullient artist Francis Picabia, a Cuban with a great deal of useful money, joined forces with young French rebels, many of whom had seen the horror of the war as medical corpsmen. Their professed objective was to release man's unconscious, long buried under the weight of conventional culture, and with that release make possible a humane world of beauty and love. Their methods were deliberately shocking and, very often, brutal; but above all they relied on derisive humor.

Very quickly, dada at Paris fell under the influence of young André Breton, a psychiatrist in the French army during the war and a close student of Freud and Jung. Under Breton's masterful direction, dada became surrealism. *Dada selon Breton* was also *Dada sans rire*. Among the surrealists, the gaiety fell away. The effort to dig back of conscious

26. Julian Green, *Diary, 1928–1957* (N.Y., 1964), pp. 5, 7.

27. Michel Sanouillet, *Dada à Paris* (Paris, 1965), has a survey of dada in Europe and America, and an excellent account of the relation of dada to surrealism; the bibliography also is good. Robert S. Short's "The Politics of Surrealism, 1910–1936," *Journal of Contemporary History*, I, 2 (1966), 3–25, gives an interesting account of the efforts of the surrealists to work with the French Communist party; the footnotes are a good guide to the literature on surrealism.

thought to the turbulent realm of the unconscious and to find ways to picture that world in words or with brush or chisel was pursued with deadly seriousness. With deadly seriousness also Breton pursued the determination to overthrow bourgeois society. In his second Surrealist Manifesto, he said the simplest surrealist act was to go into the street and fire a revolver into the crowd as often as possible. This was hyperbole, but there was a disquieting undertone of brutality mingled with surrealist talk of love. In his search for a lever with which he could dislodge the bourgeois world, Breton sought alliance with Communism in the late twenties. The results were inevitably comic. A few surrealists, notably Louis Aragon, accepted the discipline of the party, but most, and certainly Breton, could not exchange the loose shackles of the bourgeoisie for the unquestioning acceptance of discipline imposed on members of the Communist party. In the end, the surrealists not only broke with Communism but tolerated artists like Dali, who seemed much closer to Fascism.

The surrealists had, like the expressionists, a great vogue. But some sensitive artists, while recognizing the importance of the exploration of the mysteries of the unconscious, asked whether these mysteries could really be caught and expressed by the artist, whether the very effort to make conscious the unconscious did not, so to speak, invalidate the experiment. Mauriac, for instance, while acknowledging the importance of the discoveries of Freud, wondered if "the firmly outlined characters of the traditional novel" might not "enjoy a longer lease of life in the feelings and the memories of men than the work of their modern counterparts."[28] Certainly the surrealists themselves would not claim that they had effectively destroyed the bourgeois world, much less constructed the new, free world.

Corresponding in part to a figure like Jünger in Germany were those in western Europe who sought escape in action, most notably André Malraux. Unlike Jünger, Malraux was unwilling to remain within a national frame. Instead, he fought against French imperialism in Indochina, for a Communist victory in China, and for the republic in the Spanish civil war. In these experiences he made terms with man's fate—death—by merging the love of violence with service to an ideal—Communism; one has the feeling that for Malraux, as for so

28. François Mauriac, *Mémoires Intérieurs* (N.Y., 1960), pp. 60, 61.

many of his contemporaries, loneliness was the terror which hung over man, loneliness which could be banished at least temporarily by action with, and against, other men.

Where western Europe differs from central Europe is in what came after the collapse of hope during the economic depression. For the followers, though not the leaders, in central Europe, the combination of sentimental aspiration and brutal action of the Nazis seemed enough. In western Europe, where the old political forms held, both artist and intellectual looked out on a bleak future. "We are living in a demented world," the Dutch historian Johan Huizinga stated at the beginning of his survey of the European scene in 1935. On the one hand, he argued, the speed and extent of advance in scientific knowledge had made it impossible even for workers in the same field of study to understand each other; on the other hand, the advent of mass democracy gave political importance to the views of men untrained to critical thought. Huizinga recognized that the increase in scientific knowledge was a tribute to man's critical intelligence and that in time the universe as seen by science would become part of culture, if time could be had. There was the problem, he feared; in the confusion of values attendant on scientific advance and the spread of democracy, all stability had been lost. He explored the weakening of respect for reason, and the praise of "intuition," "the vital impulse," "heroism"; he ended with an ironical exploration of "puerilism," the worship of youth, and of "existentialism," which he saw as a word which "will serve to forsake the spirit all the more solemnly, a sneer at all that is knowledge and truth." On this ethical disarray, he argued, the dictators had built their political power. From this ethical disarray, there followed a worship of violence which was driving Europe toward war. And, he argued, "the world can no longer bear modern war."

In the preface to the second edition of his work, Huizinga stoutly maintained that he was an optimist, that in the end Europe would draw back from the final catastrophe. By his own admission, his readers had not drawn that conclusion; rather, he fed the pessimism which spread over western Europe as Nazism consolidated its control in Germany.[29]

The equally distinguished French historian Élie Halévy, in a discus-

---

29. J. Huizinga, *In the Shadow of Tomorrow* (N.Y., 1936).

sion with other intellectuals in November, 1936, was avowedly filled with pessimism. He went back to the way in which the need to mobilize national resources and to unite national feeling in the war of 1914 had compelled the belligerent governments to build what amounted to national socialist states. During the era of the civil war in Russia, Halévy continued, Lenin had built a tyranny, which had been perfected by his successors; the Russian example had served as a model for Italian Fascism; and Hitler had built on the example of both. Adopting an expression of the French philosopher Maurice Blondel, Halévy described Communism, Fascism, and Nazism as *"frères ennemis"* with a common father—the character of modern war. Now, timid and apprehensive, the Western democracies faced the possibility of war with these enemies which were, in essentials, brothers. If war came, the democracies would be faced with the tragic choice between defeat at the hands of the tyrannies or victory achieved through suicidal recourse to mobilization of the economy and the means of communication, as the Russians, the Italians, and the Germans had been mobilized. To fight the tyrannies, the democracies must become tyrannies.[30]

Not all observers were so despondent. At the beginning of the postwar era the Spaniard Ortega y Gasset interpreted what he called the dehumanization of art as a necessary and temporary escape from the twin burdens of an overpoweringly rich artistic tradition and the unnerving accuracy of technological achievements such as photography. To escape, the artist turned to the primitive, or he turned into himself by exploring the unconscious, or he took up the challenge of science by cubism. Above all, however, the artist renounced—for the moment—the high seriousness of art, no longer aspired to emulate Michelangelo, but instead laughed at art, if not at himself. To be accepted in the twentieth century, Ortega maintained, there must be a dash of irony in the work of art. But, he concluded, all this would pass; the ironic was itself an indication of the rich vitality of Western culture, which would move on to new artistic achievements when the artist regained his courage to portray the indomitable spirit of man.[31]

Later, at the onset of the depression, Jung in his essays on the art of

30. Élie Halévy, *The Era of Tyrannies* (N.Y., Anchor Books, 1965), pp. 265–316, esp. pp. 277, 300, 307.

31. J. Ortega y Gasset, *The Dehumanization of Art* (N.Y., Anchor Books, 1956), pp. 1–51, esp. pp. 41–48.

Picasso and of Joyce's *Ulysses* took up the same theme of the present as a disturbing but necessary break between two cultural eras. Superficially, he said, the psychologist could easily find symptoms of schizophrenia in *Ulysses* and in Picasso's paintings, but the fragmentation and disintegration were in the age, not in the artists. *"Ulysses,"* Jung pointed out, "was written between 1914 and 1921—hardly the conditions for painting a particularly cheerful picture of the world or for taking it lovingly in one's arms (nor today either, for that matter)." The present, in Jung's judgment, was one of those ages, not uncommon in Western history, when an outworn tradition was going through the necessary process of destruction so that a new age could be born.[32]

As war became first a possibility, then a probability, even such qualified optimism faded. In one form or another, western European thought and feeling, where it did not slide off into the eccentricities of surrealists like Dali, had overtones of desperation, if not of despair.

6. THE ARTIST IN BRITAIN

In Britain there was plenty of both desperation and despair, and for many artists there was an intolerable amount of boredom. Yet, more than in central and western Europe, there remained a conviction that once the hold of middle-class values had been broken, Europe could move forward again, leaving behind the awful boredom of the middle-class era.

The sense of an impending age of emancipation had been strong in Britain before 1914, and indeed the war itself had initially been greeted by many as a cleansing storm. As elsewhere, that mood of exaltation did not last. Because Britain had a volunteer army until 1916 and because so many young men of intellectual or artistic promise hastened to enlist, in Britain more than in continental countries there was a numbing conviction that the best of the young were being sacrificed. By the end, for most articulate Englishmen war had become, in Keynes's words of 1929, "a nightmare interlude, something to be permanently avoided."[33]

32. C. G. Jung, *The Spirit in Man, Art, and Literature* (N.Y., 1966), pp. 109–41, esp. pp. 117, 118, 127, 138, 139.

33. J. M. Keynes, *Essays and Sketches in Biography* (N.Y., Meridian Books, 1956), p. 174.

From survivors of the trenches came books like Siegfried Sassoon's *Memoirs of a Fox-Hunting Man* and Robert Graves's *Goodbye to All That;* in both books the memory of the gentleness of life before 1914 served to heighten the senseless sacrifice of so many men who had not been allowed time to live. From a classical scholar like G. Lowes Dickinson and a philosopher like Bertrand Russell came historical works explaining the war of 1914 in terms of the outmoded values of the years before 1914, values which had survived the holocaust and which would drive mankind to "collective suicide" unless men learned to think in terms of the world community created by science and technology.[34]

Lytton Strachey characteristically approached the problem of living in Britain from the opposite direction: by contrasting the boring present with the flawed but vigorous Victorians. The persons in his *Eminent Victorians* (1918) were on the whole not a lovable lot, but they were men and women of large stature who battled for what they wanted. His *Queen Victoria* (1921) cast the queen in this same heroic mold.

However one approached them, the twenties in Britain as seen by artists and intellectuals were unheroic years. In Aldous Huxley's early novels disenchanted speakers sat talking despondently or indulged in joyless sex. Like so many others, Huxley left England; he took his disillusionment with him and sought solace in mysticism and drugs. D. H. Lawrence, whose great novel *Sons and Lovers* was written before the war, wandered over the earth seeking, like so many European artists, fulfilling love and wholeness, and never finding either.

For many young people, Aldous Huxley gave release from what they thought the hypocrisy of their age, just as D. H. Lawrence gave them freedom from the puritan ethic. A more complex, indeed a more baffling, product of the new age was that great, sprawling story by another exile, James Joyce's *Ulysses* (1922). For some, *Ulysses* was just an inordinately long dirty story; for others it was the most successful sustained use of the "stream of consciousness" technique; for still others it was a massive indictment of Roman Catholic Ireland in particular and more generally of Western culture in decay. To a few at first, and to an ever increasing number as the years passed, what

34. G. Lowes Dickinson, *The International Anarchy, 1904–1914* (N.Y., 1926); Bertrand Russell, *Freedom versus Organization, 1814–1914* (N.Y., 1934).

mattered was the abounding vitality of *Ulysses,* the exuberant joy in the richness of language, the sweep of the symbolism which revealed its richness only as the huge complicated structure was mastered; what mattered was above all the persistent vitality of the long tradition stretching from Homer's epic to this minutely detailed account of what happened to the Dublin Jew, Bloom who had no son, and the Dublin artist, Dedalus, who had no father, on the inconsequential sixteenth of June, 1904. The surface story was one of decay, made the more appalling by the title of *Ulysses* and by the use of the structure of the *Odyssey.* Beneath that story there was strength, strength which carried the hope of new achievement.

In essentials that was the message of the other scathing indictment of that same year 1922, T. S. Eliot's "The Wasteland." Again the glories of the great ages of the Western tradition were set in harsh contrast, here to the trivial lusts of postwar London. Here again the glory was not simply something which was gone; it was a beacon summoning men to take up the story anew.

By the thirties a new generation of writers was moving toward direct involvement with more menacing times, men like W. H. Auden, C. D. Lewis, Stephen Spender, and Christopher Isherwood, or the still younger men who went off to Spain to fight for the republic. Most were at one time or another attracted to Communism, but in the end most were repelled by what they saw of Communism in action in Spain and by what they read of Russia during the Great Purge. What remained was the ironic jest, common to all artists in these desperate years, but beyond that the hope of arousing the democracies to unite in opposition to Fascism.

Nearly all of these younger artists were sons of the middle class, painfully conscious of their inability to communicate with the workman. Yet the tentative, jesting hope that the human spirit would rise against boredom at the one extreme and against terror at the other extreme was a hope they shared with a very different, but great, British artist, the cockney Charlie Chaplin. As the movies sank into the banal, relieved only by the violence of the Western and the gangster film, Charlie Chaplin's little tramp, a figure of frustration relieved by persistence and humor, moving through the world of technology and brutality, somehow lessened the terror hanging over the thirties.

To illustrate the quality of tough hope which somehow marked off the boredom of Britain from the desperation of western Europe, John Maynard Keynes may be set against Huizinga and Halévy. All through the years between the wars, from *The Economic Consequences of the Peace* of 1919, to *The General Theory of Employment, Interest and Money* of 1936, through his heart attack of 1937, and into the period of mobilization and war, the one common exhortation of Keynes was that something could, and should, be done—immediately. Possibly his most famous dictum was his 1923 dismissal of the arguments of his opponents on monetary theory: " 'In the long run' this is probably true. . . . But this *long run* is a misleading guide to current affairs. *In the long run* we are all dead."[35] Keynes's contributions to economic theory were of great and lasting importance, and his attack on traditional thinking about the futility of government action to bring the economy out of depression was eagerly taken up by most young economists. But what made Keynes loom up as a beacon of hope to his contemporaries was his confident conviction that man was not the helpless victim of historical forces, but rather that with thought and courage man could fight through to a better world—and that the fight would be exhilarating.

In a very different way, that was the impression left on many of his contemporaries by the Anglo-Irish poet W. B. Yeats. The frame within which Yeats built his picture of the world seemed silly even to many who most admired him; as a system builder, there was much more to be said for Spengler. Many also were repelled by Yeats's occasional outbursts against democracy and for rule by an elite; repellent also could be his praise of violence. But he was not a Fascist, as some said, and for all his feeling of superiority to the masses, he could speak to a wider audience than the other poets of his day. Where he was best, and almost unique, was in his portrayal of love as an obtainable boon, and in his persistent confidence that the spirit of man would prevail over the destructive forces of his age. When he died early in 1939, Auden, who on the surface had almost nothing in common with Yeats, wrote an elegy which in some measure captures the oppressive fears and the muted hopes of the years between the wars:

> In the nightmare of the dark
> All the dogs of Europe bark,

35. J. M. Keynes, *A Tract on Monetary Reform* (London, 1923), p. 80.

And the living nations wait,
Each sequestered in its hate;

Intellectual disgrace
Stares from every human face,
And the seas of pity lie
Locked and frozen in each eye.

Follow, poet, follow right
To the bottom of the night,
With your unconstraining voice
Still persuade us to rejoice;

With the farming of a verse
Make a vineyard of the curse,
Sing of human unsuccess
In a rapture of distress;

In the deserts of the heart
Let the healing fountain start,
In the prison of his days
Teach the free man how to praise.[36]

---

36. W. H. Auden, *Collected Shorter Poems 1927–1957* (London, 1966), pp. 142–43.

Chapter Nine

THE RESURGENCE OF JAPAN, SOVIET RUSSIA, AND NAZI GERMANY

I. WORLD POLITICS IN THE DEPRESSION

THROUGH the decade following the signing of the Treaty of Versailles, the divisions between and within the victorious states were clear for all to see. These divisions made it possible for Turkey to compel the abandonment of the Treaty of Sèvres and the negotiation of a new settlement at Lausanne. Other parts of the Peace of Paris were revised, most notably with regard to reparation. Through the decade, however, the beneficiaries of the peace treaties so patently had the power to enforce obedience that, except in the case of Turkey, open rebellion against the treaties could not succeed. Instead, the Washington treaties of 1922, the Locarno Pact, and the Kellogg-Briand Pact seemed to strengthen the Peace of Paris.

After 1929, rebellion against the Treaty of Versailles gathered strength in Germany. In Italy, Mussolini was increasingly vehement in his denunciation of the territorial settlement established by the Peace of Paris. As in the past, the Soviet Union continued to denounce both the territorial settlement and the League of Nations as the handiwork of capitalist imperialism. Nevertheless, when Germany's Chancellor Brüning abandoned Stresemann's policy of "understanding" and attempted a customs union between Germany and Austria in 1931, he was compelled to abandon the attempt. To most observers at the time, it seemed that after 1931 the possibility of a successful revolt of Germany against the Treaty of Versailles became more remote, that Hitler could hope for less from the victors of 1918 than Brüning.

In the event, the opposite proved true. Step by step the victors retreated, and Hitler moved from one success to another. Central to an understanding of this unexpected reversal is the effect of the depression on political life: everywhere, the depression encouraged isolation and made international cooperation more difficult. The unsuccessful efforts to cope with the Japanese seizure of Manchuria after September, 1931, were symptomatic of the barriers to cooperative action, and strengthened the barriers. Simultaneously, the disarmament conference was making painfully clear both the intensity of popular feeling in Britain and the United States against war and expenditure on armaments, and the unwillingness of those countries to undertake any obligations for the preservation of peace which might entail the use of force to prevent aggression.

With the failure of the International Economic Conference in London in July, 1933, and the collapse of the disarmament conference in October, the government and the people of Britain and of the United States turned away from collective efforts to achieve disarmament and security, and concentrated their attention on the task of coping with the depression at home. It was at this moment that the spectacular revival of German and Russian power brought into question the stability of the territorial settlement, particularly in central and southeastern Europe, imposed by the Peace of Paris. More completely than in the decade after 1919, the stability of that settlement now depended on the power and the resolution of France. By 1933, however, the depression had spread into France and was undermining both power and resolution.

2. THE BREAKDOWN OF THE "RULE OF LAW" IN EAST ASIA, 1929–1933

Between the summer of 1931, when financial panic forced President Hoover to propose a moratorium on the debt payments of Germany and Austria, and the summer of 1933, when the Nazis had consolidated their hold on Germany, neither the people nor the government of Britain or the United States gave more than sporadic attention to foreign affairs; the depression was too immediately important.

The British, after a few tense weeks in the summer of 1931, settled to the task of economic reconstruction, soberly and with no apparent plan; only slowly did it become apparent that the British people were drawing in on themselves and attempting to insulate their country from Europe and from the world outside the Empire. The National government formed on August 24, 1931, was intended to tide over the crisis which had already paralyzed Austrian and German finance and which threatened the financial stability of Britain. To meet the crisis, the government prepared to balance the budget by the very orthodox method of cutting expenses. Promptly there were protests from those whose pay was to be slashed, from schoolteachers and more dramatically from the seamen of the fleet. Whether or not the disobedience of seamen at Invergordon on September 15 should be called mutiny is debatable, but it did bring action. A week later the government abruptly cut loose from financial orthodoxy. The gold standard was abandoned; the pound promptly fell to about $3.80. The decision to abandon the gold standard was followed by announcement that the wage cuts, civil and military, would be much less drastic than originally proposed. The government had retreated in face of protest.[1]

Now the appeal to unite behind the National government found a hearing. The election of October 27 returned an overwhelming majority of National candidates. However, the majority included National Liberal and National Labour members, and there were sharp divisions within the Conservative core of the government. Therefore, the prime minister, Ramsay MacDonald, and his titular deputy but actual mentor, Stanley Baldwin, had every reason to follow their natural inclination to avoid adventures, domestic or foreign. The value of the pound continued to fall slowly—it was about $3.40 at the end of the year—and while the decline stimulated exports it was thought a symptom of financial weakness.

The government was convinced that a revival of economic strength at home was dependent on closer economic ties with what was now usually called the Commonwealth. A round table conference went on through the autumn of 1931, searching without success for some accommodation with the nationalist movement in India; the concessions offered by the government were so strongly opposed by Conservatives like Winston Churchill that the rebels defied the party leadership. In December, the Statute of Westminster recognized the full autonomy of the dominions within the Commonwealth. In March, 1932, Parliament adopted a frankly protective tariff, and at a conference at Ottawa in the summer some headway was made toward increasing trade with the dominions—with the conspicuous exception of Ireland. The drift toward protection led to the resignation of some of the National Liberal and National Labour members, making the government more obviously conservative, but without much loss of national support.

1. For a good account of these events see R. Bassett's *Nineteen Thirty-one: Political Crisis* (London, 1958).

In fact, considering the meager legislative record and the continued high unemployment, the hold of the government on the country was remarkable. Probably much credit should go to the chancellor of the exchequer, Neville Chamberlain. To the distress of many of his Conservative colleagues, he quietly but steadily, by many unobtrusive decisions, bent the internal program of the government to the service of the masses of the British people. Men of property who felt that they were being pressed toward "socialism" chafed under his unrelenting pressure, but they could not ignore the success of Chamberlain's measures in holding the country from the much less attractive alternative of a Labour government. The idea of planning was in the air, popularized not least by the success of the five-year plan in Russia and given respectability in Britain by the "New Economics" of John Maynard Keynes and his disciples. If Britain must have a planned economy, it seemed far better to have the planning done by a government which was conservative in fact if not in name. So, without enthusiasm, and certainly not from affection, Neville Chamberlain came to be recognized as the future leader of British conservatism. As yet, however, he was little known to the British people. The National Liberal foreign minister, Sir John Simon, also made little impression on the country. Ramsay MacDonald had lost his standing with his old supporters when he broke with Labour to head the National government. However, his life-long devotion to peace gave a comfortable sense of security to a people hungry for quiet, and Stanley Baldwin's frank insularity gave added assurance of isolation from the storms sweeping across so much of the world outside Britain. By 1933, the rise in unemployment had at least been checked, and there were hopeful signs that the economy was reviving. The National government no longer was thought a temporary expedient; its hold on power was unchallengeable, so long as the calm continued.

The calm seemed the more precious by contrast with the turbulence of American politics in the depression years. The Congress was incapable of positive action, and President Hoover's prestige was so damaged by the depression that his proposals commanded little respect in the Congress. Viewed from Europe, it seemed that the United States was, like Germany, paralyzed by wrangling factions. In the election of November, 1932, the Democrats won a majority in both houses of the Congress, and the Democratic candidate, Franklin

Delano Roosevelt, was elected President. This merely intensified the paralysis during the months between the election in November and the beginning of the new administration in March, 1933.

Superficially, during the depression years the American people and their government were in agreement on one subject, foreign policy. The agreement was that the United States should hold aloof from the rest of the world, should, according to President Hoover's adaptation of St. Paul's injunction to the early Christians, be in the world but not of it.[2] The President and most of the people were determined that the country would not be "dragged" into another war. They hated expenditure for armaments, chiefly because they were convinced that the arms race would lead to another war, but also because the money spent on arms should be put to productive use. They had agreed to the temporary suspension of payments on intergovernmental debts in the summer of 1931 to halt the spread of financial panic, but they were determined to collect the war debts. If Europeans did not pay the debts they would simply spend the money on arms, ran the American argument; the debts were valid obligations which should be respected, just as treaties should be respected. Above all, the Washington treaties should be respected, both in their restriction of naval armament and in their guarantee of the independence and integrity of China.

Here lay the possibility of conflict. American policy was unalterably opposed to the use of force in international affairs; American policy also demanded respect for treaties, and especially the Washington treaties. How was the use of force to be prevented? And how was violation of treaties to be prevented without using force?

These questions had arisen briefly and ambiguously early in the Hoover administration. Like the British, the Americans had adopted a tolerant attitude toward the inroads of Chinese nationalism on foreign treaty rights during the triumphant northern march of the Kuomintang. The occupation of Peking by forces of the Kuomintang in June, 1928, and the transfer of the government to Nanking did not, however, bring stability. Communists controlled parts of Kiangsi and Fukien and were active underground in much of China; war lords continued

2. On American policy during the Hoover administration see A. Rappaport, *Henry L. Stimson and Japan, 1931–1933* (Chicago, 1963), and Robert Ferrell, *American Diplomacy in the Great Depression: Hoover-Stimson Foreign Policy, 1929–1933* (New Haven, 1957).

to dominate large parts of the country; Manchuria had an almost independent regime; the Kuomintang itself was rent by factions united only by their nationalism. Chiang Kai-shek continued his endeavor to turn the antiforeign sentiment against what seemed the weakest and most isolated of the Great Powers, the Soviet Union. Friction came to a climax in 1929, when Manchurian troops forcibly expelled the Russians from operation of the Chinese Eastern Railway. The Russians threatened, without result. Then Soviet troops invaded northern Manchuria and resumed control over the railway. The incident came at an awkward time, just when the Kellogg-Briand Pact for the renunciation of war was proclaimed in an elaborate ceremony in Washington. Secretary of State Stimson appealed to both the Chinese and the Russians not to use force. The Russians harshly rebuffed American intervention, and in the end the Chinese agreed to reestablishment of Russian control over the railway zone in northern Manchuria.

To Stimson, as to most Americans, the failure of the effort to invoke the Kellogg-Briand Pact and the obvious success of force in Manchuria did not invalidate or even weaken the pact. Neither did it suggest the need for mobilizing force in support of the pact. The pact should be strengthened, Stimson wrote in November, 1930, "not by seeking to add extraneous sanctions of force, but by providing the machinery for enlightening and strengthening the present sanction of public opinion."[3] That machinery was set in motion in January, 1931, by the announcement of the League council that the long-awaited disarmament conference would convene in February, 1932. Particularly in the United States and Great Britain a multitude of organizations began to mobilize support for the conference; petitions urging peace through disarmament were signed by millions of people.

Meanwhile, almost unnoticed, new tension was growing in the Far East, where Chinese nationalism was now turned against Japan. On the one hand, the Chinese built railways parallel with Japan's South Manchurian Railway to undermine the value of the treaty rights of Japan, and Chinese were encouraged to migrate to Manchuria so that the Chinese character of the province would be strengthened. On the other hand, particularly from the summer of 1931, trade with Japan was boycotted throughout China.

The Chinese pressure precipitated a crisis in Japanese political life. Through most of the years since the Washington conference, Japan had been governed by liberals who urged cooperation with Britain, the United States, and China. From the outset this policy had been attacked by military leaders who argued that the 5:5:3 naval ratio was humiliating, and by nationalists who resented the inroads of Chinese nationalism on Japanese treaty rights in China. With the Great Depression the task of keeping Japanese foreign trade abreast of the burgeoning population of the islands became increasingly difficult. The Chinese boycott complicated this task; the encroachment of the Chinese on the Japanese position in Manchuria jeopardized the future of an area which all Japanese regarded both as an outlet for population and as a center for Japanese economic growth.[4]

On September 18, 1931, Japanese army officers in Manchuria forced the hand of the liberal government by moving out from the railway zone and clashing with Chinese troops at Mukden. In the weeks following, the Japanese government repeatedly promised to withdraw to the zone of the South Manchurian Railway, but the Japanese army continued to expand its operations.[5]

News of the clash at Mukden reached Geneva on September 19, 1931. Both the council and the assembly of the League were in session, and indeed had been considering ways of alleviating suffering in China, where floods had killed hundreds of thousands and made millions homeless. Now China was suffering military attack, in defiance of the League covenant, the Washington treaties, and the Kellogg pact. At Geneva, and very generally in western Europe and the United States, sympathy for China rose, and demands were made for intervention by the League and by the United States as the sponsor of the Kellogg pact. The governments of the Great Powers held back. The "revisionist" powers, Italy and Germany, were not anxious to establish a precedent for intervention by the League. The Soviet Union was silent; the memory of encounters with Chinese nationalism was fresh. The French government had always regarded the League primarily as a means of holding Germany in check; Manchuria was, as André

4. A useful study in the formation of Japanese policy in Manchuria is S. N. Ogata, *Defiance in Manchuria* (Berkeley, 1964); see also James Crowley, *Japan's Quest for Autonomy: National Security and Foreign Policy, 1930–1938* (Princeton, 1966).

5. See Robert H. Ferrell, "The Mukden Incident," in the *Journal of Modern History*, XXVII (1955), 66–72.

Tardieu said, a long way off; so France was unwilling to go beyond conciliatory gestures.

In Britain the National government was preoccupied with the currency crisis when the Japanese army attacked at Mukden; in the weeks following, the government was preoccupied with the election; after that, the government wanted quiet while the economy was recuperating.[6] Moreover, now even more than earlier, the British government regarded Japan as a bulwark against Russian expansion in East Asia. Not only in East Asia, but in India and other British possessions, Communism was growing, and Communism was thought a tool of the Soviet government.

While there was hope that the liberal government in Tokyo might restrain the Japanese military in Manchuria, the American government was also unwilling to take strong action, and supported a Japanese proposal that an international commission investigate conditions in Manchuria. The League council set up a commission, headed by Lord Lytton, which moved with relative rapidity: its report was issued in October, 1932, less than a year after the Japanese had suggested the creation of the commission.

During these months, however, the Japanese had moved more rapidly. A new cabinet, dominated by the military, took office in January, 1932. Japanese armies occupied all of China north of the Great Wall. In an effort to break the Chinese economic boycott, Japanese naval forces landed at Shanghai. When the Chinese resisted the landing, the Chapei section of the city was bombed from the air, causing great fires and much loss of life, and sending a great wave of horror through western Europe and the United States. Undeterred by the mounting protests, the Japanese organized a puppet government in Manchuria and the other conquered areas of north China. In September, Japan solemnly recognized the puppet state, now called Manchukuo, as an independent state.

Through these events, the American government tried to hold the future open by notifying the Chinese and Japanese governments that the United States would not recognize the validity of any changes brought about in violation of the Kellogg pact, that is, brought about by

6. For a study of the impact of the Manchurian crisis on British foreign policy and newspaper opinion, see R. Bassett, *Democracy and Foreign Policy, a Case Study: The Sino-Japanese Dispute 1931–1933* (London, 1952).

force. This position, which came to be called the Stimson Doctrine of Nonrecognition, was applauded in the United States. Initially, no European government followed the American lead, but after the bombardment of Shanghai the League assembly accepted the Stimson doctrine.

The report of the Lytton Commission, while stressing Chinese violations of Japanese treaty rights in Manchuria, concluded that the province should remain part of China, with international protection for the treaty rights of other states. After futile efforts to negotiate a compromise settlement, the League assembly accepted the recommendations of the commission on February 24, 1933. A month later, Japan withdrew from the League of Nations.

So far as one can estimate, the American government and the assembly of the League of Nations had gone about as far as the American people and the peoples of western Europe were prepared to go: Japanese use of military force had been condemned, and the existence of the puppet state of Manchukuo was not recognized by members of the League or by the United States. The view was frequently expressed that the pressure of world public opinion would, in the end, be effective in restraining Japan, but this claim had an increasingly hollow sound. Instead of turning against the aggressive policy of their government, the Japanese people were angered by the censure of other governments and united behind their own government. Similarly, the Japanese economy did not crack under the pressure of hostile foreign opinion. Instead, the Japanese people accepted the lowered standard of living which followed from the decision of their government to stimulate exports by drastically cutting the value of the currency. Soon other countries were desperately seeking to stop the import of cheap Japanese goods. These efforts had small success. By 1933 Japanese exports were rising rapidly, and the efforts to exclude Japanese products merely strengthened the conviction of the Japanese people that their country must acquire more territory, by force if necessary.

Very early the states most immediately concerned with the fate of Manchuria decided that American and League censure was unlikely to change the situation imposed by Japanese arms. In May, 1933, a truce was signed by the Chinese, not only leaving Manchuria and Jehol in Japanese control, but establishing a demilitarized zone south of the Great Wall. The Soviet Union in the same month made the first of many offers to sell Russian rights in the Chinese Eastern Railway. Since the Japanese had closed the border between Manchuria and Siberia, the railway had no value to the Russians, and the Russians were not prepared to defend their rights in north Manchuria by arms against strong Japan, as they had a few years earlier against weak China.

Despite all talk of the irresistible power of public opinion, therefore, the American doctrine of nonrecognition, like the assembly vote accepting the recommendations of the Lytton Commission, had failed to turn back Japan. Manchukuo was unrecognized, but Manchuria and Jehol were now, for all practical purposes, Japanese possessions. Of even greater importance for the future was the defiant isolation of Japan, now outside the League, arming rapidly, determined to win further gains.

Few were willing to recognize these ugly facts. It was comforting to hope that Japan would, in the end, be chastened by the disapproval of world opinion or by inability to keep its economy functioning. More important, the crisis in the Far East as it slowly unfolded from the autumn of 1931 through the spring of 1933, if squarely faced, would have provided too terrible a commentary on the efforts to preserve peace by disarmament which were proceeding through the din of battle.

3. THE DISARMAMENT CONFERENCE, 1932-1933

It was hard not to conclude that the disarmament conference was rather a mockery, as Secretary Stimson said, when the opening of the conference, on February 2, 1932, was delayed for an hour so that the League council could discuss the bombs falling on the helpless population of Shanghai. After the delay the presentation of petitions and the almost endless speeches began. Slowly the usual divisions appeared.[7] The Germans again asserted the injustice of keeping Germany disarmed while others were armed. The Russians again proposed general and complete disarmament. The Italians, despite Mussolini's earlier praise of the beauty of machine guns and airplanes, again professed willingness to accept arms reductions, no matter how drastic, as long as Italian military strength had equality with that of France. The French

---

7. J. W. Wheeler-Bennett, *The Pipe Dream of Peace* (N.Y., 1935), is a history of the disarmament conference up to the summer of 1934.

presented an unusually elaborate plan for an international security system with its own police force. The British and Americans again asked for "qualitative" disarmament, that is, for the abolition or reduction of "offensive" weapons.

For six weeks the deluge of speeches and projects continued; then the conference took a long Easter recess, leaving the experts to discuss the various plans. The discussion merely deepened the old division: the Germans insisted on an equality which the French refused to accept until they had assurance of armed support if rearmed Germany attacked; the British and American governments, and peoples, supported the German demand for equality, but refused to be drawn further into the quarrels of Europe.

On June 22, against the advice of his own Secretary of State and without consulting other governments, President Hoover sought to "cut through the brush" by proposing what he called a "broad and definite method of reducing the overwhelming burden of armament which now lies upon the toilers of the world." Roughly what he proposed was the abolition of all "offensive" weapons and the reduction of all other forces by one-third. Hoover's move was dramatic, simple, sweeping. It was greeted with great enthusiasm. The Russian, Italian, and German delegates to the conference hastened to give their approval. Yet it was, as Stimson said, "just a proposition from Alice in Wonderland." The distinction between "offensive" and "defensive" weapons was easily blurred: one of the American delegates was then "sitting in the Sea Commission, blowing great clouds of smoke from his cigar and demonstrating in fervid Southern eloquence that battleships were the most defensive of all types of weapons; they became a symbol of the American home and family, they could be given to children to play with as toys, so harmless was their use and purpose."[8] At a time when the cry to overthrow the Treaty of Versailles by force was rising in Germany, Hoover called on France to reduce her armed forces more than a third. Finally, what was happening in the Far East made a mockery of Hoover's guiding principle: "The Kellogg-Briand Pact, to which we are all signatories, can only mean that the nations of the world have agreed that they will use their arms solely for defense."

8. Senator Claude Swanson, as described by Hugh R. Wilson, *Diplomat Between Wars* (N.Y., 1941), p. 268.

Very quickly, the Hoover plan was buried, and the conference adjourned for the summer.

The debate on adjournment produced a new crisis. The German delegate announced that Germany would take no further part in the conference until the principle of equality of rights was accepted. For months the British and American delegates sought to reconcile the German demand for equality with the French demand for security. Finally, a formula acceptable to all was devised: the disarmament conference would seek an agreement giving Germany "equality of rights in a system which would provide security for all nations." There now seemed only the problem of implementing these words; the conference was asked to convene again on January 31, 1933.

By then Hitler was in power and in every German city his brown-and black-shirted followers were marching in military formation shouting for freedom from Versailles. In France the spectacle of these marching columns raised new apprehension. Without repudiating the agreement of December, the French government emphasized the security system promised in the formula. To the British government, however, the very violence of feeling in Germany made more desirable some definite agreement which, by replacing the hated "dictate" of Versailles, would at once placate the Germans and set limits on German action. On March 16, MacDonald presented a detailed draft treaty to the conference. If accepted, the draft treaty would replace the disarmament clauses of Versailles and give Germany equality with other powers within five years; definite limits were set on the armament of all powers; a disarmament commission was to supervise the execution of the agreement, with full power of investigation; rather vaguely, to placate the French, the draft provided for consultation between signatories of the Kellogg pact in case there was a breach of the pact. Again, hopes rose. The MacDonald plan was accepted as a basis for discussion, and the conference adjourned for a month to enable the various delegations to study the plan closely.

Immediately MacDonald embarked on another scheme to bring the unruly Nazi government into definite agreement with other states. From Geneva, MacDonald and Simon went to Rome on March 18. There Mussolini suggested a Four-Power Pact between Italy, Britain, France, and Germany by which the members would work together to ensure the peace and in particular would give Germany arms equality "by stages" and make needed treaty revisions "within the framework of the League."[9] MacDonald took up the idea; again there was delay while the French and Germans were consulted.

During the delay, opinion shifted in Britain. In part the shift resulted from disgust with Nazi brutality toward Jews and political opponents. In part the shift resulted from fear that supposedly disarmed Germany already possessed a formidable force in the uniformed party organizations.[10] The shift in British opinion was short-lived, but the French government exploited the changed situation with skill. In successive drafts the text of the Four-Power Pact was altered so that it became, in effect, merely a reaffirmation of existing obligations under the League covenant, the Locarno treaties and the Kellogg pact. As for the Mac-Donald plan, the French withheld for the moment their own objections and merely supported the British in repelling German demands for greater freedom to arm. Rapidly, Hitler lost patience. "The disarmament question will not be solved at the conference table," he told his ministers on May 12. "There is no historical instance where a victor accorded arms to the vanquished through negotiations."[11] Rumors spread that at a speech before the Reichstag on May 17 Hitler would withdraw from the disarmament conference.

On May 16, the new American President, Roosevelt, intervened with an appeal to all governments not to take action which might jeopardize the success either of the disarmament conference or of the economic conference which was soon to meet in London. Whether or not his message made Hitler draw back is not known. Certainly Hitler's speech did not reflect his mood of a few days earlier; instead it was a most eloquent appeal for peace through disarmament, a statement of Germany's need and desire for peace which carried conviction

9. See K. H. Jarausch's well-documented dissertation *The Four Power Pact, 1933* (Madison, 1966); Charles Bloch, *Hitler und die europäischen Mächte 1933/1934: Kontinuität oder Bruch* (Frankfurt, 1966); and K. D. Bracher, "Das Anfangsstadium der Hitlerschen Aussenpolitik," *Vierteljahrshefte für Zeitgeschichte*, V (Jan., 1957), 63–76.

10. *Documents on German Foreign Policy*, Series C, Vol. I (Washington, 1957), p. 405. The shaping of the British image of Nazism is described by Brigitte Granzow in her study *A Mirror of Nazism: British Opinion and the Emergence of Hitler, 1929–1933* (London, 1964).

11. *Documents on German Foreign Policy*, Series C, Vol. I (Washington, 1957), p. 410.

to a Europe hungry to believe. Within a few days the innocuous text of the Four-Power Pact was completed; it was signed on June 8.

A change followed the "scuttling" of the London economic conference by President Roosevelt on July 3. The enthusiasm with which the President's action was greeted in the United States showed clearly that the cooperation of the American government with the League of Nations in the years just past had little popular support. The American Congress was already debating measures designed to prevent the United States from involvement in another European war.

Again, it is impossible to make a clear connection between American and German action. However, when he had set forth his views in *Mein Kampf*, Hitler had shown respect for American strength and had seen the "linguistic and cultural communion" of Britain and the United States as a unique element in British power. Just as the moderation of Hitler in May was probably influenced by the vigorous intervention of President Roosevelt in European affairs, so the increasing truculence of Hitler from the summer of 1933 was probably encouraged by the conviction that effective opposition from the United States or cooperation between Britain and America was no longer to be feared.

In any case, as the summer advanced Hitler struck out more confidently against the Jews and his other victims at home, threatened more openly to bring about the "reunion" with Austria which he had promised in the first sentences of *Mein Kampf*, showed more clearly his determination to end the Rapallo policy of cooperation with the Soviet Union, and pressed more vigorously the scarcely concealed rearmament of Germany.

The change in Germany brought a change in Britain, and in particular brought second thoughts about granting equality in armament to Germany. At the suggestion of the French, Sir John Simon modified the MacDonald plan: during a preliminary period of four years, there would be an arms truce while a permanent disarmament commission was demonstrating that a system of investigation and control was feasible; only after these four years, and after the commission had shown ability to discover and end illegal military preparation, would disarmament begin. In other words, the treaty barrier to German rearmament would continue for at least four years more, and the commission would end the illegal German rearmament which, everyone knew, was advancing rapidly. Simon introduced his revision of the MacDonald plan at Geneva on October 14. On the same day, Hitler withdrew from the disarmament conference and announced that Germany would withdraw from the League of Nations. For all practical purposes, the German withdrawal ended the conference. In form, it continued; there was one general meeting, in May, 1934, and the conference was never officially ended, but in reality the search for disarmament finally failed in September, 1933.

The moral drawn in the United States was that safety lay in the isolation made possible by two protecting oceans. In Britain the dread of war and the desire for isolation from continental rivalries were strong, but the English Channel was narrow and British sea power was of small help against air power.

The mood in which the British people confronted their changed position was expressed, and in part shaped, by a speech of Stanley Baldwin in the House of Commons on November 10, 1932, in the course of a debate on the disarmament conference. He accepted without question the assumptions of what was already called the "Douhet theory," although the writings of the Italian general Giulio Douhet had not yet been translated into English: that no effective defense against air power was possible and that bombardment of population centers would bring victory.[12] "The man in the street" must realize, Baldwin said, that "the bomber will always get through." The only defense, the only road to victory, was "to kill more women and children more quickly than the enemy." He saw no prospect that limitation on the size or use of military aircraft could end the peril. The peril would end only if "the conscience of the young men," the young men who must fly the planes and drop the bombs, recognized that this one instrument of war was evil and must go. "But when the next war comes, and European civilization is wiped out, as it will be and by no force more than by that force, then do not let them lay the blame upon the old men. Let them remember that they, they principally or they alone, are responsible for the terrors that have fallen upon the earth."[13]

So far as many of the youth of Britain were concerned, Baldwin was preaching to the converted. A few weeks later, on February 9, 1933, the Oxford Union resolved by a large majority: "That this House will in

12. Edward M. Earle (ed.), *Makers of Modern Strategy* (Princeton, 1943), pp. 489–97.
13. *Parliamentary Debates,* Commons, Fifth Series, Vol. 270, cols. 632, 638.

no circumstances fight for its King or country." When there was protest against the vote, the motion was reaffirmed by a much larger majority, and very quickly similar motions were carried at other British colleges and universities.

The failure of the disarmament conference intensified the drift of British opinion against war. In October, 1933, there was a by-election in the "safe" Conservative constituency of East Fulham. Duff Cooper, a supporter of the Conservative candidate, had just returned from the continent, and reported that "Germany was preparing for war on a scale and with an enthusiasm unmatched in history." When he addressed a meeting in East Fulham he was greeted with violent hostility; he could not be heard until police arrived and imposed order. The National candidate argued that Britain must strengthen its defenses in face of German rearmament. The Labour candidate said the issue was "Peace versus War"; his campaign posters stressed the horrors of war; his supporters equated disarmament with peace and, by inference, equated warnings against the rising military strength of Germany with desire for war. When the poll was counted, there was a Labour majority of nearly five thousand; in 1931 there had been a National majority of fourteen thousand.[14]

Later, Stanley Baldwin justified his failure to strengthen the defenses of Britain by fear of repudiation at the polls: "That feeling that was given expression to in Fulham was common throughout the country."[15] This was only part of the story. Baldwin had helped to create, and in part shared, the feeling which found expression in the East Fulham by-election. And he was not alone. With rare exceptions the political and intellectual leaders of the Western democracies moved with increasing bewilderment through the years which, on the one hand, saw the establishment of totalitarian rule in four of the seven Great Powers and the spread of dictatorship through much of Europe, and on the other hand saw a resurgence of violence in international politics and the collapse of hope of peace through disarmament.

In 1929 even an observer like Winston Churchill, who prided himself on his "realism," was confident that the treaties of Washington and

14. Alfred Duff Cooper, *Old Men Forget* (N.Y., 1954), pp. 182, 183; The London *Times,* Oct. 10, 14, 18, 19, 24, 25, 26, 27, 1933.

15. Speech of November 12, 1936. *Parliamentary Debates,* Commons, Fifth Series, Vol. 317, col. 1144.

Locarno had laid solid foundations for the building of an international community through the League of Nations and the Kellogg pact. The building did not, he believed, depend on the altruism of man, but rather on the instinct of self-preservation. The alternative to the international community was the "international anarchy" of armed states which had reached its inevitable conclusion in four years of wasting war; the return of international anarchy would mean the return of war, and there was general agreement that another war meant the end of European civilization, if not, as Churchill warned, the extermination of mankind.

By 1933 Japan, under military rule, had won Manchuria by war, had successfully defied the public opinion which Sir John Simon had called "one of the most terrific forces in nature," and was planning new wars; in Italy and Germany the marching columns of "disciplined, strong young men" were singing praise of war; in Russia, flushed with the success of the five-year plan, there was confident expectation that, as Lenin had prophesied, the twentieth century would see "a series of frightful collisions," culminating in the triumph of Communism. In face of these developments, the American government, under President Hoover and Secretary Stimson, had tried to mobilize public opinion in support of the Kellogg pact, without success. President Roosevelt had, at the outset, tried even more vigorously to provide leadership for the international community, only to draw back and cooperate with the Congress in seeking to insulate America from the conflicts which impended. Britain stood perplexed, fearful of the consequences alike of arming and of failing to arm. Undoubtedly the government was partly responsible for the passivity of British policy; as Churchill said, Baldwin's speech on the horror and decisiveness of aerial bombardment spread about "a certain helplessness and hopelessness." But the vigor with which the voters in East Fulham repelled arguments for rearmament fortified official reluctance to recognize that the international community did not exist, and that international anarchy, for all its fateful implications, was a fact. So, in public at least, MacDonald continued to hope for an arms agreement with Germany which would avert an arms race. As for France, all through 1933 the foreign minister, Joseph Paul-Boncour, had muttered threats that he would reveal German violations of the disarmament clauses of the Treaty of Versailles and force compliance with the treaty. When, however, Hitler left the disarmament conference and the League of Nations, the French government did nothing. Indeed it was hard to say that France had a government in any real sense. A cabinet crisis was beginning in France when Hitler left the conference. The cabinet formed on October 26 gave way to another on November 27, and to a third on January 30, 1934. A week later Paris was the scene of riots which seemed the prelude of civil war. Since 1918, through fifteen years, French power had towered over Europe. Now, quite suddenly, and just as German power was beginning to rise, France fell prey to factional strife which called into question the military power which had, from its signature, sustained the Versailles settlement.

4. THE SECOND FIVE-YEAR PLAN AND THE GREAT PURGE IN RUSSIA

By 1933 the first Soviet five-year plan was completed; the second started in 1932, although it was not formally adopted until the seventeenth party congress, the "Congress of Victors," in 1934. The first plan had brought a spectacular growth of industrial production. As yet, however, it was far from certain that the Soviet economy could stand the pace of enforced expansion; doubt was intensified outside of Russia by reports of famine which filtered through the rigid censorship.

In fact, the pace was not only maintained but accelerated during the years after 1933. At the time, in the absence of reliable statistics, it was impossible to measure Soviet industrial growth with any accuracy, and wildly conflicting estimates found ready acceptance. In retrospect, the growth was remarkable: according to the best estimates, from 1929 through 1936 Soviet industrial production grew at an average annual rate of 12 per cent or more, with gains of much more than this rate in each of the years from 1933 through 1936. On the other hand, it is now evident that the rate of growth slowed drastically, beginning in 1937, as resources were shifted to preparation for war and as the country was convulsed by the Great Purge.[16] This slowing was not apparent at the time.

In the great propaganda campaign which accompanied the launching of the second five-year plan, as earlier with the first, emphasis was placed on the production of consumer goods, and again the promise

16. Gregory Grossman, "Thirty Years of Soviet Industrialisation," *Soviet Survey*, No. 26 (Oct.–Dec., 1958), p. 17.

was forgotten in practice. With the good harvest of 1934 the food situation improved, and for a time rationing was ended, but for the great majority of Russians food was limited to the basic monotonous diet. Housing and other amenities were again postponed. In the second, as in the first, plan emphasis was on expanding the industrial base, but in the second plan expansion was geographical. Whole new industrial complexes—that is, everything from mining to finished products—were built in Siberia and Turkestan, far removed from the western and eastern frontiers and therefore from territory which might be overrun by invading armies. The widely separated industrial centers were linked by new roads, canals, and railroads, as well as by lines for the transmission of electricity. As before, the capital for this construction was secured by enforced saving, that is, by holding down the standard of living.

Since the first plan had already drained the great pool of surplus labor from the countryside to the cities, the second plan laid emphasis on increasing labor productivity, what each laborer produced. As usual, the campaign for increased productivity was launched with a fanfare of propaganda. On August 31, 1935, in a carefully planned and dramatically staged test, Aleksei Stakhanov mined 102 tons of coal in a single work shift, thirteen times the normal production. He was held up as a hero and exemplar. The whole year 1936 was called the Stakhanov Year; other "Stakhanovites" appeared in other fields of labor, and they also became heroes. Under cover of the organized enthusiasm, pay scales were shifted to piecework, with bonuses for production above the norm, and norms raised as efficiency spread.

Much was possible by holding out the incentive of higher wages and by depressing the basic rate to the bare level of subsistence. But even more could be accomplished by technical education and by changing work habits so that regularity and punctuality improved.

The campaign for increased productivity produced a revolution in education. Earlier, Soviet education had been, in Western terms, "permissive" and "progressive." Now the sexes were segregated, the children were put into uniform, emphasis was placed on set tasks in basic subjects, the authority of the teacher over his students was strengthened. At all levels of instruction technical and scientific subjects were given priority. By every possible inducement, the better students were pushed into technology and science; the humanities could be left to slower minds.

The lower schools produced skilled workers for the machines. There was even more pressing need for managers and engineers. In the decade 1929-39 the number of students in the higher technical schools and universities grew from fewer than 200,000 to more than 600,000. This vast expansion produced too many badly trained engineers and scientists, but the dependence of the Soviet Union on foreign specialists was ending, and, of capital importance, there were plenty of eager youngsters waiting for the jobs of those who disappeared in the Great Purge.

Behind the school was the family. Here again there was a revolution. In the early years of the Soviet Union the family had been viewed with suspicion as a transmitter of bourgeois and Christian values. Therefore divorce and abortion had been made easy to secure, and children had been regarded as charges of the state and not of the family. All that changed with the need for order, discipline, and regularity, and also with the need for more workers. Divorce and abortion were frowned upon; the family with many children became the ideal and received financial rewards; within the family both the authority and the responsibility of the parents were emphasized.

Culture was also harnessed to production. With the five-year plans, the experiment and variety of earlier Soviet music, art, and literature became a menace to the temper Stalin was inculcating. In 1929 literature came under the dictatorial control of the Association of Proletarian Writers (RAPP). The result was a deadly uniformity fatal even to propaganda effectiveness. In 1932 Stalin broke the power of RAPP and set up a Union of Soviet Writers to produce a literature based on "Soviet realism." Soviet realism was a vague term at the outset. By trial and error, costly error, Soviet writers found that what Stalin wanted was literature with a broad popular appeal, literature which ceaselessly praised the Soviet rulers and their five-year plans, literature which helped to produce the "Soviet man," that is, the model Stakhanovite who eagerly did everything he was supposed to do when he was supposed to do it.

What was true of literature was true of the other arts. All must reach the masses, all must generate enthusiasm, immediately for Stalin and his five-year plans, in a larger sense for the Soviet Union; that is, all must inculcate "Soviet patriotism."

Here was another strange hybrid. Until his death in 1932, the study of Russian history was dominated by M. N. Pokrovski, whose writings had been much admired by Lenin. Pokrovski was an economic determinist whose devotion to Communism made him depict the history of czarist Russia as a dark record of exploitation at home and aggressive imperialism abroad. In 1934 Stalin himself joined in a growing attack on Pokrovski. Soviet historians began groping for a new interpretation which would make Bolshevism the legitimate heir and the culmination of earlier Russian history. So Peter the Great became the first Bolshevik; czarist generals who had repelled invaders like Napoleon became ancestors of the Red army; even Ivan the Terrible became the heroic discipliner of the Russian people. Soviet patriotism, then, was pride in what Russians had done, what they were doing in the five-year plans, and what their country would be when, under Stalin's benign direction, its industrial power matched the greatness of the historic Russian character.

Inevitably, it was hard to fit religion into Soviet patriotism; the ideological and practical difficulties of an accommodation were almost insuperable. In the thirties atheism continued to be preached, churches were closed, and the clergy were among the groups hardest hit by the Great Purge. But already there was the suggestion that in the past Orthodox Christianity had been a civilizing influence, and there were tentative hints of accommodation with a properly Sovietized Orthodoxy, if that could be achieved. In the Stalin constitution of 1936, for the first time, priests were given the right to vote.

The results of all these changes were encouraging. In impressive numbers, the new "Soviet man" was emerging, a man very like an early Victorian middle-class Englishman, except in his enthusiastic obedience to the will of his government. The rewards for conformity were great. The ideal of equality of income was discarded and denounced even for party members. A new "intelligentsia" of technicians, engineers, and scientists, of plant managers and administrators, of artists, writers, and musicians, of film actors and directors, of journalists and radio commentators, of police and military officers, was growing in both numbers and affluence. By 1939 possibly 10 million Soviet citizens were in this "stratum," to use the Soviet euphemism for what would be called a class in capitalist society. They constituted less than 15 per cent of Soviet workers, yet they received more than a third of the national income, more than all the city workers, more even than the peasants who were still more than half of the population. Moreover, there were signs that this was becoming a hereditary "stratum." Until 1933 almost two-thirds of the students in the higher schools were required to be children of workers; by 1938 the children of workers made up only about a third of the student body, and they were far outnumbered by students from the "stratum" of the intelligentsia.

Viewed from one side, therefore, a new and "socialist" society was taking form with breathtaking speed and changing agricultural Russia into an industrial giant. The capstone of this Russia was set in place by the new Stalin constitution. The decision to replace the constitution of 1924 was made in 1935. Stalin was chairman of the drafting committee; Nikolai Bukharin and Karl Radek, soon to be purged, did a large part of the drafting. The draft was approved by the party central committee on June 1, 1936. Soviet citizens were then invited to suggest changes. Meetings were held in every part of the Soviet Union; about 150,000 suggestions were made, and a few were considered seriously. In November, 1936, the finished document was unanimously adopted by the Eighth Congress of Soviets.

The new constitution made several changes in the formal structure of government. The suffrage was to be equal and universal, and voting was to be secret. Citizens voted directly for the two houses of the Supreme Soviet—the Soviet of the Union and the Soviet of Nationalities. In joint session, the two houses elected the Presidium, whose chairman was to be the titular head of state, and the Council of Ministers, which was, in form, the equivalent of a Western cabinet. The Soviet Union was declared to be a federal state of eleven republics which were said to have the right to secede from the union.

The citizens were declared to have great rights: the right to work; the right to rest and leisure; the right to maintenance in old age, sickness, or incapacity; the right to education; and freedom of speech, of the press, of assembly, and of street processions and demonstrations. Women had equal rights with men; all nationalities and races were said to have equal rights; "freedom of religious worship and freedom of anti-religious propaganda is recognized for all citizens." The Communist party was described as "the vanguard of the working people in their struggle to strengthen and develop the socialist system," and as "the leading core of all organizations of the working people, both public and state."

It is impossible to know why Stalin had a fundamental law prepared which stood in such glaring contrast to the reality of Soviet life. Probably, in part, he was holding before the Russian people a vision of what might be when the Great Purge had eliminated all traitors and when the five-year plans had brought abundance; he had used this diversion earlier, when he promised riches to the peasants whose standard of living he was forcing down. Probably, in part, the constitution was written with an eye to public opinion in the West, now that Stalin was advocating a popular front against Fascism. After all, in practice his power was not impaired by a clause guaranteeing "the inviolability of the homes of citizens and privacy of correspondence," a clause which, read in western Europe or America, sounded so liberal, and a clause the good faith of which could be impugned only by the laborious, boring, and inconclusive accumulation of examples of homes entered and correspondence opened. The propaganda effectiveness of the verbal grant of rights in the constitution can be measured by a comparison of the space given in Western writings at the time, and even later, to the provisions of the constitution, and to the Great Purge.

The Great Purge was the other side of Soviet Russia.[17] Despite the patient study of many experts, there is much about the Great Purge which remains "inexplicable and mysterious," as Khrushchev was to say in his speech on the "Cult of the Individual" at the twentieth party congress on February 25, 1956. The mystery begins with the murder of Stalin's "protégé," S. M. Kirov, the young party boss of Leningrad, on December 1, 1935. For long it was believed, on Stalin's authority, that Kirov was murdered by the Left opposition because he was reputed to be Stalin's heir. Another of Stalin's young men, Andrei Zhdanov, went to Leningrad to weed out the plotters. There were executions, and thousands were sent to prison camps. Khrushchev, in his speech, hinted strongly that Kirov's murder was instigated by the secret police, known by 1935 as the NKVD, the People's Commissariat of Internal Affairs. Some Western scholars go further than Khrushchev and say Stalin ordered Kirov murdered because he had protested against the terror used to compel fulfillment of the five-year plans.

After the penalties exacted for Kirov's murder, there was a lull. Then, in August, 1936, came the Trial of the Sixteen. These were Old

17. Robert Conquest, *The Great Terror: Stalin's Purge of the Thirties* (London, 1968), sifts a mountain of evidence and comes as close to being "definitive" as one can hope, considering how much can never be known.

Bolsheviks—that is, Bolsheviks before the October revolution—who were accused of plotting with Trotsky. All, including prominent figures like Zinoviev and Kamenev, were executed. During the trial the defendants made elaborate confessions, in which they implicated other Soviet leaders in their supposed plots. Shortly afterward, one of those implicated, the old head of the trade unions, M. P. Tomski, was said to have committed suicide.

Such confessions became routine in later trials. When the confessions were subjected to analysis by foreign experts, it became obvious that many of the admissions were demonstrably false. Why the defendants made these "confessions" remains a matter of conjecture. Remarkably, in all the trials only one defendant repudiated his supposed confession in court, and even in this case, after a hasty adjournment of the proceedings, the next day he affirmed the truth of the confession he had repudiated.

The next show trial, of the Seventeen, in January, 1937, introduced a new note, plotting with foreign powers to destroy the Soviet Union. One of the defendants was the internationally famous journalist Karl Radek; his confession was unusually full of denunciations of other Soviet leaders, and he received only a prison sentence. Next, in June, 1937, it was the turn of the military. The leading generals, headed by Marshal Tukhachevski, were tried secretly, possibly because they could not be forced to accept the confessions prepared for them, and all were executed. The last of the show trials, of the Twenty-one, came in March, 1938; after this trial, the leaders of the Right opposition were killed.

These were the elaborately staged trials of men whose names were known to all Russians. Most of the victims, even most of the famous, died without public trial. Some of the Soviet leaders who were reported to have committed suicide or to have died of natural causes were probably killed. Others simply disappeared. By the time the Great Purge subsided in 1938, all of Lenin's Politburo except Stalin and the exiled Trotsky were dead; Trotsky was assassinated in Mexico in 1940. Khrushchev, in his famous speech, used another yardstick. The seventeenth party congress, he pointed out, was known as the Congress of Victors, and 80 per cent of the delegates were Bolsheviks before 1921. Yet of the 1,966 delegates, most were arrested during the Great Purge. Of the 139 members and candidate members of the Central Committee at the congress, 98 were killed. Other yardsticks have been used. They all tell the same story. By 1939 there had been a clean sweep of all who might conceivably challenge Stalin's dictatorship, right down to the chief of the NKVD under whom the purge began, Yagoda, and his successor Yezhov, who was replaced by Beria in 1938 and later killed. The chief prosecutor, Andrei Vishinsky, survived; a decade later he represented the Soviet Union at the session of the United Nations which adopted the Universal Declaration of Human Rights.

If the Great Purge had killed only the Old Bolsheviks and other party leaders who might have challenged Stalin's dictatorship, then the explanation of his biographer, Isaac Deutscher, would be plausible: that at a time when momentous and inevitably controversial decisions loomed ahead in foreign affairs, Stalin was eliminating all those around whom opposition could coalesce.[18] But the purge did not stop at the top. The terror spread out and down to touch the lives of the most obscure. According to the more conservative estimates, 7 or 8 million were arrested; other estimates range up to twice that number. Relatively few of those arrested were killed. In the years of the Great Purge the forced labor camps expanded mightily. It is estimated that there were 5 or 6 million persons in the camps in 1935-37, and about 10 million in the early forties. The NKVD administered this great pool of slave labor, which was available for the building of canals and railways or other public works in regions where free labor could not be had, or for use in mining or other hazardous occupations. On the basis of Soviet documents captured first by the Nazis and then by the American armies, it has been estimated that one-sixth or more of all new construction in the Soviet Union was done by the NKVD, using these hapless creatures.

Undoubtedly the camps were not filled just to get labor for use in northern Russia or Siberia; fear of being sent to the camps was a guarantee of the good behavior of the ordinary Soviet citizen, just as the execution of potential leaders was a guarantee of the good behavior of those in responsible positions. The shadow of terror never left the consciousness of the residents of the Soviet Union.

The elimination of so many of the old wielders of power undoubtedly was a drain on the efficiency of party, government, industry, and particularly of the armed forces. But in ever increasing numbers the

18. Isaac Deutscher, *Stalin* (N.Y., Vintage ed., 1960), pp. 375–78.

Soviet school system produced administrators, engineers, technicians, and military and police officers, who, in return for unquestioning obedience, advanced rapidly through ranks depleted by the purges. By the end of 1938, when the fury of the purges subsided, obedience was universal, and it continued, nourished by the memory of the consequences of even the suspicion of disobedience.

5. THE NAZI REVOLUTION, 1933–1939

Nazi achievements between 1933 and 1939 can be compressed into two sentences. Economically, Germany in 1933 was close to collapse, with more than 6 million—more than a third of the working population—unemployed; by 1939, German industrial production had more than doubled, and there were an estimated 2 million jobs for which no workers could be found. In 1933 Germany was a disarmed and isolated power; by 1939 all Europe trembled in fear of German power.

Seen in retrospect, the cost of these achievements can be compressed into two words, freedom and honor. Yet in 1939 to all except a few Germans it seemed that what had been won was exactly those two words, freedom and honor.

There is an inseparable connection between the shift in the economic and in the international position of Germany. It is doubtful whether the economic burdens laid on the German people would have been borne if they had not been accompanied by the dazzling successes of Hitler's diplomacy. Conversely, from the first the central objective of the Nazi economic program was rearmament, rearmament, as Hjalmar Schacht put it, "at once, out of nothing, and at first under camouflage."

In 1937, when the necessity for camouflage had ended, a German military periodical described Hjalmar Schacht, with reason, as "the man who had made the reconstruction of the Wehrmacht economically possible." His appointment as head of the Reichsbank in 1933 and as minister of economics in 1934 showed two things about Hitler. It showed that Hitler, unlike Mussolini and to a much greater extent than Stalin, was prepared to work with men of demonstrated ability. Schacht had pulled the German currency out of the morass into which it had sunk by 1923, and as president of the Reichsbank from 1923 to 1930 he had presided over the boom years of the German economy. Of greater significance, Schacht's appointment showed that if Hitler had ever taken seriously the promises of social revolution contained in the "immutable" Nazi program, he was now determined to subordinate everything to the task of rearmament.[19] The appointment of Schacht was a clear indication that, economically, the task was to be performed within the traditional structure of business and society. Similarly, the retention of the old Reichswehr leaders was clear indication that, militarily, the task was to be performed within the traditional military structure as designed by Seeckt in the early days of the Weimar Republic.

Hitler's repeated statements that the revolution was completed and his cooperation with the old industrial and military leaders ran counter to the views of a large proportion of his followers, and particularly to the plans of Ernst Röhm, the commander of the Storm Troopers (SA). The armed youths of the SA had been a great asset while the Nazis were fighting for power; now that the Nazis had power, the disorders of the Storm Troopers were a nuisance. More serious was the fact that all those who wanted a "second revolution" now joined the SA; its membership swelled to an estimated 4½ million. Finally, Röhm aspired to the headship of a "people's" militia, including both the SA and the Reichswehr. How far his plans had developed is unknown, but the Reichswehr was alarmed and demanded that Hitler suppress his ambitious subordinate. For months Hitler hesitated, probably in part because he always put off unpleasant decisions, but in part also because he always felt more secure himself when he stood as arbiter between rivals.

In the end, it was probably fear of a crisis after the obviously impending death of President Hindenburg which compelled a decision. On June 30, 1934, Hitler struck at the SA, using the rival Black Shirts (SS) and the secret police of Himmler and Heydrich as executioners. For three days there were murders, not only of Röhm and his chief followers and the rebellious Nazi Gregor Strasser, but of enemies of Hitler like Generals Schleicher and Bredow, of the chief assistants of Papen (Papen himself had shown signs of insubordination, but was apparently still considered useful), of the Catholic leader Erich

---

19. On the social changes—largely of a subjective nature—caused by Nazi rule, see *Hitler's Social Revolution: Class and Status in Nazi Germany, 1933–39*, by David Schoenbaum (Garden City, N.Y., 1966). See also the biography of Schacht by E. N. Peterson, *Hjalmar Schacht: For and Against Hitler: A Political and Economic Study of Germany, 1923–1945* (Boston, 1954).

Klausener, and even of the Bavarian leader Kahr, who had refused to join the Hitler putsch of 1923. Possibly a couple of hundred were killed in all; the whole episode is still shrouded in obscurity and apparently the records were carefully destroyed.

On July 3 the Reich government issued a law saying the murders were legal acts of "self-defense of the State." For its services, the SS was made an independent organization. Now began the rise of Heinrich Himmler as the chief instrument of Nazi terror, and of the SS as the elite of the party. As for the Reichswehr, it had stood aside passively during the murders; the generals were silent even about the murder of two of their number. Possibly in return for the suppression of the SA, the military applauded when, after President Hindenburg's death on August 2, Hitler assumed the power of the presidency; thereafter, all members of the armed forces swore an oath of loyalty to Adolf Hitler, not simply to the nation. At one stroke, on June 30 Hitler had broken all opposition within the Nazi party; in gratitude, the only rival center of power, the military, placed itself under his power. As for the German people, they ratified Hitler's assumption of supreme power in a plebiscite, by a vote of nearly 38½ million out of a total of 45½ million. Thereafter, individuals might oppose Hitler. Schacht, for instance, was to call for a slowing of the pace of rearmament, and he, like the others who challenged Hitler's policies, was dismissed. Other individuals disappeared into concentration camps. Small groups met secretly to plot the overthrow of the Nazis. But opposition of dangerous proportions never reappeared until Germany was nearing defeat in the Second World War.

The "second revolution" had been averted, but under the pressure of rearmament, revolutionary change did take place almost unnoticed. There was change in economic relations with the rest of the world. All imports and exports were controlled by the state, and Schacht's financial genius was shown by his skill in so balancing imports and exports that German industry received all essential imports and enough foodstuffs were imported for current needs and military stockpiles without impairing the value of the currency. Within Germany, controls were no less complete. A Food Estate controlled agricultural production, distribution, and prices. The peasant was glorified as the truest representative of the German race, and he was protected against foreign competition. However, despite the provision of cheap fertilizers and other favors, there was little increase in agricultural production; like Soviet totalitarianism, Nazi totalitarianism was least successful in agriculture.

Industry came under a dual control—by type and by region. Businessmen who had expected greater freedom of action under Hitler were disillusioned. Particularly after revival had produced competition for raw materials, labor, and capital, controls were steadily tightened. The businessman was told what to produce, in what quantity, and with what materials, and where he was to sell, at what price. He was told what to do with his profits, how much could be disbursed as dividends, how much must be reserved for plant expansion. Despite the abolition of trade unions, the businessman was told the wages he must pay, what work conditions must be, and how many workers he must employ or, after the labor market tightened, how many he could employ. By 1938, a close observer of the German economy could compare it to the Russian. The difference, he wrote, was "a mere matter of method." Under both, the capitalist entrepreneur was transformed "into a pensionable civil servant." All planned economies, he concluded, "are achieved at the price of liberty."[20]

The German worker also lost his freedom. Collective bargaining in the traditional sense ended in 1933; by 1939 it was difficult to move from one job to another. But there were advantages. The most obvious and the most precious was the possession of a job. The ending of unemployment was, from the point of view of the worker, the greatest achievement of the Nazis. Then there was all the color and the excitement of the "Strength through Joy" organization, an obvious imitation of the Italian Dopolavoro, but built into an enormous and varied enterprise with its own ships and hotels, its concerts and plays, its myriad activities for the lengthened vacations ordered by the government. All of the old social services continued, and most were improved. Wages were fixed, but so were prices. If all the various enforced "contributions" are taken into account, the worker on full time was likely to find his real wages lower; but now full time was general. On balance there was probably little change in the actual condition of the worker, except that he had a job, that there was more color in his life—and except that he had lost his freedom.

20. W. F. Bruck, *Social and Economic History of Germany* (Cardiff, 1938), pp. 210–12.

Taking the German people as a whole, they found less to think about, and far less time to think. Culture was regimented, more than in Italy, less than in Russia. Every writer or actor or artist had to belong to the organization of his craft; if he stepped out of line, he was dismissed from the organization and could not follow his calling. The results in literature and the arts were lethal. The banal reigned. In scholarship, historical study suffered most because of the dogma of racism, but the other humanities suffered almost as much. Much more than in Russia, scientific study was impaired, because so many German scientists were "non-Aryans."

What was lost in quality was, in all fields of German life, replaced by quantity. With a sure instinct, the regime set out to keep people busy. For instance, more than a million people gave "voluntary" assistance in the charitable work called "winter help." Undoubtedly winter help did provide an outlet for charitable impulses and did benefit those helped. But it also kept people occupied in their leisure time, kept them too busy to think. There were an infinite number of other distractions. There were huge spectacles such as the annual Nürnberg party rally. There were the Olympic games in 1936 (marred by the victories of the American Negro, Jesse Owens). Never had there been such circuses.

Most impressive of all, there were the obvious evidences that the outside world, which had shown scant respect for the Weimar government, took the Nazi government very seriously: in a steady stream foreign statesmen came to pay court to Hitler; foreign diplomats even came to the Nürnberg party days.

It is a remarkable fact, and a fact which must not be forgotten if the history of Europe in these years is to be understood, that until after 1939 the Nazi revolution was relatively bloodless. When we read of Lloyd George returning from a talk with Hitler filled with praise for his host; when we recall the kind words Churchill had for what Nazism was doing within Germany even while he was warning of the menace of Nazi foreign policy; when we reconstruct the many lauda-tory things Lord Halifax, so kindly and decent a man, said in his conversations with Hitler in 1937; and when we note that the same enthusiasm can be found in supposedly discerning observers from other countries, then we marvel, because we see, marching endlessly to their death, the millions of victims of Nazi racism. We forget that this death march, while it began even before the Nazi seizure of power, was of a relatively few easily ignored victims until after 1939. Jews were excluded from German national life and from the professions, at first without much uniformity, then systematically after the adoption of the Nürnberg Laws of September 15, 1935, which painstakingly defined who was a Jew and what a Jew could not do. But physical persecution of Jews was sporadic until the pogrom of November 10, 1938, and few Jews were killed even in that episode, which did send a premonitory chill across Europe.

Some outside of Germany could see clearly what was happening in Germany. Jews could see, very early, because they knew what their fellow Jews were suffering, even though that suffering was as yet short of death. More slowly, religious leaders saw, as their hope of accommodation with "the movement" was dissipated by harsh experience with the worthlessness of Nazi promises. Pope Pius XI's encyclical of March 14, 1937, "On the Condition of the Catholic Church in the German Reich," forced the attention of some Christians, but not all Christians and not even all Catholics, to the racism and paganism which were coming to be recognized not simply as the eccentricity of some Nazis but as central characteristics of Nazism. Some trade union leaders, like Ernest Bevin in Britain, never forgot the suppression of the German unions on May 2, 1933, and never wavered in their conviction that Fascism was the enemy of the working man. However, some pacifist leaders of the British Labour party, like George Lansbury, clung to the hope that Hitler could be persuaded to recognize the wisdom of disarmament and peace. Everywhere the pacifism of the non-Communist left blurred the unfolding picture of Nazi glorification of war. Foreign businessmen were infuriated by the cavalier treatment of their investments in Germany and by the devious business methods of the Nazis, but they hesitated to risk the loss of all their stake in the German economy, they shared in the prevalent dread of war, and they were impressed by the argument that the Nazis had saved Germany, and Europe, from Communism.

So it went, and if so many of the leaders of other countries were unable, or unwilling, to see what was happening in Germany, it is not strange that all except a small minority of Germans thought Hitler was restoring, and not destroying, German freedom and German honor. Of course, any disposition to doubt or to question was quickly checked by fear. By comparison with the Great Purge, the Nazi terror was still bloodless, but it was there and it was never forgotten, at least by Germans who had political consciousness. The "German look"—the nervous jerk of the head to make sure no one was listening—was a bitter jest in Germany as well as abroad. The abbreviation for the German secret police, Gestapo, had the same sinister sound for Germans as NKVD had for Russians, and was never used in jest, as Italians jested with the letters OVRA. Nazi Germany had its concentration camps, in the thirties fewer and much smaller than their Soviet counterparts. From them came the same tales of torture and death, with the same deterrent effect on the mass of the nominally free population. In them, Nazi agents and particularly the SS men were producing the mentality and perfecting the techniques needed for the mass terror and extermination of the war years.

By 1939 only the Christian churches had escaped complete "coordination." The churches were particularly dangerous to the Nazi regime because, implicitly if not explicitly, Christianity was hostile both to Nazi racism and to the Nazi "leadership principle." Even when Christian ministers were unconscious of this conflict of ideals, as many were, or were silent about the conflict, as most were, the very existence of independent Christian churches was a challenge to totalitarianism, particularly after all other loyalties had been uprooted or assimilated. Against the churches a campaign, now open and violent, now silent but deadly, was waged. Individual ecclesiastics were hounded out of office, expelled from Germany, or sent to concentration camps. So-called morality trials sought to turn public sympathy against churchmen. In countless ways churchgoing was made difficult for young people. There were reports that Hitler intended to set up a new "German" church, to which all must belong.[21]

Always, however, Hitler drew back from a clear break with the Christian churches, just as the churches refrained from open war on Nazism. Tacitly, both sides looked to time for a favorable verdict. Hitler consoled himself with the thought that as the older generation died off, Christianity would lose its hold on the German people. The churches, by avoiding an open break which would cut the Germans completely from the Christian tradition, could hope to regain the loyalty of the German people when the Nazi fever passed. Since, in

21. See J. S. Conway, *The Nazi Persecution of the Churches, 1933–1945* (London, 1968).

practice, religion did not greatly hamper his freedom of action, Hitler could afford to wait. The churches, while Germans were rejoicing in each new advance toward national "freedom" and "honor," had no real alternative to waiting.

If it is hard to keep clearly in mind both the fact that Stalin industrialized Russia and the fact that the cost was millions killed or imprisoned and all terrorized into submission, it is still harder to see clearly what Hitler did and what was the cost. In Germany, until 1939, relatively few had been killed or even imprisoned, and the surface of German national life had a color and enthusiasm absent from Russian life below the "stratum" of the intelligentsia. The economic achievement of the Nazis was comparable to that of Stalin, and the shift in the international position of Germany was more obvious than the rise of Russian national power. Yet when there has been a time interval sufficient for the historian to see those years in perspective, it is likely that the cost of Hitler's revolution will be placed higher than that of Stalin's revolution, just because the German people participated in Hitler's revolution so much more willingly, for the most part so much more gladly. Indeed, the future historian may conclude that while the ferocity of Stalin turned Russia from an agricultural state into an industrial state, it was Hitler who—by his attempt after 1941 to exterminate the people who encumbered the Russian land he needed for "living space"—gave the Russian people for the first time a sense of identity with the Stalin regime they had passively endured for so many years.

In 1932, walking among the trees of the Hofgarten in Munich, one might have come suddenly on a sunken stone court. On the walls were inscribed the names of the 13,000 men of Munich who were killed in the world war. Standing there in the silence, looking up from this hole in the ground to the surrounding trees, one could think that this was the Germany left, not just by the war, but also by the years since the war, a stone foundation of frustrated, outraged nationalism. In the next six years, with the aid of the German people, Hitler built a prison for Germans, for every German, on that foundation. Then, after 1939, the prison became a fortress, a fortress from which the German people, their "freedom" and their "honor" restored, moved in disciplined formation to attempt the subjugation of Europe and the extermination of the "inferior" peoples who occupied ground needed for the "living space" of the master German race.

Chapter Ten

THE DEMOCRACIES IN THE GREAT DEPRESSION, 1933–1936

I. THE END OF THE POSTWAR ERA

FROM 1933 to 1939 Europe lived under the shadow of Russia and Germany, the two great powers which had emerged exhausted and broken from the world war.

This sudden shift affected, first of all, the 100 million people who lived in the *cordon sanitaire,* the buffer zone stretching from Finland and the Baltic to Turkey and the Mediterranean. Russia and Germany, while they were weak, could be ignored with impunity by the small states. As the strength of the giants revived, neutrality became difficult if not impossible for their neighbors, particularly since, in these same years, the strength and the resolution of France were increasingly questioned.

The dilemma of the small states was not simply that they were increasingly pressed to ally with Russia or Germany; sooner or later all were forced to recognize that alliance meant acceptance of one or the other of the two totalitarian systems, Communism or Nazism. Most Czechs hoped that, fortified by alliance with France, alliance with Russia was possible without embracing Communism. The Polish government, also fortified by alliance with France, thought it safe to maintain close relations with Germany. Austria and Hungary, and more waveringly the states of southeastern Europe, hoped for safety through reliance on the Italian counterweight to German power; but after 1936 few could fail to see that Italy was becoming a satellite of Germany, with decreasing ability to pursue an independent policy. Finland and the Baltic states—and less obviously the Scandinavian states—were reduced to silence and abandonment of any initiative in international affairs, to the desperate hope that by avoiding offense they would remain unnoticed, and safe. Everywhere, however, even in Czechoslovakia, there was agreement—active agreement among members of the ruling groups, passive agreement among most others, except the members of Communist parties—that if a choice must be made,

Nazi rule would be less horrible than Soviet rule. The logic of this choice seemed obvious to all in the upper and middle classes who, from close range, had seen what had happened to their sort of people in Russia, but even most workers and peasants found little to envy in the convulsive changes going on in Russia. So, increasingly, it was the deepening shadow of German power which lay on central and south-eastern Europe.

Everyone in these countries with ability to see beyond the frontier of his own state had known from the first that the security of his country resulted in large part from the weakness of Germany and Russia after 1918. Therefore the revival of these giants awakened immediate apprehension in central Europe. In western Europe, and also in the United States, things were not usually seen in this harsh, clear light. To a dangerously great degree, this was because people simply did not want to see. In the West, transcending all the differences between parties and groups, one conviction was general: the First World War had shaken Western civilization and another world war would destroy Western civilization; therefore, there must not be another world war. What was going on in Germany, and less obviously in Russia, was daily heightening the possibility, even the probability, of another general war; therefore there was an increasingly desperate determination not to see what was going on, or more usually to see only part of what was going on. Those who hated and feared Russia saw the famine of 1932–33 and saw that the Great Purge was killing off the most famous military commanders. It was easy to conclude that Russia was weak, to ignore the vast increase in Soviet industrial power. Those who regarded Russia as the leader in the progress of the working man denied that there was a famine and saw Russia strengthened by the elimination of traitors in the Great Purge. Similarly, it was easy to take a partial and distorted view of Germany, to see only the falling curve of unemployment and the smiling faces of the youngsters who looked out from newsreels, or to see only the beating of helpless Jews by Nazi bullies and the trucks which broke down during the Nazi invasion of Austria.

If it was easier for many Americans to see things steadily, that was because most Americans were confident that if war came the United States could stand aside, with the road to war barred by the Neutrality Law. The Netherlands, Switzerland, and, after 1936, Belgium also clung, like the Scandinavian and Baltic countries, to the hope of neutrality. Even in Britain and France some had this hope, but most realized that if there was a war, they would be in it. A few, like Winston Churchill, ceaselessly urged that all resources be mobilized for war as the one way to avoid war, and their number grew, slowly until 1938, very rapidly in 1939. Until 1939, however, most recoiled from this remedy since the conviction was widespread that preparation for war produced war. Until March, 1939, there was general agreement in Britain and France both that war must be avoided and that war could be avoided; the argument was over means to achieve the agreed end, passionate argument which split all the usual groupings in both countries.

2. THE RIGHT AND THE LEFT IN FRANCE
DURING THE GREAT DEPRESSION

Through 1931 most Frenchmen seemed content to shrug aside charges of militarism and to accept with some complacency praise of the rich and complex civilization of France—even themselves to speak *du bonheur d'être Français*—particularly when the economic blizzard swept over Europe and America, and France remained prosperous.[1] Then, in 1932, the tourists did not come, the luxury exports fell off, and the world collapse of agricultural prices was felt by French farmers, despite high tariffs. When the British and the other countries of the "sterling bloc" devalued their currency, they gained an export advantage over French goods, and they also bought less from France because French goods were too expensive in terms of depreciated pounds.

By 1932 it was evident that supposedly immune France had been hit by the depression. Compared to Germany or Britain there was not much unemployment; the millions of foreign workers went home, and large numbers of French workers, when their jobs disappeared, went to the country to live with their peasant parents or brothers. There was no financial panic, as in America. There was simply a slow, steady fall of production, intensified in 1933 when the dollar was devalued and the German mark became a "managed" currency.

The French groped for a way out. Immediately they discovered that the relative tranquillity of domestic politics during the years of prosperity and security had been a tranquillity which did not result from

1. See the remarks of Raoul Girardet on French opinion in 1930–33 in *Bulletin de la Société d'Histoire Moderne,* 14th series, No. 5 (1968), pp. 14–19.

domestic harmony but rather from ability not to press too hard on jealously suspicious groups. French society had hardened into a pattern which few French politicians were willing to disturb.

By 1933, when most of the rest of the world had resorted to currency devaluation as one way of coping with depression, France was at a disadvantage in international trade, but French politicians were too afraid of the electorate to imitate the currency devaluation of the British, the Americans, the Germans, and almost everyone else. At the same time, Frenchmen with money to invest suspected that some day the franc would be devalued and therefore began to ship their funds abroad. As a result, there was little new investment in France and little new construction; fear of future devaluation of the franc resulted in a deepening of the depression within France. The flight of capital could be checked, as it was being checked in Germany, by rigid exchange controls; but again French politicians drew back, fearful of antagonizing segments of the French electorate. If the French government had been willing to resort to a vast program of public works, "pump priming," as it was called in America, the decline of production might have been halted, but here again fear of deficit financing, with the possible risk of uncontrollable inflation, prevented action. Since every positive course of action involved the certainty of antagonizing some part of the electorate, the government did nothing to cure the depression.

As the economic horizon darkened for France, the international horizon also darkened, with the rise of the Nazis in Germany and with the ever more bellicose tone of Italian Fascism. Here also, under pressure, French policy was showing unexpected weakness and division. Through the first decade after the Peace of Paris, French policy had proclaimed that the treaty settlement in western Europe would endure only as long as the map of central Europe remained intact. Therefore, the French argued, to protect their own frontiers they must protect the frontiers of the states to the east of Germany, if necessary by invading Germany; to make possible the occupation of German territory, the Rhineland must be permanently demilitarized and French military strength must be greater than German. To the French, these were self-evident truths, truths which they repeated at every international conference on armaments or security, through the collapse of the disarmament conference in 1933.

By then, however, doubt had arisen whether, in fact, France was prepared to act on these supposedly self-evident truths. The most obvious reason for skepticism was the building of a great chain of fortifications from the Swiss frontier, all across northern France, to link up with fortifications being built by Belgium, the ally of France; this was known as the Maginot Line, begun in 1929.[2] The French government denied that the decision to build these fortifications meant any shift in French foreign or military policy; the Maginot Line merely provided a secure defense behind which the French army could be mobilized for movement into the demilitarized Rhineland. This argument sounded increasingly hollow during 1933, as German rearmament proceeded in defiance of the Treaty of Versailles, as Germany shook off the restraints of membership in the League of Nations—and as France did nothing to compel Germany to abide by treaty or covenant. Now the building of the Maginot Line seemed one of many indications that the French were concerned only with the defense of their own frontiers and were not prepared to defend their eastern allies. In January, 1934, Marshal Pilsudski drew what seemed the obvious conclusion. Without consulting his French ally, he accepted Hitler's proposal for a nonaggression pact. By this agreement, which was to remain in force for ten years, Germany and Poland agreed to work toward "good neighborly relations" and to settle all disputes by peaceful means; the two governments promised that "in no circumstances" would they "proceed to use force in order to settle such disputes."

As the depression dragged on, and as the resolution of France to defend the Peace of Paris was increasingly questioned, Frenchmen became more suspicious of one another. The divisions passed almost unnoticed until they suddenly exploded in bloody riots.

3. THE FRENCH RIGHT AND FASCISM

In December, 1933, a French racketeer, Serge Alexandre Stavisky, was accused of defrauding investors in the shares of the municipal pawnshop in Bayonne. He had been arrested before; indeed for years he had been under indictment, but never tried. This immunity was rumored to be the result of his intimate connection with some members of the Chamber of Deputies and of the lenient view which the

2. Vivian Rowe, *The Great Wall of France: The Triumph of the Maginot Line* (London, 1959).

courts took of his activities because he had these political connections. In January, 1934, he was said to have committed suicide to avoid arrest; rumor said that he had been killed so that he could not implicate his protectors. Immediately thereafter, the mangled body of the government attorney who had been pursuing the case was found. Supposedly he had been run over by a train; rumor said he had been murdered. The newspaper of Charles Maurras' royalist organization Action Française and the Communist journal *Humanité* eagerly took up the case to discredit the government.[3] Much was made of Stavisky's Russian-Jewish origin. Through January, 1934, there were minor riots almost nightly in Paris.

The cabinet then in office was dominated by the middle-class Radical Socialist party. The elections of 1932 had been won by a coalition of Radicals and Socialists, and although the Socialists followed their traditional policy of refusing to enter a coalition government, they did support the Radical cabinet with their votes in the Chamber of Deputies.[4] In face of the January riots, the cabinet was reorganized. Edouard Daladier became premier. He had a robust stocky figure and a heavy impassive face; these were thought to signify strength of character and will.

The new cabinet was to face the Chamber on February 6, 1934. Rightist organizations called on their followers to show, by demonstrations on that day, the disgust which the French people felt for political corruption. There were many such organizations. Some were frankly modeled after the Italian Fascists or the German Nazis; these were small. The direction and the mass support were provided by Maurras' Action Française and by Colonel de La Rocque's Croix de Feu, which had started as an elite veterans' organization but had now become the refuge of Frenchmen, and particularly young Frenchmen, who had lost faith in parliamentary government.

The riots on February 6 were violent and bloody; there were deaths and more than a thousand were injured. Within the Chamber also

---

3. See Eugen Weber's scholarly account, *Action Française: Royalism and Reaction in Twentieth Century France* (Stanford, 1962).

4. Francis de Tarr, *The French Radical Party from Herriot to Mendès-France* (London, 1961), and Peter Larmour, *The French Radical Party in the 1930's* (Stanford, 1964); John T. Marcus, *French Socialism in the Crisis Years, 1933–1936: Fascism and the French Left* (N.Y., 1958), and Nathanael Greene, *Crisis and Decline: The French Socialist Party in the Popular Front Era* (Ithaca, 1969).

there was violence, and the session was adjourned. The Socialist leader, Léon Blum, offered continued support to the cabinet, but the supposedly imperturbable Daladier was shaken, and he resigned. A new cabinet, called a government of national union, but really representing the center and right parties, was formed by the ex-president of the republic, Gaston Doumergue; the strongest and most popular figure in the cabinet was the hero of Verdun, Marshal Pétain.

On the surface, events had followed a familiar pattern. There had been corruption in earlier years of the Third Republic; the corruption had at times led to a violent popular reaction; and then public opinion had rallied to the support of the republic. Supposedly, the Doumergue government was just such a drawing together of the supporters of the republic. In fact, however, the rioters had accomplished their immediate objective, to end government by the coalition of left and center parties which had won the election of 1932.

On the left there was, and long remained, a firm conviction that much more was involved in the riots, that the riots were part of a Fascist plot to overthrow the republic and set up a Fascist state.[5] To show that the French people were not prepared to surrender passively to Fascism, as the German people had surrendered a year earlier, the Socialist party and the Socialist trade unions called for a brief general strike and a demonstration on February 12. The Communists were still bound by the Comintern dictum that the first Communist objective was to destroy the Socialists. Adherence to this dogma had cost the French Communist party much of its popular support in the elections of 1932, but the party adhered to the instructions from Moscow during the riotous days which culminated on February 6; indeed, Communists participated in the riots. One result of the refusal of the Communist party to oppose the "fascists" was the desertion of the dynamic leader Jacques Doriot, who, after the pattern of Mussolini, ended by himself forming a Fascist party, the Parti Populaire Française (PPF). When the call came for a general strike on February 12, the response among the French workers was so strong that the Communist party leaders,

---

5. On French "fascism" in general, see Robert J. Soucy, "The Nature of Fascism in France," *Journal of Contemporary History*, I, 1 (1966), and Raoul Girardet, "Notes sur l'esprit d'un fascisme français 1934–1939," *Revue française de science politique* (July–Sept., 1955), pp. 529–46, as well as the studies of René Rémond and others in the bibliographical essay.

after wavering, joined the demonstration; momentarily, the breach between Socialist and Communist seemed healed when leaders of the two parties addressed the demonstrators, an estimated 150,000, from the same platform.[6]

The Stavisky affair, unlike earlier affairs such as the Panama Canal scandal, had not ended with an overwhelmingly strong rally to the republic; rather, the riot of February 6 and the strike of February 12 seemed to show a deep, unbridgeable chasm between the France of the right and the France of the left.

In actuality, the divisions were not as clear as they appeared in the myths which were accepted as facts. Almost certainly the riot of February 6 was not the result of a Fascist plot. Indeed, a large proportion of the demonstrators were protesting nothing more important than Daladier's dismissal of the Paris prefect of police, Jean Chiappe. Similarly, there was no left-wing plot to destroy all those who stood for the stability of the Third Republic, as many on the right maintained.

The question of Fascism in France depends largely on definition of terms. If the word "fascism" is taken to mean a disillusionment with parliamentary government, a readiness to embrace simple and even violent solutions for political problems, a disposition to say that the wisdom of the old was an excuse for inaction, while the passion, the idealism, the confidence in the future, and the physical strength of youth were the true wisdom—then there was much fascism in France, and everywhere in Europe in the thirties, when parliamentary rule had disappeared in many countries and was on the defensive in most, and when the cult of youth, what the Dutch historian Johan Huizinga derisively called "puerilism," was rampant everywhere. Mussolini and Hitler were certainly contemptuous of parliamentary democracy, were able to use idealistic youngsters to exterminate their opponents, and were constantly diverting the attention of the people they were subjugating by great cloud pictures of future wealth and glory. So, however, was Stalin.

Such a broad definition of fascism obscures and distorts the distinctive qualities of the interwar years. These were certainly years when,

6. For the riot of February 6 and the counterdemonstration of February 12, see Georges Lefranc, *Histoire du Front Populaire (1934–1938)* (Paris, 1965), pp. 12–35; René Rémond, "Explications du 6 février," *Politique*, II (July–Dec., 1959), 218–30; and Marcel Le Clère, *Le 6 février* (Paris, 1967).

particularly after the depression had stimulated social and national strife, parliamentary government was difficult at best. But the kind of military dictatorship which Pilsudski set up in Poland, or King Alexander set up in Yugoslavia, was not something new. Similarly, the proliferation of armed bands in support of parties or politicians, from one end of Europe to the other, was certainly symptomatic of the decay of parliamentary government, of the growing acceptance of violence as a method of settling disputes, and also of Huizinga's "puerilism." However, while the youths of the Action Française or the Croix de Feu acted like Storm Troopers and Black Shirts, that did not make them Fascists.

If Italian Fascism and German Nazism are taken as the norm, Fascism was, first of all, a mass movement centering in large segments of the middle classes which felt their position menaced both by the upper middle classes and by, in Marxist terminology, the proletariat; in particular, these segments felt themselves in danger of losing their middle-class status and of being pushed down into the proletariat. In the second place, these segments of the middle classes identified their plight with the plight of their nation and thought it their mission, as a preliminary step, to gain complete control over their nation and then to exalt the position of their nation in the world. They looked to the past for inspiration concerning the peculiar nature and mission of their nation, but they did not want to go back. They were neither conservatives nor reactionaries—they were emphatically revolutionists who were disgusted by what their nation was in the present, who were determined to smash ruthlessly all of the present and to move on to the realization of what the nation was ideally, to their "myth," as Mussolini put it, emphasizing the contempt for reason, the faith in the irrational which was an essential part of the movement. It is these two aspects of Fascism—the mass middle-class base and the proudly irrational nationalism—which most clearly distinguish Fascism from Communism. Fascism and Communism were alike in their totalitarianism, in their fanatical determination to create a new man, a new society, a new culture, all permeated, saturated, with the new ideal. They were also alike in the working out of what the Nazis called the "leadership principle" and what the Communists called "democratic centralism"; in both, control and direction were from the top down. In both, the top position was occupied by a charismatic leader ("charismatic," like "myth," is a distinctive word of the interwar years), a leader to whom godlike wisdom was attributed, a ruler who exercised the power of life and death not only over his subjects but over all members of the party. Khrushchev was later to claim that the "cult of personality" was Stalin's perversion of democratic centralism, but (to remain within the interwar years) the difference between Stalin and Lenin was a difference of temperament and not of political conviction.

The spirit of Fascism can be found in France, and everywhere in Europe west of Russia. Fascist organizations existed in France: Doriot's PPF was Fascist and was, appropriately, subsidized by Mussolini. Similar organizations can be found in other countries: Sir Oswald Mosley's British Union of Fascists, Léon Degrelle's Rexists in Belgium, Cornelius Codreanu's Iron Guard in Rumania and José Antonio Primo de Rivera's Falange in Spain. Almost every country had a Fascist league, large or small. Yet not even the Spain of Franco was Fascist, by the test of Italian and German Fascism.[7]

Despite their hatred for the Third Republic and their cult of youth, neither the Action Française nor the Croix de Feu was Fascist, judged by the models of Germany and Italy. The Action Française had no mass lower-middle-class base, and its "myth" was reactionary—the restoration of pre-1789 France. The Croix de Feu was middle class, but it showed little of the revolutionary ardor or the irrational nationalism common to Nazism and Fascism.

France was not menaced by a Fascist plot, as Socialists and Communists maintained. Neither was France menaced by a conspiracy of the left, as the parties of the right maintained. The French Socialist party was by now rather less "revolutionary" than the British Labour party or the American New Deal Democrats. The French Communist party had, like all European Communist parties, become completely subject

7. For a discussion of Fascist movements, including those outside Germany and Italy, see Francis Carsten, *The Rise of Fascism* (Berkeley, 1967); the essays in the issue of the *Journal of Contemporary History* devoted to "International Fascism 1920–1945" (Vol. I, No. 1, 1966); and Eugen Weber, *Varieties of Fascism* (Princeton, 1964), a compact study with documents. Weber edited with Hans Rogger a useful collection of essays, *The European Right: A Historical Profile* (Berkeley, 1965). Ernst Nolte's *Three Faces of Fascism: Action Française, Italian Fascism, National Socialism* (English trans., London, 1965) has been the center of vigorous discussion. Cf. Wolfgang Sauer's bibliographical essay, "National Socialism: Totalitarianism or Fascism?" *American Historical Review*, LXXIII (Dec., 1967), 404–24. For the working of French political institutions, see the writings of Goguel and Hoffmann in the bibliographical essay.

to orders from Moscow; the French party officials were obedient bureaucrats, not revolutionary leaders. For the rank and file, the party provided a "home away from home"; it was trade union, political party, social club, mutual-help organization, organizer of sports, everything except an actively revolutionary force. After 1934 an increasing number of workers and peasants, even petty bourgeois, voted Communist. But this flood of recruits was, in itself, testimony to the lack of revolutionary ardor in the party: most were voting against a government which had failed to produce prosperity, and not for the abolition of private property.

Possibly, as some of the most acute students of French politics maintain, the failure of France to make effective progress toward the solution of either domestic or foreign problems in the thirties is largely explained by the political institutions of the Third Republic. Certainly these institutions—and particularly the firm grip of the parliament on the executive as well as the legislative functions of government—were an effective barrier to rapid change. When the Republic was taking form after 1871, the dominant middle classes and their peasant allies had been, in general, satisfied with their own situation and fearful of a disturbance of that situation, whether by the old ruling classes on the right or by the temporarily weakened, but potentially powerful, city workers on the left. To ensure the perpetuation of the consensus, the rules of the parliamentary game had been so drawn that stalemate was easy to produce, but strong action most difficult. In a crisis, temporary decree powers could be voted, as they were to Clemenceau in 1917, and as they were to Poincaré when the franc threatened to collapse; only in such extreme situations was decisive action possible.

According to this institutional view of French politics, the unstable short-lived governments characteristic of the Third Republic were of slight importance so long as all parties except the extreme right and the extreme left had roughly the same views and interests. But after the war, and especially during the depression, dissatisfied voters tended to vote for these parties of the right and left. In 1924, in 1932, and in 1936, the elections were won by coalitions of center and left parties. As soon, however, as the parties of the left threatened the position, and especially the property, of the middle-class consensus, the "radical" groups of the center moved into alliance with the right; this happened in 1926, in 1934, and again in 1938.

In a rough way, it is probably true that the political traditions and institutions of the Third Republic worked increasingly badly as the old middle-class consensus broke down, and as property ceased to seem sacred to voters who had no property and did have votes. But much more was involved. In any explanation of the combination of immobility and instability characteristic of France in the thirties, room must be left both for refusal to surrender the international position achieved at such cost in 1919 and for refusal to face the possibility that another war might be the only means to maintain the international settlement of 1919. Room must be found for the confusion and uncertainty inevitably resulting from alliance with Communist Russia, which had deserted France in 1917, and which, in theory, was committed to the overthrow of capitalist France, along with all other capitalist states; for the confusion and uncertainty inevitably resulting also from enmity toward the Nazi regime, which was pledged, in theory, to the defense of capitalism against godless Communism. Finally room must be left for the doctrinaire economic views of middle-class politicians who—despite what was going on in Britain and America—insisted on equating Communism and economic planning, as well as for the doctrinaire views of socialist politicians who saw a capital levy as the only proper remedy, even though the capital levy made political alliance with parties of the left center impossible. In short, room must be found both for France as one of the oldest and most distinctive cultures of Europe and for France as an aggregation of fiercely competing, even antagonistic, interest groups.

4. THE DIPLOMATIC OFFENSIVE OF BARTHOU AND LAVAL, 1934–1935

The so-called government of national union which took office in France after the riots of February 6 had no program for ending the depression. Instead, the government concentrated its efforts on rebuilding the international position of France. The foreign minister, Louis Barthou, was a man of great energy who prided himself on his "realism," that is, on his single-minded devotion to French national interest, without regard for sentiment or ideology. He recognized that in the first year of Nazi rule the drift of international politics had been unfavorable to France. From intelligence reports, he was aware of the clandestine rearmament of Germany. He was aware also that British opinion blamed France rather than Germany for the failure of the disarmament conference, and that the British sympathized with German demands for modification of the Treaty of Versailles. Finally, he could not ignore the uneasiness of the smaller states to the east of Germany.

To Barthou, the opportunities presented by Nazi policy were more important than the dangers. Germany was rearming, but was militarily still weak. Moreover, the dissension within the Nazi party which was to culminate in the blood purge of June 30, 1934, and the still precarious state of the German economy made the survival of the Nazi regime doubtful. Of greatest hope from the French point of view was the effect of Nazi policy on Russian and Italian foreign policy.

After initial wavering, Hitler moved to end the ties between the Reichswehr and the Red army. Neither the Rapallo agreement nor the Treaty of Berlin of 1926 was formally denounced; indeed, the Treaty of Berlin was renewed in 1933. But by the summer of 1934 all good will was gone from the relations of Germany with the Soviet Union. As relations with Germany worsened, Russian attacks on the League of Nations ended, and on September 18, 1934, the Soviet Union joined the League. Already France and Russia were moving toward political cooperation. Through the summer they pressed for an "Eastern Locarno," that is, a guarantee of the frontiers of the states to the east of Germany. When the German government, without actually refusing to negotiate, made clear its intention to talk the proposal to death, Barthou began to discuss seriously a revival of the prewar Franco-Russian alliance. As a "realist," he refused to consider the old argument that alliance with Communism was impossible.

Neither did he take seriously the view that Fascist Italy and Nazi Germany were natural allies. Separating the two was Austria, and the whole question of primacy in the Danube basin. By exploiting this situation, Barthou hoped to revive the alliance with Italy and complete the encirclement of Nazi Germany.

Events in Austria supported Barthou's reasoning. As the Austrian Catholics and Socialists watched events in Nazi Germany, they lost their enthusiasm for Anschluss. The efforts of Hitler to force Austria into submission by economic pressure and by encouraging Austrian Nazis to hope for help from Germany merely drove the Austrian chancellor, Engelbert Dollfuss, to seek Italian aid. He visited Rome in

March, 1934, and there, with Hungary, negotiated the Rome Protocols with Mussolini, agreements which bound the two Danubian states economically to Italy in return for the promise of Italian political protection. At home, Dollfuss set up a "Fatherland Front" in alliance with the Heimwehr, the private army of Prince Ernst Rüdiger von Starhemberg and other Austrian reactionaries; he also sought Vatican support by building the Fatherland Front along the "corporative" lines which had won praise in papal encyclicals. Under pressure from Mussolini he set out to break the power of the Socialists who ruled in Vienna and had great influence in other Austrian cities. By February, 1934, the private army of the Socialists, the Schutzbund, was driven to fight back. In Vienna the municipal housing projects were the center of Socialist resistance; they were subjected to artillery fire by the government, and with their capture Socialist resistance collapsed. On April 30, the corporative constitution went into effect. Dollfuss was dictator over a country where all opposition except that of the Nazis had been broken, but he had lost the support of a large proportion of the people, in fact, the Austrian corporative state could survive only so long as it had the support of Italian Fascism.

In 1934 that support was firm, and Mussolini's determination to preserve Austrian independence was an effective bar to alliance between Germany and Italy. That was demonstrated when Austrian Nazis seized control of government buildings in Vienna and murdered Dollfuss on July 25. Within a few hours the revolt collapsed. Kurt von Schuschnigg assumed the chancellorship, promising to continue the policy of Dollfuss. The Italian army was concentrated along the Austrian frontier. In western Europe the murder of Dollfuss, coming less than a month after the German blood purge of June 30, was accepted as proof of Nazi barbarism. Hitler vehemently denied any connection with the murder, but his protestations did not carry conviction; after all, the Munich radio had, night after night, called for a rising against Dollfuss. When, on September 27, Italy, France, and Britain issued a joint declaration in support of Austrian independence, it seemed that the international consequence of Nazism had been to isolate Germany and to bring about a revival of the wartime alliance against Germany.

French confidence was momentarily shaken when Barthou and King Alexander of Yugoslavia were assassinated by Croatian terrorists at

Marseilles on October 9, and there was new uneasiness in November when Doumergue, unable to hold together the parties in his coalition government, resigned as premier. Confidence revived, however, as Barthou's successor as foreign minister, Pierre Laval, set out to complete the alliance system.[8]

Laval was careful to give Germany no provocation. He scrupulously lived up to the provisions of the Treaty of Versailles which required that the inhabitants of the Saar decide by plebiscite whether they wished to be part of Germany, to remain under League administration, or to be administratively joined to France. The plebiscite was held on January 25, 1935. More than 90 per cent of the inhabitants voted for union with Germany, and on March 1 the Saar was again joined to Germany.[9] Repeatedly, Laval stressed his willingness, indeed his eagerness, to further the Nazi demand for "freedom," if by freedom the Germans meant release from the restrictions on German sovereignty imposed by the Treaty of Versailles, including the restrictions on German armament; in return, however, Germany must give binding assurance that freedom would not be used to attack the freedom of the eastern neighbors of Germany. Only the demilitarization of the Rhineland was expressly excluded from the discussions Laval was eager to begin. The demilitarization of the Rhineland, the French insisted, no longer rested on the "dictate" of Versailles, but had been freely accepted by Germany in the Locarno Pact.

Hitler always stated his willingness to begin negotiations, but always evaded actual discussion of the French proposals. Others were more impressed with Laval's program. In January, 1935, he came to Rome. There, on January 7, he concluded an agreement on outstanding colonial disputes between Italy and France. The two governments also concluded a consultative pact, promising to discuss common action if the independence of Austria were threatened; other governments were invited to join this agreement. Finally, Laval and Mussolini undertook to work for the conclusion of a general agreement between the states concerned with central Europe, an agreement promising noninterven-

8. Geoffrey Warner's *Pierre Laval and the Eclipse of France* (London, 1968) is primarily concerned with foreign policy. For Laval as a symbol of politics in the interwar period, see Alfred Cobban, "Laval and the Third Republic," *The Cambridge Journal*, II (Feb., 1949), 279–87.

9. See Helmut Hirsch, "The Saar Plebiscite of 1935," *South Atlantic Quarterly*, XLV (Jan., 1946), 13–30.

tion in the affairs of the states of that area. In veiled form, what Laval and Mussolini proposed was that Hitler be asked to abandon the union with Austria which in *Mein Kampf* he had made the first task of German foreign policy, and also be asked to accept as final the German frontiers with Czechoslovakia, Poland, and Lithuania. In return, Laval and Mussolini, again in veiled form, offered to remove the restrictions on German rearmament.

A month later, Laval was in London. Here again he was successful in winning support for an "Eastern Locarno," although the British refused themselves to guarantee the eastern territorial settlement. Again, the promise of arms equality was held out to Germany as a reward for the stabilization of Germany's eastern frontiers.

The German reply was swift and defiant. On March 9, very casually, announcement was made that Germany already had an air force, although under the provisions of the Treaty of Versailles Germany was to have no air force. On March 16, again in defiance of the Treaty of Versailles, the German government introduced conscription. In short, Hitler had taken the concessions which Britain, France, and Italy had been prepared to offer him in exchange for agreements stabilizing the frontiers in central Europe—without agreeing to stabilize the frontiers. When, on March 25, Sir John Simon visited Berlin, he repeatedly asked the size of the German air force. Hitler's reply shattered the easy optimism of British estimates: "We had reached parity with Britain."

Momentarily, the open violation of the Treaty of Versailles by Germany and the revelation of the extent of German secret rearmament completed the isolation of Germany. In April, 1935, there was a conference of the British, French, and Italian leaders at Stresa which ended with a declaration that the three countries would "act in close and cordial collaboration" to oppose treaty violations "which may endanger the peace of Europe." On May 2 a further stage in the isolation of Germany seemed attained when the French and Soviet governments concluded a mutual assistance pact which provided that if either country were the victim of unprovoked aggression, the other ally would give military assistance.[10] On May 16 a similar agreement was signed between Russia and Czechoslovakia, with the significant reser-

10. *Alliance Against Hitler: The Origins of the Franco-Soviet Pact,* by William Scott (Durham, N.C., 1962), is a history of relations between France and the Soviet Union in the early 1930's.

vation that Russian aid would be forthcoming only after France had come to the assistance of Czechoslovakia. Stalin also sought to ease Laval's task at home. The French Communists had consistently fought against the military budgets and had denied that the French workman had any interest in fighting the battle of French capitalists against Nazi Germany. On May 15 Stalin issued a statement praising efforts to strengthen the military defenses of France against Nazi aggression; promptly the leaders of the French Communist party became advocates of increased military expenditure.

On paper, Germany was isolated and encircled by the formidable union of France with Britain, Italy, and the Soviet Union. At home, Laval's prestige had risen, and on June 7 he became premier in a cabinet which was given almost dictatorial power to end the economic depression. The policy he chose to combat the depression was deflation, that is, the forcing down of expenditures, to bring the budget into balance, and of prices, to enable French products to compete in international trade. Whether, in the light of the failure of deflation in Britain, the United States, and Germany, Laval's effort to bring the French economy into balance by cutting expenditures and forcing prices down could have succeeded under the best of circumstances is questionable. Deflation pressed most obviously on the workingman, the peasant, and the small businessman and shopkeeper; in a democracy, these groups could register their discontent at the polls. When Laval became premier, the Socialists and Communists were already drawing together, and the search for unity was facilitated by the shift of Comintern policy in the summer of 1935 from war against the Socialists to a "popular front" of all left parties against "fascism." In September the Socialist and Communist trade unions in France agreed to merge. Through the autumn, the leaders of the Socialist and the Communist parties, together with some Radicals, labored to formulate a program broad enough, and vague enough, to satisfy Socialists and Communists and also to draw the middle-class Radical Socialist party away from allegiance to Laval's coalition government.

5. FASCIST AGGRESSION AND THE FAILURE
OF LEAGUE SANCTIONS

Laval's reconstruction of the old union of France, Britain, Italy, and Russia was formidable in appearance; against such power, Hitler could not hope to win—if these four powers, and their allies in central Europe, were prepared to fight in the event of German aggression. From the outset, however, both the fact of union and the willingness to fight were open to question.

Whether the Red army would have advanced beyond the frontiers of Russia to defend the map of central Europe seemed doubtful in 1935; certainly, few in central Europe—or in Britain or France or Italy—were willing to see the Red army move into central Europe.

The British people and government wanted no armies to move anywhere. The temper of British opinion was made clear by what was called the Peace Ballot, a public opinion poll in which more than 11½ million voted between the autumn of 1934 and the announcement of the final result on June 27, 1935. On propositions such as peace through the League, "all-around reduction in armaments," and economic sanctions against aggression, the vote was overwhelmingly favorable. Even collective military measures to restrain an aggressor were approved, three to one—although on this question there were many abstentions.

Since there was to be a general election in the autumn of 1935, the returns on the Peace Ballot were followed closely by political leaders. The Labour party was divided. The pacifist wing, led by the leader of the parliamentary party, George Lansbury, and supported by the leader of the left wing, Sir Stafford Cripps, opposed sanctions because sanctions might lead to war. The pacifists were defeated in a dramatic debate at the annual conference of the party, on October 1, 1935, after Ernest Bevin put the issue squarely on the treatment which trade unions had received in Fascist countries. Lansbury resigned and was replaced by Clement Attlee. Thereafter, the Labour party, while opposed to rearmament, stood for peace through League action, including as a last resort sanctions.

The National government—more because there seemed no other way to hold the electorate than from conviction—publicly espoused similar principles. On June 7, 1935, the cabinet was reorganized in preparation for the election. Stanley Baldwin replaced the infirm Ramsay MacDonald as prime minister. Simon was replaced by Sir Samuel Hoare as foreign secretary, with the young and popular Anthony Eden beside him as minister for League of Nations affairs. This strange division of foreign affairs among two offices was recognition of the popular conviction that the League was the bulwark of peace and the hope for disarmament.

On armament, the government was caught between the cost of the expansion of military strength, particularly in the air, necessitated by German rearmament, and the intensity of the popular demand for disarmament. The government sought to escape by taking up Hitler's offer to Sir John Simon that the size of the German fleet not exceed 35 per cent of the British fleet. An Anglo-German naval agreement was concluded on June 18, 1935, and was applauded in Britain as evidence of the National government's concern for arms limitation.[11]

To the French, the Anglo-German naval agreement was treachery. In March, at Stresa, Britain had joined with France and Italy in condemning German rearmament as a breach of the public law of Europe. Now, in June, by signing the naval agreement, Britain accepted German rearmament as an accomplished fact; the French were certain the British action would encourage Hitler to expect British acquiescence in new violations of international agreements. Moreover, the naval agreement had been concluded without consulting France; this did not encourage belief in British loyalty to the alliance against German aggression.

Before June ended, the British had failed also in their effort to satisfy Mussolini's ambition for empire without impairing the prestige of the League. For months, tension had been rising between Italy and Ethiopia, ostensibly because of clashes along the ill-defined frontier between Ethiopia and Italian Somaliland.[12] Stories were current that when he went to Rome in January, 1935, Laval gave at least tacit approval to the Italian conquest of Ethiopia as the price for the agreements with Italy. Probably he had. In any event, after Laval's visit, Italy began to send more and more troops to Somaliland, the contingents sent on their way with fiery declamations by Mussolini about Italian honor.

In June, Anthony Eden went to Rome to propose a compromise settlement: if Mussolini would be satisfied with a part of Ethiopia adjacent to Italian Somaliland and some economic advantages, then

---

11. There are two concise studies of the naval accord: Charles Bloch, "La Grande-Bretagne face au rearmement allemand et l'accord naval de 1935," *Revue d'histoire de la deuxième guerre mondiale,* No. 63, and D. C. Watt, "The Anglo-German Naval Agreement of 1935: An Interim Judgement," *Journal of Modern History,* XXVIII (June, 1956), 155–75.

12. The best history of the events preceding the outbreak of war in Ethiopia is George W. Baer's *The Coming of the Italo-Ethiopian War* (Cambridge, Mass., 1967). Baer has included an exhaustive bibliography.

Britain would compensate Ethiopia with a port and a corridor for a railway in British Somaliland. Tactfully, Eden made clear British opposition to the armed conquest of Ethiopia. Mussolini refused the offer, and now the Fascist press began a campaign against British "hypocrisy," charging that after subjugating a quarter of the globe by violence, the British now preached the virtues of peace and nonaggression to the Italians, who, before Fascism, had been too weak to share in the colonial scramble.[13] The Italian people were convinced. The depression and all the blighted promises of Fascism were forgotten. The Italian people were united, united in rejecting the condescending friendship of Britain.

By September, war between Italy and Ethiopia obviously impended, and the dispute was at last placed before the assembly of the League. Sir Samuel Hoare began the discussion by stating that "the League stands, and my country stands with it, for the collective maintenance of the Convenant in its entirety, and particularly for steady and collective resistance to all acts of unprovoked aggression." Laval announced that France would fulfill its obligations under the covenant; quite obviously, however, he remained determined to find some formula which would preserve the French alliance with Italy without sacrificing the French alliance with Britain. And, despite Hoare's brave words, he also was determined not to allow sanctions to lead to war.

Undeterred by the opposition of the League, and with every evidence of the enthusiastic support of the Italian people, including leading representatives of the clergy, Mussolini attacked Ethiopia on October 11, 1935. The League, with Anthony Eden playing a leading part in the proceedings, declared that Italy had violated the covenant and began the imposition of sanctions. Without opposition, the export of arms to Italy was prohibited; more reluctantly, loans and credits to Italy were prohibited, and imports from Italy were banned; some other exports to Italy were also banned, but these did not include important products like coal, steel, and the one essential of twentieth-century warfare, oil. No suggestion was made that a mortal blow be dealt to Italian communication with east Africa by closing the Suez Canal. Moreover, the British and French representatives made plain their continued hope to arrange a peaceful settlement by friendly negotiations with Italy.

13. See Mario Toscano's essay, "Eden's Mission to Rome on the Eve of the Italo-Ethiopian Conflict," in A. O. Sarkissian, *Studies in Diplomatic History and Historiography in Honor of G. P. Gooch* (London, 1961).

At the time, little attention was paid to these limitations on League action. Instead, every indication of Italian weakness was hailed in western Europe and the United States as evidence of the effectiveness of League pressure. Much was made of the slow progress of the Italian armies, and indeed to secure action Mussolini was forced to remove the incompetent Fascist general, Emilio De Bono, and replace him by a professional soldier, Marshal Pietro Badoglio. It took Badoglio the remainder of the year to organize his forces for attack. In the absence of victories, grumbling began in Italy; to supporters of the League this was a favorable sign. The lira was devalued drastically, and this was hailed as evidence that sanctions were working.

In the weeks of waiting, the British election took place. The firm support which the National government was giving the League was stressed in the campaign, and Stanley Baldwin sought to eliminate rearmament as an issue by pledging that while the national security must be protected, there would be "no great armaments." The Labour party was at a hopeless disadvantage. Economic conditions were improving, and for this the National government claimed credit. Labour claimed to be the peace party, but quite apart from the obvious division within the party on the best way to preserve the peace, the National government could point to the naval agreement with Germany as evidence of leadership in the cause of disarmament, and to the vigor of Hoare and Eden at Geneva as evidence of leadership in pursuit of peace through the League. The election took place on November 14, 1935; the National government was returned to office with a diminished but substantial majority.

During the British electoral campaign, representatives of the French and British governments had been at work in Paris under the close supervision of Laval, seeking to formulate a compromise settlement in Ethiopia. For Laval, time was running out. On the one hand, he desperately needed some success before the French elections; on the other hand, the lull in the fighting in Ethiopia would end when Badoglio had completed his preparations for attack. Laval was in communication with Mussolini, who threatened retaliation if oil was placed on the sanctions list or if the Suez Canal were closed. The threat was taken seriously by the Anglo-French working group in Paris; indeed, it was believed that the prestige of Fascism in Italy would be fatally impaired if Mussolini retreated in face of League pressure. Undoubtedly, France and Britain could defeat Italy, but only at what seemed ruinous cost. If Mussolini became an enemy or, still worse, if Fascism in Italy was replaced by a left-wing government dependent on Communist Russia, then France would be isolated and Laval would be repudiated by the French electorate. Within the British government there was fear that if Italy did fight to prevent the imposition of effective League sanctions, then British naval forces in the Mediterranean would be badly mauled by Italian air power, which had supremacy in that area. To the British government, Ethiopia was not worth a serious sacrifice of sea power at a time when German military power was growing and when the Japanese were threatening new moves in China.

Neither the French nor the British government was prepared to carry sanctions to the point where there was serious likelihood of war with Italy. Yet pressure within the League for the addition of oil to the sanctions list was mounting rapidly. The pressure from other members of the League merely irritated Baldwin and Laval: after all, if war came, it would not be the smaller League powers which would do the fighting, but Britain and France. What really troubled the British and French governments was the probable reaction of opinion, particularly in Britain, if Ethiopia were crushed by Italy while the imposition of effective sanctions was blocked by the two governments.

Almost certainly arguments such as these guided the Anglo-French working party in Paris in formulating a compromise solution. Only such arguments could make defensible the solution which was proposed: the outright cession of large parts of Ethiopia to Italy, the designation of much of the remainder as an Italian sphere of influence; with a corridor to the sea as the only compensation to Ethiopia—a "corridor for camels," as it was soon contemptuously called. When Sir Samuel Hoare passed through Paris on his way to Switzerland for a vacation, he agreed to the submission of these terms to Mussolini and to the Ethiopian government; since Laval had been in communication with Mussolini, his acceptance was probable.[14]

What came to be called "the Hoare-Laval deal" was signed on December 8, 1935; on December 9, possibly because Laval hoped to prevent any British attempt to modify the terms, the agreement was

14. H. Braddick's essay, "The Hoare-Laval Plan: A Study in International Politics," *Review of Politics*, XXIV (July, 1962), 342–64, is a concise, well-documented account of this episode.

"leaked" to the French press. In Britain the terms aroused, first, stunned disbelief, then indignation too strong to be resisted. On December 18 Hoare resigned; on the following day Baldwin announced that the Hoare-Laval proposals had been abandoned; a few days later Anthony Eden, whose reputation as a defender of the League was untarnished, became foreign secretary. The Baldwin government received a grudging vote of confidence in the Commons. For a time opinion in Britain was distracted by the Christmas holidays, then by national mourning when King George V died on January 20, 1936. But tension soon mounted again. In February, the Italian forces began to move ahead rapidly in Ethiopia, their advance facilitated by the use of poison gas against native forces devoid of defense against gas. The pressure for the imposition of an embargo on exports of oil to Italy mounted once more, and in face of that pressure the refusal of the British government to consider any measure which might lead to hostilities with Italy once more became apparent.

Tension was mounting in France also. The failure of Laval to reconcile the Italian and British allies of France determined the fate of his government. The Radical Socialist party at last decided to throw in its lot with the Socialists and Communists in the elections. Laval lost his majority and resigned on January 19. A caretaker government, with Albert Sarraut as premier and Pierre Étienne Flandin as foreign minister, was installed to prepare the elections. This government at last submitted the French alliance with Russia to the Chambers for ratification. The debate showed how the diplomatic defeats of the last year had divided the French people. When Laval had concluded the alliance with Russia his action had the support of the parties of the right, which took pride in their devotion to the national interests of France. In May, 1935, the Russian alliance had seemed the logical completion of the alliances with Britain and Italy, all designed to prevent the expansion of Nazi Germany. By February, 1936, the alliance with Italy was lost, and confidence in British support was badly shaken; in central Europe, Poland and Rumania made no secret of their unwillingness to permit the passage of Soviet troops through their territory in case of a war between Russia and Germany. Above all, the probability of a Popular Front victory in the impending elections meant, to the parties of the right, that French Communists would be able to place French foreign policy in the service of international Communism. In these changed circumstances, French conservatives turned against the Russian alliance; the Chamber of Deputies voted to ratify the alliance on February 27, but the large number of negative votes and abstentions threw a harsh light on the lack of unity in France.

6. THE NAZI REMILITARIZATION OF THE RHINELAND

With France, Britain, and Italy divided from one another, and with public opinion in France and Britain divided and distracted over questions of foreign policy, Hitler made his decisive move to regain German "freedom." On March 7, 1936, he announced that since the Franco-Russian alliance was incompatible with the Locarno agreements, those agreements were "dead," and that to protect the frontiers of Germany, German troops were moving into the Rhineland, into the territory which, according to the Treaty of Versailles and the Locarno Pact, was to be permanently demilitarized. As usual, he announced his willingness to make a whole series of new agreements—for demilitarized zones on both sides of German frontiers in the West, for nonaggression pacts with the eastern as well as the western neighbors of Germany, and for insurance against attack from the air.

The remilitarization of the Rhineland was a flagrantly illegal act. Moreover, it drastically altered the balance of power, destroying French security against a surprise attack and jeopardizing French capability to march into Germany in case of a German attack against the eastern allies of France. Finally, the reoccupation of the Rhineland was a gamble: German rearmament had not progressed to the point where the German army could hope successfully to resist a French invasion.[15]

The French did not fight. Some, at least, of the members of the French cabinet knew that the whole position France had won in the world war was at stake. The events of the days which followed the German action have been subjected to minute examination. Although there is much conflict of testimony and many gaps in the evidence, what emerges clearly is unwillingness among the military as well as the civilian leaders of France to take responsibility for resuming the bloodshed ended at such terrible cost on November 11, 1918. Many, including

---

15. The German forces which reoccupied the Rhineland were, presently available evidence suggests, under orders to fight if French troops entered German territory; whether, in fact, Hitler would have resorted to war at this early date is uncertain; cf. D. C. Watt, "German Plans for the Reoccupation of the Rhineland: A Note," *Journal of Contemporary History* I (Oct., 1966), 193–99.

Flandin, the foreign minister, professed eagerness to act if sure of the support of Britain, and the discussions in Paris were broken off with obvious relief while the British were consulted. The results of that consultation were known in advance: immediately following the German action the British government, the British opposition leaders, and almost the whole British press spoke firmly against resort to force. Consultation with the British government, therefore, merely confirmed what the French cabinet already knew, that Britain was not prepared to support the use of force. So, after much talking and threatening, the French government did nothing. The Chamber of Deputies and, so far as anyone could estimate, the French people acquiesced in the decision to do nothing; indeed there was every evidence of popular reluctance to risk a war to prevent the militarization of the Rhineland.[16]

At first sight, the results of the French elections held on April 26 and May 2 told a different story: in the new Chamber the anti-Fascist Popular Front would hold 380 seats and the parties of the center and right only 237 seats. From these results one could conclude that the French people had turned decisively against the National Front which since the riots of February, 1934, had ruled France, and which had so clearly failed either to restrain the Fascist powers or to restore prosperity in France. On close examination, however, the verdict was not so clear. If the Communists had made spectacular gains, so had the parties of the right; there had been a tendency for voters to move to the two extremes. The center had lost heavily; in particular, the Radical Socialists had dropped from 159 to 116 seats. Yet, so far as control over the Chamber was concerned, they still had their old pivotal importance: with 265 deputies on their left and 237 deputies on their right, the Radical Socialists could end the Popular Front at any time by moving into alliance with the right. Another weakness became evident when the Communist party announced that it would not participate in the Popular Front government; in other words, that Communists would claim all rights as members of the Popular Front but would not accept responsibility for the actions of the government. Beyond these doubts

16. French policy with regard to the remilitarization of the Rhineland is examined in the light of the French diplomatic documents by Jean-Baptiste Duroselle and John C. Cairns in Evelyn M. Acomb and Marvin L. Brown, Jr. (eds.), *French Society and Culture Since the Old Regime* (N.Y., 1966), pp. 243–68, 283–88. Still useful is the thoughtful essay by W. F. Knapp, "The Rhineland Crisis of March 1936," in James Joll (ed.), *The Decline of the Third Republic* (London, 1959), pp. 67–85.

concerning the dependability of the Radicals and the Communists, there was the massive problem of reconciling the interests of the small businessmen and shopkeepers who voted Radical, the bureaucrats and schoolteachers who voted Socialist, and the workers and peasants who had sent the Communist vote soaring.

None of this was clear in the hopeful days of May, 1936, when most Frenchmen felt that the years of sterility and defeatism were ending and that France, like the United States a few years earlier, was about to receive a "new deal."

As for the German people, they gave their verdict on the foreign policy of Hitler in a plebiscite held on March 29. Almost unanimously, 98.7 per cent of those voting, they gave their approval. Whatever allowance is made for fear, there can be no doubt that the remilitarization of the Rhineland greatly enhanced the popularity of the Nazi regime with the German people.

In Ethiopia, while the attention of Europe was fixed on the Rhine, the Italian offensive gathered momentum. The last resistance collapsed at the beginning of May, and Emperor Haile Selassie fled to Europe. On May 9, from his balcony on the Palazzo Venezia, Mussolini announced that the King of Italy was now the Emperor of Ethiopia and that the conquest of Ethiopia was only the beginning of the great age of Fascist imperialism.

At the end of June, the assembly of the League of Nations heard Emperor Haile Selassie plead for aid in organizing resistance to the Italians. The assembly then voted the end of sanctions. With that vote, hope of attaining collective security through the League of Nations ended. The League, which to Woodrow Wilson was the great achievement of the Peace of Paris, was thereafter ignored in the crises of European and world politics.

Chapter Eleven

THE WESTERN DEMOCRACIES, 1936–1938

I. FRANCE: THE POPULAR FRONT

IN the hopeful spring days following the elections of 1936 in France, revolutionary change was in the air.[1] Industrial workers in particular were convinced that at last the time had come to break the control of men of property, of the "two hundred families," over France. In accordance with the traditions of revolutionary syndicalism and in imitation of the "sit-down" strikes in the United States, French workers took possession of factories and halted production to force acceptance of the Popular Front program. The Socialist premier, Léon Blum, as soon as he had organized his government, summoned employer and labor representatives to his official residence, the Hôtel Matignon, and there pounded out an agreement calling for the recognition of trade unions, for collective bargaining, and for wage increases varying from 7 to 15 per cent.[2]

The Matignon Agreement conceded nothing which had not been commonplace in many European countries; in France, where the divided and weak labor organizations had been unable to secure recognition, the agreement seemed revolutionary to both workers and employers. Encouraged, French workers by the millions joined the General Confederation of Labor, the central organization of the now united Socialist and Communist unions. The Chamber of Deputies was impressed and somewhat frightened by the new militancy of the

1. The best account of the Popular Front is Georges Lefranc's *Histoire du front populaire, 1934–1938* (Paris, 1965). G. Dupeux, *Le Front populaire et les élections de 1936* (Paris, 1959), is valuable. See also James Joll's assessment, "The Front Populaire— After Thirty Years," in the *Journal of Contemporary History*, I, 2 (1966), 27–42, and his essay "The Making of the Popular Front" in Joll (ed.), *The Decline of the Third Republic* (London, 1959). The January–March, 1966, issue of *Le mouvement social* is devoted to the Popular Front.

2. On Blum, see J. Colton, *Léon Blum: Humanist in Politics* (N.Y., 1966), and G. Ziebura, *Léon Blum: Theorie und Praxis einer sozialistischen Politik*, Vol. I, 1872–1934 (Berlin, 1963), which has been translated into French (Paris, 1967). *Léon Blum, chef de gouvernement, 1936–1937*, the product of a symposium, was published as No. 155 of the *Cahiers de la Fondation Nationale des Sciences Politiques* (Paris, 1967).

unions. In a rush, laws were passed implementing the Matignon
Agreement and establishing a forty-hour work week and vacations
with pay. Other legislation brought the Bank of France under government control, broke up the political leagues such as the Croix de Feu,
sought to end corruption of the press, permitted the nationalization of
armaments industries, and authorized a huge public works program.

Even the Senate, which did not have a secure Popular Front
majority, acquiesced in these measures. But private investors, fearful of
inflation and an unbalanced budget, resorted to the hoarding of gold
or to the export of their capital. Prices inched upward, destroying the
effects of wage increases and pressing on those with fixed incomes.
Blum was urged to push on, to take firm control over the economy and
particularly over the export of capital, above all to take measures which
would expand the stagnating production of France.

Before these proposals, Blum and his radical allies drew back. To
take the road to a "managed" economy was, to him, to take the road
Germany was traveling, the road to Fascism. Moreover, any effort to
guide and control the economy would affront a host of interests, all the
way from finance capital down to the little shopkeeper who might be
approaching starvation as his trade fell off, but who clung to his shop
because it was his and because it signified he was an independent
proprietor and not a workman. The same spirit, fearful of any change,
which kept the parish priest closed within his little world, imprisoned
the shopkeeper or tradesman or manufacturer, and also the farmer,
with his exhausted fruit trees and his production falling below other
countries of western Europe. Each had his little world, and each was
prepared to defend that little world. So, in February, 1937, when a
belated and reluctant devaluation of the franc had failed to check either
the flight of capital or the rise of prices, Léon Blum proclaimed a
"pause" in reform, hoping in vain for a rise in production.

It was not alone in his thinking on economics and society that Blum,
in office, showed himself caught in traditions which he had earlier
condemned. On the problem of defending France against the rising
strength of Germany, Blum the pacifist reached conclusions much like
those of Marshal Pétain the professional soldier. The thought of both
men was anchored in the stark statement: "Fire kills."

Pétain could not free himself from the memory of the world war.
Through four years, fire from artillery and machine guns had killed

the Frenchmen who tried to break through the line of trenches which stretched across northern France from Switzerland to the Channel. Pétain and his followers were determined that France should not again see its sons killed by the million, and they were convinced that such sacrifice was unnecessary. In another war France must stand on the defensive. Moreover, Pétain believed, it was not necessary for France to pour its wealth and its resources into military preparation, as Italy and Germany were doing. Italy and Germany were bent on conquest; to conquer, they must win in war. France wished only to protect itself. That was a far easier task, because the world war had demonstrated the superiority of defense over offense. If war came, France need only repel attack, sheltered behind the Maginot Line, an infinitely stronger defensive system than the trenches and barbed wire which had resisted attack through four years. Another war would again be a test of staying power; during the war France could mobilize its fresh resources and draw on the resources of the world outside Europe; German resources, already strained by preparation for war, would be unable either to muster the force necessary to break through the defenses of France or to hold out through years of fighting. With the same massive calm which had made him a tower of strength at Verdun and during the French mutinies of 1917, Marshal Pétain watched unafraid the military preparations of Nazi Germany; by the very intensity of their preparations, the Germans were preparing their own defeat. The arguments of those who, like Colonel Charles de Gaulle, urged that the plane and the tank had restored the superiority of the offensive were brushed aside. When, after the German remilitarization of the Rhineland, the Belgians withdrew from their alliance with France and resumed their old neutrality, the French general staff merely concentrated on the problems of extending the defenses of the Maginot Line to the English Channel.

The representative of the middle-class Radicals, Daladier, who was minister for war in the Popular Front government, accepted this military plan which husbanded the resources, human and material, of France, although Daladier, characteristically, also listened to de Gaulle. Blum was won by Pétain's arguments and repelled by the arguments of de Gaulle. To Blum, war was in essence bad, an evil to be averted. De Gaulle, with his plans for an elite force of professional soldiers poised for offensive action, suggested not the defense of French soil by the sons of France but dreams of Napoleonic conquest. So the Popular Front meant no break in limited and defensive military preparation.

More remarkably, there was no shift in foreign policy. Blum did not share the hatred for Communism of the parties of the right, and even of many of the Radicals in the Popular Front; for him, the rank and file of French Communists were misguided and too enthusiastic fellow Marxists. From experience, however, he had learned to mistrust the leaders of the French Communist party, and saw back of them the hated totalitarianism of the Soviet regime.[3] So, no more than the conservatives who had preceded him, was he inclined to begin the military conversations which were necessary if the alliance with Russia was to have real meaning. Even in relations with Germany and Italy he made no break with the past. Of course, he did not share the rising enthusiasm of many French conservatives for the Fascist leaders as crusaders against Communism and as bulwarks of European civilization against the disorders of the age, including the demands of labor.[4] But just as his pacifism brought him close to military leaders like Pétain, so his humanitarianism brought him to seek a reconciliation with the dictators. He was desperately aware that the rising tensions in Europe threatened to precipitate a war which would bring misery and death to every home in every land. As one who was completely convinced that all men everywhere were brothers, and that all men were much alike, he believed that if he offered friendship and reconciliation his offer would be accepted. And so, over and over, he affirmed his desire to regain Italian friendship and to remove the legitimate grievances of Germany. These offers were not made out of fear, except as he feared for the future of mankind if war came. No less than his military advisers, he was convinced that the military expenditures of Mussolini were driving Italy into bankruptcy and that Hitler was taking Germany on the same path, while France, by conserving its strength, was in an ever stronger position.

Possibly, given time and experience in government, Blum might

3. For studies of the parties making up the Popular Front, see Daniel Brower, *The New Jacobins: The French Communist Party and the Popular Front* (Ithaca, N.Y., 1968), and the studies of the Radical and Socialist parties cited above, Chap. X, n. 4.

4. Charles Micaud studied the drift of the French right toward pacifism in *The French Right and Nazi Germany, 1933–1939* (Durham, N.C., 1943).

have modified the ideas which he shared with so many of his fellow intellectuals. When he had been in office only a few weeks, however, he was confronted with the necessity to make decisions for which his intellectual training offered no guidance, decisions which ensured the failure of the Popular Front. On July 20 he received an open telegram from the premier of the Popular Front government of the Spanish Republic: "Are surprised by a dangerous military *coup*. Beg of you to help us immediately with arms and aeroplanes. Fraternally yours Giral."

2. THE SPANISH CIVIL WAR AND THE DICTATORS

The Spanish Popular Front government had come to power after elections in February, 1936.[5] In these elections the Communists, Socialists, and various liberal parties had supported a common list of candidates; many even of the anarchists, so numerous in Spain and traditionally so hostile to Socialists and Communists, supported the list. Whether or not the Popular Front and its Basque nationalist allies received a majority of the popular vote is a matter of controversy. In terms of seats won, however, the Popular Front had a decisive majority, not only over the National Front of the rightist parties, but over the combined seats of the National Front and the Center. A moderate republican cabinet now took office, but few expected it to endure. Not to go further back in the turbulent history of Spain, the five short years

5. Hugh Thomas' well-balanced history, *The Spanish Civil War* (London, 1961), is the standard account; Gabriel Jackson, *The Spanish Republic and the Civil War, 1931–1939* (Princeton, 1965), is valuable. An excellent study of the roots of the conflict is Gerald Brenan's *The Spanish Labyrinth: An Account of the Social and Political Background of the Civil War* (Cambridge, 1960). Dante Puzzo, *Spain and the Great Powers, 1936–1941* (N.Y., 1962), is a diplomatic history of the civil war; the older study by P. Van der Esch, *Prelude to War: The International Repercussions of the Spanish Civil War, 1936–1939* (The Hague, 1951), is also useful.

On Russian policy, see David Cattell, *Soviet Diplomacy and the Spanish Civil War* (Berkeley, 1957); on German policy, see the dissertation of Manfred Merkes, *Die deutsche Politik gegenüber dem spanischen Bürgerkrieg 1936–1939* (Bonn, 1961), and the Marxist study by Marion Einhorn, *Die ökonomischen Hintergründe der faschistischen deutschen Intervention in Spanien* (E. Berlin, 1962). Einhorn has used the rich Potsdam archives and the archives of the Deutsches Wirtschaftsinstitut of Berlin.

For intellectuals and the Spanish civil war, see the perceptive study of Peter Stansky and William Abrahams, *Journey to the Frontier: Julian Bell and John Cornford; Their Lives and the 1930's* (London, 1966), and the review article by Stephen Spender, "Writers and Revolutionaries: The Spanish War," *New York Review of Books,* XIII (Sept. 25, 1969), 3–8.

of the republic had been years of rising violence. Hard on the fall of the monarchy and the victory of the republicans in 1931, rightist groups had attempted a revolution in 1932; when the elections of 1934 gave a majority to the right, there had been leftist uprisings; the government of 1936 stood uneasily between those who called for and were attempting a social revolution and those who regarded any left government as a menace to the Church, the army, and not merely the aristocracy but the fearful middle classes. In the weeks and months following the elections of February, the record of violence and, most ominously, the roll of assassination and counterassassination lengthened.

To distribute blame in so tangled a story is impossible. All that can be said with certainty is that the old governing classes, and the Church and military which were inseparably allied to the old governing classes, had become the object of passionate hatred to most of the city workers and a large part of the peasantry and had also lost the support of most of the intellectual and cultural leaders of Spain. Certainly there were many workers and peasants who were loyal to the Church, just as there were priests and higher ecclesiastics who rebelled against the alliance of the Church with what they thought the blindly selfish exploiters of the poor. Beyond that, there was the tragedy of the Basque country, intensely Catholic and intensely loyal to the Popular Front. But, by and large, the generalization holds: Catholicism, which had once been inseparably connected with Spanish national feeling, had come to be identified with the rich who were hated by the poor.

One more generalization is now possible. The rapid descent of Spain, first, into violent disorder, and then into civil war, was an affair of the Spanish people, and not of outsiders, whether the U.S.S.R. or Nazi Germany or Fascist Italy. All three swung into action once the civil war began and greatly influenced the course and the outcome of the civil war; but the civil war was the outcome of hatreds which, over the course of more than a century, had been building up ever more explosively among the people of once proud and powerful but now weak and impoverished Spain.

On July 17, 1936, there was a rebellion of army leaders in Spanish Morocco, followed by revolts of army officers in one Spanish city after another. Within a few days, northern Spain, except for the coastal provinces along the Bay of Biscay and a deeper strip in the east along the frontier of France and the Mediterranean was in rebel hands; the rest of Spain, including Madrid, was in government control; in both parts there were still pockets of resistance. Throughout the country, each side attempted to exterminate adherents of the other side.

The importance for Europe as a whole of the ferocious struggle which raged in Spain for nearly three years cannot be exaggerated. The civil war was, in its inception, the outcome of Spanish history, but it became the testing ground for all of the larger issues dividing Europe. Mussolini and Hitler intervened at once, and possibly decisively. The crews of Spanish naval vessels mutinied against their rebel officers, so that the government had, temporarily, control of the sea approaches to Spain; if rebel troops had not been ferried from North Africa by Italy and Germany, the revolt might have foundered.

Mussolini claimed that he aided the rebels to prevent the spread of Communism, but it is doubtful if this was his major motive. One obvious motive was to place an ally athwart the sea lane between France and French Africa; Mussolini tried very hard to secure naval and air bases for Italy in the Balearic Islands. Probably even more important was the desire to raise Fascist prestige, already heightened by the Ethiopian war, to new heights in Italy by new military victories. The result was the opposite. The Italian people, and still more the hapless conscripts sent to fight in a cause for which they had no understanding, were impressed chiefly by the mounting costs of Italian intervention. By mid-1937 there were about 50,000 Italian troops in Spain; support of this army was a heavy drain. In every way, Italy was weakened by the Spanish adventure, not least by the fact that Italian freedom of diplomatic action, already impaired by the Ethiopian war, was further diminished as the Spanish civil war dragged on.

The Nazis never became deeply involved; probably there were never more than 10,000 Germans in Spain. Of these, 6,000 were in the Condor Legion. The Germans went in chiefly to complicate the strategic situation of France. Once there, the Nazis used the opportunity to test their military theories, and particularly their theories of air and tank warfare, under combat conditions. In 1932 the bombing of the civilian population of Shanghai by Japan had aroused disgust and horror throughout the world. From the systematic bombardment of Madrid from the air in 1936 to the final victory of the rebels in 1939, the Nazis repeatedly subjected Spanish cities to bombardment from the air, on occasion even bombarding a city when its capture was already imminent, so that the effects on the civilian population could be subjected to careful analysis while these effects were still fresh.

German and Italian policy in Spain can be described with some confidence, because extensive evidence is available. Soviet policy can only be surmised, because there is so little evidence, and much even of this is suspect. At the outset, Stalin moved hesitantly, probably in part because he was waiting to see what Britain and France would do, and in part because he was preoccupied with preparations for the first of the show trials of the Great Purge. When he did move to support the government cause in Spain, he had two unique assets. The first was the international apparatus of the Comintern, which went into action everywhere, except of course in Italy and Germany. A host of committees sprang up to provide various kinds of assistance to the Spanish government, usually headed by non-Communists and with largely non-Communist membership, but with Communists in positions which ensured control. The most famous of these organizations were the international brigades of volunteers to fight in Spain. In the brigades most of the volunteers were Communists, and some of the remainder were merely adventurers eager for excitement, but many were non-Communist idealists eager to fight for freedom—and a large proportion of the Communists in the brigades were idealists who identified Communism with freedom. In addition to organizing the international brigades, the committees sponsored by the Comintern collected money and supplies and munitions to support the brigades.

The other Soviet asset was the small Spanish Communist party. In journalistic accounts, Spanish Communism was symbolized by the dramatic figure of the woman universally known as La Pasionaria. In actuality, the party was a severely disciplined group which early in the civil war received an infusion of foreign leaders such as the Italian Palmiro Togliatti, and which in the autumn of 1936 came under the tight control of the Soviet embassy, whose expanding personnel included agents of the NKVD.

By the autumn Stalin had laid aside his initial caution and was sending substantial aid to the Spanish government, but only after a shipment of Spanish gold arrived at Odessa to ensure payment. Just as German aid in the first days may have been decisive in preventing the crushing of the rebellion, so the international brigades, the discipline of the Communist party, and Soviet supplies may explain the failure of the rebels to take Madrid in the great battle which opened in November, 1936. The brigades and the Russian tanks and planes took the lead in the fighting, while the party made sure that there was no rising of the "fifth column" of rebel sympathizers within the city, upon which General Mola had counted to give victory to his four columns of troops.

Thereafter, the Communist party, although it represented only a small minority of the Spanish people, rapidly attained almost complete control over the Spanish government, or over the Loyalist government as it came to be called now that there were obviously two governments in Spain (the rebel government will hereafter be referred to as Nationalist). It is easy to understand the growing Communist ascendancy. The Popular Front was made up of factions which were divided from each other only less than they were separated from the Nationalists—liberals, socialists, anarchists, Communists, Trotsky Communists, Basque and Catalan separatists; these groups had no love for one another. Among the groups, the Communists alone had both discipline and a realization that an attempt to impose social revolution on the Spanish people would produce a civil war within the larger civil war. The Communists, acting on orders from Moscow, were determined to postpone the social revolution until the Nationalists had been beaten. To achieve their end, the Communists imposed a reign of terror on all who tried to bring about a social revolution. They were successful, partly because they were disciplined, partly because they were ruthless, but chiefly because everyone in the Loyalist camp knew that unless Soviet aid continued, the Loyalists were certain to lose.

Remarkably, the Nationalists avoided domination by either Germany or Italy, even though the Nationalists were also divided among themselves. At the outset the Nationalists had no positive program and they scarcely had a government. They did not even have a leader. Only slowly did the plump, insignificant figure of Francisco Franco emerge from the group of rebel generals who ran Nationalist Spain like an army camp. Still more slowly, Franco's brother-in-law, Ramón Serrano Suñer, emerged as the organizer of some sort of conservative program for the essentially negative Nationalist regime. Possibly it was Franco's bored indifference to all ideological discussion, and his jealous suspicion of all, including the leaders of the Fascist Falange, who sought to impose a body of beliefs on their followers, which explain Franco's ability to prevent explosive conflicts within Nationalist Spain. More probably, his success was ensured by the lack of any disciplined group in the service of Germany or Italy; the Falange, an imitation of the black- and the brown-shirted Fascists, never won a large popular following. Whatever the explanation, Franco successfully repelled the efforts of the Germans and the Italians to control him, although he was as dependent on their aid as the Loyalists were on Soviet aid. In the last months of the civil war, when stalemate was ended only by massive German assistance, Franco did give the Germans extensive economic concessions. Even then, he avoided political subservience, even political intimacy.

3. FRANCE AND THE SPANISH CIVIL WAR

This difference in the evolution of Loyalist and Nationalist Spain helps to explain the policy of France and Britain during the civil war. At the outset, the Popular Front government in France was eager to heed the appeal of the Spanish Popular Front for aid.[6] Most of Blum's supporters were convinced that if the Popular Front were overthrown in Spain, Fascism in France would take the offensive; to save the Popular Front in France, the Popular Front in Spain must be saved. Blum, therefore, agreed to the Spanish request for planes, guns, and ammunition.

Immediately, there was a violent reaction, beginning on the right, but spreading to include many Radical-Socialists. French Catholics, like Catholics everywhere, were horrified by reports of the murder of priests and the pillaging of churches. Few Catholics knew anything about Spain or the Spanish church; for most, the fact that in Loyalist territory churchmen were being murdered and churches destroyed sufficed. Within a few weeks this view hardened as the murders mounted and Pope Pius XI denounced the "truly satanic hatred of God" of the Loyalists. Other Frenchmen of the right or center supported the Nationalists because the Loyalists included Communists, anarchists, and Trotskyites. This was true in other countries; as Winston Churchill was to say later, he could not be expected to favor those who would have murdered him and his family and friends.[7]

6. See J. Bowyer Bell, "French Reaction to the Spanish Civil War, July–September 1936" in L. P. Wallace and W. C. Askew, *Power, Public Opinion and Diplomacy* (Durham, N.C., 1959).

7. Winston Churchill, *The Gathering Storm* (London, 1950), p. 192.

If it had been only a question of left against right in France, Blum probably would have persisted. Very quickly, however, warnings came from Britain, at first only warnings to be prudent, but quickly rising to a blunt threat that if French aid to the Loyalists resulted in war with Germany, Britain would stand aside.

The warnings fell with doubly crushing force on Blum and his government. The prospect of war with Germany without British help was bound to strike terror into any Frenchman. In some ways more paralyzing for Blum was that one word—war. In his thought—as in the thought of most French socialists, in the thought of most British laborites, and for that matter in the thought of most Western liberals— war was a part of the old capitalist order, which was bad partly because it was connected with war. Now, by competing in the provision of arms to the rival forces in Spain, Blum risked one object of his hatred, war; on the other hand, by refusing to give arms to the Loyalists he might ensure the success of hated Fascism.

Blum tried to escape the dilemma by proposing on August 2 that all governments agree to a "nonintervention pact." At the same time, the French frontier remained open for the "private" shipment of arms to the Loyalists, including some shipments which were, in veiled form, from French government sources. The British government welcomed the nonintervention proposal, but insisted that the danger of war would continue so long as the French frontier remained open. Forced at last to choose, Blum contemplated resignation; in the end, on August 8, the French cabinet bowed to British pressure and closed the frontier. On September 9, the first meeting of the nonintervention committee was held in London. Already, what a German diplomat said of the Italian government—that it obviously did not intend to live up to the nonintervention agreement—was no less obviously true of the German government, and also of the Soviet government.

The decision of Blum was angrily denounced by the Communists and also by other adherents of the French Popular Front, as well as by his fellow intellectuals in all Western countries. Most refused to acknowledge the cruel choice with which he felt himself confronted: between his devotion to peace and his devotion to international social- ism. Possibly, if the French had capped each infusion of German and Italian men and arms by an infusion of French men and arms, the end would not have been war. If Blum had been, like his critics, only a

French intellectual commenting from the sidelines, he might himself have said the alternatives were not war, without British help, or the closing of the frontier. But in 1936 Blum the intellectual had become Blum the premier, and as premier he was not prepared to gamble on the peaceful outcome of a race to ensure the victory of one side or the other in a civil war in which both sides preferred an international war to defeat.

So far as the French Popular Front government was concerned, the closing of the frontier was a fatal blow. As the Spanish civil war dragged on, with victories now for one side and then the other, but with the tide of battle running relentlessly against the Loyalists, and with German and Italian aid moving with less and less concealment to strengthen the Nationalist cause, the French tradesmen and peasants and workers and schoolteachers and intellectuals who had combined to bring the Popular Front to power in France quarreled with one another. Blum fell in June, 1937. The Popular Front continued in form, to disintegrate finally in a government crisis which left France leaderless just as the Nazis marched into Austria in March, 1938.

The Popular Front failed for many reasons: because of timidity in measures to cope with the financial and economic ills of France; because of the relentless and unscrupulous opposition of those who hated any left government; and because of the inevitable fissures in a grouping which sought to achieve cooperation between Radicals, Socialists and Communists; but the sense of mission, the confidence of victory, was drained away in the months after August, 1936, when Léon Blum was forced to choose between his devotion to peace and his devotion to socialism.

Thereafter, France was incapable of effective action. At home, the drift to the extreme right and extreme left was intensified. On the right, there was lamentation over the loss of friendship with Fascist Italy and willingness to go to almost any length to regain that friendship. Increasingly, among conservatives, the old nationalist hatred for Germany was replaced by admiration for what the Nazis were doing to impose "order" on the German people and to prevent the spread of Communism in Europe. Laval, having failed in his efforts to build an alliance system against Germany, was moving toward the thought of alliance with Germany. Flandin, despite repeated rebuffs from the Nazis, was sure that he could arrange a "reasonable" settlement of

Franco-German differences. Within the government, after the end of the Popular Front, Foreign Minister Georges Bonnet played a most ambiguous role; at the least he was defeatist. The premier, Daladier, alternated between moods of resistance and moods of despair in his negotiations with Germany; it was only in his determined resistance to the demands of French labor that he showed the vigor imputed to him.

Among French workers, and many intellectuals and students, there was increasing adulation of Soviet Russia, together with a revival of the old argument that war against Germany would serve the interests only of French capitalists; workmen had nothing to gain, no matter who won. Economic production revived somewhat when the fall of the Popular Front brought a return to more orthodox methods of balancing the budget by reducing expenses, including wages. Since they did not participate in the revival, the French workers felt no inclination to further the revival, or even to increase arms production, by working harder than was necessary. The middle classes did participate in the revival, but showed by rather forced gaiety an uneasy consciousness that time was running out for the Third Republic.

Between 1934 and 1936 the parties of the right failed, failed in their efforts to combat the depression at home, failed in their efforts to restrain the revival of German power by paper pacts which had no force behind them. In 1936 the Popular Front failed, failed either to unite France behind a program of social reform at home or to unite the country in resistance to Fascism in Spain. After 1936 French leaders continued to insist that in a crisis Frenchmen would forget those things which divided them at home and unite in resistance to Germany as they had united in 1914. French leaders, with equal vehemence, insisted that the Maginot Line was insurance against a repetition of the war of attrition, against another and fatal outpouring of the blood of young Frenchmen.

Behind these vehement protestations, however, there was an increasing consciousness that what confronted France immediately was not an invasion of France by Germany, but German determination to dominate central Europe. Over and over, the Germans said that if the French would abandon their eastern alliances, then Germany and France could be friends. Few Frenchmen were willing to accept the German demand that friendship be purchased by acquiescing in

German domination of central Europe: once Germany was triumphant in the east, France would be at the mercy of Germany; then the Germans would be in a position to demand at least the return of Alsace-Lorraine and probably to demand also that control of northern France of which German leaders had dreamed in the years before November, 1918. French leaders could not agree to the surrender of central Europe to Germany, but French leaders quailed at the thought of fighting to prevent Germany from dominating central Europe, of moving out of the defenses of the Maginot Line to assault the West Wall which the Germans were frantically building. If, in an invasion of France, Germany would bleed to death in front of the Maginot Line, would not France bleed to death in front of the West Wall?

French statesmen could not bring themselves to abandon their eastern allies. Neither could they nerve themselves to an invasion of Germany to protect their eastern allies—certainly not without assurance of British support, and the hope of that Russian and American support which had been essential for victory in 1918. Caught between fear of abandoning and fear of supporting their eastern allies—caught also between the demand of the French people that the position won at Versailles be maintained and the refusal of the French people to make sacrifices for the building of the defenses of France—the rulers of France, in effect, surrendered control of French foreign policy to Britain. Where Britain led, France followed, complaining and expostulating, but helpless.

4. BRITAIN AND THE SPANISH CIVIL WAR

Superficially, the Spanish civil war divided British opinion no less than French opinion.[8] At the outset, when the British government espoused nonintervention, there was little dissent. As the ferocity of the struggle mounted, however, and as it became evident that Germany, Italy, and Russia were participating in the fighting, a confused debate began in Britain.

Government spokesmen argued that the aid being given to one side and the other in Spain was deplorable but impossible to prevent; for Britain and France also to intervene would be to bring back to European politics the passions of the age of the religious wars, with fatal

8. See K. W. Watkins, *Britain Divided: The Effect of the Spanish Civil War on British Political Opinion* (London, 1963).

consequences for European civilization. Moreover, in the view of men like Stanley Baldwin, British interests would not be seriously hurt no matter which side won in Spain: the victor would show the proud determination to eliminate foreign influence that Spaniards had always shown; the totalitarian states would be forced to withdraw, without reward for their sacrifice of blood and treasure. These arguments were repeated with confidence even after the intervention of Italy and Germany began to tilt the scales in favor of Franco. Indeed, little effort was made to conceal the conviction of most members of the British government that while the most desirable outcome was a stalemate followed by a peaceful settlement effected through British mediation, a Franco victory was preferable to a "red" victory.

Just as government policy can be described as noninterventionist with a bias toward the Nationalist side, so Labour policy was, at the outset, noninterventionist with a bias toward the Loyalist side. And if the government had a secure majority in Parliament behind its policy, Labour had the support of most British intellectuals. A poll taken in 1937 showed that fewer than a half dozen of the British intellectual leaders who responded were on the side of the Nationalists, and fewer than a dozen and a half professed neutrality; a hundred favored the Loyalists. Probably if the poll had been extended to include less conspicuous figures such as scientists and other scholars and their students, the proportion would have been much the same. Here was an asset far greater than numbers would suggest, because these were men and women trained to speak, to write, to persuade, men and women who were, most of them, passionately devoted to the Loyalist cause. To these people, Spain was a struggle between all that was old, unjust, oppressive in Europe, and all that was new, clean, free. "The struggle in Spain," wrote W. H. Auden, "has X-rayed the lies upon which our civilization is built."[9]

Despite this depth of feeling, the opponents of the Baldwin government were unable to unite on an alternative to the policy of nonintervention. Pacifism had been officially repudiated by the Labour party during the Ethiopian crisis, but the appeal of pacifism was still strong, particularly among intellectuals. In 1937, Aldous Huxley was a supporter of the Spanish Loyalists and also the editor of *An Encyclopedia*

9. Thomas, *op. cit.,* pp. 220–22.

of Pacifism, which preached the folly of war and argued that in another war "the chief use of the army will be, not to fight an enemy, but to try to keep order among the panic-stricken population at home."[10] In April, 1937, at a pacifist meeting, Bertrand Russell declared that if the Germans invaded England they should be welcomed like tourists and treated in a friendly way, because the damage done in resisting them would be greater than the damage they would do. He concluded: "The Nazis would find some interest in our way of living, I think, and the starch would be taken out of them."[11] On the other hand, Labour party leaders like Hugh Dalton and Ernest Bevin had come to the conclusion that what had happened in China, Ethiopia, and Spain had demonstrated the folly of unilateral disarmament and pacifism, and that the dictators could be stopped only by force. The leader of the Labour party, Clement Attlee, tried to straddle the issue by insisting that a firm stand by the powers loyal to the League in Spain and elsewhere would mean not war but peace: "The dictators were not intending, and were in no condition, to engage in war."[12]

On the question of cooperation with Communists there was also division. Many of the intellectuals who supported the Spanish Loyalists were Communists or fellow travelers, or at least were convinced that in Russia the future was being built and that the West had no higher purpose than to recapture a dead past. Evidence to support this conviction seemed abundant. In Russia the curve of industrial production was shooting up; in the West each advance was succeeded by a falling back. In Russia there was work for all, and the Stakhanovites moved from one triumph to another; in Britain men decayed on the dole, and the highest aspiration was to recapture the position Britain once occupied, not to scale new heights. Russia was described as the unhesitating and unswerving supporter of free government in Spain, while Britain at best was doing nothing, and even seemed an ally of the foes of freedom. In 1936 the British intellectuals who thought of themselves as the builders of a new and free society were almost as hostile to the Labour party, which to them seemed dominated by a stagnant trade union mentality, as they were to the National government, which was described as the ally of Fascism in Spain and elsewhere.

As the Communists moved into control of Loyalist Spain, however,

10. Aldous Huxley (ed.), *An Encyclopedia of Pacifism* (N.Y., 1937), p. 13.
11. *New York Times,* April 2, 1937, p. 9.
12. London *Times,* July 12, 1937, p. 14.

disillusionment spread among British intellectuals. It was fed by stories told by idealists in the International Brigades about the relentless fight of the Communists against the Spanish Trotskyites and anarchists, and above all by the recall to oblivion in Russia of exactly those Communist leaders who had shown most sympathy for the sufferings of the Spanish people.

When the Great Purge began in Russia, it was easy for sympathizers in Britain to argue that the victims really were traitors and that the Soviet Union could now better serve the Communist cause. As, however, the purge was intensified, as the Old Bolsheviks made their fantastic confessions, and as reports of the spread of terror multiplied, only the most hardened advocates of the Soviet cause could push the evidence aside. For some British as well as French and American intellectuals, the controversy which raged around André Gide's *Retour de l'U.R.S.S.* during the summer of 1937 was a turning point. Gide went to Russia in 1936 a Soviet sympathizer; he was disillusioned by what he saw and sadly told of his disillusionment in his book. Until the book appeared, Communists had lavished praise on him and his work; now he and his writings were covered with abuse. One unintended effect of this abuse was to communicate Gide's disillusionment to British intellectuals like the young poet Stephen Spender, who had been a member of the Communist party for a brief period in the winter of 1936–37.[13]

By the autumn of 1937 the pressure of events had moved most Labour members of Parliament to the point where they voted for the arms budget. At the annual Labour party conference in October, an overwhelming majority voted, as in the past, against a new effort to form a Popular Front with the Communist party. But the tradition of pacifism continued strong in the Labour party and among British intellectuals. Strong, too, remained the disposition to interpret all European problems as a struggle between "Fascism" and "freedom," with the Soviet Union as the leader of the forces of freedom.

5. BRITAIN: THE END OF THE BALDWIN ERA

Stanley Baldwin had no difficulty defending his policy of nonintervention in Spain against opponents who were busy fighting each other. As Hitler and Mussolini intervened more and more openly in Spain,

13. Cf. Spender and Gide in *The God That Failed*, ed. by Richard Crossman (N.Y., 1950).

however, Baldwin recognized the drift of Europe toward war. "We have two madmen loose in Europe," he told the Imperial Conference which was in session when he retired in May, 1937. "Anything may befall."

Later the accusation was to be made that Baldwin had failed to make military preparations for the perils he saw ahead because he was afraid of losing office. This legend will live on because it is repeated in Winston Churchill's epic history of the Second World War and because events were to show that Britain should have begun rearmament before 1935 and should have armed much more rapidly after 1935.

The legend has no foundation, but the problem remains: Baldwin, nearly all members of his cabinet (including Neville Chamberlain, his successor and one of the early advocates of rearmament), and most members of Parliament saw no great danger in the placid pace of British military preparations in 1937. Even those who were uneasy, like Alfred Duff Cooper and Anthony Eden, showed little recognition that speed was desperately urgent; certainly they did not show sufficient alarm to carry the case to the British public, as Churchill had done since 1933. This is the more remarkable because men like Duff Cooper and Eden were aware, as most Englishmen were not, that an interval of years must intervene between the decision to produce weapons and the production of weapons. The German decision to produce had been taken in the first years of the Nazi regime, and in 1937 German production was rising to a flood. By then it was apparent that the British decisions of 1935 and 1936 would never produce a comparable flood. This disparity was pointed out by Churchill and a few others, but government spokesmen and most of the publicists who were known to speak with full knowledge of the facts accepted with equanimity the widening gap between German and British military power.

In Britain, as in France, argument hinged on the supposed superiority of defense over attack. On April 3, 1937, a leading editorial in the London *Times,* written by the most distinguished British military commentator, B. H. Liddell Hart, argued that the battles of the Spanish civil war, like the battles of the world war, demonstrated that "defense is paramount." Indeed he argued that in Spain "perhaps the most probable alternative to a stalemate is that continued attacks may turn the scales of war against the attacking side."[14]

14. London *Times,* April 3, 1937. This editorial appeared, under Liddell Hart's name, in the *New York Times* on the same day.

In other writings, Liddell Hart applied this dictum to Europe as a whole and argued that since Britain wished only to defend itself, while Germany must seek victory, in a war between the two countries Germany would need vastly greater forces. Moreover, he said, the next war would be long, an endurance test. In such a contest, success must come to the side with the greater staying power rather than to the side with the greater initial strength. Germany and Italy were already suffering from the burden of military preparations and they did not possess assets sufficient to sustain a long war. Britain should not imitate their exhausting preparations, Liddell Hart argued, but should conserve the strength needed, not only to parry the aggressor's thrust and to fight a long war, but to give continued leadership after the war.[15]

In the light of this reasoning, it is easier to understand the strange combination of foreboding and confidence evident in Britain during Stanley Baldwin's last months of office. The foreboding resulted immediately from the increasing recklessness of German and Italian intervention in Spain, and more generally from the obvious determination of Hitler and Mussolini to upset the European, and world, balance of power. For this situation Baldwin saw no remedy, and if war did come he saw Europe engulfed in general ruin. On the other hand, Baldwin plainly believed he had prepared Britain, and the Empire, for war, not by the weight of British arms but by the unity of the British people, the unity essential for survival in a long war which no one could hope to win but which he was confident that a united British Empire would not lose.

For Baldwin, therefore, the crisis in the last months of 1936 over the plan of King Edward VIII to marry a divorced American woman was of incomparably greater importance than the mounting succession of crises over foreign intervention in Spain, of greater importance than the increasingly vehement demands of the controlled German press that Germany be given a free hand in central Europe and that Germany regain the colonies lost in the world war. The marriage plans of the king, Baldwin believed, threatened the unity of the Empire; about Germany and Italy there was nothing to be done. When King Edward had abdicated, when the new king, George VI, had been crowned, and when the statesmen of the British Commonwealth, assembled for the coronation, gave assurance that the Empire, like Britain itself, had

15. Liddell Hart, *The Defense of Britain* (N.Y., 1939), pp. 25, 26, 42, 43, 48, 49.

emerged united from the crisis, then Baldwin could feel that his task was accomplished. On May 28, 1937, he resigned. His successor was Neville Chamberlain, who had, since the formation of the National government in 1931, been the strongest and most original mind in the cabinet, and who had waited with increasing impatience for the day when he could give a new direction to British foreign policy.

6. CHAMBERLAIN AND THE APPEASEMENT POLICY

With Chamberlain, "appeasement" became British policy.[16] It was not a new word. It had been used earlier, by Briand for instance, as something both desirable and possible. To Chamberlain, however, the word meant much more than to Briand the conciliator, much more than to Baldwin, whose success through a long career is in large part explained by his ability to appease opponents.

Chamberlain had been one of the first and most consistent advocates of British rearmament. Like Baldwin, however, he believed that rearmament which jeopardized financial stability or social reform was dangerous and unnecessary. Like Baldwin, he was in 1937 a pessimist about the consequences of war for European civilization and an optimist about the ability of Britain to avoid defeat in war without concentrating British resources on rearmament.

So far, only the dwindling minority of British pacifists and the even smaller number of advocates of all-out rearmament disagreed with Chamberlain. He, however, was determined to end what he regarded as the policy of passive drift in foreign affairs, and to move vigorously toward reconciliation with Germany and Italy.

When he took office, Germany and Italy were united in what was called the Rome-Berlin Axis, formed in October, 1936. In November, 1936, Germany and Japan concluded what was called the Anti-Comintern Pact.[17] In all three countries there was talk of a formal alliance of turning the "axis" into a "triangle." To many in Britain, the logical answer to the union of the "dictators" was a union of the

---

16. K. Feiling, *The Life of Neville Chamberlain* (London, 1946), remains the best biography; valuable material, particularly from Chamberlain's diary, is in Iain MacLeod, *Neville Chamberlain* (London, 1961). W. N. Medlicott, "Neville Chamberlain," *History Today,* II (May, 1952), 345–50, is an excellent summary of Chamberlain's foreign policy.

17. Cf. below, pp. 325–326.

"democracies." Chamberlain was convinced that such a union was neither desirable nor attainable.

In 1937 the American Congress passed a permanent neutrality law designed to insulate the United States from the quarrels of the rest of the world. In the Congress there was strong support for the Ludlow Resolution, which would require a popular referendum before the United States could enter a war.[18] Chamberlain recognized the potential power of the United States, but he saw no reason to make sacrifices to win American favor since he could hope for nothing "but words" in return. As for Russia, he thought it ludicrous to speak of the Soviet Union as a democracy, and he believed the Great Purge was both revealing and increasing the weakness of Russia. Above all, while there is no convincing evidence to support the accusation that he wanted a war between Russia and Germany, there is conclusive evidence that he believed Russia wanted to embroil the "capitalist" countries in war with each other. Even France seemed to him a weak and unreliable ally: "She never can keep a secret for more than half an hour, nor a government for more than nine months!"[19]

Chamberlain thought a union of the "democracies" was neither desirable nor attainable; he thought the union of the dictators was neither solid nor permanent. German and Japanese interests clashed in the Far East, he argued, and Germany and Italy were separated by Austria; in 1934 Mussolini had shown clear recognition of the dangers which a union of Austria with Germany would entail for Italy.

While Chamberlain rejoiced at the lack of a clear division between the "dictators" and the "democracies," he recognized that the international situation was dangerous. In his view, the recurrent crises were symptomatic of a fevered temper in Germany and Italy which had its origins in the peace settlement of 1919.

That settlement, Chamberlain believed, by its denial of the justifiable grievances of Germany and Italy, had resulted in a truly neurotic condition in those countries, a condition which must be met not by the use of force but by removing the grievances. Over and over, the Germans asserted their right to colonies. Chamberlain believed this

18. The search for a way to avoid entanglements, commercial and otherwise, which might result in the United States being drawn into war is described by Robert Divine in *The Illusion of Neutrality* (Chicago, 1962), with a useful bibliographical essay.

19. Feiling, *op. cit.*, pp. 322–25.

right could be acknowledged, not by the return of the precise territory taken from Germany—opposition in the Empire and within his own party made that impossible—but by making Germany a partner in great colonial enterprises and thereby removing the stigma of Versailles. Some concession must also be made to the demand that the Germans in Austria, Czechoslovakia, and Poland be given the self-determination denied to them in 1919. Finally, concessions must be made to the demand for recognition of the "natural" predominance of Germany in central Europe; so long as German influence spread peacefully, Britain could only rejoice. In Chamberlain's view, as Germany became economically prosperous, as Germany attained equality as a colonial power, and as Germans lost the feeling their fellow Germans in other countries were treated unjustly, the neurotic excitability which made Germany a difficult neighbor would subside. Then Germans would recognize that they, no less than the British, had everything to gain by peace and disarmament, and everything to lose by ruinous expenditure on arms, and above all by war.

Italy, Chamberlain was convinced, could also be appeased. After all, the conquest of Ethiopia was a fact; why not placate the Italians by agreeing to address their king as Emperor of Ethiopia? The Italians were obsessed by the feeling that their country had not been treated as a great power; why not make a special effort to show recognition of the fact that Italy was the great Mediterranean power? Then the Italians would recognize that their security was menaced not by British naval power but by German claims to dominance in central and south-eastern Europe.

When he reviewed the international situation at the Guild Hall on November 9, 1937, Chamberlain contrasted the alternatives facing mankind: whether to move toward peace and prosperity or toward a "perpetual nightmare" of armament and war. "One has only to state these two alternatives," he concluded, "to be sure that human nature, which is the same all the world over, must reject the nightmare with all its might and cling to the only prospect which can give happiness."[20]

During the years when he had waited for power, Chamberlain had, in the imagery of diplomacy, "made a picture." The world created by the Peace of Paris, he believed, was doomed. Japan in the Far East, Italy in the Mediterranean, and Germany in central Europe were in violent

20. London *Times*, Nov. 10, 1937, p. 8.

rebellion against the position allocated to them by the treaty arrangements of the past. To oppose their violence with violence would mean, in his judgment, first an arms race which would devour resources needed to ensure peaceful social change, and then war which would end in common ruin. Only the rulers of the Soviet Union could hope to gain if mankind took the path to war; Communism, he was convinced, would be the sole beneficiary from war.

In office, Chamberlain set about the task of translating his picture of the world into reality. He moved without doubt or hesitation. Opposition at home he treated with impatience which quickly changed to contempt, whether the opposition came from the Labour party, from dissidents in his own party like Churchill, or from the foreign office. Completely confident of his own judgment, he came more and more to mistrust the slow, patient processes of professional diplomacy, and to look for results through direct negotiations between important personages, that is, between men on whom rested final responsibility for the welfare of their country, men like himself. In these negotiations, he scorned quibbling over what he thought details; he was concerned, he said, only with the large picture.

During 1937 Chamberlain took no overt steps to appease Hitler or Mussolini, but he did, repeatedly, affirm his belief that appeasement was possible. In Britain there was opposition to his views. Inevitably, those who believed Fascism was the enemy of democracy were outraged by his affirmation that differences of political creed need not be an obstacle to friendly relations. There was opposition also to his contention that German and Italian friendship could be won by granting at least part of the demands of Hitler and Mussolini. The opposition was, however, confused and divided. Conservatives who were prepared to ignore what Hitler and Mussolini were doing at home objected vehemently to colonial concessions to Germany and Italy. Many who believed that any territorial expansion of Nazi Germany was an expansion of slavery were troubled by the conviction that Germans, like other peoples, were entitled to the right of self-determination. Those who were disposed to believe that the "dictators" could be stopped only by mobilizing and uniting the strength of the "democracies" were tortured by the belief that war came in 1914 because Europe had become divided into furiously arming alliance systems. In this clash of opinion, it is probable that what the mythical "average Englishman" thought was well expressed by the most revered of British historians in a letter printed in the London *Times* on August 12, 1937. "Dictatorship and democracy must live side by side in peace, or civilization is doomed," wrote George Macaulay Trevelyan. "For this end I believe Englishmen would do well to remember that the Nazi form of government is in large measure the outcome of Allied and British injustice at Versailles in 1919."

As he worked on the task of preparing concrete proposals to be presented to Germany and Italy, Chamberlain showed complete confidence that despite the demand of Labour and its allies among the intellectuals for a firm stand against the dictators in Spain, and despite the misgivings even of some members of his cabinet like Anthony Eden, he did have the support of his countrymen, and he did have on his side, in his labors for appeasement, "human nature, which is the same all the world over."

Chapter Twelve

NAZI DYNAMISM, 1936–1938

1. GERMAN NATIONALISTS AND GERMAN NAZIS

CHAMBERLAIN's hatred of war and of the dissipation of resources on preparation for war, like his willingness to put national pride to one side in the hope that by removing the feeling of injustice he could bring rebellious peoples to a realization of the suicidal nature of war, was rooted in the memory of the world war. Like most of his countrymen, he saw clearly that despite victory Britain had lost from the war, and like his countrymen, he drew the conclusion that war was an evil to be avoided at almost any cost.

Germans, at least those who controlled the destiny of Germany, drew a different conclusion. "The debate about the significance of war and the ideal of eternal peace, the conflict between the heroic and the pacifist conception of the world, in Germany is over and done with," wrote Hermann Foertsch, a colonel of the general staff. "The hard facts of an unworthy peace, after an unfortunate war, have waked our people from an uneasy dream, and the accomplishments of National Socialism have once more quickly taught us that only the weak need fear a war, while the strong are safe by reason of their very strength."[1]

By 1937, no one active in German political life would deny Foertsch's dictum that, as a fact of nature, "in the life of nations, we find both peace and war."[2] In public, there was also agreement on what Germany demanded and what Germany would, if necessary, fight to obtain. What Germany demanded was "justice," justice for the Germans who were denied the right of self-determination promised them by Woodrow Wilson, and justice through the return of the former German colonies to their rightful owner. That was all Germany demanded. Beyond these demands, Germany asked only that the other powers unite with Germany in the defense of civilization against the

---

1. Hermann Foertsch, *The Art of Modern Warfare* (N.Y., 1940), p. 5. This book appeared in Germany before war began in 1939.
2. *Ibid.*, p. 3.

EUROPE

AFTER MARCH 15, 1939

Spheres of interest agreed to in Secret Additional Protocol to Russian-German Treaty of August 23, 1939

Russian interest

German interest

Areas of German "complete political disinterestedness"

Map by Harry Scott

advance of Bolshevism, instead of allying with Bolshevism, as France and Czechoslovakia had done, to deny Germany its "rightful" influence in central Europe.

Behind the façade of unity, and sometimes breaking through the façade, debate proceeded on the objectives of German policy and the means to attain these objectives. On one side, very roughly, were those who believed that primacy in central Europe would satisfy German national needs, and that primacy was the extreme goal obtainable without a war in which German defeat was likely.

Schacht, from his experience in shaping the German economy, argued that by 1937 the limit of the economy had been reached; to continue to divert so much of the national product to rearmament would mean uncontrollable inflation and economic collapse. He could marshal impressive evidence. Full employment had been reached and competition for labor between employers was rising. Competition for raw materials, domestic and imported, was pressing ever harder against Schacht's intricate controls. Funds needed for the rebuilding of over-worked plants were still siphoned into the production of armaments. The conclusion which inexorably followed, Schacht maintained, was that the impressive economic achievement effected since 1933 must be consolidated. Further expansion must wait.

The army chief, Fritsch, the chief of the general staff, Beck, and the war minister, Blomberg, argued that the expansion of the armed forces was proceeding too rapidly. In their view, the quality of the officers was declining. Efficient planning was impossible with everything in flux. The training of recruits was inadequate. In every way, they argued, the quality of the armed forces was below what Germany had attained in the past, and below what would be required to defeat France and Britain. Again, it was necessary to halt expansion, to consolidate the gains made since 1933.

Less openly and less vigorously, but insistently, most German diplomats, headed by the foreign minister, Neurath, argued that the international position of Germany must be consolidated while the Soviet Union was weakened by the Great Purge, while the United States was struggling with the depression and in an isolationist mood, while France was beset with social strife, and above all while Britain was bent on appeasement. In the opinion of the foreign ministry, Italy and Japan were weak and reckless; because they were weak and reckless, they were allies of limited value and doubtful loyalty. To delay the consolidation of German gains would be hazardous. Already the opposition to Chamberlain was uniting in Britain. From the United States, the German ambassador reported over and over that if Germany became involved in war with Britain and the position of Britain was threatened, then the United States would intervene, with as decisive effect as in the world war.

Whether their conclusion followed from economic or military or political arguments, those who would stop to consolidate the gains made since 1933 reasoned within the framework of traditional German nationalism. What they were saying was that Germany, without war, now had within its grasp the victory which had been unobtainable in 1918 after four years of terrible fighting. Without fighting, Germany could have a position in Europe higher than that Bismarck had won in three wars.

To those within "the movement" these were cowards' arguments.[3] The generals, argued the SS leaders, wished to halt the expansion of the armed forces because the "dynamism" of Nazism, already animating the new air force, was spreading into the army and the navy now that the flood of recruits and the expansion of the officer corps were breaking the hold of the outworn aristocratic traditions of the old officers. When Schacht said the limit of the possible had been reached, argued Göring, he was only saying that the cleverness of the economist could do no more. There remained the argument of force; fear could restrain the pressures on the economy and make possible further expansion. As for the international position of Germany, that also could be maintained and enhanced only by force, according to Ribbentrop, the party expert on foreign affairs. Ribbentrop was appointed ambassador in London in October, 1936. At the outset he seems to have hoped that a division of spheres of influence could be arranged, with Britain conceding supremacy in central Europe to Germany in return for a guarantee of the imperial position of Britain. Very quickly, however, he concluded that the British would acquiesce in German dominance on the continent only if confronted with overwhelmingly superior force. He had earlier advocated a German alliance with Italy

3. Roger Manvell and Heinrich Fraenkel have published biographies of three leaders of the Nazi movement: *Hermann Göring* (N.Y., 1960); *Doctor Goebbels* (N.Y., 1962); and *Heinrich Himmler* (London, 1965).

and Japan; now that alliance and the concentration of all German energy on armament became, for him, the one way to compel British acceptance of the position to which Germany aspired in Europe.

To those who thought in terms of traditional German nationalism, the "dynamism" of the party had been a means to the recovery of Germany's position as a great power. By 1937 that position was attained. Now a continuation of the strained effort, so necessary in the years after 1933, was thought not only unnecessary but dangerous, involving the risk of collapse at home and defeat by a coalition of the powers menaced by the prospect of German hegemony. To the party, "dynamism" was the essence of Nazism; to halt or even to slow the progress of "the movement" would be to invite attack from the enemies of the party at home and abroad.

In this clash of wills, Hitler at first kept silent, or more usually allowed each of the rivals to believe he had the Führer's support. The trend of successive decisions, however, was steadily toward those who argued that everything should be subordinated to the accumulation of power for use in war. The trend was most obvious in the direction of the German economy. Schacht soon recognized that he had lost control; in December, 1937, he resigned as economic dictator, but remained as head of the Reichsbank. In name, he was succeeded by a Nazi figurehead. In fact, Göring was now in control, and he proceeded on the assumption, as he bluntly told German industrialists, that war had already begun, although the shooting had not started.[4]

In diplomacy, the trend was toward alliance with Italy and Japan. To clear the way for agreement with Italy, a "gentlemen's agreement" was concluded with Austria on July 11, 1936, setting forth a series of specific steps which the German and Austrian governments would take "for the reestablishment of normal and friendly relations." With the Austrian question temporarily out of the way, and with the growing need for joint action with Italy in the Spanish civil war, a first step was taken toward alliance. The Italian foreign minister, Ciano, came to Germany in October, 1936, and during his visit the secret Berlin Proto-

4. How swiftly in fact did the Germans prepare for war? This question has given rise to extensive debate, much of which has been ably summarized and evaluated by T. W. Mason in "Some Origins of the Second World War," *Past and Present*, No. 29 (Dec., 1964), esp. pp. 76–85. See also Alan Milward's *The German Economy at War* (London, 1965). Milward argues that the Germans prepared only for a short war; they had not rearmed "in depth."

cols were signed. The Protocols were merely a series of policy statements on specific problems, and not an alliance or even a general consultative pact. The Protocols did not preclude agreements with other powers, as the Italians demonstrated in January, 1937, when they concluded a short-lived and ineffective "gentlemen's agreement" with the British to preserve the status quo in the Mediterranean. In public, Mussolini made much of what he called the Rome-Berlin Axis; he still hoped, however, to play between Germany and Britain.[5] As for Germany, the foreign office continued to oppose alliance with Italy, and Hitler seemed content for the moment to watch Italy sink deeper into the morass of the Spanish civil war.

The German foreign office was equally opposed to alliance with Japan, but Hitler evidently did want an alliance, so the foreign office was simply kept in ignorance of the negotiations Ribbentrop conducted through 1936.[6] When it became evident that the Japanese government was unwilling to accept any treaty which might involve a collision with Britain or the United States, a public agreement was signed on November 25, 1936, by which Germany and Japan agreed to oppose the activities of the Comintern. Other powers were invited to join this Anti-Comintern Pact. Secretly, Germany and Japan agreed to make no political agreements with the Soviet Union and, in case one signatory became involved in war with the Soviet Union, to consult on the possibility of joint action. On November 6, 1937, Italy joined the Anti-Comintern Pact; the Italians were not told of the secret agreement between Germany and Japan.

When the Anti-Comintern Pact was signed, German advisers were training the Chinese army, Germany was shipping arms and other supplies to China, and economically Germany and Japan were rivals rather than allies in the Far East. In July, 1937, Japan undertook new and large-scale military operations against China, and soon the Japanese begin to press for an end to German aid to China. At first, the

5. The literature on the Rome-Berlin Axis is reviewed in D. C. Watt, "The Rome-Berlin Axis, 1936–1940: Myth and Reality," *The Review of Politics*, XXII (Oct., 1960), pp. 519–43.

6. For the relations between Germany and Japan, see Theo. Sommer, *Deutschland und Japan zwischen den Mächten, 1935–1940* (Tübingen, 1962), which has a useful bibliography; Frank Iklé, *German-Japanese Relations, 1936–1940* (N.Y., 1956); and Ernst L. Presseisen, *Germany and Japan: A Study in Totalitarian Diplomacy, 1933–1941* (The Hague, 1958).

German foreign office successfully resisted this pressure, but in 1938 Hitler ordered a change of policy. Manchukuo was recognized; shipment of military supplies to China was first reduced and then ended; the German military advisers were ordered to leave China. As the foreign office pointed out, these concessions brought no reciprocal concessions from Japan, but to Ribbentrop and apparently to Hitler this was short-sighted reasoning. To Ribbentrop, the Anti-Comintern Pact and the concessions to Japanese wishes fortified Japan in the conviction that the conquest of China could be safely undertaken, and this advance was inevitably bringing Japan into collision with other powers. By the end of 1937 the openly contemptuous affronts of the Japanese military to British and American interests and nationals had produced severely strained relations. With the Soviet Union, the Japanese advance was producing armed clashes; from July, 1938, undeclared war was waged sporadically along the Manchurian frontier. While Britain, the United States, and the Soviet Union were preoccupied with the Far East, they were less likely to take a firm stand in Europe. In Ribbentrop's thinking, this was an advantage for Germany which more than outweighed the sacrifice of German interests in the Far East.

Like Schacht, when Hitler spoke, Neurath had no possibility of resisting his will; therefore the foreign office could, at best, only delay the drift of Germany toward alliance with Italy and Japan. The German military seemed in a stronger position. Hitler made no secret of his contempt for professional diplomats; but the military, in an age when warfare was wedded to technology, felt themselves masters of a field in which Hitler was an amateur. Moreover, the military commanders had under their control the armed forces of Germany, which were as yet outside party control. Therefore, the military leaders—Blomberg, Fritsch, and Beck—repeatedly spoke up in opposition to Hitler's commands.

One such clash occurred at a four-hour conference in the Reich Chancellery on November 5, 1937. Those present were Hitler, Neurath, Blomberg, Fritsch, Göring, naval commander Raeder, and Hitler's adjutant Colonel Hossbach, who prepared the minutes of the meeting.[7] Hitler began with a lengthy analysis of Germany's position in Europe and of the policies needed to strengthen that position. There were, he

7. The minutes appear in *Documents on German Foreign Policy*, Series D, Vol. I (Washington, 1949), pp. 29–39.

said, 85 million Germans packed in the center of Europe. The security and prosperity of these Germans could not be ensured by "autarchy," that is, by self-sufficiency within the existing frontiers; even under strict National Socialist leadership, he maintained, "autarchy is untenable in regard both to food and to the economy as a whole." Neither could a solution be found by participation in the world economy, even if Germany acquired colonies; both trade and colonies would be vulnerable to attack in time of war. In any case, the "two hate-inspired antagonists, Britain and France," would never give Germany the colonies.

The only solution, Hitler concluded, was the acquisition of living space in Europe. The space could be won only by "resort to force with its attendant risks." He was resolved to move no later than 1943–45; all must be ready by then at the latest for the solution of the problem of living space by force.

He thought action might be possible earlier, even in 1938. If France were paralyzed by civil strife or became involved in a war with Italy over Spain, then Germany must seize Austria and Czechoslovakia. Almost certainly Britain, and probably France, had already decided not to fight over Czechoslovakia, so in his judgment Germany could move at any time. If Germany moved swiftly, Russia would probably stay out; in any case, fear of Japan made Russian intervention doubtful. The seizure of Austria and Czechoslovakia would provide foodstuffs, shorter and better frontiers, and manpower for military service.

In the discussion which followed Hitler's speech, Blomberg and Fritsch made clear their conviction that the German armed forces could not defeat France and Britain, even if those powers were at war with Italy. Neurath cast doubt on the possibility of a war of France and Britain against Italy.[8]

Within a few months, those who had offered objections to Hitler's

8. The so-called Hossbach Protocol summarizing the discussion at the conference of November 5, 1937, became the subject of vigorous controversy following the publication of A. J. P. Taylor's *The Origins of the Second World War* (London, 1961). The controversy quickly widened to a reexamination of British appeasement policy and of German foreign policy in 1937–39. The voluminous literature is ably summarized in T. W. Mason's "Some Origins of the Second World War," *Past and Present,* No. 39 (Dec., 1964), pp. 67–87, and in D. C. Watt's "Appeasement: The Rise of a Revisionist School?" *The Political Quarterly,* XXXVI (April–June, 1965), 191–213. See also Alan Bullock's excellent analysis of the question of Hitler's responsibility, "Hitler and the Origins of the Second World War," *Proceedings of the British Academy,* LIII (1967), 259–87.

arguments were out of office. According to his later testimony, Neurath tried repeatedly to resign because he was not in agreement with the views Hitler expressed on November 5. On February 4, 1938, his resignation was accepted, and Ribbentrop was appointed foreign minister. On the same day, the military leaders were forced out of office, Blomberg ostensibly because his second wife was reputed to be a prostitute, and Fritsch on a totally false charge of sexual relations with a man. With the leaders went their subordinate followers, generals, and diplomats. To ensure his complete control over the military, Hitler assumed direct command and set up a new High Command of the Armed Forces (O.K.W.) as his military staff, headed by a pliant tool, General Keitel.

2. SOME MOOT QUESTIONS ON EUROPE IN 1938–1939

The bloodless but macabre Nazi purge of February 4, 1938, was the end of one story, the advance of Nazism to control over all parts of German national life. That story can be told with confidence because the evidence is abundant and clear.

A new story now began, the story which opened with the stormy meeting of Hitler and the Austrian Chancellor Schuschnigg at Berchtesgaden on February 12, which proceeded through a year and a half of almost unrelieved tension punctuated by moments of acute crisis, and which ended in war in September, 1939. That story cannot be told with complete confidence. The evidence is sometimes conflicting. More serious, while the evidence is voluminous, there are gaps. Before proceeding to the telling of this story it is necessary to take a position on three debatable but crucial questions. The first concerns Hitler's objectives. The second is the nature of Soviet foreign policy. The third, intimately connected with the others, is whether the story need have ended in a second great war.

The bulk of the evidence on German foreign policy in the months from February, 1938, to September, 1939, is enormous, but it does not permit a categorical statement of Hitler's intentions. Clearly, he was determined to speed the pace of German diplomatic action after the relative lull of the preceding two years. He was certainly resolved on speedy solution of the Austrian, Czech, and Polish problems. There is ample room for disagreement, however, on what he meant by "speedy," on what he meant by "solution," and on what he meant by "problems." It is unlikely that he had any definite plan of campaign, much less any set timetable. Probably he would have been content, at least temporarily, if he could have reduced the three eastern neighbors of Germany to the position of obedient satellites, although it is difficult to believe that any independent state could have given the kind of obedience he evidently expected. In summary, from February, 1938, he believed the international situation favorable for the imposition of control over the eastern neighbors of Germany, with no more than an acceptable degree of risk that German expansion would precipitate the war with France and Britain which he hoped at least to postpone.

At no point did Hitler believe there was serious risk that German expansion in central Europe would result in war with the Soviet Union. The fragmentary evidence on Soviet foreign policy, while not conclusive, strongly suggests that Hitler's judgment was correct. For Stalin, German expansion eastward came at a most dangerous time, when by the Great Purge he had eliminated the old political and military leaders, and before the new men had demonstrated the capacity to lead.[9] Moreover, while overt popular resistance to the five-year plans had been crushed, Stalin almost certainly recognized that he had won no more than passive acquiescence from the peasants and the city workers. The memory of the destruction which the German army had inflicted on Russia in the great war was still fresh; Stalin had every reason to avoid a new war which would jeopardize all his achievements.

Like Hitler and unlike Chamberlain, Stalin accepted war as a fact of international life. In Communist thinking, the only question was whether, in the final crisis of capitalism, the capitalist states would war against one another or unite to destroy the Soviet Union. When the decision to embark on the five-year plan was taken in 1928, it had seemed that a long period of stabilization lay ahead, and that war, whether war between capitalist states or war against the Soviet Union, was improbable. Almost immediately, capitalist stabilization gave way to economic depression, and international tensions rose, first in Manchuria, then in Ethiopia, then in Spain, then once more in China, and

9. Soviet policy in 1938 and the "anti-Red" explanation of British policy are analyzed in Donald Lammers, *Explaining Munich: The Search for Motive in British Policy* (Stanford, 1966).

now in central Europe. In Asia, Russian and Japanese armies were by 1938 fighting sporadic but large-scale battles. Undoubtedly if the Reichswehr invaded Soviet territory, the Red army would fight. But while Russian Communists believed the "Second Imperialist War" had already begun, and while they had every reason to encourage the resistance of other states to "Fascist" aggression, this was in their view emphatically a war between capitalist states, and Stalin evidently believed his first task was to keep the war from spilling over into Russia.

In Western countries, there was a widespread belief that in return for a firm alliance with Britain and France, Stalin would engage in war with Germany for the defense, first of Czechoslovakia, and later of Poland. The French government waveringly held to that belief; the British government seems at times to have hoped this was true. The German government did not believe that, short of an invasion of Russia, the Red army would be sent against the Reichswehr. In the German view, the open refusal of the Polish and Rumanian governments to allow the Red army to cross their territory made it easy for Stalin to talk largely of helping the enemies of Fascism, with complete confidence that if war came in central Europe the Red army could remain aloof. In August, 1939, Hitler paid a high price for the so-called nonaggression pact with Russia, but he wanted the pact, not because he feared Russia would fight, but because he wanted to show Britain and France that Russia would not fight.

At this point, the problem of Hitler's intentions merges with the problem of whether the end of the story need have been war. Again, just as it is impossible to say categorically what Stalin would have done if the British and French had followed a different policy, so it is impossible to say categorically what Hitler would have done if faced with the certainty of invasion both from the east and from the west. It can be said with something approaching certainty, however, that Hitler would have pushed ahead in 1938 even if the British and French governments had announced their determination to give military support to Czechoslovakia. In such a situation, Hitler was convinced that Russia would not send the Red army to invade Germany from the east. As for the west, French and British military planning and rearmament were based not on a war to defeat Germany by offensive action but on defense against a German attack. Therefore, even in the unlikely event

that Britain and France intervened to prevent German expansion eastward, "lightning action" by Germany would overwhelm the prey and
bring home to the British and French the futility of an attempt to
reverse the verdict already achieved by German arms.

This logic did not convince many of Hitler's political and military
subordinates. The purge of February 4, 1938, did not silence the opposition; his opponents did not stop short even of treasonable communication with British leaders in their determination to avert a war which,
they believed, Germany would lose. At the summit of the military
command, the chief of the general staff, General Beck, resigned in
October, 1938, when he was unable to convince Hitler that his policy
was certain to result in war and that Germany must lose the war.

On the surface, the issue separating Hitler from the German opposition was whether the impending war would be long or short. All
Hitler's planning was based on the conviction that the war would be
short; his opponents feared the war would, like the war of 1914–18, be a
war of attrition. This was not simply a difference of opinion about the
efficacy of new arms or new strategy; it was a moral difference. The
German opposition believed that Europe, if faced with a German bid
for hegemony, would resist, as Europe had resisted the Hapsburgs in
the sixteenth century, Louis XIV in the seventeenth century, and
Napoleon at the beginning of the nineteenth century. Europe would
resist, and would summon up the moral and physical strength, including the colossal strength of the United States, to defeat Germany.

Hitler recognized that the balance of potential physical power lay
heavily on the side of Britain and France, especially if Russia and the
United States rallied to their side. But he had only contempt for the
Communist rulers of Russia, and he was convinced that the United
States was becoming a mongrel country dominated by Jews. France
alone he did not fear; in population, resources, and leadership Germany was much the stronger. For the record of the British in history
he had the highest respect, but in his judgment Britain was ruled by
most unheroic leaders who thought only in terms of financial profit
and loss, and who would not hazard the existence of Britain in a war
to the finish with Germany. Hitler seems to have believed that the
British people would turn to leaders worthy of their country's past if
the security of the British Empire were clearly in jeopardy, but he had
no intention of offering such a clear challenge. Ever since the peace

conference of 1919, the successive rulers of Britain had said they would not fight over the fate of central Europe, and there had been no popular dissent from that view. Even in the unlikely event that a shift of popular opinion brought someone like Winston Churchill to power, the defensive armaments of Britain and France could not prevent German conquests in central Europe.

Such was Hitler's reasoning, so far as it can be discerned from the available evidence. The evidence suggests, therefore, that Hitler would not have been deterred in 1938 or 1939 by any action Britain or France could take. To weaken British and French resolution, that is, to avert or postpone war, he would settle temporarily for less than he had intended, as he did at Munich. But he would not stop and he would not even lose the momentum of his advance. In May, 1936, when he occupied the Rhineland, a resolute stand by Britain and France probably would have compelled Hitler to retreat; by 1938 it was too late.

3. AUSTRIA DESTROYED

On February 12, 1938, a week after Hitler had removed those of his advisers who opposed Nazi "dynamism," the Austrian chancellor came to Berchtesgaden in the hope of easing friction by discussion with Hitler.[10] Schuschnigg found the military leaders of Germany assembled there, and Hitler threatened to invade Austria unless freedom of action was given to the Austrian Nazi party, and unless Austrian Nazis were given strategic posts in the government. Schuschnigg's courage failed. In the hope of averting armed conquest, he accepted the demands. Soon, in Austrian cities Nazi gangs roamed at will and the terrified opponents of Nazism began to turn their assets into cash, preparatory to flight. Austria, it seemed, would collapse without an invasion.

The mounting violence sent a wave of apprehension across Europe. In Russia the last of the mass trials of the Great Purge impended, and in France the final break-up of the Popular Front had begun; neither government took strong action to maintain Austrian independence. In Britain the crisis precipitated a break between Chamberlain and

10. A clear and thorough account of the events culminating in Germany's annexation of Austria is found in Jürgen Gehl, *Austria, Germany, and the Anschluss, 1931–1938* (London, 1963). *Anschluss: The Rape of Austria* (London, 1963), by Gordon Brook-Shepherd, and *Von Dollfuss zu Hitler* (Wiesbaden, 1955), by Ulrich Eichstädt, are useful studies.

his foreign secretary, Anthony Eden. For months Eden had vainly been pushing for more rapid rearmament, for military conversations with France, and above all, for more intimate cooperation with the United States. These differences had not seemed of decisive importance. In particular, it was hard to believe the American government was prepared to go beyond talking about the evils of aggression. In October, 1937, President Roosevelt made a speech in Chicago calling for a "quarantine" of aggressors, but he hastily drew back when there were protests in the Congress and the press. When, therefore, Roosevelt very secretly informed Chamberlain, in January, 1938, of a plan to meet with the diplomatic corps in Washington to discuss ways of relaxing international tensions, Chamberlain asked the President to wait until the possibility of an accord between Britain, Italy, and Germany could be explored. Eden, who was on the continent and was not informed of Roosevelt's proposal until it had been rebuffed, was sure a mistake had been made; in his judgment, American isolationism could be weakened only by welcoming every American initiative, even if the proposals promised no immediate result. Almost unconsciously, Eden was moving to the side of those who believed that to restrain the "dictators" an alliance of the "democracies" was essential.

While Eden was still arguing that Chamberlain's rebuff to Roosevelt must be withdrawn, the Italians gave notice that the German threat to Austria made an Anglo-Italian agreement essential. Chamberlain agreed; Eden strongly disagreed, arguing that to negotiate with Italy while Italian troops were in Spain would merely encourage the Italians to demand new concessions. At last the difference was clear. Just as Eden had come to believe that the advance of the dictators could be halted only by massing overwhelming strength against them, so he was now convinced that appeasement of the dictators merely led to a demand for further concessions.

The issue, once joined, was laid before the cabinet, which, after efforts to evade decision by blurring the issue, supported Chamberlain. On Sunday, February 20, 1938, Eden resigned. He was succeeded by Lord Halifax, who in India had won the reputation of a conciliator. Parliament gave a vote of confidence to the Chamberlain government, although some fifty members on the government side did not vote.

The negotiations with Italy were taken up by Lord Halifax, and on April 16 an agreement was signed. The most significant provisions were Italian renunciation of territorial ambitions in Spain and British recognition of Italian rule in Ethiopia. The agreement was to go into effect only after the problem of foreign "volunteers" in Spain had been solved. Eventually, in November, with the Italian "volunteers" still in Spain, the British agreed to bring the agreement into force. By then it was obvious that the agreement had not effected a reconciliation between Britain and Italy. Neither had it, as Chamberlain hoped, made Italy a barrier to German expansion in central Europe. By then, Austria was gone and Czechoslovakia dismembered.

The end of Hitler's Austrian policy came more quickly and more awkwardly than he intended. Within a few days of Schuschnigg's return from Berchtesgaden on February 12, Hitler's agents reported that the violence in Austria was getting out of hand. To regain control, Hitler ordered the leaders of the Austrian Nazi party to come to Germany and remain there. On February 21 he outlined his plans. He rejected a revolution in Austria: "It would not be possible to choose a time for action." Force he also ruled out as dangerous and unnecessary. An "evolutionary" solution was much safer. Indeed, if the protocol signed by Schuschnigg was carried out, "the Austrian problem would be automatically solved." The Austrian police were now in the hands of a Nazi sympathizer, Seyss-Inquart, of whom Hitler had a good opinion: "He was not too strong a man."[11]

Hitler could wait, but Schuschnigg could not. To halt the headlong plunge toward complete control by Germany, he announced in a speech at Innsbruck on Wednesday, March 9, that there would be a plebiscite on the following Sunday. The Austrian people would say whether they favored a "free, independent, social, Christian and united Austria."

Hitler, with his intimate knowledge of the management of plebiscites, resolved that the voting must not take place. On Thursday a plan for the invasion of Austria was hastily improvised. A letter was sent to Mussolini asking his support. On Friday morning Schuschnigg was presented with a demand that the plebiscite be postponed. After wavering for a few hours he gave way, but almost at once he was confronted with a German demand that he resign. Again he gave way. Next came a German demand that Seyss-Inquart be made chancellor. The Austrian president gave way to this demand shortly before mid-

11. *G.D.*, Series D, I, 541, 549.

night. Before he capitulated, the Germans ordered Seyss-Inquart to assume the chancellorship and to ask Germany to send troops "to prevent bloodshed."

Once installed in office, Seyss-Inquart tried to halt the invasion, but the German troops moved in at dawn on Saturday; news that Mussolini acquiesced in the German conquest of Austria removed the last barrier to action. The German troops met with no resistance, but there were embarrassing breakdowns of mechanized equipment, testimony to the haste with which the invasion had been mounted.

On Saturday afternoon Hitler came to Linz, where he was once a schoolboy, and announced that he had now fulfilled the mission laid on him by Providence, "to restore my dear homeland to the German Reich." The next day, the Sunday on which Schuschnigg had planned to hold his plebiscite, the new Nazi Austrian government issued a proclamation (prepared by the Nazi German government) stating that "Austria is a province of the German Reich" and announcing a plebiscite on April 12 to ratify the union. The German government ordered that a plebiscite be held in Germany on the same day. The voting produced the desired result in both Austria and Germany: ninety-nine out of every hundred voted for the union of Austria with Germany.

In the intervening weeks, Himmler's Gestapo and SS contingents headed by Heydrich arrested those suspected of opposition to the Nazis and herded them into the inevitable concentration camp. Less exalted Nazis amused themselves by publicly subjecting Jews to obscene indignities. The pace of Nazi terror, like the pace of Nazi policy, was quickening. In weeks instead of years, Austria went through all the phases of "coordination," to the horror of observers who had scarcely noted the slower process in Germany. Not only was the pace quickening; there was also a new indifference to world opinion. In the seizure of Austria there had, to be sure, been some effort to cloak each step in the appearance of legality, and a few minor concessions—such as allowing Sigmund Freud to go into exile—were made to protests against the wholesale arrests and the brutality following the annexation. But the emphasis now was on Nazi power to crush resistance, swiftly and implacably.

The harsh tone of German diplomacy was effective. The French and British protests against the annexation of Austria were almost perfunctory. The British government did say that negotiations for an

Anglo-German agreement must be deferred until popular indignation over the events in Austria had subsided, but assurance was given that desire for an agreement continued.

4. THE ISSUE JOINED IN CZECHOSLOVAKIA

While the invasion of Austria was being mounted, the German government gave repeated assurances that Germany had no designs on Czechoslovakia. A few days after the conquest of Austria, Hitler began a campaign both to stimulate and to control the demand of the Sudeten German minority in Czechoslovakia for "justice."[12] On March 29, the leader of the Sudeten Germans, Konrad Henlein, and his deputy, Karl Frank, conferred with Hitler and other Nazis. Hitler said he "intended to settle the Sudeten German problem in the not-too-distant future." He appointed Henlein his "viceroy" and promised him full support. At the end Henlein summarized, and Hitler approved, the tactics to be used: "We must always demand so much that we never can be satisfied."[13]

As in Austria, so in Czechoslovakia, Hitler hoped for an "evolutionary" solution. Indeed, the need to move with care was much greater. Austria had no allies, except for the frayed ties of the Rome Protocols with Italy and Hungary. Czechoslovakia had a military alliance with France and an alliance with Russia calling for Soviet military assistance once France was committed to action. The difference in the view taken by world opinion of Austria and Czechoslovakia was in some ways more important. To most people, Austrians were Germans, and therefore union with Germany seemed natural. Moreover, the authoritarian government of Austria was burdened with the memory of the bloody suppression of the Socialists in 1934. On the other hand, by general agreement of Western observers, Czechoslovakia was the most successful democracy in central Europe. This achievement seemed the more remarkable because few coun-

---

12. On the background of the Sudeten crisis, see Johann Wolfgang Brügel, *Tschechen und Deutsche, 1918–1938* (Munich, 1967); Helmut K. Rönnefarth, *Die Sudetenkrise in der internationalen Politik. Entstehung, Verlauf, Auswirkung* (2 vols., Wiesbaden, 1961); and Boris Celovsky, *Das Münchener Abkommen, 1938* (Stuttgart, 1958). See also Brügel's article, "German Diplomacy and the Sudeten Question before 1938," *International Affairs*, XXXVII (July, 1961), 323–31.

13. *G.D.*, Series D, II, 198.

tries had such complicated nationality problems. Under the temperate leadership of Masaryk the nationalities lived in relative peace with one another for a decade. This situation began to change after 1929 when the economic depression, which set men's tempers on edge everywhere, stimulated quarrels between the nationalities in Czechoslovakia. Beginning in 1933, Nazism spread rapidly among the Sudeten Germans, who were already unhappy because the economic depression hit with especial force the industrial areas they inhabited. The movement of an increasing proportion of the Germans of Czechoslovakia into the Nazi Sudeten German party inclined the Czechs to discriminate economically and politically against this potentially traitorous minority. When the Czech government sought to strengthen its position by alliance with Russia in 1935, a new source of discord was added. Many Czech and Slovak groups, and particularly many Catholics, were uneasy at alliance with Communist Russia, and inevitably the alliance gave a new weapon to Henlein.

In December, 1935, Czechoslovakia lost its greatest symbol of unity when age compelled Masaryk to turn the presidency over to Eduard Beneš, who had been his trusted lieutenant. Beneš was respected at home and abroad for his intelligence and for the skill with which he had conducted Czech foreign relations. However, he was not a patriarchal figure, and he could not hold the loyalty of discordant groups as Masaryk had done. Through 1936 and 1937 the German press conducted an intermittent but increasingly strident campaign against Czechoslovakia as a Soviet airfield in the heart of Europe and against the Czechs as oppressors of Germans. Within Czechoslovakia there were sporadic clashes between the Czech police and Henlein's followers, and at the end of 1937 the Sudeten German deputies left the parliament, demanding autonomy for the German population.

The increasingly tense situation at home and abroad did not greatly alarm the Czech government. The alliance of Czechoslovakia with France stood firm, buttressed by the pact with Russia, and the military strength of Czechoslovakia was formidable. Above all, as Hitler must recognize, world opinion would be outraged by a German attack on Czechoslovakia. Therefore the Czech government remained calmly confident when the German invasion of Austria touched off wild demonstrations among the Sudeten Germans.

On April 24, 1938, in a speech at Karlsbad, Henlein openly affirmed the Nazism of his party, demanded a total revision of Czech foreign policy, and set forth changes which must be made in the internal structure of Czechoslovakia, the end result of which would be to give autonomy to the Sudeten Germans. The Czech government, which had been seeking some basis for agreement, made clear its determination not to accept the "Karlsbad eight points." The two sides settled down to a test of strength. Violence began to build up. There were to be municipal elections in late May. The Sudeten party leaders were determined to show that they alone spoke for the Germans of Czechoslovakia. Like the Nazis in the Weimar Republic, they set out to achieve their goal by preventing anyone else from speaking. The result was increasingly frequent clashes with the Czech police.

All this was reminiscent of what had happened in Austria a few months earlier. There was one apparently overriding difference, the attitude of the Great Powers. As soon as violence began in March, the French stated that they would fight in case of a German attack on Czechoslovakia, and the Soviet Union not only said it too would give armed assistance but also called for a conference of the powers to halt aggression.

On March 24, in Parliament, Chamberlain gave a carefully prepared statement of the British position. On the one hand, he said Britain would make no binding commitment to aid France in case of a war over Czechoslovakia and would not take part in a conference which tended to divide Europe into "exclusive groups of nations." However, he said, if war did come, "other countries besides those which were parties to the original dispute, would almost immediately be involved." This, he emphasized, was especially true of Britain and France, with their long friendship and their devotion "to the same ideals of democratic liberty."[14]

Chamberlain's statement of March 24 was close to a promise of support for France. So far as one can make a firm statement about an event which did not take place, one can say that if Germany had attacked Czechoslovakia and if France had come to the military assistance of Czechoslovakia, then Britain would probably have intervened on the side of France immediately and would almost certainly have

14. House of Commons, *Parliamentary Debates*, Fifth Series, Vol. 333, cols. 1404–6.

intervened if there was danger of a French defeat. This was true not only in March but throughout the Czech crisis to the settlement at Munich.

It was even more demonstrably true, however, that Chamberlain did not at any time think a war over Czechoslovakia was justified, and that he was determined to go to any length to prevent a war over Czechoslovakia. He was convinced that if war did come, nothing could prevent Germany from a rapid and complete conquest of Czechoslovakia. He was sure no effective aid would come from Russia; indeed he thought he had sound evidence for his belief that the Soviet Union was "stealthily and cunningly pulling all the strings behind the scenes to get us involved in war with Germany." As for Britain and France, "nothing that France or we could do could possibly save Czechoslovakia from being overrun by the Germans, if they wanted to do it."[15]

Chamberlain, and Halifax also, went further. They believed that a state containing many nationalities which was, like Czechoslovakia, dominated by one nationality had no possibility of continued existence; it could survive only if transformed into a nation of nationalities like Switzerland. As the crisis developed, Chamberlain and Halifax lost hope of attaining even this goal. At first tentatively and indirectly, then with increasing openness and firmness, they advanced the idea that to avert war the Sudeten Germans should be given to Germany.

From March, therefore, British policy moved on two planes. Chamberlain's warning on March 24, that if there was war between Germany and France, Germany must not count on British neutrality, remained one basis of British policy. At the same time, the conviction that a war to preserve Czechoslovakia could not be won, and was not justifiable, led Chamberlain and Halifax to ever more desperate efforts to avoid war.

At the end of April, when the long governmental crisis in France had ended, the premier, Daladier, and his foreign minister, Bonnet, came to London seeking a firmer promise of British support to France and Czechoslovakia. Hitler, they said, wanted not the reform but the destruction of Czechoslovakia. If Czechoslovakia disappeared like Austria, then Hitler would make new demands until, supreme in the east, he could turn with invincible strength against Britain and France.

15. Feiling, *op. cit.,* pp. 347, 348.

On the other hand, Daladier argued, if Britain and France stood firm, "then the peace of Europe might be saved." Chamberlain retorted that to threaten war in expectation of a German retreat would be "bluff," and he was not willing to bluff because "it was not money but men with which we were gambling."

In the end, agreement was reached on the policy to be followed by Britain and France. Pressure would be exerted on the Czechs to reach agreement with the Sudeten Germans. The Germans would be told of this pressure and asked to take no action which might impede agreement. If, however, peaceful agreement was not reached, and war threatened, then the British would tell the Germans that if they resorted to force, France would fight and the British "could not guarantee that they would not do the same."

The first two parts of the agreed policy were immediately implemented. Increasingly strong pressure was put on the Czechs to meet the demands of the Sudeten Germans. The German government was informed of this pressure and asked—without success—to facilitate the Anglo-French action by moderating the demands of the Sudeten Germans. The Czechs, on the other hand, slowly gave way. On Wednesday, May 18, the Czechs gave assurance that they were already in contact with the Sudeten parliamentary leaders and that Henlein had been invited to a conference.

At this point the Anglo-French efforts were suddenly interrupted by two seemingly connected developments.[16] On Thursday, May 19, from widely scattered points in Germany, there were reports of German troop movements. These reports were accepted as reliable by the British. The Czech government ordered partial mobilization on May 20. Simultaneously there was an intensification of the violent clashes of the Sudeten Germans with the Czech police. On Friday, May 20, the Sudeten German party used these clashes as justification for breaking off negotiations with the Czech government.

On Saturday, May 21, the situation was so tense that the German minister in Prague asked for permission to begin the burning of secret papers, the usual preliminary to war. The French ambassador reminded the German government of the alliance commitments to Czechoslovakia. The British ambassador reminded Ribbentrop of

16. The evidence is reviewed in Gerhard L. Weinberg, "The May Crisis, 1938," *Journal of Modern History*, XXIX (Sept., 1957), 213–25.

Chamberlain's statement of March 24, and said that if German aggression forced French intervention, Britain might be "forced in by circumstances or by political necessity." Ribbentrop retorted that if war came, there would not be "a living soul" left in Czechoslovakia, France would be defeated, and Britain and Germany would "fight to the death."[17]

The crisis passed as quickly as it had arisen. Investigation showed that there had been no unusual German troop movements; the origin of the reports remained—and remains—a mystery. The effects of the "May scare" were far-reaching. The widespread belief that Hitler had retreated in the face of firm action infuriated him. Secretly, he informed the military of his "unalterable decision to smash Czechoslovakia by military action in the near future." Keitel said the preparations must be completed "by October 1, 1938, at the latest."[18]

5. MUNICH

The German government, far from concealing Hitler's fury, stressed his determination not to tolerate another such blow to his pride.[19] If there was an "explosion" in Czechoslovakia, said Ribbentrop, the Germans would move with "lightning speed" to protect their racial brothers. Openly, military preparations were made to give effect to this threat. Great numbers of workers toiled day and night to strengthen the West Wall. German officers talked freely with foreign military attachés about troop movements and military exercises.

In other words, a war of nerves now began. There was plenty of time to wear down British and French nerves; preparations for the invasion of Czechoslovakia were to be completed only after summer had ended. As Goebbels once remarked, in the war of nerves Nazi nerves would prove stronger.

His prophecy proved true, so far as the British and French governments were concerned. In public, right up to the end, the French ministers continued to affirm their loyalty to the alliance with Czechoslovakia. Privately, however, Bonnet very early assured the British of

17. *G.D.*, Series D, II, 316–18.

18. *Ibid.*, p. 358.

19. The most vivid and most thoughtful account of the Munich crisis remains John Wheeler-Bennett's *Munich—Prologue to Tragedy* (London, 1948). There is a good review of the literature in Francis L. Loewenheim (ed.), *Peace or Appeasement? Hitler, Chamberlain, and the Munich Crisis* (Boston, 1965).

his willingness to force concessions from the Czechs. Chamberlain believed that the British warning of May 21 had prevented a German blow against Czechoslovakia. He also believed, however, that it had been a "d——d close-run thing," and he had no desire for another test of strength. His conviction that Britain could not allow France to be defeated was not shaken, but, more strongly than ever, he was convinced that Czechoslovakia was not worth a war. Therefore, he redoubled his pressure on the Czech government. Probably at Chamberlain's suggestion, the London *Times* hinted, rather vaguely on June 3 and more definitely on subsequent days, that to preserve peace it might be necessary to allow the Sudeten Germans to decide their own fate by a plebiscite. Halifax began to suggest on June 18 that the Czech government "accept the services of an independent British expert who would try and reconcile the two parties."[20] The Czechs showed no enthusiasm for this idea, which put the Czech government and the Sudeten minority on an equal footing and which would, in effect, be an abdication of Czech sovereignty, but what amounted to an ultimatum from Lord Halifax forced Beneš to give way. On July 26, Chamberlain announced that Lord Runciman was going to Czechoslovakia, at the invitation of the Czech government, as an independent mediator.

While Runciman was pushing the Czechs toward the transformation of Czechoslovakia into a "nation of nationalities," Chamberlain and Halifax tried to circumvent "extremists" like Ribbentrop and to warn Hitler directly that an attack on Czechoslovakia was likely to result in a general European war. A variety of approaches was attempted, without eliciting a reply from Hitler. On August 27 a public appeal was attempted. In a speech at Lanark, Sir John Simon stressed the eagerness of the British government for peace and appeasement, but warned that if war came it was likely to spread like "a fire in a high wind."

By now intelligence reports were pouring in, all agreeing that there would be a crisis in September and most stating that Hitler intended to attack Czechoslovakia. During the second week of September, the Nazi Party Day would take place, and Chamberlain feared that when Hitler spoke he would take a position which would make war inevi-

20. *B.D.*, Series 3, I, 501.

table. Lord Runciman was urged to avert this tragedy by making his report before Hitler spoke. Bonnet thoroughly approved of this course of action. He said that if, when Runciman reported, the British proposed a solution, the French government would support the proposal, "whatever it was." If the Czechs refused to go along, "tant pis pour eux."[21]

Under pressure from Halifax, Runciman went to Beneš with the British minister on September 4. They warned Beneš that war impended, that if war came Czechoslovakia would be devastated, that whatever the outcome of the war "it was more than doubtful" if Czechoslovakia would be reestablished, and that to avert these disasters Czechoslovakia should, if necessary, accept the Karlsbad program.

On September 6, Beneš and the Czech cabinet capitulated. On September 7 the Czech proposals were given to the Sudeten leaders, who told the German government that the proposals met 90 to 95 per cent of the Sudeten demands—yet broke off negotiations with the Czechs, claiming that a Sudeten deputy had been beaten by the police.

On that day also the London *Times* definitely proposed the cession of the Sudeten districts to Germany, a proposal which the *Times* reiterated two days later. In the view of the German embassy in London, these suggestions might have been prompted by Chamberlain; but the embassy stressed that the British public was in a mood reminiscent of 1914, resigned to war if Chamberlain said war was necessary.

On Monday, September 12, Hitler made his long-awaited speech at Nürnberg. It was a violent speech, full of abuse of Czechoslovakia, full of laments for the supposed sufferings of the Sudeten Germans, full of threats that if the Czechs did not end these sufferings Hitler would. But it did not say when or how he would act.

The action came within Czechoslovakia. As soon as Hitler had ceased speaking, rioting began in the Sudeten region. During the night rioting assumed the proportions of an insurrection. Since spring, the German government had said, over and over, that if there was an "explosion" in Czechoslovakia, Germany would act with "lightning speed."

The "explosion" had come, and the French and the British governments each moved to avert German action. During Tuesday afternoon,

21. *Ibid.*, II, 194.

the British ambassador spoke with Bonnet, who said that "peace must be preserved at any price as neither France nor Great Britain were ready for war." Bonnet's collapse seemed "so sudden and so extraordinary" that the ambassador asked to see Daladier and found him only less desperately determined to avoid war. "I fear the French have been bluffing," concluded the ambassador. Whether these reports, which were received by telephone in the early evening, influenced British action is uncertain. Later in the evening, Chamberlain took a step which he had contemplated for a fortnight. He asked Hitler to see him at the earliest possible moment.[22] During the afternoon of Wednesday, Hitler agreed to see Chamberlain on Thursday, at Berchtesgaden.

Hitler did most of the talking, and his talk centered on what he insisted was his moderation. In face of the brutality and the arrogance of the Czechs, he asked only that the Sudeten Germans be allowed self-determination. He said this was his last territorial demand in Europe. He made vague references to the need to satisfy the just claims of the Poles and Hungarians, and also to the resentment of the Slovaks against Czech rule. He also insisted that the Czech alliance with Russia must be ended. Chamberlain repeatedly sought, without success, to get a precise statement of Hitler's demands. By the end, Chamberlain concluded that, territorially, Hitler would be satisfied by the transfer to Germany of regions in which more than half of the inhabitants were German. Chamberlain proposed to return to Britain and discuss the cession of these regions with his colleagues, with the French, and with the Czechs. Hitler agreed and promised that unless there were some outrageous incident, he would not move against Czechoslovakia before his next meeting with Chamberlain, which was to take place at Godesberg in western Germany.

On Friday, September 16, Chamberlain returned to London; on Sunday he and Halifax discussed with Daladier and Bonnet what should be done. That night the Czechs were told they must surrender to Germany "areas with over 50 per cent of German inhabitants." The existing alliance treaties of Czechoslovakia must be replaced by "an international guarantee of the new boundaries of the Czechoslovak State against unprovoked aggression"; Britain would join in this guarantee. The Czechs accepted these terms early on Wednesday, after

22. *Ibid.*, II, 310–12, 314.

they had been warned that rejection, or even an attempt to alter the terms, would mean attack by Germany. On Thursday, September 22, Chamberlain came to the meeting at Godesberg confident that he had successfully negotiated a settlement.

Hitler, in form, still asked only "freedom" for the Sudeten Germans; but now he said this freedom must be achieved by the withdrawal of the Czechs from regions designated on a map which he showed to Chamberlain; the German army would occupy these regions by October 1. Only after the Germans were in possession of the designated districts would an international commission be permitted to settle details such as plebiscites in doubtful areas and the transfer of minorities. Hitler scarcely bothered to reply to Chamberlain's angry protest that this was not what had been agreed at Berchtesgaden, that this was not self-determination but an imposed settlement.

While he was trying to decide what to do in face of Hitler's adamant stand, Chamberlain learned that Hitler's agreement not to use force against Czechoslovakia was, in substance, being violated. When, following Hitler's speech of September 12, rioting began in the Sudeten areas, Henlein had dropped the pretense that he had no connection with Germany and wanted only autonomy within Czechoslovakia. He and many of his followers fled to Germany and announced that only union with Germany would satisfy the Sudeten Germans. A Sudeten "Free Corps" was hastily organized and equipped by the German military. While Hitler was meeting with Chamberlain, the Sudeten Free Corps moved across the German frontier and began the seizure of Czech towns.

When the British government heard on September 22 of the invasion of Czech territory, the British cabinet asked the French government and Chamberlain, at Godesberg, whether it was not necessary to withdraw the advice not to mobilize given earlier to the Czechs. The French government immediately agreed; the next day, when he became convinced that Hitler would make no concessions, Chamberlain reluctantly agreed.

The Godesberg conference ended in the early hours of Saturday, September 24. Although Hitler had refused to modify his demands, Chamberlain said he was still hopeful of a peaceful solution for the Sudeten crisis and of a general agreement between Germany and Britain. Hitler said he had similar hopes: "As he had already stated several times, the Czech problem was the last territorial demand which he had to make in Europe."[23]

During the day following, Sunday, the French ministers again conferred in London. At the end, Chamberlain's confidant, Horace Wilson, was sent to Germany to tell Hitler that if Germany attacked Czechoslovakia, the French would aid Czechoslovakia and the British would aid the French. To Beneš, Chamberlain sent a message saying that unless the Czechs accepted the German terms, Czechoslovakia would be attacked and overrun; this time, however, he refused to advise the Czechs on the action they should take. The British warning received emphasis from Hitler's speech of September 26, which was possibly the most violent he had ever made. Chamberlain's radio address to the British people on the next day pitched on a very different key: "How horrible, fantastic, incredible it is that we should be digging trenches and trying on gas-masks here because of a quarrel in a far away country between people of whom we know nothing."

It is impossible to determine whether Chamberlain would have accepted Hitler's Godesberg terms if he had not been held back by fear of repudiation by Parliament and the people. Certainly he had not given up hope of averting war. Within a few hours of his radio address he was again urging Hitler to convene another conference and urging Mussolini to support his plea. The next day, as he was addressing the Commons, word was brought that Hitler had agreed to confer at Munich with representatives of Britain, France, and Italy. When he told the Commons of the invitation there was general rejoicing. Apparently no one noticed that the fate of Czechoslovakia was to be decided without the Czechs.

The conference at Munich which went on from noon on Thursday, September 29, into the early morning was a confused affair. Mussolini presented a draft agreement for discussion; the draft had been prepared in the German foreign office. In essentials, the conference accepted this draft, and in essentials the Munich agreement was close to the terms Hitler had demanded at Godesberg.

Before returning to London on Friday, September 30, Chamberlain had a talk with Hitler. At the end, Chamberlain produced a draft declaration. The draft said the Munich agreement was "symbolic of the

23. *G.D.*, Series D, II, 907, 908.

desire of our two peoples never to go to war with each other again," and concluded with the resolve to deal with all questions by "the method of consultation." Hitler readily agreed to sign this declaration.

6. BRITAIN AND FRANCE AFTER MUNICH

On their return from Munich, Chamberlain and Daladier were received by applauding crowds. When, a few days later, the British Parliament debated the settlement, doubts had appeared. During the debate in Commons, Chamberlain was savagely attacked. With few exceptions, however, his attackers at least implicitly took the position that if Chamberlain had been firm both peace and Czechoslovakia could have been preserved; in other words, these attacks were based on the assumption that Hitler was bluffing. To most Englishmen, this thesis did not carry conviction. In their view, war impended on September 27; at Munich on September 29 Chamberlain averted war. For this, they were grateful.[24]

Mingled with applause for Chamberlain's untiring and successful efforts to preserve peace, there was shame, shame that to avoid war Britain had sacrificed a democracy. There was also fear, fear that Hitler had made up his mind to dominate Europe by force, and fear that Britain did not have the military strength to force Hitler to abandon his determination to dominate Europe. Even Chamberlain gave expression to this fear. Through the months which culminated in Munich he had, in public, defended the extent and pace of British rearmament. Now he admitted that when British military power was mobilized in September, inadequacies became apparent which must be repaired by increased expenditure on arms. But he still gave no hint that the need was great or the time short.

During the September crisis, as the German embassy repeatedly warned, an ominous mood of calm resolution had taken hold in Britain. There had been no panic and few had shown willingness to buy peace at any price. In France there had been panic, and very many had given way to despair, or worse. If, mingled with the applause for Chamberlain, there was an uneasy feeling that 1938 was not a year upon which Englishmen would look back with pride, in France there was a numbing sense of failure. It had been a failure not alone of the

24. On the debate over "appeasement" in England, see William R. Rock, *Appeasement on Trial: British Foreign Policy and Its Critics, 1938-1939* (Hamden, Conn., 1966).

government. It had been a failure of the national will to preserve for France the position won by the suffering and death of so many Frenchmen in the world war.

Now the French alliance system was in ruins. Worse, the French people were divided against one another, and there appeared no cure for the divisions. There was not even a united resolution to repair the deficiencies in the French military which had become so glaringly apparent during the crisis. The debate on Munich in the Chamber of Deputies was listless and lasted only a few hours. There was little searching criticism of Daladier or even of Bonnet. Except for the Communists, most deputies seemed actually unwilling to uncover the truth. After Munich, as before, France drifted.

The contrast between Britain and France was illustrated by the rearmament effort of the two countries during the months following the Munich settlement. In both countries there was alarm at the deficiencies in the armed forces revealed by the mobilization in September, and recognition of the need for much greater expenditure on defense.

In Britain there was effective action, particularly in defense against air attack. The Czech crisis had come just as opinion was shifting from the conviction that "the bomber will always get through" over to the conviction that effective defense against air attack was possible. On November 1, 1938, Sir John Anderson became minister of civilian defense. In the months following, his driving energy and the funds which were now made freely available repaired the deficiencies revealed in September. The production of bomber and fighter planes was also speeded, now that the yardstick of appropriations was not what was left over after the needs of other departments had been met, but what was needed by the military services to prepare for war. A beginning was also made on the enlargement of the army. Slowly, the doctrine that France must shoulder the burden of defense on the ground was giving way to a recognition that a British expeditionary force was essential if the vital channel ports were to be kept out of German hands. The navy was thought strong enough, particularly since the German navy had been relatively neglected during German rearmament.

The speeding of British rearmament was impressive, but it was, as Churchill continued to complain, far short of what would have been possible if British resources were mobilized for war. In part the still limited effort was explained by continued belief that concentration on armaments would make war more probable. It was partly explained also by continued belief that what counted in modern war was not striking power but staying power. There was one other brake, the suspicion with which Chamberlain and his close advisers were regarded by the Labour party and the trade union leaders. Mobilization would put enormous power in the hands of the government, power which could be used against domestic as well as foreign opponents. Despite the fact that Chamberlain had earlier forced the National government to accept social reforms resented by many Conservatives, as prime minister he was regarded with suspicion by labor leaders. Many years earlier, Stanley Baldwin made a comment which Chamberlain had carefully recorded, but had not heeded: "I always gave him the impression, he said, when I spoke in the House of Commons, that I looked on the Labour Party as dirt."[25] Chamberlain's authoritarian manner, under which many besides labor leaders writhed, now proved a handicap in mobilizing British strength.

The pace of British rearmament after Munich was open to criticism, but it was the quickened pace of a country which was, despite all suspicions and differences, essentially united. France was incapable of such an effort. In the midst of the Czech crisis, on July 11, 1938, a National Service Law was passed which put great power over the economy in the hands of the government, but required that the power be exercised in consultation with the leaders of management and labor. In November the minister of finance, Paul Reynaud, issued a series of decrees intended at once to revive the economy and to speed rearmament. One of the reforms, in effect, removed restrictions on hours of work. To the trade union leaders, the forty-hour work week was the last remnant of the Popular Front reforms, and labor had not agreed to Reynaud's decree. The General Confederation of Labor ordered a one-day general strike in protest. The strike, on November 30, was a failure. Some workers were glad to see the end of the forty-hour week because now they could make more money working overtime. Much more serious, the strike brought the ideological divisions within the labor movement into the open. The Communist labor leaders tried to turn the strike into a protest against the failure of the government to defend

25. Iain MacLeod, *Neville Chamberlain* (London, 1961), p. 203.

Czechoslovakia; the syndicalists and pacifists would not support the "war policy" of the Communists; the trade unionists who were not Communists, syndicalists, or pacifists wavered in confusion between the militant factions. On the other hand, Daladier showed willingness, almost eagerness, to use force against the strikers.

With the failure of the strike, the strength of the General Confederation of Labor collapsed; from more than 5 million members in the days of the Popular Front, the membership fell to 2 million. The old divisions within labor continued: of the organized workers, possibly one-third followed the Communists; possibly another third, including strategically placed unions like the schoolteachers, were pacifist or syndicalist opponents of a "capitalist" war; the remainder, on questions of foreign policy, supported the government. As for the rank and file of workers, whatever the views of their leaders, they sank into an apathy which, because strikes fell off, was mistaken by the middle classes and the government for social peace. In order not to disturb that peace, the government refrained from effective measures to speed military preparations, even though, as Reynaud said, France took eighteen months to build a submarine while Germany could build one in eight months. Tacitly, the Daladier government, like its predecessors, drew back from action which might disrupt the close network of jealous interest groups in France, even while recognizing that action was essential and that the time for action was running out.

Chapter Thirteen

THE COMING OF WAR, 1938–1939

I. GERMANY AFTER MUNICH

IN THE months after the Munich settlement German gestures continued to be violent and German pronouncements continued to be strident. With complete certainty, it can be said that one major purpose in this new stage of the war of nerves was to create confusion concerning the next German move, and another purpose was to frighten opponents. Both these objectives were abundantly achieved. By January, 1939, the governments of France and Britain were thoroughly confused and frightened.[1]

Certainly also, British rearmament after Munich came as an unpleasant surprise for Hitler. Between 1933 and 1938 he had performed the astounding feat of building the most formidable military machine in Europe, while maintaining a high level of civilian production and actually extending the social services upon which so much of the popularity of the Nazi regime rested. Schacht and others had warned that the economy could not support this triple burden. While their protests had been pushed aside, the cost of German rearmament did begin to level off during 1938 and it seemed that an opportunity had come to stabilize the economy. When, however, British expenditure on armaments spurted after Munich, it became necessary to accelerate German expenditures also. Again Schacht protested, until he was removed from direction of the Reichsbank in January, 1939.

To discourage British rearmament, Hitler, through his speeches and through the press, heaped abuse on "warmongers" like Churchill, Eden, and Duff Cooper, and built up fear of a German attack.[2]

1. For a clear and well-documented account of European diplomacy in the year and a half preceding the outbreak of war, see Christopher Thorne, *The Approach of War, 1938–39* (London, 1967). An older study by L. B. Namier, *Diplomatic Prelude, 1938–1939* (London, 1948), is still useful. In *Die Entfesselung des zweiten Weltkrieges* (Frankfurt, 1964), Walter Hofer lets the documents tell the story of international relations from the invasion of Prague to the outbreak of war. I have used parts of my review article, "The Last Months of Peace," *Foreign Affairs*, XXXV (April, 1957), 507–24.

2. Cf. *G.D.*, Series D, IV, 309–12.

Through many channels, reports of military plans and activities which could portend an attack reached British intelligence. Ribbentrop's now unconcealed efforts to weld the loose ties between Germany, Italy, and Japan into a firm, and public, military alliance were probably also designed to convince the British that resistance to the eastward advance of Germany would mean an attack of overwhelming power all over the globe against the British Empire. The draft of a treaty of alliance was given to the Italians at the Munich conference. Mussolini hung back then, because he still hoped to win concessions from the British. The British did agree in November, 1938, to bring the agreement recognizing the Italian conquest of Ethiopia into force, but by the time Chamberlain and Halifax visited Rome in January, 1939, Mussolini had decided that greater gains could be made by alliance with Germany and Japan. The Japanese, however, continued to delay; as the German ambassador in Tokyo reported in March, Japan was still too dependent economically on the United States and Britain to risk a complete break.

Finally, the increased indifference of the Nazis to what world opinion thought of events within Germany was probably a deliberate effort to paralyze opposition by fear. This indifference was most clearly shown in the reprisals which were exacted for the murder of a German diplomat by a Polish Jew in Paris in November, 1938.[3] First, there was a "spontaneous" pogrom in Germany in which some Jews were killed and enormous damage was done to Jewish property. Immediately afterward, the German government laid economic penalties on the Jewish community which came close to making life in Germany impossible for Jews and made the emigration of Jews from Germany next to impossible unless they left with only the clothes on their backs. Englishmen who expressed their disgust were vilified in the Nazi press and by Nazi leaders. Those attacks included the still revered Baldwin, who raised his voice against man's inhumanity to man and called for international help for Jewish emigration from Germany. Momentarily, even Chamberlain was driven to doubt Hitler's sanity.

Toward the British, the Nazis directed threats and invective; toward the French, they were gentle. Unlike the British, the French had not united to strengthen their defenses, and paralyzing civil discord con-

3. On this, see *Pogrom, 10 November 1938*, by Lionel Kochan (London, 1957).

tinued in France. The mood of the French was satisfactory from the Nazi point of view and was encouraged by soft words. The German press, while berating the British, said little about French protests against the pogrom. Ribbentrop journeyed to Paris and signed a Franco-German declaration on December 6 which was similar to the declaration signed by Hitler and Chamberlain at Munich. Later, Ribbentrop was to contend that during the discussions in Paris, Bonnet said France would not interfere with German plans for central Europe; Bonnet denied he had made such a statement. Given the record of the two men, it is impossible to decide which told the truth.

In any case, during the months after Munich the Germans not only refrained from abuse of France, they showed a disposition to hold Italy back from action against France. Emboldened by French desertion of Czechoslovakia, Mussolini began to press for concessions. On November 30 there was a "spontaneous" demonstration in the Italian chamber, the deputies shouting for Nice and Savoy, Tunis and Corsica, and for Djibouti in French Somaliland. When the French made clear their determination to fight rather than yield to Italian threats, the German government counseled the Italians to be patient.

After Munich, Hitler, like Mussolini, certainly felt contempt for the rulers of Britain and France. Contempt for the men of Munich, and the bellicose gestures of late 1938 and early 1939 do not, however, demonstrate an intention or even a desire to launch an attack on Britain and France, as was widely feared at the time and as some historians have concluded. Despite occasional boasts, Hitler almost certainly remained convinced that war with Britain would be long, hard, and to the death, and therefore should be avoided until the German position in the east was strengthened. It is safe to conclude, therefore, that his threats to Britain after Munich, like his gentleness to France, were designed to ensure British and French neutrality when Germany again moved east.

2. PRAGUE

Evidence to support the contention that Hitler was contemplating an attack on the west is slight. There is ample evidence that immediately after Munich he began to plan new moves eastward. What is not clear is when the direction of the advance was decided and why that direction was chosen.

On October 24, 1938, Ribbentrop told the Polish ambassador that the time had come to dispose of the issues separating Germany and Poland.[4] He asked for Danzig and for a German highway and railroad across the Polish Corridor to connect Germany and East Prussia. He suggested also that Poland join the Anti-Comintern Pact. Rather vaguely he held out hope of German assistance to Poland in a war against Russia to conquer the Ukraine. After a delay of nearly four weeks, the Poles declined the German offer; Ribbentrop repeated his suggestions, but said there was no hurry. Early in January, 1939, in the course of a friendly conversation with Beck, the Polish foreign minister, Hitler reiterated the German requests and again held out the prospect of gains at the expense of Russia. Beck gave an evasive reply. Later in the month, Ribbentrop went to Warsaw and more insistently pressed for satisfaction of the "extremely moderate" German demands; again, he held out the bait of the "Greater Ukraine." Beck did not flatly reject the German demands, but he showed more consciousness of the risks than of the advantages of joining Germany in an anti-Soviet policy.

The Poles were silent about the German demands, but showed their uneasiness by their actions. Late in November, the nonaggression treaty between Poland and Russia was reaffirmed; in other ways also the Poles showed eagerness to improve their relations with Russia. After Ribbentrop's visit to Warsaw, Beck made arrangements to visit England.

Obviously, Polish relations with Germany were deteriorating. The Germans showed clearly also that Czechoslovakia was not to enjoy a more secure existence now that it had become, in the words of the London *Times,* "a more homogeneous state." The Czechs had no illusions. The demand of the Poles for Teschen was granted by the Czechs. When Ribbentrop and Ciano met in Vienna on November 2, 1938, and fixed the frontiers between Hungary and Czechoslovakia, the Czechs accepted the award without demur. The alliances with France and Russia were ended. At home, constitutional changes gave autonomy to the Slovaks and the Carpatho-Ukrainians; Czechoslovakia became Czecho-Slovakia. Beneš resigned and went into exile. Sudeten Germans who had opposed Henlein and who had fled into Czecho-

4. For a study of the background of the Danzig question, see Ludwig Denne, *Das Danzig-Problem in der deutschen Aussenpolitik 1934–39* (Bonn, 1959).

Slovakia were, on German demand, rounded up and shipped back to the regions ceded to Germany. Every effort was made to prevent the Czech people from discriminating against the German minority, which the German government insisted must remain in Czecho-Slovakia.

Repeatedly the Czech government sought to learn what more must be done to earn German favor. These efforts merely brought denunciation of the "Beneš spirit," which, the German government contended, still survived. The uncertainty of relations with Germany was a barrier to stability within Czecho-Slovakia. Instead, with Nazi encouragement, Slovak and Carpatho-Ukrainian politicians clamored for still more freedom from Czech control. Meanwhile, German military plans for the seizure of Czecho-Slovakia were revised so that the conquest could be effected quickly by the peacetime forces of Germany.

By the end of January, 1939, the violent language of the Nazis, the intelligence reports of German military activities, and strained German relations with Poland and Czecho-Slovakia had created an expectation of immediate war in London: the only question seemed whether Hitler would strike east or west. Then, on January 30, Hitler made a speech full of kind words for Britain and France. As everyone was quick to note, his speech was free of the usual Nazi diatribes against the Soviet Union; in fact he said nothing about Russia. His reassuring words found echo in the sources from which foreign diplomats and military attachés drew indications of German intentions. Pacific reports from Germany encouraged optimism in France and Britain. Soon Bonnet was commenting on the "immense improvement" in the position of the Western democracies. Chamberlain, by mid-February, was "very optimistic" and hopeful that economic talks with the Germans would lead to political reconciliation. He even said publicly that he was "inclined to believe" the arms race was unnecessary. The optimism of political leaders carried conviction to their peoples.

The Soviet reaction to the sudden collapse of tension found Delphic expression in a speech of Stalin's on March 10. According to the British ambassador in Moscow, Stalin was much harsher in his references to the "so-called democracies" than to the "Fascist dictators"; Stalin made clear that from the Soviet point of view there was nothing to choose between the two sides of the "Second Imperialist War" which, he said, was already raging from Spain to China. The ambassador closed his report with the hope that "innocents at home" who thought Stalin was eager to ally with the West would ponder Stalin's advice to his party: "To be cautious and not allow Soviet Russia to be drawn into conflicts by warmongers who are accustomed to have others pull the chestnuts out of the fire."[5]

The lull ended as suddenly as it began. On Sunday, March 12, the German press was filled with accounts of the intolerable sufferings of the German minority in Czecho-Slovakia. The next day Monsignor Tiso, a Slovak ecclesiastical politician, was brought to Berlin and told to proclaim the independence of Slovakia; independence was dutifully proclaimed on March 14.

In an effort to placate the Germans, the president of Czecho-Slovakia, Emil Hácha, asked for an interview with Hitler. The interview took place during the early hours of March 15. Hácha was told that German troops had already crossed the Czech border; a mass invasion would begin at dawn; to avoid useless slaughter he must sign an agreement making Bohemia and Moravia a protectorate of Germany. There is conflicting evidence concerning the extent and nature of the pressure exerted on Hácha. In the end, he agreed to sign away the independence of his country. The German troops met with no resistance as they moved in.

Every effort was exerted to make the German conquest seem a natural "reunion" of Bohemia and Moravia with the German community. Hácha remained as president of the protectorate. Neurath, who was still regarded abroad as a German statesman and not as a Nazi, became the titular head of the German administration in the protectorate, screening the usual work of the Gestapo and the SS in the concentration camps. On March 16, by an exchange of telegrams between Tiso and Hitler, Slovakia was taken under German protection; a treaty confirming this status was signed on March 23. Meanwhile, Hungary was permitted to annex Carpatho-Ukraine. Almost overnight Czecho-Slovakia had disappeared from the map. The Czech provinces were part of Germany; the Slovaks were under German protection; the easternmost fragment of this state which, only a year before, had seemed so strong was now part of Hungary.

Without a pause, Hitler pushed on. After Lithuania had given way to a German ultimatum, Germany annexed Memel on March 23. Two days earlier, Ribbentrop had suggested to the Polish ambassador that

5. *B.D.*, Series 3, IV, 411–19.

Beck make an early visit to Berlin to discuss the return of Danzig to Germany and "the establishment of extraterritorial rail and road connections between the Reich and East Prussia." This time the compensation offered to Poland was in Slovakia. Ribbentrop intimated there was no time to lose: "The Führer had felt nothing but amazement over Poland's strange attitude on a number of questions; it was important that he should not form the impression that Poland simply was not willing."[6]

Why Hitler decided to annex Bohemia and Moravia (an action which could not be justified by appeal to the right of self-determination) before he had secured Danzig and Memel (which had predominantly German-speaking populations) is not known. Probably he decided that although Beck had refused the hazardous compensation of German aid in a war against Russia to conquer the Ukraine, the Poles would give way if Hitler offered them part of Slovakia in exchange for Danzig and a passage across the Corridor. On March 21, Ribbentrop did offer compensation in Slovakia, and on March 25 the German High Command of the Army voiced "the impression" that Hitler would "use Slovakia as a political bargaining counter between himself, Poland and Hungary."[7]

What can be said with confidence is that Hitler did expect Poland to give way without fighting and did not expect that his moves from March 15 to March 23, 1939, would decisively affect German relations with the other Great Powers. Even when, on March 26, the Polish ambassador returned from Warsaw with a conciliatory but definite rejection of the German demands, Ribbentrop thought the Poles were merely trying to "get off as cheaply as possible."[8] Similarly, there seemed no uneasiness in Berlin over the initial reaction of the Great Powers; there had so often been protests in the past, and the protests had always ended in acquiescence. There seemed no reason to believe the old sequence would not be repeated.

3. THE END OF APPEASEMENT

The French and the British governments did not seem greatly perturbed when German troops marched into Prague. On March 15, Bonnet said Britain and France should do nothing. In the House of

6. *G.D.*, Series D, VI, 70–72.
7. *Ibid.*, p. 118.
8. *Ibid.*, p. 122.

Commons, Chamberlain said that the moral guarantee of Czechoslovakian independence undertaken by Britain after the Munich conference did not apply to a situation of internal dissolution.

Public opinion, particularly in Britain, took a different view. Support for appeasement collapsed overnight. The violent reaction is partly explained by the fact that the annexation of Bohemia and Moravia could not be justified by an appeal to the principle of self-determination; on March 15, Hitler did not free Germans, he subjugated Czechs. Another element was collapse of confidence in Hitler's promises. In 1938 he had said he had no further territorial demands in Europe; he had said he did not want to rule over Czechs; he had agreed to settle disputes not by force but by negotiation. All these promises he broke on March 15; confidence in his word disappeared.

There was another consideration. The "chemical dissolution" of Czecho-Slovakia into quarreling fragments which had prepared the way for subjugation by Hitler could be repeated in one country after another. According to the Rumanian minister in London, Germany was already beginning to put pressure on Rumania. Poland and Yugoslavia, like Rumania, had restive minorities; so did states in western Europe like Belgium. In every state there were social tensions which could open the way for subversion. Since 1917, the accusation that the Communist rulers of Russia sought to turn the peoples of other states against their governments had been a barrier to normal diplomatic relations with the U.S.S.R. Since the outbreak of the Spanish civil war, fear of the Fascist "fifth column" had competed with fear that the Communists of every country were agents of the U.S.S.R. Now, after German troops entered Prague, fear of the Nazi fifth column mounted.

Even in Italy there was fear. "What weight can be given in future to those declarations and promises which concern us more directly?" Ciano asked. Within a few days, realization that Italian imperial expansion at the expense of France depended upon German support brought Mussolini back into line. He took revenge by not informing Hitler before he seized Albania on Good Friday, April 7. But many Italians undoubtedly echoed the derisive comments of their king that he could not see the point of a military invasion of Albania to "grab four rocks," and that in Munich Mussolini was called Hitler's "Gauleiter for Italy." Even in the Fascist Grand Council, Italo Balbo, a leader of the March on Rome in 1922, told Mussolini: "You are shining

Germany's boots." However, on the surface the policy of unswerving loyalty to the Axis prevailed. By now, there was no alternative for Fascist Italy.

The revulsion in Britain and France was deeper, and lasting. On March 17—only two days after his tepid comment on the German occupation of Prague—Chamberlain raised the decisive question: was the destruction of Czecho-Slovakia "a step in the direction of an attempt to dominate the world by force?" The ambassador in Berlin was instructed to say that Britain regarded the German action "as a complete repudiation of the Munich Agreement," and then to return home "for consultation." The French ambassador was also told to enter a protest and to return home.

In the days following, fear of new German moves mounted, fed by the German seizure of Memel and by reports of German demands on Rumania and Poland. The British government made hurried efforts to bring Britain, France, Russia, and Poland into a consultative pact to resist German aggression. When it became evident that agreement could not be quickly achieved, Chamberlain announced in Parliament on March 31 that in the event of an action which clearly threatened Polish independence, and which Poland was determined to resist, Britain would give all possible assistance to Poland.[9] France, Chamberlain said, joined in this promise. A few days later, when the Polish foreign minister Beck was in London, the Polish government undertook reciprocal obligations in case of aggression against Britain or France.

When Mussolini seized Albania and fear rose of an Axis thrust into southeastern Europe, the British and French governments promised support to Rumania and Greece also. A few days later Denmark, the Netherlands, and Switzerland were included in the lengthening list of countries whose independence would be defended by Britain and France. In more usual diplomatic fashion, negotiations proceeded on treaties of mutual assistance between Turkey, Britain, and France; these were completed during the summer.

To underscore British determination, on April 19 a ministry of supply was created to coordinate all military preparations, and on April

9. On the origins of the British guarantee, see T. Desmond Williams, "Negotiations Leading to the Anglo-Polish Agreement of 31 March 1939," *Irish Historical Studies*, X (1956), 59–93, 156–92.

26 Chamberlain announced that a bill would be introduced authorizing <u>conscription</u>. These measures were deprived of some of their intended effect on opinion abroad by the opposition they encountered from Liberal and Labour members of Parliament and from some trade union leaders, but it was soon apparent that the opposition had little support in the country. In France there already was conscription, but Daladier, probably because of fear of reviving the opposition of French labor, refused to create a ministry of supply. In both Britain and France appropriations for arms production were increased.

Behind Chamberlain's rush of activity was the conviction that Hitler would draw back from war once Britain was committed to fight. He, and Halifax, continued to believe that Britain and France could not win a war against Hitler in the sense of achieving positive results worth fighting for. They also believed, however, that Britain and France would not lose: in the end superior resources and maritime supremacy would exhaust German powers of resistance. War would wreck European civilization, but in the common ruin Germany would suffer most. All this was seen so clearly by Chamberlain that he was sure it must be seen by Hitler. When the crisis had dragged on through four tense months, Chamberlain told the American ambassador that "Hitler is highly intelligent and therefore would not be prepared to wage a world war."[10]

In March, when the crisis began, Daladier and even Bonnet shared this confidence. Bonnet's confidence soon collapsed, and it seems probable that, had he dared, he would have urged capitulation. Daladier also became increasingly skeptical of the chances of success. By the end of the crisis his confidence was gone, but he remained convinced that France must fight; capitulation, he contended, would be the end of French independence. So far as can be discerned, while some Frenchmen shared Bonnet's views, most agreed with Daladier that France had no alternative, and must fight.

The American government sought to heighten confidence in British and French ability to wage war by asking the Congress to modify the Neutrality Law so that, as in the world war, the Western powers could draw freely on the productive capacity of the United States. Soon it became evident that the Congress would not act. While German representatives in the United States reported home that if war came,

10. United States Department of State, *Foreign Relations of the United States, 1939*, Vol. I (Washington, 1956), p. 288.

and there was danger of a British defeat, the Neutrality Law would be swept aside, officials in the German embassy also said that American military strength was so slight that no effective help could be given to Britain and France for at least six months after the American decision to intervene. When Roosevelt sent Hitler a telegram on April 14 asking him to promise that he would not "attack or invade" a long list of states, his request was treated with contempt in Germany. Nowhere did the President's telegram greatly bolster confidence that the enormous potential resources of the United States would, at the decisive moment, enhance the capability of Britain and France to thwart a German attack on a central European state.

In Parliament and in the press, critics of Chamberlain's new policy insisted with increasing vehemence that only one country could give effective aid in case of an attack on one of Germany's eastern neighbors. That country was Russia. And, said these critics, by guaranteeing British assistance to Poland and Rumania before securing a promise of Russian military aid, Chamberlain surrendered his most effective lever for obtaining a promise of Soviet aid.

These arguments left Chamberlain unmoved. The essential, he contended, was to let Hitler know Britain would fight. Furthermore, the Poles and the Rumanians refused to consider any agreement which might permit Soviet troops to cross their borders. Repeatedly, British diplomats stressed "the horror and hatred of Bolshevism that prevails among those countries which have suffered from it, got rid of it but are still next-door neighbors to it."[11] Chamberlain had complete sympathy for these fears. "I must confess to the most profound mistrust of Russia," he wrote privately on March 26. He thought the Soviet objective was merely to divide the other powers, and he did not believe Russia could "maintain an effective offensive, even if she wanted to."[12] Finally, immediately after the British guarantee to Poland on March 31, Hitler began to denounce the "encirclement" policy of Britain: would not a firm alliance of Britain and France with Communist Russia, the object of Hitler's hatred long before 1933, drive Hitler to precipitate the war Chamberlain was desperately eager to avoid? Chamberlain feared that would be the result.

The initial British proposal to Russia, on April 14, clearly reflected

11. *B.D.*, Series 3, V, 236, 237.
12. Feiling, *op. cit.*, p. 403.

Chamberlain's feelings: Russia was simply to announce that if a European neighbor of Russia was attacked, Russian help in repelling the aggression would be given "if desired." The Soviet counterproposal of April 17 seemed to confirm all Chamberlain's fears: there must be a defensive alliance among Britain, France, and Russia, operative in case of attack by a European power; the three allies were to give military assistance in case of aggression against a European neighbor of Russia; the political agreement defining these obligations would go into effect only after the conclusion of a military pact stating the extent and forms of assistance to be given by each.[13]

There followed three weeks of confused discussion within the British government and between the British and French governments. The British thought the Soviet counterproposal justified German charges of "encirclement." The European neighbors of Russia were bound to object to an agreement sanctioning Soviet military intervention whether or not the assistance was wanted. Above all, the British suspected a trap in Soviet insistence that the political agreement become binding only after the completion of a military agreement: the complex bargaining on military terms could be used either to exact one concession after another or to obtain knowledge of British and French military resources and plans without any intention of completing the agreement.

The French government, on the other hand, was coming to believe more and more strongly that the only hope either of averting or of winning a war with Germany was to secure a Soviet promise of military assistance. And many in Britain, including articulate critics like Churchill and Lloyd George, were coming to the same conclusion.

While the debate went on, the British and French ambassadors returned to Berlin and sought some clue to German intentions. In Berlin they encountered a wall of silence. On April 3, immediately after the British and French had promised aid to Poland, German missions abroad were instructed not to discuss relations between Germany and Poland. The Polish ambassador was told that Hitler's "generous" offer would not be repeated. Thereafter, German officials were silent, or at most made remarks about the "incomprehensible" policy of Britain, France, and Poland.

13. *B.D.*, Series 3, V, 206, 228, 229.

On April 28, Hitler made a speech. He said that the "encirclement policy" was incompatible with the German-Polish Non-Aggression Pact of 1934 and the Anglo-German Naval Treaty of 1935; these agreements had, therefore, ceased to have validity. He was, he said, ready to make new agreements. With irony verging on ridicule, he dismissed Roosevelt's peace appeal as meaningless. About Russia he said nothing.

On the whole, Hitler had reason to believe the "war of nerves" was going as well in 1939 as it had in 1938. Someone with access to British diplomatic dispatches was keeping the German embassy in London fully, accurately, and promptly informed of the communications between London and Moscow, so Hitler knew that British hopes of winning a quick agreement with Russia had been disappointed. On the other hand, the Soviet ambassador in Berlin had suggested on April 17—the very day the Russians had made their counterproposals to the British—that ideological differences need not be a barrier to normal relations between Germany and Russia, and "out of normal relations could grow increasingly improved relations."[14] This hint strengthened the hope aroused by Stalin's speech of March 10 that the Soviet Union might remain neutral if war came. Orders to make plans for a war with Poland so that operations could start on September 1 had been given to the armed forces on April 3; the detailed directive, dated April 11, stated that war with Poland was only a possibility, to be avoided if possible. At the end of April, the date set for the possible initiation of war against Poland was still four months away. Before then, it seemed, the nerves of the opposition must crack; as Hitler said, "one could only yell for a certain time."

4. COMPETITION FOR SOVIET FAVOR, MAY, 1939

On May 3, a flurry of activity in all capitals followed the announcement that the Soviet commissar for foreign affairs, Maksim Litvinov, had been replaced by the chairman of the Council of People's Commissars, Vyacheslav Molotov. The change came without warning, and no one took seriously the solemn assurances of the Soviet press that foreign policy was unchanged. The shift at least meant that Stalin now regarded foreign affairs as much more important than in the past. Litvinov was a cosmopolitan who was on easy terms with Western

14. *G.D.*, Series D, VI, 266, 267.

statesmen and diplomats, but he was not high in the councils of the Communist party, and he was a Jew, which was a handicap in dealings with Nazis. Molotov had no experience in foreign policy, and few in the Moscow diplomatic corps even professed to know what was behind his slablike face, which seemed even more impenetrable when lighted by a wintry smile. But all knew that he was one of the few Old Bolsheviks to survive the Great Purge and that he was regarded as Stalin's closest adviser. Also, as the German ambassador noted, he was not a Jew.

Very quickly the British learned that Molotov was impervious to argument. He questioned, endlessly. He was voluble in his complaints. But he did not discuss his own demands; in response to every objection, he simply repeated his demands. On May 8 the British ambassador explained at length to the new foreign commissar why not merely the British and French governments but the Poles and Rumanians as well thought the Soviet proposals of April 17 too far-reaching, and even likely to precipitate the German attack all wanted to prevent. The ambassador suggested that Soviet fears of becoming involved in a war with Germany without assurance of British and French support could be removed by a slight modification of the original British proposal: the Soviet promise of aid to Poland and Rumania could be made operative only after the British and the French were committed to action. Molotov listened; he asked questions; he complained of British slowness. Then, a few days later he said the British proposal was unacceptable and repeated the Soviet proposals of April 17: a mutual assistance pact between Britain, France, and Russia; guarantees against aggression to be given by these three to all the European neighbors of Russia; a military agreement.

The German government could take comfort not only from this rebuff (of which it was immediately informed by the "reliable source"), but from indications that Molotov would like to begin discussions with Germany.[15] The change of foreign ministers in Moscow came just as word was received in Berlin that the Japanese, because of their economic dependence on Britain and the United States, were unlikely to agree to a general alliance with Germany and Italy, although they would be happy to make an alliance against Russia. Ribbentrop and

15. For the Nazi-Soviet negotiations in 1939, see Gerhard Weinberg's study, *Germany and the Soviet Union* (Leiden, 1954).

Ciano decided to wait no longer for the Japanese and instead to conclude a military alliance between Germany and Italy; this Pact of Steel was signed with much ceremony in Berlin on May 22.[16] Meanwhile, the German ambassador in Moscow, Schulenburg, was brought home for consultation. On his return to Moscow he indicated to Molotov on May 20 that Germany was ready to resume the negotiations for an economic agreement with Russia which had been in suspense for some months. Molotov listened, asked questions, complained of past Nazi actions, and then said that economic negotiations must wait until a "political basis" had been found. Schulenburg exhausted his ingenuity in efforts to discover what was meant by "political basis," but Molotov had said all he intended to say. He had also learned all that he needed to know: that the possibility existed for agreement with Germany as well as for agreement with Britain.

Probably—in the absence of solid evidence, nothing can be said with confidence about Soviet policy—it was this knowledge which encouraged Molotov to raise his price for agreement with Britain and France.

On May 27, the British and French ambassadors presented proposals which their governments hoped would meet Molotov's objections. There was to be a mutual assistance pact between Britain, France, and Russia, formulated in accordance with the principles of the League covenant and operative not only in case of a direct attack in Europe but also in case one of the allies was fighting to defend a small state which it was pledged to protect; the three allies were to "concert" on methods of making effective the aid and support each ally was to give. As the ambassadors explained, the covenant was brought in to avoid the charge of encirclement; the formula on small states was designed both to avoid naming states which did not want to be named and to include small Western states like Belgium, Holland, and Switzerland; the promise to "concert" was to make clear the intention to have military conversations without holding up the political agreement until the complicated military conversations were concluded.

Molotov objected. He objected to mention of the League. He objected to vagueness on what small states were to be protected. He objected to vagueness about the military pact. Then, on May 30, he

16. On this, see M. Toscano, *The Origins of the Pact of Steel* (Baltimore, 1968), and M. Magistrati, "Berlino 1939: da Praga al Patto d'acciaio," in the *Rivista di Studi Politici Internazionali* (1952), pp. 597–652.

brought in a new objection: the British plan did not protect small states against "indirect aggression," against the sort of thing that had happened in Czechoslovakia—"Did we," he asked, "mean not to cover German absorption of such States nominally with their consent?" The British ambassador responded vehemently that neither the British government nor British opinion would impose on the small states of Europe "guarantees of protection against their will." Such guarantees, he said, "would amount to menaces, not protection against aggression."[17]

Back of the ambassador's immediate and violent rejection of the idea of protection against "indirect aggression" was knowledge of a note which the Soviet government had sent to Estonia on March 28. The note, after affirming Soviet interest in Estonian independence, had warned that any impairment of Estonian independence by any other country, even with the consent of the Estonian government, would be "intolerable" for the Soviet Union and would automatically terminate all agreements barring Soviet intervention in Estonian affairs. In diplomatic language, the note asserted the right of the Soviet Union to take any action, including military action, at any time the Soviet Union chose to say there was danger of an impairment of Estonian independence. Molotov's injection of the need to protect the Baltic states against indirect aggression was seen in "the lurid and sinister light of that Note," as the American ambassador in Paris put the matter.[18]

Now there were two barriers to agreement between Britain, France, and Russia. The old barrier, Soviet insistence that the political agreement go into effect only after the military agreement was completed, remained formidable. Even more formidable was Soviet insistence that the Baltic states be guaranteed against "indirect aggression," which was interpreted in London and Paris as a demand that Britain and France help establish Soviet supremacy in central Europe. Closely linked with this new barrier was the problem of finding some way of defining the states to be guaranteed against aggression, when these states were adamant in their refusal to be named in any Soviet guarantee, indeed hinted at a preference for German protection if faced with the possibility of having Soviet troops on their soil.

As usual, Molotov was unmoved by British and French objections.

17. *B.D.*, Series 3, V, 701, 702, 722.
18. *Ibid.*, pp. 775, 776.

Instead, on May 31 he made a public speech in which he set forth the Soviet conditions for agreement with Britain and France—and added a hint that negotiations for an economic agreement with Germany might soon be resumed.

After two months of crisis, on May 23 Hitler surveyed the international situation in a speech to German military commanders. By now he had enlarged his objective. Poland was to be attacked at the first suitable opportunity and destroyed. "It is not Danzig that is at stake. For us it is a matter of expanding our living space in the East and making food supplies secure and also solving the problem of the Baltic States." The campaign against Poland could be a success only if Britain and France stood aside. There were indications that "Russia might disinterest herself in the destruction of Poland," but to restrain Russia it might be necessary to have closer ties with Japan. In any case, the task was to isolate Poland, and there must not be a simultaneous showdown with France and Britain. That showdown would come, but later. It would be a hard and probably a long fight, involving the very existence of Germany; it was time to begin preparations for that fight. He was therefore setting up a small planning staff, which would work in complete secrecy and would study all aspects of the problem of preparing for the life-and-death battle with Britain. He gave no date for the war with the West, but in response to a question from Göring he stated that the armaments program would be completed by 1943 or 1944.[19]

5. THE SOVIET DECISION, JUNE AND JULY, 1939

June and July were months of probing. By late July, in Berlin even Hitler had apparently come to the conclusion that Britain and France would fight to save Poland unless Russia could be brought over to the German side. In Paris the conviction hardened that Hitler was determined to crush Poland and that France and Britain must secure Russian aid at any cost, if not to avert war, to avert defeat. In London Chamberlain and Halifax continued to maintain that payment of the price demanded by Russia for an alliance would destroy the moral position of Britain without securing any compensating military advantage; they also continued to hope that Hitler would, in the end, accept

19. *G.D.*, Series D, VI, 574-80.

the solid advantages of British economic aid rather than plunge the world into war. Behind them, however, British opinion was hardening against any concessions to Germany, and there was a growing disposition to blame Chamberlain and Halifax for failure to win alliance with Russia. The debate which went on within the Soviet government is not known, but before the end of July the Soviet government had decided to negotiate with Germany, without breaking off negotiations with Britain and France.

Early in June, the British government sought to hasten negotiations with Russia by sending to Moscow the foreign office official who had been most intimately concerned with the negotiations, William Strang. Strang had both knowledge and judgment, and he was imperturbable in diplomatic argument. Possibly, as many have maintained, Stalin would have been more impressed if Halifax or someone like Eden had been sent, but, surveying Stalin's later diplomatic career, this seems doubtful: Stalin was not easily impressed, and when he was ready for agreement he used the means at hand. Strang brought a proposal that the naming of states to be guaranteed, and also the question of a guarantee against indirect aggression, be avoided by providing for consultation among Britain, France, and Russia in case one of the three believed its vital interests were endangered by threats to a small European state. The Moscow press cryptically reported that the result of Strang's conversation with Molotov on June 15 was "not entirely favorable."

Two days later the Germans presented to the commissar for foreign trade a formal proposal to open negotiations for an economic agreement with Russia. With irony which was not overlooked, Mikoyan expressed his regret that the German proposal was "not entirely favorable."

The Soviet tactics produced much the same effect on Halifax and on Hitler. The American ambassador in London reported on June 27 that Halifax was disposed "to tell Russia to go jump into the Baltic Sea," but friends told him failure to secure a pact with Russia would be "psychologically bad for England." As for Hitler, on June 29 he issued instructions to end negotiations with the Soviet Union. Almost invariably such instructions were obeyed without question. Now, however, the officials of the German foreign office persisted, and soon the weary task of answering Russian questions and listening to Russian complaints was resumed.[20]

The Russian negotiators professed impatience with the slowness of both the British and the Germans, but their tactics suggested that their real objective was to prolong the negotiations. In their discussions with the Germans, the Russians quietly dropped the demand for the building of a "political basis," but they haggled over details of the conditions for starting economic negotiations. Probably the German ambassador was correct in his surmise that the Russians, like others, believed August would be a critical month, and "till then they will prefer not to commit themselves."[21]

Strang was finding his stay in Moscow "a humiliating experience." Step by step, the British were forced to retreat in order to keep alive the hope of agreement. They were even forced to agree to use of the words "indirect aggression," although they insisted that the expression must be defined so as to exclude any possibility of interfering with the independence or neutrality of a state.[22]

On the surface, the second half of July was a quiet period in the long crisis which had gripped Europe since March 15. In secret, however, the final decisions were being taken and the decisive moves made. We know much about what was said and done; we have no full understanding of what led to the decisions and actions.

In Berlin, Hitler's resolution to break Polish resistance hardened; indeed by now retreat would be a serious blow to his prestige, at home and abroad. The German embassy in Warsaw reported that the Polish government would neither surrender without fighting nor allow itself to be provoked into rash action which would be accepted abroad as an excuse for German military intervention. By mid-July it was also clear that the British and French governments would declare war if Germany attacked Poland. In Berlin the belief persisted that, if confronted with the certainty of Japanese intervention, the resolution of the British and French governments might weaken; repeatedly, the Japanese were pressed to conclude a military alliance with Germany and Italy, but without success. There remained Russia. The British and French

20. *Foreign Relations, 1939*, Vol. I, p. 276; *G.D.*, Series D, VI, 810, 820, 821, 870, 871.
21. *Ibid.*, p. 895.
22. *B.D.*, Series 3, VI, 422–26.

people still believed that in the end Russia would fight beside Britain and France to defend Poland. Hitler seems to have become convinced that if this belief could be destroyed, then Britain and France would not fight. By July 22, the German government decided to seek not just an economic agreement with Russia but a political agreement as well. In the days following, there were repeated conferences of Hitler and his diplomatic and economic advisers out of which, events were to show, emerged a decision to pay whatever price Russia might demand for a political agreement with Germany ensuring Russian neutrality.

Almost certainly Hitler's thinking was influenced by knowledge that the French government had also decided to pay whatever price the Russians might demand for an alliance. On July 19, the French views were presented to the British. Immediately thereafter "leaks" to the press stressed French willingness to meet all of Molotov's demands and blamed the British for failure to achieve alliance with Russia.

These rumors in the press came at an awkward moment for Chamberlain. On July 22 even more sensational stories were circulating: that a British official, Robert Hudson, had offered a visiting German official, Helmuth Wohlthat, great concessions, including a huge loan, if Hitler would agree not to attack Poland. By Monday, July 24, these stories had aroused so much protest that Chamberlain was forced to deny in the House of Commons that any "deal" with Germany was planned. Actually, Hudson—and Chamberlain's close adviser, Sir Horace Wilson, with whom Wohlthat had also talked—had said only what Halifax had publicly said earlier, that if Germany left the path of armed aggression, Britain would be glad to cooperate with Germany in the economic reconstruction of Europe. And on July 21, before the newspaper rumors of a "New Munich" began, Halifax had made a great concession to the Soviet position by agreeing that the political agreement between Britain, France, and Russia should go into effect only after the military agreement had been completed. This left only the definition of "indirect aggression" to be settled. Probably this crowning concession was made more to placate the French and critics of the government in Parliament and the press than with hope that the alliance would now be completed; Chamberlain's skepticism about the possibility of securing real assistance from the Russians continued unabated.

Whether or not that skepticism had been justified earlier, it was now.

On July 22, before the British ambassador told Molotov of the British concession, the Soviet press suddenly announced that "Soviet-German negotiations with regard to trade and credit have been resumed." When Molotov did receive the British and French ambassadors, on July 24, and was told of the concession on the military convention, he immediately and persistently pushed aside discussion of the political agreement and asked that British and French military missions come to Moscow to begin the military conversations. The British and French governments were bewildered, and also suspicious, about Molotov's motives, but on July 27 they agreed to send military missions to Moscow.

Because they were convinced that a firm alliance with Russia was necessary to deter Hitler from war, Daladier and Bonnet were frightened by the delay which the military discussions must entail and pushed for speed in getting the missions to Moscow. The British, who were skeptical of the success of the negotiations but convinced that Hitler was unlikely to attack so long as the negotiations continued, were in no hurry and insisted on sending their mission by sea. Neither government seriously considered the possibility that Molotov's real motive for beginning the military discussions was to gain time for political discussions with Germany. The American government, which had a "reliable source" in the German embassy in Moscow, hinted repeatedly at the possibility of a Nazi-Soviet agreement, but could not speak openly for fear of compromising the "reliable source." So the American hints had little effect.

While he waited for the British and French military missions to arrive, Molotov also waited for the Germans to show their hand. In public, the Soviet government spoke in language calculated to keep alive the hopes, and the fears, of both sides. On July 30, the Soviet newspaper *Izvestia* compared the Europe of July, 1914, with the Europe of July, 1939. *Izvestia* argued that it was not accurate to say another world war impended; the Second Imperialist War had been in progress for many years, with battlefields in China, in Ethiopia, in Spain, in Austria, in Czechoslovakia. In this Second Imperialist War, the Soviet Union stood apart, strong and vigilant, ready to cooperate in a "general peace front" to halt further "Fascist aggression," determined to repel any attempt to carry "the Second Imperialist War across the borders of the land of the Soviets."

In London and Paris these words were interpreted as evidence of willingness to join the Anglo-French peace front; to Berlin, they suggested a decision to remain aloof unless Soviet interests were directly involved.

6. THE NAZI-SOVIET PACT, AUGUST, 1939

August, everyone in Europe had said for months, would see the climax of the Polish crisis. In preparation for the crisis, the British, the French, the Polish, and the Germans scheduled maneuvers which would make possible the initiation of military operations without waiting for mobilization. In Britain and France hope persisted that while their representatives continued discussions for an alliance with Russia, Hitler would not precipitate war. On August 4, the British Parliament recessed until October. Many, even among the Conservatives, opposed the recess, and Labour and Liberal members made little effort to conceal their fear that, freed from the necessity to defend themselves in debate, Chamberlain and Halifax would seek peace by appeasing Germany. Chamberlain insisted on adjournment, but he did reiterate that a German move against Poland, including Danzig, would mean war with Britain. Then he left for Scotland, and Halifax for Yorkshire; most other political leaders also left London. Doubters were reassured by reports of the great naval maneuvers and by the cordial reception given the British and French military missions on their arrival in Moscow on Friday, August 11. There were also comforting reports that Ciano, who met that day with Ribbentrop in Salzburg, preparatory to conversations with Hitler at Obersalzberg on Saturday and Sunday, would urge the necessity for a peaceful solution of the crisis; these reports seemed plausible because there was no evidence of military activity in Italy.

Ciano also had been optimistic until a few days before he came to Salzburg, optimistic because through all the months since March every German communication to the Italian government had insisted that the Polish crisis would be solved peacefully and that Hitler, like Mussolini, wanted some years to complete his military preparations before resorting to war. Because the Pact of Steel explicitly required consultation between the allies in any situation likely to result in war, Ciano had accepted the German assurances that there would not be war. For weeks, the Italian ambassador in Berlin warned vainly of information from reliable sources that Hitler intended to attack Poland; finally, to clear up the situation, on August 7, Mussolini agreed to ask for a meeting.[23]

At Salzburg on August 11, Ribbentrop bluntly told Ciano that "the conflict between Germany and Poland is inevitable" and that "Europe will be an impassive spectator." Russia, he said categorically, "will not intervene," and for the first time he revealed that "conversations of a fairly definite character are now in progress between Moscow and Berlin." Hitler was equally categorical in stating his determination to begin operations against Poland by the end of August, in affirming his conviction that "the conflict will be localised," and in his confidence that "Russia will not make any move."[24]

Ciano returned to Italy an angry and frightened man. He was angry because, as usual, Hitler had made his decision without consulting Mussolini. Ciano was frightened because he was convinced Britain and France would fight, and he knew Italy could not hope for victory in war. He and other Fascist leaders set out to convince Mussolini that Italy must remain neutral. After all his talk of Italian military prowess, after all his glorification of war, Mussolini must be made to face the fact that Fascism had not done what he had boasted Fascism would do—make Italy a strong military power. Instead he was forced to acknowledge that war meant defeat and the end of the Fascist regime. Mussolini stormed; he talked of loyalty and of shame; he searched for an opportunity to step dramatically on the stage as arbiter, as he had done in 1938. The opportunity never came.

On Saturday, August 12—the day the British and French military missions had their first formal discussions with the Russians in Moscow, and the day on which Hitler told Ciano of his determination to settle the Polish question by the end of August—the negotiations between Germany and Russia reached a decisive stage. Ten days earlier, in a conversation with the Soviet chargé in Berlin, Ribbentrop had said that "from the Baltic to the Black Sea, there was no problem which could not be solved to our mutual satisfaction." Repeatedly

23. See M. Toscano, *L'Italia e gli Accordi Tedesco-Sovietico dell'Augusto 1939* (Florence, 1952), and M. Magistrati, "Salisburgo 1939," in the *Rivista di Studi Politici Internazionali* (1949), pp. 479-509.

24. The quotations are from Malcolm Muggeridge (ed.), *Ciano's Diplomatic Papers* (London, 1948), pp. 297-304.

during the following days, in both Moscow and Berlin, German officials reiterated this idea. At last, on Saturday, August 12, the Soviet chargé said he had received instructions to state that his government was prepared to begin discussions in Moscow; he implied that the discussions would take some time. On Monday, Ribbentrop replied, stressing the necessity for speed and saying that he was prepared to come to Moscow himself "to lay the foundations for a final settlement of German-Russian relations."[25]

At Obersalzberg on that Monday, Hitler reviewed the political and military situation. Russia, he said, would keep out of the war. France would follow Britain. "While England may talk big, even recall her ambassador, perhaps put a complete embargo on trade, she is sure not to resort to armed intervention in the conflict."[26]

By now, Hitler was doing his utmost not to conceal, but to drive home, his determination to crush Poland. On August 8, the German press suddenly and with one voice opened a barrage of threats against the "criminal war agitation" of the Poles. During the week following, the barrage mounted in intensity, but in Britain and France it was overshadowed by reports of Ciano's "peace mission" to Hitler and of the cordial atmosphere surrounding the arrival of the British and French military missions in Moscow. On Tuesday, the fifteenth, the French ambassador appeared at the German foreign office and said flatly that "a conflict between Germany and Poland would automatically involve France"; on the same day, the British ambassador gave a similar warning. Press reports from Britain and France indicated that the people of both countries regarded the situation as "serious but not alarming"; as if to confirm this estimate, Halifax, who had returned briefly to London, resumed his vacation on Thursday, the seventeenth.

More than ever, it appeared that what Russia decided would be decisive for Britain and France; and in this situation German need was Russian opportunity. When, on August 15, Schulenburg presented Ribbentrop's offer to come immediately to Moscow to settle every question from the Baltic to the Black Sea, Molotov blandly stressed the need for "adequate preparation" before the arrival of so distinguished a visitor, and asked whether Germany was prepared to conclude a non-

25. G.D., Series D, VI, 1048–50; VII, 58, 59, 62–64.
26. Ibid., pp. 551–56.

aggression pact and to influence Japan in the direction of better relations with the Soviet Union. Two days later, his terms were accepted,
and the need for speed was again stressed. Molotov reiterated his
conviction that everything must be done in orderly stages and asked for
a draft of the nonaggression pact the Germans had in mind. New and
more frantic German emphasis on the need for speed, because war
might come at any moment, brought some results. The interminable
haggling over details of the Russo-German economic agreement ceased,
and the treaty was signed during the night of Saturday, August 19;
earlier in the day, Molotov agreed that Ribbentrop might come to
Moscow on August 26 or 27.

Already the day, August 20, on which Hitler had hoped to launch
the attack on Poland was at hand. To speed action, Hitler himself
intervened with a telegram to Stalin. More strongly than ever he
stressed the imminence of war. He asked that Ribbentrop be received
on August 22 or August 23; Ribbentrop would come with full powers
to draw up and sign a nonaggression pact and a political agreement.
On August 21, Stalin replied, agreeing to the arrival of Ribbentrop on
August 23. Immediately, in the early hours of Tuesday, August 22, the
German government issued a communiqué telling of the impending
conference and of the intention to conclude a nonaggression pact. The
Soviet government, on the other hand, was evidently determined to
play the game out to the end. On that Tuesday morning, "competent"
Soviet sources gave assurance to the press "that the arrival of Herr von
Ribbentrop for the conclusion of the Non-Aggression Pact was in no
way incompatible with the continuation of negotiations between the
British, French and Russian military missions for the purpose of
organizing resistance against aggression."[27]

Even the published text of the Russo-German nonaggression pact of
August 23 was hard to reconcile with this assurance. Unlike other such
agreements concluded by the Soviet Union, the agreement signed by
Molotov and Ribbentrop contained no "escape clause" in case one of
the signatories launched an aggressive war; the promise not to support
a third power in war was binding "should one of the Contracting
Parties become the object of belligerent action by a third Power."

27. *Ibid.*, VII, 208–9.

The "Secret Additional Protocol" to the pact delineated spheres of influence in central and southeastern Europe "in the event of a territorial and political transformation" in those areas. Finland, Estonia, Latvia, and part of Poland were to be in the Soviet sphere of influence; Lithuania and the remainder of Poland were to be in the German sphere of influence. In southeastern Europe, Russia affirmed "its interest" in Bessarabia, while Germany declared "complete political *désintéressement* in these territories."[28]

7. WAR, AUGUST AND SEPTEMBER, 1939

Hitler had played the final card. It was a costly move. The price he was willing to pay for Soviet support had mounted rapidly since May, when consideration for Soviet interests in Poland had been the highest price mentioned; even as late as August 16, Ribbentrop offered, so far as the Baltic states were concerned, only a joint guarantee of their independence. Now Hitler had been forced to surrender his claim to hegemony in the Baltic and in southeastern Europe.

The cost was high, but again Hitler was confident that he could crush Poland without fighting a general war. On August 22, before Ribbentrop reached Moscow, Hitler called his military leaders together once more. Again, he expatiated on the weaknesses of France and Britain militarily and in leadership, as contrasted with the strength of Germany and Italy. To compensate for their weakness, Britain and France had counted on Russian aid; now he had destroyed this hope. Moreover, now there was no need for Germany to fear a blockade; access to the resources of Russia was assured. "Poland has been manoeuvred into the position that we need for military success." The German attack, he said, would probably begin on Saturday morning, August 26. It was not necessary to find a plausible excuse for attack; what counted was victory, and the victor would not be asked whether or not he told the truth. His commanders must close their hearts to pity and act brutally, with the greatest harshness. What was at stake

---

28. *Ibid.*, pp. 245–47. By a secret additional protocol to a Russo-German treaty signed on September 28, 1939, Lithuania was placed in the Soviet sphere of influence, and Germany received a larger share of Poland (*ibid.*, Series D, VIII, 166). On June 24, 1940, in a memorandum for Hitler, Ribbentrop explained the background of the reference to "political *désintéressement*": "When the Southeastern European problems were discussed I declared very generally that Germany was *politically* disinterested in 'these areas,' i.e., in the Southeast of Europe" (*ibid.*, Series D, X, 11).

was the secure existence of 80 million Germans; the aim was not this or that frontier line, but the annihilation of Poland.[29]

How much Hitler was troubled by the breath-taking cynicism of his pact with Russia it is impossible to say. Since his obscure beginnings in Munich, he had carefully built up the image of Nazism as the bulwark against the flood of Bolshevism, with Hitler as the knight in armor, fearlessly facing the Communist hordes which threatened to overwhelm European civilization. At home and abroad this image had given him strength. Now, by the Nazi-Soviet pact, that image was destroyed. There is evidence, in the hurried shorthand notes which General Halder kept during these frantic days, that Hitler was worried by the impact of the blow in Germany. Halder's notes on a conference of Hitler with Reichstag and party notables on August 28 include the following:

. . . Soviet Pact widely misunderstood by Party. A pact with Satan to cast out the Devil. . . .

"Applause on proper cues, but thin."

Personal impression [of Führer]: exhausted, haggard, croaking voice, preoccupied. "Keeps himself completely surrounded now by his SS advisers."[30]

The disastrous consequences abroad—the fury of the Japanese and the humiliation of the Italians, who had been kept in ignorance, the angry disillusionment of conservatives everywhere—could be disregarded if the Nazi-Soviet pact broke British and French courage, whether immediately or after a quick conquest of Poland. This Hitler insisted must be the result. On August 23, the attack on Poland was definitely set for Saturday, August 26.

Even more than Hitler, Stalin had betrayed what he had said was the moral foundation of his cause. Through all the years of Hitler's rise, Stalin and his followers had contrasted Soviet resistance to Fascist aggression with the cowardice, or worse, of the appeasers—and this contrast had been accepted by millions everywhere, not least in France and Britain. Now Stalin, by the nonaggression pact of August 23, had agreed to stand aside while Hitler subjugated Poland, and although the terms of the secret additional protocol were unknown, everywhere

29. *G.D.*, Series D, VII, 200-6, 557-60.
30. *Ibid.*, pp. 563, 564; quotation marks as in text.

there was suspicion that Stalin had agreed to share the spoils with Hitler. As in Nazi Germany, opinion in the U.S.S.R. could be controlled. The German ambassador reported a few weeks later that opinion in Russia was doubtful and confused by the sudden shift from enmity to friendship, but "the Soviet Government has always previously been able in a masterly fashion to influence the attitude of the population in the direction which it has desired, and is not neglecting the necessary propaganda this time either."[31] Opinion abroad at first received no clear justification of the Nazi-Soviet pact; only after Poland was conquered and partitioned did propaganda from Moscow take a clear line against the British and French "warmongers" who insisted on prolonging a war which had no meaning for the suffering peoples of the world.

In France, the Nazi-Soviet pact deepened social divisions. Forgetting their own earlier admiration for Fascist "order," the representatives of the middle and upper classes turned in righteous wrath against French Communists and Communist-led trade unions. A few Communist leaders, like Thorez, fled to Russia, but most French Communists and fellow travelers floundered about, trying to reconcile their Communism and their patriotism, while the French workers and French peasants who had looked to Russia for leadership in the fight against Fascism were stunned by the sudden swing of Stalin to the side of Hitler. Pushing aside the advice of those who urged conciliation of these workers and peasants, who must now fight the battles of France, the Daladier government suppressed the Communist and leftist press and treated all those who had followed Communist leadership as enemies of France.

Apparently some of those who denounced the lack of patriotism of French workers were themselves disposed to act as Hitler expected them to act. The American ambassador reported that while he was talking with an official of the French foreign ministry on August 22, "politicians kept calling him on the telephone urging that it would be folly to go to war in support of Poland in view of the agreement between the Soviet Union and Germany." To the American ambassador, however, Daladier said the Nazi-Soviet pact, "the secret clauses of which were unknown, placed France in a most tragic and terrible situa-

31. *Ibid.*, Series D, VIII, 13.

tion." Without help from the east, Poland would soon be defeated; thereafter, since the British would not have a large army for two years, France would bear "the entire brunt of the war on land." War, then, would mean "sacrificing the lives of all able-bodied men in France in a war, the outcome of which would be to say the least doubtful." On the other hand, if France did not support Poland, all central Europe would fall to Germany, and then "Germany would turn on France and England with all the economic resources of these countries at her disposal."[32]

Chamberlain's view was much the same. On August 23 he told the American ambassador, "I have done everything I can think of and it seems as if all my work has come to naught." After reviewing the situation, he concluded, "The futility of it all is the thing that is frightful; after all they cannot save the Poles; they can merely carry on a war of revenge that will mean the destruction of the whole of Europe."[33]

In Britain, the Nazi-Soviet pact had the opposite of the effect intended by Hitler: the country became more united, more determined that there must be no return to appeasement. Within the government there apparently persisted some hope that Hitler would, at the last moment, draw back from war. In Parliament, however, while there was evident a feeling among the opposition parties that a more forthright policy by Chamberlain might have won alliance with Russia, resolution to accept war was general. For some supporters of the government, and more obviously for some in the dominions overseas, the failure of negotiations with Russia was welcome and made easier the acceptance of the necessity for war. The often-quoted cry of a die-hard Tory as a Labour member rose to speak at a moment when Chamberlain appeared reluctant to face the necessity for war—"Speak for England!"—caught the temper of the house and of the country.

On Thursday, August 24, Germans in Danzig made the first of the moves planned as preludes to the attack scheduled for Saturday. During Friday afternoon, however, there came two heavy blows: the Anglo-Polish Mutual Assistance Agreement was signed, and Mussolini made it plain that Italy would not fight if Germany became involved in war with France and Britain. In the evening, the order to attack was canceled.

32. *Foreign Relations, 1939,* I, 301–4.
33. *Ibid.,* p. 355.

There followed a week of confused negotiations. Much has been written of the "offers" made by Hitler during that week, but their purpose was succinctly noted by Halder in his diary: "Führer has hopes of driving wedge between British, French and Poles." On August 29, Halder even laid out the planned timetable:

> 30.8 Poles in Berlin
> 31.8 Blow up [*Zerplatzen*]
> 1.9 Use of force.[34]

The Poles refused to come, as the Austrians and Czechs had come, but in the evening of August 31, Halder reported Hitler still "expects France and England will not take action." The next morning, September 1, the German attack on Poland began. On September 3, first Britain and then France declared war on Germany.

Over and over, through the spring and summer of 1939 the British and French governments had said they would fight if Germany attacked Poland. These warnings went unheeded. In justification for his refusal to heed the warnings from London and Paris, Hitler invariably came back to the same arguments: Britain and France were militarily unprepared for war, and certainly for a war to protect Poland; they had threatened before and had drawn back at the end; the men in power in 1939 were the same men whose will had earlier collapsed in face of firm resistance. As he repeatedly boasted, he had bluffed and won before; what he had done when Germany was weak he could do again with confidence now that Germany was strong.

These boasts had an increasingly hollow sound from the last week of July. But by then the whole world had come to regard the question of Danzig as a decisive test of strength. Through the years since 1933 Hitler had advanced from one victory to another by convincing his opponents that if they did not surrender he would annihilate them and, if necessary, bring what Bonnet called the house of Europe crashing in ruins. Now Hitler was confronted by the despised Poles; they not only remained steady through the war of nerves, but, despite all provocation, they avoided rash action which would place the onus of aggression on them. If they were able to defy him with impunity, the tide which had carried him from success to success would turn.

In a last desperate effort to break the will of his opponents, Hitler

34. *G.D.,* Series D, VII, 567.

promised the hated Bolsheviks more for neutrality than he could win from war against Poland. Even under this pressure the courage of the Poles did not collapse. Retreat was now more impossible than ever. And so the diplomatic moves of March, intended at the outset only to advance Germany another stage along the road to supremacy in Europe, led inexorably, step by step, to war against the West in which the very existence of Germany was at stake.

Hitler concealed his failure even from himself—Britain and France would recognize the futility of fighting once Poland was destroyed; when convenient, the secret agreement dividing the spoils with Russia could be disregarded, as earlier agreements had been discarded when they had served their purpose.

Chamberlain made no effort to conceal his failure, indeed his address to Parliament on September 3 was less a call to battle than a lament for peace lost: "Everything that I have worked for, everything that I have hoped for, everything that I have believed in during my public life, has crashed into ruins." In his confession of failure, he united the British people as he had never done when he had been sure of success. A young poet, who had earlier seemed closer to the Soviet Union than to the Britain of Baldwin and Chamberlain, listened to the speeches of September 3. He heard a Labour and a Liberal leader talk "about gallant Poland, our liberties, democracy, etc." He noted in his diary: "Personally, I prefer Chamberlain's line to all their sanctimoniousness, which is that he has done his best to give Hitler everything but now feels that he can give nothing more."[35]

35. Stephen Spender, "September Journal," *Partisan Reader* (New York, 1946), pp. 394–95.

BIBLIOGRAPHICAL ESSAY

The volume of writing on the years from 1919 to 1939 is already enormous, and new publications appear at what seems accelerating speed. In part this situation is explained by the availability of new evidence. More important, the rapid changes of the last three decades inevitably lead to changing estimates of the decades before 1939. Above all, many of the issues, and events, and names, of the years between the first and second world wars still evoke passionate response, so that one interpretation inevitably leads to opposing interpretations. In this situation a "definitive" bibliography would be quickly outdated. It would also be misleading, because no list, no matter how bulky, could be even substantially complete—and also because no one person could possibly read all that has significance for an understanding of these years.

Representative recent special studies and biographies have been cited in the footnotes; nearly all of these provide guidance for further reading. Here I have tried to include studies with good bibliographies, recent interpretive works which help to an understanding of all or a major segment of the period, and accounts which, though in some ways outdated, give part of the story as it looked to those who lived through those years.

Several journals give excellent lists of books and articles as they appear. Possibly the best are those in the *Vierteljahrshefte für Zeitgeschichte*. The *Journal of Contemporary History* frequently contains articles surveying research; similar thoughtful surveys appear in the *Journal of Modern History*, the *Revue historique*, the *Revue d'histoire moderne et contemporaine*, and the *Historische Zeitschrift*. For the English-speaking reader, the *American Historical Review* and the *Journal of Modern History* review most of the important works; most of the journals listed above review a substantial number. The *American Historical Review* lists articles printed in other journals; from these lists, the student can identify important specialized journals such as *Foreign Affairs*, the *Journal of Economic History*, and the *Economic History Review*, and journals which defy precise classification such as *Annales: Economies, sociétés, civilisations*.

An essential source of information not only on published historical studies but on aids to bibliographical information is *A Guide to Historical Literature*, prepared for the American Historical Association by G. F. Howe and others (New York, 1961).

D. C. Watt (ed.), *Contemporary History in Europe, Problems and Perspectives* (London, 1969), is a unique and invaluable study of university course offerings, scholarly publications, and research in progress in each of the European countries. There is good material on the difficulties of research on recent history, and on ways in which these difficulites can, in whole or in part, be surmounted. Aside from the unevenness inevitable in a volume with more than a score of contributors, there are two major defects: few of the essays take account of events or publications since 1966, and there is no index.

There is no satisfactory general survey in English. The volume in *The New Cambridge Modern History* (Vol. XII, *The Era of Violence, 1898–1945,* ed. by David Thomson, Cambridge, 1960) contained excellent chapters, but was so obviously incomplete that a second edition was undertaken under the editorship of C. L. Mowat (*The Shifting Balance of World Forces, 1898–1945,* Cambridge, 1968.

A suggestive topical survey, *An Introduction to Contemporary History,* analyzing the years roughly from 1890 to 1960 as a transition from "modern history" to the "contemporary era," was published by Geoffrey Barraclough in 1964 (Penguin ed., Baltimore, 1967); the footnotes are a good introduction to the bibliography of the period. Theodore H. Von Laue, *The Global City: Freedom, Power and Necessity in the Age of World Revolutions* (Philadelphia, 1969), is a thoughtful attempt to relate technological change to social and cultural history. A pioneer effort at understanding is Hajo Holborn, *The Political Collapse of Europe* (N.Y., 1951).

The best interpretive survey is Maurice Crouzet, *L'époque contemporaine: A la recherche d'une civilisation nouvelle* (*Histoire générale des civilisations,* Vol. VII, 5th ed., Paris, 1969). Valuable, and much more detailed, is Maurice Baumont's *La faillite de la paix* (*1918–1938*) (*Peuples et Civilisations,* Vol. XX, in 2 parts, 5th ed., Paris, 1967–68). Both have excellent bibliographies. Volume IX of the *Propyläen Weltgeschichte* (*Das zwanzigste Jahrhundert,* ed. by Golo Mann, Berlin, 1960) is a cooperative work, with chapters by German and American scholars. The volume is vigorously written and beautifully illustrated.

The most ambitious study is *L'Europe du XIXe et du XXe siècle, interprétations historiques,* ed. by Max Beloff, Pierre Renouvin, Franz Schnabel, and Franco Valsecchi (7 vols., 1959–67). Volumes V–VII deal with the years since 1914. Some of the essays are valuable, and several have excellent bibliographies, but the coherent development promised by the analytical table of contents does not emerge.

The *Annual Bulletin of Historical Literature,* published by the Historical Association (London), gives all significant publications. A good discussion of the more important publications is Henry Winkler, "Some Recent Writings on Twentieth Century Britain," *Journal of Modern History,* XXXII (1960), 32–47.

There are several recent single-volume surveys. The first to appear, Charles L. Mowat, *Britain Between the Wars, 1918–1940* (Chicago, 1955), manages to combine a multitude of facts into a story of sustained interest. David Thomson's *England in the Twentieth Century, 1914–1963* (London, 1964) is brief and thoughtful. The most vigorous and engrossing is A. J. P. Taylor, *English History, 1914–1945* (N.Y., 1965). W. N. Medlicott, *Contemporary England, 1914–1964* (London, 1967), is a balanced political account.

Two interesting and suggestive retrospective studies are Robert Graves and Alan Hodge, *The Long Week-end: A Social History of Great Britain, 1918–1939* (N.Y., 1941), and Malcolm Muggeridge, *The Thirties (1930–1940) in Great Britain* (London, 1940). One of the best ways to get a "feel" for these years in Britain is through biographies and autobiographies, some of which have been listed in the text. The official royal biographies, Sir Harold Nicolson, *King George the Fifth: His Life and Reign* (London, 1952), and Sir John Wheeler-Bennett, *King George VI: His Life and Reign* (London, 1958), were written by perceptive observers of British life and give a good view of political history.

G. D. H. Cole, *A History of the Labour Party from 1914* (London, 1948), is both sympathetic and scholarly. The history of the trade union movement dominates the first volume of Alan Bullock's *The Life and Times of Ernest Bevin,* Vol. I, *Trade Union Leader, 1881–1940* (London, 1960). A good diplomatic survey is F. S. Northedge, *The Troubled Giant: Britain among the Great Powers, 1916–1939* (N.Y., 1967). There are two excellent publications of the Royal Institute of International Affairs, both entitled *Survey of British Commonwealth Affairs,* the first by W. K. Hancock (2 vols. in 3, London, 1937–42), the second by Nicholas Mansergh (2 vols., 1952–58).

The tangled questions of British military thought and action are discussed by Robin Higham in *Armed Forces in Peacetime: Britain, 1918–1940* (Hamden, Conn., 1962), and *The Military Intellectuals in Britain: 1918–1939* (New Brunswick, N.J., 1966). Brief but valuable comments on the quantity and quality of British preparation for war are in D. K. Hancock and M. M. Gowing, *British War Economy* (London, 1949), and M. M. Postan, *British War Production* (London, 1952).

FRANCE

The Comité française des sciences historiques publishes a *Bibliographie annuelle de l'histoire de France.* There is an excellent bibliographical article by René Rémond, "La France de 1914 à 1945," in the *Bulletin de la Société des professeurs d'histoire et de géographie,* No. 188 (October, 1964), pp. 101–10. John C. Cairns showed that a bibliographical article can by itself evoke a period by his "Along the Road Back to France 1940," *The American Historical Review,* LXIV (April, 1959), 583–603.

There is a fascinating analysis of the difficulties involved in trying to understand French foreign policy in the thirties by Pierre Renouvin, "La politique extérieure de la France de 1933 à 1939; Progrès et lacunes de l'information historique," Académie royale de Belgique, *Bulletin de la classe des lettres et des sciences morales et politiques,* 5th series, XLIX (1963), 199–221.

Equally interesting and valuable is Annie Kriegel, "L'historiographie du communisme français; Premier bilan et orientation de recherches," *Le mouvement social,* No. 53 (Oct.–Dec., 1965), pp. 130–42. Kriegel's "Le parti communiste sous la IIIᵉ Republique," *Revue française de science politique,* XVI (1966), 5–35, is an effort to "quantify" party membership.

Marc Bloch's *Strange Defeat* (Oxford, 1949) is an intensely personal statement written by a major historian in 1940; it is essential for an understanding of France between the two world wars.

There are several excellent surveys in English. The treatment in Gordon Wright's *Modern France* (Chicago, 1960) is brief but penetrating. Paul A. Gagnon, *France Since 1789* (N.Y., 1964), is good and more detailed. An older study, D. W. Brogan, *France Under the Republic: The Development of Modern France (1870–1939)* (N.Y., 1940), is remarkable for its combination of searching criticism and compassion. An unusually successful and valuable collaborative work is E. M. Earle (ed.), *Modern France: Problems of the Third and Fourth Republics* (Princeton, 1951).

Jacques Néré, *La Troisième République (1914–1940)* (Paris, 1965), is the best brief political and social history with an equally good brief bibliography. The best detailed study is J. Chastenet, *Histoire de la IIIᵉ République,* Vols. V–VII (Paris, 1960–63). One of the most interesting and suggestive accounts is by the economic historian Claude Fohlen, *La France de l'entre-deux-guerres, 1917–1939* (Paris, 1966).

The increasingly obvious inability of the political institutions and the party system of the Third Republic to cope with the problems of government after World War I has been examined in several excellent studies. Possibly the best is François Goguel, *Les institutions politiques françaises,* lectures delivered in 1967–68 (Paris, 1968), pp. 51–96; valuable is his *La politique des partis sous la IIIᵉ République* (Paris, 1958). The most suggestive essay in English is by Stanley Hoffmann, "Paradoxes of the French Political Community," in *In Search of France,* by Hoffmann and others (Cambridge, Mass., 1963), pp. 1–117; much of Hoffmann's essay, and still more the other essays in the volume, is concerned with the years after 1939, but valuable light is thrown on the years 1919–39. An attractive indirect approach to the subject is Rudolph Binion, *Defeated Leaders: The Political Fate of Caillaux, Jouvenel, and Tardieu* (N.Y., 1960).

Some party histories are cited in the text. René Rémond's masterly study of the French right (Paris, 1954) has been revised for the English edition, *The Right Wing in France from 1815 to de Gaulle* (Philadelphia, 1966). George Lichtheim, *Marxism in Modern France* (Columbia Paperback ed., N.Y., 1968), is an interpretive essay with emphasis on the years since 1945 but with insight on the twenties and thirties. Good general histories are Daniel Ligou, *Histoire du socialisme en France (1871–1961)* (Paris, 1962), Georges Lefranc, *Le mouvement socialiste sous la Troisième République (1875–1940)* (Paris, 1963), and Jacques Fauvet, *Histoire du parti communiste français,* Vol. I, *De la guerre à la guerre, 1917–1939* (Paris, 1964).

On the French military, there are two interesting impressionistic accounts: Jacques Nobécourt, *Une histoire politique de l'armée,* Vol. I, *1919–1942, de Pétain à Pétain* (Paris, 1967); and Paul-Marie de La Gorce, *The French Army, a Military-Political History* (English trans., N.Y., 1963). More substantial accounts, with bibliographies, are R. Challener, *The French Theory of the Nation in Arms, 1866–1939* (N.Y., 1962), and P. C. F. Bankwitz, *Maxime Weygand and Civil-Military Relations in Modern France* (Cambridge, Mass., 1967).

ITALY

There is an excellent bibliographical article by Geneviève Bibes, "Le fascisme italien: État des travaux depuis 1945," *Revue française de science politique,* XVIII (1968), 1191–1244. Earlier review articles are Emiliana Noether, "Italy Reviews Its Fascist Past: A Bibliographical Essay," *American Historical Review,* LXI (July, 1956), 877–99, and Charles Delzell, "Benito Mussolini: A Guide to the Biographical Literature," *Journal of Modern History,* XXXV (Dec., 1963), 339–53.

The best account in English is Denis Mack Smith, *Italy: A Modern History* (Ann Arbor, 1959). F. Chabod's *A History of Italian Fascism* (London, 1963) is brief but good; this is a translation of lectures which first appeared in a French and then in an Italian edition. Two other brief introductions are H. Stuart Hughes, *The United States and Italy* (Cambridge, Mass., rev. ed., 1965), and Elizabeth Wiskemann, *Fascism in Italy: Its Development and Influence* (N.Y., 1969).

The most comprehensive general study in Italian is L. Salvatorelli and G. Mira, *Storia d'Italia nel periodo fascista* (Turin, 1957).

On church-state relations there are three excellent works in English: D. A. Binchy, *Church and State in Fascist Italy* (London, 1941), R. Webster, *The Cross and the Fasces: Christian Democracy and Fascism in Italy* (Stanford, 1960), and A. C. Jemolo, *Church and State in Italy, 1850–1950* (Oxford, 1960). The last is an abridgment of Jemolo's *Chiesa e stato in Italia negli ultimi cento anni* (Turin, 1949).

On the resistance to Fascism, the best study is C. F. Delzell, *Mussolini's Enemies: The Italian Anti-Fascist Resistance* (Princeton, 1961).

The most detailed biography of Mussolini in English is Ivone Kirkpatrick, *Mussolini: A Study in Power* (N.Y., 1964). Three volumes of the biography by Renzo de Felice have appeared: *Mussolini il rivoluzionario, 1883–1920; Mussolini il fascista: 1. La conquista del potere, 1921–1925,* and *2. L'organizzazione della stato fascista, 1925–1929* (Turin, 1965, 1966, 1968); de Felice's interpretation has evoked controversy.

Two contemporary accounts by exiles are valuable: A. Rossi (the pseudonym of the former Communist Angelo Tasca), *The Rise of Italian Fascism, 1918–1922* (London, 1938); and Gaetano Salvemini, *Under the Axe of Fascism* (N.Y., 1936).

Christopher Seton-Watson, *Italy from Liberalism to Fascism, 1870–1925* (London, 1967), is suggestive on the early years of Fascism and, in the Epilogue, on the later years; but the treatment of the period after 1918 is not as searching as the account of earlier Italian history.

On foreign policy, perhaps the best way to understand Fascism is to see it through Galeazzo Ciano's eyes: Hugh Gibson (ed.), *The Ciano Diaries, 1939–1943* (N.Y., 1946); Malcolm Muggeridge (ed.), *Ciano's Diplomatic Papers* (London, 1948); and Andreas Mayor (trans.), *Ciano's Hidden Diary, 1937–1938* (N.Y., 1953).

GERMANY

To keep abreast of current research, it is necessary to study the bibliographical notes in the East Berlin *Zeitschrift für Geschichtswissenschaft* as well as the Munich *Vierteljahrshefte für Zeitgeschichte*. There are also useful review articles in *Geschichte in Wissenschaft und Unterricht*. There is a thoughtful study by G. Badia of trends in German scholarship concerning the history of Germany from 1918 to 1945, part of a series on German historiography since 1945, in *Annales: Economies, sociétés, civilisations*, XXII (March–April, 1967), 449–62. More general review articles are G. Castellan,

"Histoire de l'allemagne depuis 1914," *Revue historique,* CCXXXI (April–June, 1964), 417–56; Eric C. Kollman, "Reinterpreting Modern German History: the Weimar Republic," *Journal of Central European Affairs,* XXI (Jan., 1962), 434–51; and Wolfgang Sauer, "National Socialism: Totalitarianism or Fascism?" *American Historical Review,* LXXIII (Dec., 1967), 404–24.

There are two general works which show clearly the indelible impression left on those who lived in Germany through even part of the period. The third volume of Hajo Holborn's *A History of Modern Germany* (N.Y., 1969) is somber in tone. Golo Mann's *The History of Germany since 1789* (London, 1968) accents cultural changes and is marked by irony which seems at times a refuge from disgust.

On the Weimar period, S. William Halperin's *Germany Tried Democracy: A Political History of the Reich from 1918 to 1933* (N.Y., 1946) remains a good introduction. Arthur Rosenberg's *A History of the German Republic* (London, 1936) has the power of an outraged contemporary. Much more detailed is Erich Eyck's liberal interpretation, *A History of the Weimar Republic* (2 vols., Cambridge, Mass., 1962–63).

For the Nazi period, there is the analytical study of K. D. Bracher, *Die deutsche Diktatur: Entstehung, Struktur, Folgen des Nationalsozialismus* (Cologne, 1969); the footnotes and bibliography give a comprehensive view of writing on the subject. Probably the best introduction in English is Alan Bullock's *Hitler: A Study in Tyranny* (rev. ed., London, 1965). One can sense the incomprehensible nature of the Nazi era from reading Adolf Hitler's *Mein Kampf* (Sentry Edition, Boston, 1962). The impact on the mind of a historian whose memory reached back to the days of Bismarck's wars is recorded in Friedrich Meinecke's *The German Catastrophe* (English trans., Cambridge, Mass., 1950). A coldly rational description of the organization and operation of terror in Nazi Germany is given by Helmut Krausnick, Hans Buchheim, Martin Broszat, and Hans-Adolf Jacobsen in *Anatomy of the SS State* (N.Y., 1968; German ed., 1965). A classic analysis of the working of the Nazi political system is Hannah Arendt, *The Origins of Totalitarianism* (N.Y., Meridian Books, 1958).

Most scholarly writing is still confined to studies of part of the field; some major studies are cited above in the text. Some of the best interpretations are in the form of volumes made up of essays by experts; an example is T. Eschenburg and others, *The Path to Dictatorship, 1918–1933* (N.Y., Anchor Books, 1966); the authors include outstanding German scholars. This volume is admirably adapted to a general audience; the essays originated as radio lectures. A similar collection, but drawn mostly from scholarly journals, is Gotthard Jasper (ed.), *Von Weimar zu Hitler, 1930–*

1933 (Köln, 1968). Both of these volumes have a wider time span than the titles indicate. A perceptive popularization of recent research, with excellent bibliographical footnotes, is J. C. Fest, *Das Gesicht des Dritten Reiches* (Munich, 1963; English ed., N.Y., 1970). Fest approaches the problem of understanding Nazi Germany through sketches of individuals and types.

On labor, a good recent survey, with bibliography, is Pierre Waline, *Cinquante ans de rapports entre patrons et ouvriers en Allemagne,* Vol. I, *1918–1945* (Paris, 1968). Two very different approaches to the control of public opinion are Oron J. Hale, *The Captive Press in the Third Reich* (Princeton, 1964), and Z. A. B. Zeman, *Nazi Propaganda* (London, 1964). For Nazi justice, there is a brief guide, with bibliography, centering on the experience of Hamburg, Werner Johe, *Die gleichgeschaltete Justiz* (Frankfurt, 1967).

On foreign policy there is a general survey of the Weimar years, Ludwig Zimmermann, *Deutsche Aussenpolitik in der Ära der Weimarer Republik* (Göttingen, 1958), and a rigorously documented examination of the structure of Nazi foreign policy operations, Hans-Adolf Jacobsen, *Nazional-sozialistische Aussenpolitik, 1933–1938* (Frankfurt a.M., 1968).

On the history of the German military establishment, there is a thoughtful review article, Pierre Ayçoberry, "Le corps des officiers allemands, de l'Empire au Nazisme," *Annales: Economies, sociétés, civilisations* (March-April, 1967), pp. 370–84. Two pioneer studies marked by distinction of thought are Sir John Wheeler-Bennett, *The Nemesis of Power: The German Army in Politics, 1918–1945* (London, 1954), and Gordon A. Craig, *The Politics of the Prussian Army, 1640–1945* (N.Y., 1956). Of the many recent studies, the following are excellent, and their bibliographies furnish guidance for further study: F. L. Carsten, *The Reichswehr and Politics, 1918 to 1933* (Oxford, 1966; a revision of the German edition published in 1964), and Robert J. O'Neill, *The German Army and the Nazi Party, 1933–1939* (N.Y., 1966). There is a detailed technical study of German disarmament, with bibliography: Michael Salewski, *Entwaffnung und Militärkontrolle in Deutschland, 1919–1927* (Munich, 1966).

THE STATES BETWEEN RUSSIA AND GERMANY

Histories of the states of central and southeastern Europe have been over-shadowed by first Nazi and then Soviet power in the area. The results may be seen in two of the best books on parts of the region.

The first, Hugh Seton-Watson, *Eastern Europe Between the Wars, 1918–1941* (3d ed., Hamden, Conn., 1962), was written in 1942–43 and only slightly modified thereafter; the book reflects the hope for continued Anglo-Russian cooperation after Nazi power had been broken. The states included in Seton-Watson's survey are Poland, Czechoslovakia, Hungary, Rumania, Yugoslavia, and Bulgaria. The second, Robert Lee Wolff, *The Balkans in Our Time* (Cambridge, Mass., 1956), was completed in 1955, when Russian power overshadowed the area. The states included are Yugoslavia, Rumania, Bulgaria, and Albania. There are good summary accounts of the history of these countries, and in addition Greece, in L. S. Stavrianos, *The Balkans Since 1453* (N.Y., 1965).

The best introduction to both the history of, and the writing concerning, the states stretching from the Baltic to the Mediterranean is C. A. Macartney and A. W. Palmer, *Independent Eastern Europe: A History* (London, 1962). The states included are Finland, Estonia, Latvia, Lithuania, Poland, Czechoslovakia, Austria, Hungary, Rumania, Yugoslavia, Bulgaria, Greece, Albania, and Turkey; the period covered is 1914 to 1941.

Among C. A. Macartney's many, and uniformly good, studies of south-eastern Europe, the most outstanding is *October 15: A History of Modern Hungary, 1929–1945* (2d ed., 2 vols., Edinburgh, 1961). The first volume covers all of the interwar period. The American edition is called *A History of Hungary, 1929–1945*. There are two complementary studies of Rumania, both excellent: David Mitrany, *The Land and the Peasant in Rumania: The War and Agrarian Reform, 1917–1921* (New Haven, 1930), and H. L. Roberts, *Rumania: Political Problems of an Agrarian State* (New Haven, 1951). John H. Wuorinen, *A History of Finland* (N.Y., 1965), is a thoughtful survey; about a third of the volume is devoted to the years 1919–39. Wuorinen's views in this and his other works have been challenged as too faithfully reflecting "official" views; but writings on the states caught between Soviet Russia and Nazi Germany are almost inevitably affected by this tragic circumstance.

On the Baltic states, there is a brief informative study by the Royal Institute of International Affairs: *The Baltic States: A Survey of the Political and Economic Structure and the Foreign Relations of Estonia, Latvia, and Lithuania* (London, 1938). On Poland, there is a collaborative volume edited by Bernadotte E. Schmitt, *Poland* (Berkeley, 1947), and a translation of a German study of 1961 by Hans Roos (pseud. of Hans Otto Meissner), *A History of Modern Poland* (London, 1966). For Czechoslovakia, two works written in wartime—R. W. Seton-Watson, *A History of the Czechs and the Slovaks* (London, 1943), and S. Harrison Thomson, *Czechoslovakia in European History* (2d ed., 1953)—give a brief history of the interwar years and may be compared with a later, more detached, account by Jörg K. Hoensch, *Geschichte der Tschechoslowakischen Republik 1918 bis 1965* (Stuttgart, 1966).

On Austria, there is a good collaborative study under the editorship of

Heinrich Benedikt, *Geschichte der Republik Österreich* (Munich, 1954); C. Gulick, *Austria from Hapsburg to Hitler* (2 vols., Berkeley, 1948), is vigorously written with sympathy for the socialists.

On Yugoslavia, there is a brief historical account in Robert J. Kerner (ed.), *Yugoslavia* (Berkeley, 1949). J. B. Hoptner, *Yugoslavia in Crisis, 1934–1941* (N.Y., 1962), is vigorous and controversial. Brief histories of Greece are Edward S. Foster, *A Short History of Modern Greece, 1821–1956* (3d ed., London, 1958), Nicolas Svoronos, *Histoire de la Grèce moderne* (Paris, 1953), and C. M. Woodhouse, *The Story of Modern Greece* (London, 1968).

RUSSIA

An indispensable guide to current research is *Survey: A Journal of Soviet and East European Studies* (earlier, *Soviet Survey*), now a quarterly, published in London. Review essays on many aspects of Russian studies, originally published in the January and April, 1964, issues of *Survey*, were republished: Walter Z. Laqueur and Leopold Labedz (eds.), *The State of Soviet Studies* (Cambridge, Mass., 1965). Later, Laqueur wrote a stimulating review of historical writing on, and in, the Soviet Union: *The Fate of the Revolution: Interpretations of Soviet History* (N.Y., 1967). In both books, stress is laid on the peculiar problems of research on the Soviet Union, the most important being deficiencies in the evidence available and the difficulty of forming a settled judgment on a revolution while it is still in progress.

General accounts inevitably lean toward a skeptical or optimistic view of the continuing revolution. Donald W. Treadgold, *Twentieth Century Russia* (2d ed., Chicago, 1964), is an excellent example of the former, with a good bibliography. Examples of the optimistic view are Frederick L. Schuman, *Russia since 1917: Four Decades of Soviet Politics,* with bibliographical footnotes (N.Y., 1957), and Isaac Deutscher's impressionistic lectures, *The Unfinished Revolution: Russia, 1917–1967* (London, 1967).

The most ambitious and most important general history is E. H. Carr, *A History of Soviet Russia* (London, 1950–   ). To date, the following have appeared: *The Bolshevik Revolution, 1917–1923* (3 vols., 1950–53); *The Interregnum, 1923–1924* (1954); *Socialism in One Country, 1924–1926* (3 vols., 1958–64); *Foundations of a Planned Economy, 1926–1929* (with R. W. Davies, Vol. I in 2 parts, 1969).

Paradoxically, one of the best ways to understand Russia is through biographies of the three leaders, Lenin, Trotsky, and Stalin. Although it ends before the revolution, Bertram D. Wolfe's *Three Who Made a Revolution: A Biographical History* (4th rev. ed., N.Y., 1964) is a good introduction.

The most recent, and the best, biography of Lenin is Adam B. Ulam, *The Bolsheviks: The Intellectual and Political History of the Triumph of Communism in Russia* (N.Y., 1965); Louis Fischer's *The Life of Lenin* (N.Y., 1964) is a vigorous account by a veteran journalist. For Trotsky, the best biography is the partisan study by his disciple, Isaac Deutscher, *The Prophet Armed, Trotsky, 1879–1921* (N.Y., 1954); *The Prophet Unarmed, Trotsky, 1921–1929* (N.Y., 1959); and *The Prophet Outcast, Trotsky, 1929–1940* (N.Y., 1963). Deutscher's *Stalin, A Political Biography* (2d ed., Oxford paperback, N.Y., 1967) is less good, but probably the best life of Stalin.

A recent, and good, history of Soviet foreign policy is A. Ulam, *Expansion and Co-existence: A History of Soviet Foreign Policy* (N.Y., 1968). Other suggestive studies centered on foreign policy are Hugh Seton-Watson, *From Lenin to Khrushchev: A History of World Communism* (Praeger Paperbacks, N.Y., 1960); and George F. Kennan, *Russia and the West under Lenin and Stalin* (Mentor Books, N.Y., 1962). Party history is the center in Leonard Schapiro, *The Communist Party of the Soviet Union* (London, 1960); R. N. Carew Hunt, *The Theory and Practice of Communism* (rev. ed., N.Y., 1962); and Robert V. Daniels, *The Conscience of the Revolution* (Cambridge, Mass., 1960). The question of nationalism is explored in F. C. Barghoorn, *Soviet Russian Nationalism* (N.Y., 1956), as in Richard Pipes's study of Communism and nationalism, referred to in the text. The relation between Communism and politics is explored in Barrington Moore, Jr., *Soviet Politics: The Dilemma of Power, the Role of Ideas in Social Change* (Cambridge, Mass., 1950), in two studies by Merle Fainsod, *How Russia Is Ruled* (rev. ed., Cambridge, Mass., 1965), and *Smolensk under Soviet Rule* (Cambridge, Mass., 1958); and in Robert Conquest (ed.), *The Politics of Ideas in the USSR* (London, 1967). Ideas are more to the center in Alfred G. Meyer, *Leninism* (Cambridge, Mass., 1957), and Richard Pipes (ed.), *The Russian Intelligentsia* (N.Y., 1961). A sympathetic effort to interpret the ongoing revolution is made in T. H. Von Laue, *Why Lenin? Why Stalin? A Reappraisal of the Russian Revolution, 1900–1930* (Philadelphia, 1964).

Representative of efforts to see the Soviet period as part of Russian history is Nicholas V. Riasanovsky, *A History of Russia* (rev. ed., N.Y., 1969).

The shifting currents in Russian historical writing are described in John Keep and Liliana Brisby (eds.), *Contemporary History in the Soviet Mirror* (N.Y., 1964), and Cyril E. Black, *Rewriting Russian History: Soviet Interpretations of Russia's Past* (2d ed., rev., Vintage Books, N.Y., 1962). The first of these books grew out of a conference of Western scholars held in Geneva in 1961. The second reprints a long review of the first (1956) edition which appeared in the journal *Istoriya SSSR* in 1959.

A good review of military history, with bibliography, is John Erickson, *The Soviet High Command: A Military-Political History 1918–1941* (London, 1962). A shorter study, a revision of a French edition of 1959, is Michel Garder, *A History of the Soviet Army* (N.Y., 1966).

INTERNATIONAL RELATIONS

The Foreign Affairs Bibliography (Vol. I, 1919–1932, ed. by William L. Langer and Hamilton Fish Armstrong, N.Y., 1932; Vol. II, 1932–1942, ed. by Robert Gale Woolbert, N.Y., 1945; Vol. III, 1942–1952, ed. by Henry L. Roberts, N.Y., 1955) is the most complete. A selective bibliography of works published between 1920 and 1970 is now being prepared under the editorship of Byron Dexter for the (American) Council on Foreign Relations, the publisher of the *Foreign Affairs Bibliography* and of the quarterly *Foreign Affairs,* which contains bibliographical notes in each issue. *Foreign Affairs* is invaluable for an understanding of the way in which contemporaries viewed events. The Council also sponsored, beginning with 1931, a series entitled *The United States in World Affairs,* of which (for this period) volumes on 1931, 1932, 1933, 1934–35, 1936, and 1939 were published. While these volumes center on American policy, they give an excellent view of the impact of world politics on informed observers; there is a topical guide to the series in the volume for 1939.

Invaluable also is the series issued under the auspices of the (British) Royal Institute of International Affairs, *Survey of International Affairs,* ed. by Arnold Toynbee and others. Two of the volumes for this period are especially important, for very different reasons. The first is *The World After the Paris Peace Conference* written by Toynbee (Oxford, 1925), which in fewer than a hundred pages surveys the world as it looked to an informed British observer in 1924, when the gloom of the early postwar years was lifting. The other is *The World in March 1939* (London, 1952), which is a recapitulation, in the light of new evidence, of the history of the interwar years, with emphasis on international affairs and armaments but with much excellent material on the political and social history of the period. In addition to the annual *Survey,* the Royal Institute, beginning with 1928, published annual volumes of *Documents on International Affairs.*

The best diplomatic survey is Pierre Renouvin, *Les crises du XXe siècle,* I. *De 1914 à 1929;* II. *De 1929 à 1945* (Vols. VII and VIII of *Histoire des relations internationales,* Paris, 1957, 1958; there is an inadequate English translation, 2 vols., N.Y., 1968). A shorter French account is J.-B. Duroselle, *Histoire diplomatique de 1919 à nos jours* (Paris, 1953). The Soviet point of view is presented in Vol. III, 1919–1939, of *Histoire de la diplomatie,* published under the direction of V. Potemkin (French trans.,

Paris, 1947). A brief and concentrated presentation of the Soviet position is A. D. Nikonov's *The Origin of World War II and the Prewar European Political Crisis of 1939* (Russian and English text, Moscow, 1955).

The Carnegie Endowment for International Peace sponsored two large collections, both under the editorship of James T. Shotwell. One, *The Economic and Social History of the World War,* contains studies whose scope extends through the peace settlement and into the years between the two world wars, such as two cited in the text: David Mitrany's volume on the effects of the war in southeastern Europe, and Albrecht Mendelssohn Bartholdy's penetrating examination of the effects of the war on German society. The other series, *The Paris Peace Conference: History and Documents,* contains valuable studies, with documents, of individual countries at the Paris conference, and also topical studies such as Philip Burnett's two volumes on reparation, also cited in the text.

One of the best of the many studies sponsored by the Royal Institute of International Affairs was F. P. Walters, *A History of the League of Nations* (2 vols., London, 1952). Walters was a member of the League secretariat from 1919 to 1940, and he writes both as a participant and as a scholar.

In Winston Churchill's two volumes on the years between the wars, it is the participant who dominates the narrative, but the participant is also a great historian. *The Aftermath, 1918–1928* (N.Y., 1929) is the concluding volume of Churchill's *The World Crisis,* a history of the First World War. It was written at the climax of the Locarno era. All but a few pages of this large volume are concerned with the years 1918–23, but those few pages convey better than any pacifist tract the dread of another great war which explains so much of the history of the years between the two world wars. *The Gathering Storm* (London, 1948) is the first volume of Churchill's *The Second World War.* More than half the volume is concerned with the interwar years and forms a sustained indictment of the foreign policy of the Western democracies. Churchill did not write impartial history, but he did write of events as they were seen by a statesman of great intelligence and passionate conviction.

In a much lower key, but invaluable for an understanding of interwar scholarly opinion on the problems of peace, security, and disarmament, is William E. Rappard's *The Quest for Peace Since the World War* (Cambridge, Mass., 1940), written in the summer, autumn, and winter of 1939. Rappard was then director of the Graduate Institute of International Studies in Geneva; he was, as he said in his preface, describing "the birth, the growth and the mournful destiny of the idea that lasting peace should result from the World War."

Another work completed just after the outbreak of war in 1939, and which has stood up remarkably well not only as the testimony of a witness but as a scholarly analysis, is Arnold Wolfers' *Britain and France Between Two Wars: Conflicting Strategies of Peace Since Versailles* (N.Y., 1940).

A pioneering cooperative effort to rethink the diplomacy of the interwar years is *The Diplomats, 1919–1939*, ed. by Gordon A. Craig and Felix Gilbert (Princeton, 1953). Many of the chapters are still essential.

The only major effort in English to cover international relations between the two world wars in the light of the new evidence is A. J. P. Taylor's *The Origins of the Second World War*, discussed in the text. Nearly all other studies are confined to special topics or the foreign policy of a single country.

ECONOMIC HISTORY

The most lively studies of the economic problems of the interwar period were published before 1939. These are often the works of men involved in the effort to solve the economic problems Europe faced at the time. Since the authors sought to persuade, and not merely describe, their arguments are easy to follow; their analyses sharply illuminate the central problems of the European economy in the interwar years.

Few works are more valuable in this regard than those of John Maynard Keynes. The famous exposition of his ideas, *The General Theory of Employment, Interest and Money* (London, 1936), is hard for the general reader to understand. But anyone can grasp the argument of his pamphlet *The Means to Prosperity* (London, 1933), an explanation of what was wrong with the economy and what should be done about it. Another readable formulation of Keynes's fundamental ideas is the "Programme of Expansion" he wrote for Lloyd George in 1929; it is published in Keynes's *Essays in Persuasion* (London, 1932). The essays in this book brilliantly analyze many of the crucial economic problems of the period. Possibly the best of the many books on Keynes are Lawrence Klein, *The Keynesian Revolution* (2d ed., N.Y., 1966), and Roy Harrod, *The Life of John Maynard Keynes* (N.Y., 1951).

Gustav Cassel was a Swedish economist who sat as an expert on international commissions in the interwar period. His writings reveal the way an intelligent liberal understood the central economic problems of the 1920's. In 1926 he wrote a concise, tightly reasoned memorandum for the League of Nations Preparatory Committee for the International Economic Conference: *Recent Monopolistic Tendencies in Industry and Trade, Being an Analysis of the Nature and Causes of the Poverty of Nations* (Geneva, 1927). Five years earlier Cassel published an important and sometimes fascinating study of monetary and financial problems, *Money and Foreign Exchange After 1914* (London, 1922). Howard S. Ellis, *German Monetary Theory, 1905–1933* (Cambridge, Mass., 1937), contains an excellent study of the diverse ways economists—not just German economists—explained changes in the price level and in the exchange rates. Cassel's ideas, which played an important role in the debate arising from this divergence of opinion, are closely examined by Ellis.

Ernest Minor Patterson, in *The World's Economic Dilemma* (N.Y., 1930), discusses the difficulties of realizing an international division of labor, upon which he believes the welfare of mankind is based, in a world dominated by conflicting nationalisms. A similar theme runs through Herbert Feis's lectures, *The Changing Pattern of International Economic Affairs* (N.Y., 1940). Feis tries to explain the failure of the world economic community to organize itself along liberal lines: he argues that the failure resulted not from the intrinsic unworkability of the free-trade scheme, but from political passions and special interests that proved more powerful than the advice of experts.

Perhaps the best of the more recent studies is the chapter on the economic history of the interwar years in David Landes, *The Unbound Prometheus: Technological Change and Industrial Development in Western Europe from 1750 to the Present* (Cambridge, 1969). In spite of the subtitle, Landes is concerned in this chapter with economic history as a whole and devotes a good deal of attention to the financial and monetary questions which dominate the economic history of the 1920's.

A fundamental study, on which Landes and other writers rely, is I. Svennilson, *Growth and Stagnation in the European Economy, 1913–1945* (Geneva, 1954), a work especially valuable for its statistical tables.

W. A. Lewis, *Economic Survey, 1919–1939* (London, 1949), is a brief nontechnical account of the "ebb and flow of economic activity" and discusses government efforts to meet the economic challenges of the interwar years.

A League of Nations study, written in large part by Ragnar Nurkse, *The Course and Control of Inflation: A Review of Monetary Experience in Europe after World War I* (Geneva, 1946), contains a judicious and well-informed analysis of European monetary problems.

The best study of the reparation question is Etienne Weill-Raynal, *Les réparations allemandes et la France* (3 vols., Paris, 1949). Hjalmar Schacht, *The End of Reparations* (N.Y., 1931), is a forceful presentation of the German point of view.

There is no completely satisfactory study of the Great Depression. What caused it is still a matter for debate. *The Journal of Contemporary History,* IV, 4 (1969), has nine articles on the Great Depression. The articles are mainly accounts of its effects on particular nations or regions and of the measures governments took to combat them.

There are a number of good, informative histories of the British economy covering this period. The most useful are W. Ashworth, *An Economic History of England, 1870–1939* (London, 1960), and Sidney Pollard, *The Development of the British Economy, 1914–1950* (London, 1962).

The best work on France is Alfred Sauvy, *Histoire économique de la France entre les deux guerres,* Vol. I: 1918–1931 (Paris, 1965), Vol. II: 1931–1939 (Paris, 1967). A third volume, as yet unpublished, will mainly cover social history and will contain an extensive bibliography. Sauvy, like Cassel, likes to expose the economic fallacies and delusions that dominated the minds of politicians, economists, and common people during these years— delusions which prevented both right and left from coming to grips with and solving economic problems.

The chapter on Fascist economic policy in Shepard Clough, *The Economic History of Modern Italy* (N.Y., 1964), is a good outline of the history of the Italian economy in the interwar period. There are also two books by Epicarmo Corbino that can be profitably consulted: *L'economia italiana dal 1860 al 1960* (Bologna, 1962) and a collection of articles, *Cinquante ans de vie économique italienne (1915–1965)* (Naples, 1967).

The chapters on the interwar years in G. Stolper, K. Häuser and K. Borchardt, *The German Economy, 1870 to the Present* (2d ed., N.Y., 1967), are a good introduction to the economic history of Germany. For many years the standard work on the German inflation has been C. Bresciani-Turroni, *The Economics of Inflation* (London, 1937). Karsten Laursen and Jørgen Pedersen, *The German Inflation, 1918–1923* (Amsterdam, 1964), challenge Bresciani-Turroni's fundamental conclusions: Laursen and Pedersen argue that the German government had no viable alternative to the policy it pursued. Rolf E. Lüke, *Von der Stabilisierung zur Krise* (Zurich, 1958), is an excellent study mainly of monetary questions, covering the decade 1923–33. On the Nazi economy, see René Erbe, *Die national-sozialistische Wirtschaftspolitik 1933–1939 im Lichte der modernen Theorie* (Zurich, 1958), and Wilhelm Treue, *Deutsche Wirtschaft und Politik 1933–1945* (Hannover, 1963); C. W. Guillebaud, *The Economic Recovery of Germany, 1933–1938* (London, 1939), is still useful. Karl Erich Born (ed.), *Moderne deutsche Wirtschaftsgeschichte* (Cologne and Berlin, 1966), has five articles on the interwar period and a good bibliography.

Maurice Dobb, *Soviet Economic Development Since 1917* (6th ed., London, 1966), is an excellent introduction. Alec Nove, *The Soviet Economy: An Introduction* (N.Y., 1963), is an analysis of the Soviet economic system. Naum Jasny, *Soviet Industrialization, 1928–1952* (Chicago, 1961), is an important work, the product of years of study by one of the outstanding scholars in this field. A. Baykov, *The Development of the Soviet Economic*

System (N.Y., 1947), and Peter Wiles, *The Political Economy of Communism* (Oxford, 1962), are also valuable.

SCIENCE AND TECHNOLOGY

A good general study is René Taton (ed.), *History of Science,* Vol. IV, *Science in the Twentieth Century* (N.Y., 1966; the French edition was published in 1964), with bibliography. There are several periodicals devoted to the history of science, none of which concentrates on the twentieth century. Articles on this period are listed together in the extensive critical bibliographies in *Isis.*

There are many excellent short studies which attempt to make the history of science and the place of science in history intelligible to the "layman." One of the most successful is James B. Conant, *Modern Science and Modern Man* (Anchor, Garden City, N.Y., 1953). Another is Lincoln Barnett, *The Universe and Dr. Einstein* (2d rev. ed., Mentor, N.Y., 1957). Somewhat more technical, but clear and with an emphasis on the scientists as a community, is George Gamow, *Thirty Years That Shook Physics: The Story of Quantum Theory* (Anchor, Garden City, N.Y., 1966). A comparable study of relativity is James A. Coleman, *Relativity for the Layman* (N.Y., 1954; Pelican ed., 1959), and for genetics, L. C. Dunn, *A Short History of Genetics: The Development of Some of the Main Lines of Thought: 1864–1939* (N.Y., 1965).

More definitely concerned with the cultural impact of scientific change are Werner Heisenberg, *Physics and Philosophy: The Revolution in Modern Science* (N.Y., 1958); Hans Reichenbach, *From Copernicus to Einstein* (Wisdom Library, N.Y., 1942); and Sir E. John Russell, *Science and Modern Life* (London, 1953).

Three studies which give a synthesis of aspects of the scientific situation roughly at the end of this period are J. D. Bernal, *The Social Function of Science* (London, 1939); Julian Huxley, *Evolution: The Modern Synthesis* (Science Editions, N.Y., 1964; this is the 1942 ed. with a new introduction); and Theodosius Dobzhansky, *Genetics and the Origin of Species* (N.Y., 1937).

In a class apart as both an exposition and a battle cry of the war between the older humanistic culture and the new scientific culture which was building up in the interwar period is C. P. Snow, *The Two Cultures: And a Second Look* (Cambridge, 1964). The first edition of 1959 occasioned furious retorts, to which Snow replied with vigor in "A Second Look"; the footnotes give guidance to some of the more formidable participants in the controversy.

On technology, there is a cooperative survey edited by Melvin Kranzberg and Carroll W. Pursell, Jr., *Technology in Western Civilization*, Vol. II, *Technology in the Twentieth Century* (N.Y., 1967); the section on "Readings and References," pp. 709–39, is an excellent guide. The quarterly journal *Technology and Culture* frequently emphasizes some significant aspect of this relationship; one of the best of these theme issues is "Toward a Philosophy of Technology" (VII, 3, Summer, 1966), and includes an essay by Lewis Mumford, a pioneer in the history of technology, on "Technics and the Nature of Man." An interesting effort to demonstrate that technological change culminates in "the socialist countries," i.e., the U.S.S.R. and other Communist states, is made in Samuel Lilley, *Men, Machines and History: The Story of Tools and Machines in Relation to Social Progress* (rev. ed., N.Y., 1966); this approach may be contrasted with that of the contributors to the volume edited by Kranzberg and Pursell, who make the American experience central. There is a more generally European orientation in Maurice Daumas (ed.), *L'histoire générale des techniques*, Vol. III, *L'expansion du machinisme* (Paris, 1968).

ARTS AND LETTERS

Obviously, the best way to come to understand the world of the thinker and the artist is to read what he wrote and to look at what he painted or shaped. Moreover, one of the distinguishing features of the interwar period is the effort of thinkers and artists to understand the age in which they were living. Here, therefore, it will be enough to indicate a few guides who can start an explorer on what Stuart Hughes called "the obstructed path" (H. Stuart Hughes, *The Obstructed Path: French Social Thought in the Years of Desperation 1930–1960*, N.Y., 1968). Hughes's earlier volume, *Consciousness and Society: The Reorientation of European Social Thought, 1890–1930* (N.Y., 1958), introduced the thinkers who, more or less directly, shaped the intellectual's and the artist's view between the first and second world wars.

A writer-participant who has written much and well on the relation of the artist to his time is Stephen Spender. Of his many books on this subject, possibly the most comprehensive is *The Struggle of the Modern* (London, 1963), but the theme pervades shorter writings like *The New Realism* (London, 1939), which explores the artist's relation to the middle classes and the workers. Another writer-participant is Hannah Arendt, who has a less irenic temper and a more difficult style, but who is always a vigorous expositor, particularly on the intellectual life of central Europe, as in *Men in Dark Times* (N.Y., 1968). Vigorous and perceptive also are the writings of the Communist critic Georg Lukács, as in *The Meaning of Contemporary Realism* (London, 1962; the German edition appeared in 1957). For the experience of writers who lost faith in Communism, see Richard Crossman (ed.), *The God That Failed* (N.Y., 1950; later paperback editions). One of the contributors to that volume, Arthur Koestler, in his novels and his memoirs, has recaptured the attraction of Communism for young people of the interwar years, and the tragedy of disillusionment. A similarly revealing record of experience with Nazism, by an architect trained in value-free technology, is given in Albert Speer, *Erinnerungen* (Berlin, 1969).

Other critics who have written with great perception on these years, usually in several works, are Renato Poggioli, *The Spirit of the Letter: Essays in European Literature* (Cambridge, Mass., 1965); Joseph Chiari, *Landmarks of Contemporary Drama* (London, 1965); Lionel Trilling, *Beyond Culture, Essays on Literature and Learning* (N.Y., 1965); Nathan A. Scott, Jr., *The Broken Center: Studies in the Theological Horizon of Modern Literature* (New Haven, 1966); and Erich Heller, *The Artist's Journey into the Interior* (N.Y., 1965).

An anthology which is an extended introduction to the whole subject, including the visual arts, is Richard Ellmann and Charles Feidelson, Jr. (eds.), *The Modern Tradition: Backgrounds of Modern Literature* (N.Y., 1965).

Two works on drama which are not primarily concerned with these years, but which are valuable for an understanding of the period, both with good bibliographies, are Robert Brustein, *The Theatre of Revolt* (Boston, 1964), and Martin Esslin, *The Theatre of the Absurd* (Anchor, Garden City, N.Y., 1969).

Nearly all the works on literature have something to say about the visual arts. Two who wrote cogently about art in the twentieth century, from very different points of view, are Herbert Read, *The Philosophy of Modern Art* (Meridian ed., N.Y., 1955), and Leon Trotsky, *Literature and Revolution* (N.Y., 1925). Alfred H. Barr, among many other thoughtful works, edited a volume of pictures and objects in the New York Museum of Modern Art: *Masters of Modern Art* (3d ed. rev., N.Y., 1958). Another collection, photographs of works exhibited at the Brussels World Exhibition of 1958, with an introduction by Emile Langui, is *50 Years of Modern Art* (N.Y., 1959). Other profusely illustrated interpretive works are G. H. Hamilton, *Painting and Sculpture in Europe, 1880–1940* (London, 1967); Edward B. Henning, *Fifty Years of Modern Art, 1916–1966* (Cleveland, 1966); and H. L. C. Jaffé, *Twentieth Century Painting* (Lausanne, 1963). The Skira *Modern Painting*, with text by Maurice Raynal (London, 1960), is a picture book, with excellent color reproductions, arranged so that a developing story emerges.

On writing in central Europe, another work by Erich Heller—*The Dis-*

inherited Mind: Essays in Modern German Literature and Thought (Cambridge, 1952)—is valuable. A vigorous and thoughtful study is Ronald Gray, *The German Tradition in Literature* (Cambridge, 1965). On the tangled question of ideology, see George L. Mosse, *The Crisis of German Ideology: Intellectual Origins of the Third Reich* (N.Y., 1964); and István Deák, *Weimar Germany's Left-Wing Intellectuals: A Political History of the Weltbühne and Its Circle* (Berkeley, 1968).

Three pioneering studies in European cultural history which throw light on the whole of Europe, and which are valuable for an understanding of the interwar years even when the central concern is with earlier years, are Klemens von Klemperer, *Germany's New Conservatism, Its History and Dilemma in the Twentieth Century* (Princeton, 1957); Leonard Krieger, *The German Idea of Freedom: History of a Political Tradition* (Boston, 1957); and Fritz Stern, *The Politics of Cultural Despair: A Study in the Rise of the Germanic Ideology* (Berkeley, 1963).

A most suggestive effort to interpret German thought and action is Peter Gay, *Weimar Culture: The Outsider as Insider* (N.Y., 1968). An essay by Gay with the same title, but using some other materials, is in the valuable volume on exiles from German-speaking lands and Hungary: Donald Fleming and Bernard Bailyn (eds.), *The Intellectual Migration: Europe and America, 1930–1960* (Cambridge, Mass., 1969). More of a catalogue than a critical estimate, but suggestive of the magnitude of the intellectual and artistic drain from Europe, is Laura Fermi, *Illustrious Immigrants: The Intellectual Migration from Europe, 1930–41* (Chicago, 1968).

On France, good introductions are Georges Lemaitre, *From Cubism to Surrealism in French Literature* (Cambridge, Mass., 1941), Joseph Chiari, *Contemporary French Poetry* (Manchester, 1952), Henri Peyre, *The Contemporary French Novel* (N.Y., 1955), Germaine Brée and Margaret Guiton, *The French Novel from Gide to Camus* (N.Y., 1962), and Harry Levin, *The Gates of Horn: A Study of Five French Realists* (N.Y., 1963).

For Britain, there is nothing comparable to the critical comments of the poets and novelists of the time, or to the biographies of these poets and novelists. For instance, Harry T. Moore's *The Intelligent Heart: The Story of D. H. Lawrence* (N.Y., 1954; Penguin ed., 1960) gives an incomparable picture of England as seen in the novels of this expatriate—"a grey, dreary-grey coffin sinking into the sea." There is a good introduction, and a selection which gives the "feel" of the period, in Robin Skelton, *Poetry of the Thirties* (Harmondsworth, Penguin, 1964). A special issue of the *Review*, nos. 11–12 (Oxford, n.d.), has several suggestive essays.

On Russia, the best introduction is Gleb Struve, *Soviet Russian Literature* (Norman, Okla., 1951). Other valuable studies are Renato Poggioli, *The*

Poets of Russia, 1890–1930 (Cambridge, Mass., 1960); Patricia Blake and Max Hayward, *Dissonant Voices in Soviet Literature* (N.Y., 1962); and Avrahm Yarmolinsky, *A Treasury of Russian Verse* (N.Y., 1949).

The peculiarity of the history of Soviet Russia is, of course, the theoretical commitment of the regime to an all-embracing philosophical position. Therefore valuable clues to Soviet culture may be found in works on science and the Communist party such as R. A. Bauer's *The New Man in Soviet Psychology* (Cambridge, Mass., 1952), or David Joravsky's *Soviet Marxism and Natural Science, 1917–1932* (N.Y., 1961).

The most attractive favorable estimates of Soviet cultural life are to be found in the writings of Trotsky, Lukács, and Ehrenburg. A good general favorable estimate is J. P. Nettl, *The Soviet Achievement* (N.Y., 1967). An effort to place Soviet culture into the whole of Russian history is made in the concluding sections of James H. Billington, *The Icon and the Axe: An Interpretive History of Russian Culture* (N.Y., 1966).

A cooperative work containing papers by some of the most perceptive writers on Russian literature is Max Hayward and Leopold Labetz (eds.), *Literature and Revolution in Soviet Russia, 1917–62* (London, 1963).

INDEX